Zero Carbon Homes

Housing is a major contributor to CO2 emissions in Europe and America today and the construction of new homes offers an opportunity to address this issue. Providing homes that achieve "zero carbon", "carbon neutral", "zero-net energy" or "energy-plus" standards is becoming the goal of more innovative house-builders globally, whilst energy providers seek to decarbonise the energy supply to new and existing development.

Various new technical systems for achieving these goals are beginning to emerge. For example, the passive house with energy requirements for space heating and cooling of almost zero; the smart grid that has revolutionised the management of energy whilst enabling the connection of small-scale, renewable energy producers and electric vehicles to the grid; or the European super-grid which will enable zero carbon energy to be generated in the Sahara desert and stored in Norway.

This book explores the diverse approaches that are being adopted around the world to delivering zero carbon homes and the different societal systems and geographic circumstances in which they have developed. It postulates a road-map for delivering zero carbon homes, together with a toolkit for policy-makers and practitioners to suit particular national and local circumstances.

A series of case studies are presented that offer lessons for delivering zero carbon homes. These examples are also used to demonstrate how prototype systems can move into the mainstream. The book highlights some of the instruments and mechanisms that could be used to support this transformation and addresses the wider implications of introducing these innovative systems in terms of industry, lifestyle and urban form.

The book will be relevant to professionals in urban planning, architecture, construction and the energy sector and will be a useful resource to students in these areas.

Jo Williams is a Senior Lecturer in sustainable development at University College London, where she is the Director of the Sustainable Urbanism masters programme. She is also the Principal Investigator for the Zero Carbon Homes project and is an expert contributor to various international advisory bodies in the field of sustainable development.

Zero Carbon Homes

A road-map

Jo Williams

publishing for a sustainable future

Contents

Figures

Figures marked P can be found in the plate section between pages 206 and 207.

Abbreviations and acronyms

AGR	advanced gas cooled reactor
ASHP	air source heat pump
BedZED	Beddington Zero Emissions Development
BMU	Federal Environment Ministry (Germany)
BRE	building research establishment
BWEA	British Wind Energy Association
CAP	Climate Action Plan
CAS	compressed air storage
CCGT	combined cycle gas turbine
CCS	carbon capture and storage
CEC	California Energy Commission
CERT	Carbon Emissions Reduction Target
CHP	combined heat and power
CLG	Department of Communities and Local Government
CO_2	carbon dioxide
CS	carbon sequestration
CSI	California Solar Initiative
CSP	concentrated solar power
DECC	Department of Energy and Climate Change
DINK	dual income no kids
DTI	Department of Trade and Industry
EC	European Commission
EEA	European Environment Agency
EIA	Energy Information Administration (USA)
EPA	Environmental Protection Agency
ESCO	energy service company
ESP	edge of service provider
ETF	environmental transformation fund
EU	European Union
EU ETS	European emissions trading scheme
EWEA	European Wind Energy Association
FIT	feed-in tariff

GDP	gross domestic product
GdW	Federal association of *German* housing and real estate enterprise
GHG	greenhouse gas
GMV	Greenwich Millennium Village
GSHP	ground source heat pump
GW	gigawatt
GWe	gigawatts electric
HOA	home owners association
ICLEI	International Council for Local Environmental Initiatives
IEA	International Energy Agency
IOCs	international oil companies
IOU	investor-owned utility
IPCC	International Panel on Climate Change
IVL	Swedish Environment Research Institute
Kgoe	kilograms of oil equivalent
kWh	kilowatt hours
LCBP	Low Carbon Buildings Programme
LEED	Leadership in Energy and Environmental Design (USA building accreditation programme)
LEH	low energy house
LIP	local investment programme
LZC	low or zero carbon
MCC	Malmo City Council
Mt CO_2eq	million tonnes carbon dioxide equivalent
MUSCO	multi service company
MVHR	mechanical ventilation with heat recovery
MWe	mega watts electric
NAHB	National Association of Home Builders
NREL	National Renewable Energy Laboratory
NSHP	New Solar Homes Partnership
OPEC	Organisation of Petroleum Exporting Countries
PH	passive house
PHS	pumped-hydro storage
PIER	Public Interest Energy Research
POU	publicly owned utility
PPM	parts per million
PUC	public utilities commission
PV	cell photovoltaic cell
PWR	pressurised water reactor
RE	renewable energy
REE	rare earth elements
RO	renewables obligation
RPS	renewable portfolio standard

SME	small and medium-sized enterprise
Toe	tonnes oil equivalent
TWh	terrawatt hour
WWF	World Wide Fund for Nature

Table 1.3 Interview feedback

	Chapter	Academics environmental consultants/ research institutions	Government – national and municipal	Built environment professionals	House-builders	Utilities / ESCOs	Property agents	Residents	Finance institutions
Technical solutions	2	☑		☑	☑	☑			
Demand and deployment	6	☑			☑	☑		☑	☑
Supply and scaling up	7 and 8	☑	☑	☑	☑	☑	☑		☑
Policy instruments	9	☑	☑	☑	☑	☑	☑	☑	☑
Impact on built form	10			☑		☑			
Role of planning	10		☑	☑	☑	☑	☑		
Living with zero carbon	11	☑			☑	☑	☑	☑	

Source: Author's own.

wholesale changes that would be needed in both the energy and house-building industries to deliver zero carbon homes universally. Nor have the spatial implications, post-occupancy problems, issues of market creation and resilience been discussed. This book addresses all of these issues.

It also has an international dimension. It presents the experiences of four different countries in delivering LZC development. The UK, Germany, Sweden and USA offer very different policy approaches to delivering zero carbon, energy-plus (solar, zero-net energy) and low-energy houses as well as a LZC energy supply (heat and electricity). The regulatory, institutional, economic, cultural, political, physical and technical context in each case is very different, yet many common barriers and solutions to overcoming those barriers are demonstrated by the case studies. These more generic lessons are drawn out in the book.

This book should appeal to a very wide audience. It can be read by academics, students, practitioners and lay readers as a critical analysis of the perils of introducing a very progressive environmental policy within a market context. It could be used by policy-makers to identify more successful political strategies, instruments and institutions for delivering low-carbon development. For practitioners it might provide insight into the ownership and management structures, processes, partnerships and expertise required to deliver zero carbon homes. For planning practitioners it will provide guidance on the models for zero carbon homes, spatial implications and offer insight into how the planning system can become more proactive in facilitating zero carbon development.

The book divides into three parts. Part 1 provides an outline of possible technical options for delivering zero carbon homes. Part 2 is largely descriptive, presenting the international case studies. Part 3 analyses what is needed to successfully deliver zero carbon homes in the future, drawing on the case studies presented in Part 2, the experience of the key stakeholders interviewed, databases and literature.

The book is organised as follows:

Part I

Chapter 2 discusses various generic technological options for achieving zero carbon emissions from housing. It focuses on improving the energy efficiency of stock and decarbonising the energy supply (using decentralised and centralised infrastructural systems). It discusses how technological systems might be combined effectively in different locations and at different scales to deliver zero carbon housing.

Part 2

Chapter 3 discusses four national programmes that have produced low/zero carbon (LZC) housing in Sweden, Germany, the UK and USA. These programmes represent a range of technical models (low-energy, passive and solar houses) and offer a variety of approaches to deployment (from regulation and large state subsidies to green mortgages and tax incentives). Some generic lessons for industry and policy-makers for the development of LZC housing and refurbishment of existing communities are drawn from the case studies.

Chapter 4 presents a variety of LZC energy systems from Europe and the USA. These examples represent a range of LZC energy systems that can be adopted at a variety of scales. Potential demand for and deployment of the systems are discussed. The scale of industrial transformation required to deliver the systems is evaluated. The policy instruments needed to drive this transformation and the impact on lifestyle are investigated. Some generic lessons for industry and policy-makers planning to develop LZC energy systems in new and existing communities are drawn from the case studies.

Chapter 5 introduces various examples of LZC neighbourhoods from Europe and the USA. The neighbourhoods display a range of technological systems to reduce carbon emissions. In each case these systems are managed, operated and maintained in different ways. The resident also adopts a variety of roles from being a passive consumer, to a being actively involved in the management and production of energy. This chapter touches on how residents interact with new technical systems to reduce carbon emissions and demand for LZC neighbourhoods. Some generic lessons for industry and policy-makers for the creation of LZC neighbourhoods are drawn from the case studies. The extent to which these demonstration projects have scaled up or informed future developments is also discussed.

Part 3

Chapter 6 analyses the factors influencing demand for zero carbon energy and low-energy, passive, energy-plus, solar, zero-net energy and zero carbon houses based on the European and American case studies. It identifies the current characteristics of the market and the current position in terms of deployment of these new technical systems. It postulates how demand can be enhanced and deployment encouraged, using a variety of marketing, publicity and costing strategies.

A revolution in the house-building and energy industries will be needed to deliver zero carbon homes (discussed in Chapters 7 and 8). It will require that new supply chains, construction processes, expertise and partnerships are developed. It will result in a cultural shift and institutional changes within both industries. The role of players within industry may change and new players may emerge. Longer-term horizons for financial reward and level of resident involvement in the production process will also fundamentally change the nature of both industries.

Rarely will markets for new products develop without some form of intervention. Chapter 9 compares policy instruments that could be used to encourage the delivery and the creation of markets for zero carbon homes, drawing on experience from the case studies. The appropriateness of policy instruments varies significantly depending on the contexts in which they operate, ranging from market-based to more interventionist systems. Policy instruments adopted internationally, nationally, regionally and locally are considered and the relative benefits of each in terms of encouraging innovation are evaluated. The merits of focusing instruments on increasing supply or demand are discussed, as is the need to use a combination of fiscal, regulatory and educational instruments.

In Chapter 10 the spatial impacts of achieving zero carbon are discussed and illustrated by the case studies. The geography of zero carbon development and impact on urban form are discussed. Planning offers a spatial regulatory tool for delivering zero carbon development. The strengths and weaknesses of planning as a tool for delivering zero carbon development are evaluated and innovative planning approaches are presented.

In chapter 11 zero carbon lifestyles are discussed. The conflicts between quality of life and zero carbon technical systems are assessed. The difficulties encountered at the user-technology interface are investigated. Options for encouraging a paradigm shift, moving passive consumers towards becoming engaged energy citizens (living zero carbon lifestyles in zero carbon homes), are explored using lessons drawn from the European and American case studies.

The final chapter concludes with an overview of the key changes needed in industry, society and policy to support movement towards zero carbon homes and lifestyles. It reflects on the progress made to date and highlights the pitfalls. It postulates a series of scenarios for delivering zero carbon homes together with a toolbox of policy instruments for implementation.

Happy reading!

though most definitions refer to the operational phase of a home, household activities are not considered in calculations. Thus the total consumption of energy and release of CO_2 emissions over the life-cycle of a building are not fully considered. This can in part be justified by the fact that 80%[2] of the energy and CO_2 emissions are generated during the operational phase of a building. Regardless, to classify developments as being 'zero carbon' or 'zero energy' is misleading unless the boundaries and parameters are clearly defined.

For the purpose of this book a zero carbon home will be defined as follows:

'A home from which there are zero-net CO_2 emissions during operation.'

This is the same as the original definition adopted by the UK Government when this progressive environmental policy was first introduced. The definition focuses on the CO_2 emissions emitted from the operational phase of the life-cycle of a house. Embodied carbon is not considered, nor are the wider activities of a household that produce CO_2 emissions (e.g. travel, consumption of goods, etc). The definition concentrates on energy consumed in regulating indoor temperature, heating water and powering appliances (including lights). Furthermore, the book focuses on new buildings, rather than existing stock (although some of the lessons learnt for new build apply equally to existing stock as you will see).

Zero carbon toolbox

To achieve zero carbon emissions from housing both energy supply and household demand for energy must be tackled. Energy demand can be reduced by increasing the energy efficiency of housing stock and changing consumer behaviour (Figure 2.1). The energy supply can be decarbonised by increasing the efficiency of generating and transmission systems as well as substituting fossil fuels for low carbon energy sources (nuclear and renewable energy). A range of technologies can be used to support these changes.

The energy efficiency of housing stock is affected by the building envelope as well as the appliances and heating/cooling systems installed. The orientation and layout of buildings can also influence internal temperature and solar gain. Passive design elements can play a significant role in increasing the energy efficiency of a house. However, effective management of the energy systems and appliances operating in the home – either by the occupants or remotely by energy providers – is also very important. Smart houses offer a state-of-the-art response to this (see p. 98).

The decarbonisation of the energy supply is also central to achieving the zero carbon standard. One option is to use carbon sequestration (see p. 31); however, this is not a long-term option. Substituting fossil fuels with low carbon energy is critical to this. For renewable energy a variety of

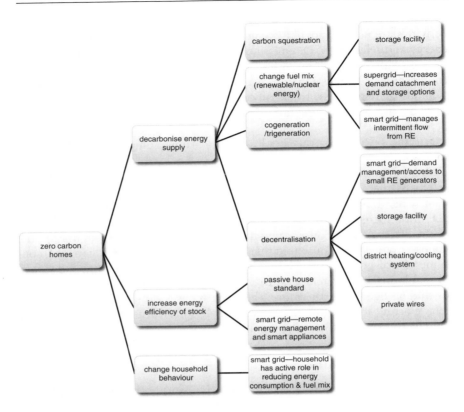

Figure 2.1 Technical toolbox for zero carbon.
Source: Author's own.

generation and storage options will need to be considered. In addition, using cogeneration and decentralised energy systems could significantly reduce transmission and generation energy losses. The introduction of smart grids (see p. 26) will help to manage energy supply more efficiently and facilitate the integration of smaller-scale generators of renewable energy into the network.

In the following sections you will be introduced to the key technological responses currently in the zero carbon toolbox.

Housing energy performance

The energy performance of housing depends on a number of factors: the airtightness of the shell; insulative capacity of the shell (walls, roofs, floors, windows); thermal bridging; heating and cooling systems; ventilation and heat recovery systems; the number of air changes; orientation and design to maximise passive solar gain. Passive house is the most energy efficient form of housing currently being built. Imposing passive house standard on new build housing in Europe[3] could as much as halve the current energy losses (IEA, 2008; Feist et al, 2001). Of course the scale of CO_2 savings will be dependent on the carbon intensity of the energy supply and the baseline energy efficiency of housing.

Passive house is a construction standard that can be met by a variety of technologies, designs and materials. It can also be adapted to cold and warm climates. Passive house standard creates a basis on which it is possible to meet total household energy demand from renewable energy sources, whilst keeping within the bounds set by limited availability of renewable energy sources and affordability.

To be a passive house a building must fulfil the following conditions:

- it must use 15 kWh/m²/annum or less ($\leq$) in heating energy;
- specific heat load for heating source at design temperature must be less than 10 W/m²;
- the building must be pressurised to 50Pa by a blower door and must not leak more air than 0.6 times the house volume per hour (n50 $\leq$ 0.6/h);
- total primary energy consumption (primary energy for heating, hot water and electricity) must not be more than 120 kWh/m²/ annum.[4]

This single definition of passive house can be used at least from 40–60° latitude. However, there will be some differences in terms of design. In colder climates passive houses must be highly insulated,[5] designed without thermal bridges,[6] have energy efficient windows,[7] be very airtight, supplied with efficient mechanical ventilation[8] systems and innovative heating/cooling technology[9] (Figure 2.2, see colour plates). In cooler climates the idea is to minimise heat loss or gain. The passive house uses free heat gains (delivered externally by solar radiation and internally by heat emissions from appliance use and occupants) to increase internal temperatures. Both the orientation of a passive house and level of occupancy can influence indoor temperatures. Cost-optimised solar thermal systems can meet about 40–60% of the entire low-temperature heat demand of a passive house. In cooler climates thermal mass, insulation, airtightness, minimisation of air changes and thermal bridging are key to minimising energy consumption and associated CO_2 emissions.

Passive houses built in warmer regions will have more poorly insulated floors, better insulated roofs and less glazing.[10] Solar control becomes more important as does some form of active cooling system. In Southern Europe single glazing is sufficient to achieve net solar gains, in fact triple glazing is not recommended south of the Alps. Orientation of buildings is much more important in Southern Europe than in northern climates. The influence of building orientation on the heating demand is typically twice as high in the Mediterranean than in Central Europe. The impact of thermal mass on heating demand is more pronounced in Southern Europe than further north. Differences in humidity may also influence design. In semi-arid climates (e.g. Spain) dehumidification will not be required, whereas in more humid coastal locations to the south and east of Nice (e.g. Italy) it will. In semi-arid climates night ventilation will be sufficient; where it is more humid supply and exhaust air ventilation systems are required.

Of course differences in design are reflected in the cost of passive houses in different locations (Table 2.2). However, cost is affected by many other factors including: economic incentives, availability of components, changes to building practices, cost of technologies and labour. The optimal design for a passive house is likely to vary a great deal. It will be dependent on climatic conditions. However, equally the availability of incentives and the regime in which the construction industry operates in each instance will have a major bearing on which options are most cost-effective.

Retrofitting some existing stock to passive house standard is technically feasible. This is very important in Europe and America where construction rates are very low. However, in some instances energetic refurbishment to passive house standard is not technically or economically feasible (Figure 2.3). The Passive House Institute compared a variety of measures in Germany to determine their effectiveness (although this will vary depending on availability of resources, incentives and market demand). Insulation is the most cost-effective measure to reduce CO_2 emissions from buildings (Enkvist et al, 2007; Hermelink, 2009; Ecofys, 2007).

The cost-optimal U-values have been calculated based on household investment in insulation and energy costs (Figure 2.4, see colour plates). The 'best practice zone' is where savings are at an optimum. A U-value outside of the 'best practice zone' means that a home-owner would be gaining

Table 2.2 Variation in passive house construction costs in Europe

	Specific construction costs		% increase	Heating demand		Cooling demand	
	Standard (Euros/m2)	PH (Euros/m2)		Standard (kWh/m2/yr)	PH (kWh/m2/yr)	Standard (kWh/m2/yr)	PH (kWh/m2/yr)
Germany	1400	1494	6.71	90	15	0	0
Italy	1200	1284	7.00	83	10.5	4.63	3.00
France	940	1034	10.00	69.6	17.4	N/A	5.00
Spain	720	740	2.85	59	8.7	23.1	7.9
UK	881	930	5.54	59	15	0	0

Source: Passive-on project, 2008.

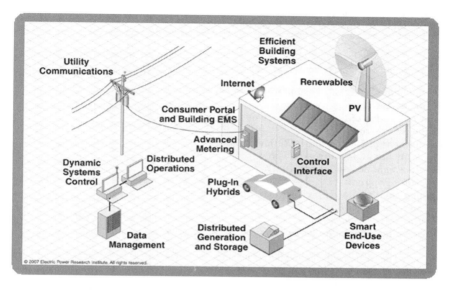

Figure 2.5 The smart grid devices.

Source: Electric Power Research Institute, 2008.

charged during off-peak periods. This energy can either be used to power the vehicle or can be returned to the grid during peak periods. Potentially if the fuel mix is low carbon this could reduce emissions from transport as well as from housing.

An analysis of potential energy and CO_2 savings that could be achieved through the introduction of the smart grid in the USA (Table 2.4) suggests it should be considered as an important tool in achieving the zero carbon standard. The study outlined nine mechanisms by which the smart grid could tackle CO_2 emissions from electricity generation and delivery (Pratt et al, 2010). While several of the mechanisms were estimated to have small or negligible impacts, five of the mechanisms could potentially provide reductions of over 1% (Pratt et al, 2010).

The combined effect of the direct mechanisms is 12%, and the indirect mechanisms total 6% of energy and emissions for the US electricity sector (Pratt et al, 2010). These correspond to 5% and 2% of the US total energy consumption and energy-related CO_2 emissions for all sectors (including electricity – Pratt et al, 2010). The magnitude of these reductions suggests that, while a smart grid is not the primary mechanism for achieving energy and carbon savings, it is capable of providing a very substantial contribution. The study also demonstrated that using a smart grid could also help to encourage the deployment of renewables.

Table 2.4 Potential reductions in electricity and CO_2 emissions in 2030 attributable to smart grid technologies

	Reductions in Electricity Sector Energy and CO_2 Emissions	
	Direct (%)	Indirect (%)
Conservation Effect of Consumer Information and Feedback Systems	3	–
Joint Marketing of Energy Efficiency and Demand Response Programs	–	0
Deployment of Diagnostics in Residential and Small/Medium Commercial Buildings	3	–
Measurement & Verification (M&V) for Energy Efficiency Programs	1	0.5
Shifting Load to More Efficient Generation	<0.1	–
Support Additional Electric Vehicles and Plug-In Hybrid Electric Vehicles	3	–
Conservation Voltage Reduction and Advanced Voltage Control	2	–
Support Penetration of Renewable Wind and Solar Generation (25% renewable portfolio standard [RPS])	<0.1	5
Total Reduction	12	6

Source: Pratt et al (2010).

The scale of savings will vary with location. The current fuel mix, efficiency of a grid system, consumers' willingness to participate in managing their own consumption, incentives offered to renewable energy generators and so on, will all influence the effectiveness of a smart grid. The American study can only provide an indication of the scale of CO_2 savings that might be made. Another study suggests CO_2 savings of around 3–9% (Electric Power Research Institute, 2008)

Carbon sequestration

Carbon sequestration (carbon capture and storage, CCS) can also be used to decarbonise the energy supply. Carbon sequestration applied to a modern conventional power plant could reduce CO_2 emissions by approximately 80–90% compared to a plant without carbon sequestration. The IPCC estimates that the economic potential of CCS could be between 10% and 55% of the total carbon mitigation effort until year 2100 (IPCC, 2005).

Carbon sequestration involves capturing CO_2 from large point sources (such as fossil fuel power plants) and storing it. There are various storage options gaseous storage in various deep geological formations (including saline formations and exhausted gas fields), liquid storage in the ocean, and solid storage by reaction of CO_2 with metal oxides to produce stable carbonates. Of course CO_2 emissions from power plants may also be absorbed within the terrestrial ecosystem by the soil or vegetation. Vegetation and soils have a large influence on atmospheric levels of CO_2 as they act as CO_2 sinks. For example tropical deforestation is responsible for about 20% of the world's annual CO_2 emissions (IPCC, 2000).

One limitation of CCS is its energy penalty. The technology is expected to use between 10 and 40% of the energy produced by a power station (Greenpeace, 2008). An energy penalty of just 20% would require the construction of an extra power station for every four built. These reductions in efficiency will require more coal to be mined, transported and burned in order for a power station to produce the same amount of energy as it did without CS. It will also use more resources. Power stations with capture technology will need 90% more freshwater than those without. This will worsen water shortages, already aggravated by climate change. Thus, wide-scale adoption of CCS may erase efficiency gains of the last 50 years, and increase resource consumption by one third (Greenpeace, 2008).

Another limitation is that safe and permanent storage of CO_2 cannot be guaranteed. Even very low leakage rates could undermine any climate mitigation effect. In addition, leakage of CO_2 could potentially degrade the quality of groundwater, damage some hydrocarbon or mineral resources, and have lethal effects on plants and sub-soil animals (IPCC, 2005). Of course release of CO_2 back into the atmosphere through leakage could also create local health and safety concerns (IPCC, 2005). The IPCC suggests that these impacts can be overcome through careful site selection, effective regulatory oversight, and an appropriate monitoring programme to provide early warning that the storage site is not functioning properly. The IPCC concludes that the proportion of CO_2 retained in appropriately selected and managed geological reservoirs is very likely to exceed 99% over 100 years and is likely to exceed 99% over 1,000 years (IPCC, 2005).

Finally there is the issue of cost. The cost of CS varies considerably depending on the technologies used and where projects are sited (IPCC, 2005). CS will increase the cost of power for several reasons. Firstly, the increased energy requirements of capturing and compressing CO_2 significantly raise the operating costs of CS-equipped power plants. In addition there is added investment or capital costs. The process would increase the fuel requirement of a plant with CS by about 25% for a coal-fired plant and about 15% for a gas-fired plant (IPCC, 2005). The cost of this extra fuel, as well as storage and other system costs are estimated to increase the costs of energy from a power plant with CCS by 30–60%, depending on the specific circumstances (IPCC, 2005). Pre-commercial CS demonstration projects are likely to be more expensive than mature technology, the total additional costs of an early large-scale CS demonstration project are estimated to be €35–50 per tonne of CO_2 abated, which equates to €0.5–1.1 bn per project over the project lifetime (McKinsey, 2008). However, with increased operating experience and scale effects this could reduce to €30–45 per tonne of CO_2 abated by 2030.

Although there are significant problems with carbon sequestration, fossil fuels are expected to continue to play a major role in the global energy mix until 2050. Carbon sequestration remains an important technology for abatement of CO_2 from stationery fossil fuel sources. However, it is essential that alternative low carbon energy sources are developed alongside this technology, which after all will be defunct when fossil fuels run out.

Low carbon energy sources

One way to decarbonise supply is to opt for energy with low carbon intensity.[11] Fossil fuels are the most carbon intensive form of energy, followed by nuclear power. Renewable energy is considerably less carbon intensive than either fossil fuels or nuclear power. Thus an energy supply based on renewable sources is preferable. A recent analysis (Sovacool, 2008) suggests that the carbon intensity of nuclear power[12] (66 gCO_2e/kWh) is well below scrubbed coal-fired plants (960 gCO2e/kWh), and natural gas-fired plants (443 gCO2e/kWh). However, nuclear energy emits twice as much carbon as solar photovoltaic cells and geothermal energy, three times as much as most forms of biofuel and six times as much as wind farms and solar thermal panels. A comparison of carbon emissions for various energy types is presented below (Table 2.5).

This analysis provides a good indication of the types of energy we need to invest in if we are to achieve a low carbon energy supply. The carbon intensity of energy supplies in the USA and Europe are generally high, reflecting their heavy dependency on fossil fuels (Figure 2.6).

In 2005 79% of primary energy consumption in the EU27 was fossil fuel based. Thus the carbon intensity of the energy supply was high. In 2005, renewable energy accounted for a mere 6.7 % of total primary energy consumption (Figure 2.7, see colour plates). Wind power constituted 75 % of the total installed renewable capacity in 2006 (excluding electricity from large hydro-power plants and from biomass). Only in Iceland, Sweden and France was 50% or more of the fuel mix based on nuclear and renewable sources[13].

Currently the quantity of energy generated from renewable sources varies considerably in Europe (Figure 2.8, see colour plates). Some member states rely heavily on hydro-power (Sweden, Norway, France, Austria and Switzerland), others on biomass (Sweden, Finland, Denmark and the UK), and some on wind (Germany, Spain and Denmark).

The consumption of renewable energy has grown in the USA in recent years. However, currently only 7% of the energy consumed comes from renewable sources. In recent years, consumption of biomass and biofuel has increased significantly, whilst hydro-power has declined. Consumption of

Table 2.5 Life-cycle estimates for electricity generators[1]

Technology	Capacity/configuration/fuel	Estimate (gCO$_2$e/kWh)
Wind	2.5 MW, offshore	9
Hydroelectric	3.1 MW, reservoir	10
Wind	1.5 MW, onshore	10
Biogas	Anaerobic digestion	11
Hydroelectric	300 kW, run-of-river	13
Solar thermal	80 MW, parabolic trough	13
Biomass	Forest wood Co-combustion with hard coal	14
Biomass	Forest wood steam turbine	22
Biomass	Short rotation forestry Co-combustion with hard coal	23
Biomass	FOREST WOOD reciprocating engine	27
Biomass	Waste wood steam turbine	31
Solar PV	Polycrystalline silicone	32
Biomass	Short rotation forestry steam turbine	35
Geothermal	80 MW, hot dry rock	38
Biomass	Short rotation forestry reciprocating engine	41
Nuclear	Various reactor types	66
Natural gas	Various combined cycle turbines	443
Fuel cell	Hydrogen from gas reforming	664
Diesel	Various generator and turbine types	778
Heavy oil	Various generator and turbine types	778
Coal	Various generator types with scrubbing	960
Coal	Various generator types without scrubbing	1050

Source: Sovacool, 2008.

Notes

1 Wind, hydroelectric, biogas, solar thermal, biomass, and geothermal, estimates taken from Pehnt (2006). Diesel, heavy oil, coal with scrubbing, coal without scrubbing, natural gas, and fuel cell estimates taken and Gagnon et al. (2002). Solar PV estimates taken from Fthenakis et al. (2008). Nuclear is taken from Sovacool, 2008. Estimates have been rounded to the nearest whole number.

wind and solar power has also increased although the quantities consumed of both are still very small (Figure 2.9, see colour plates).

There is a great deal of variation in the generation of renewable energy between states in America (Figure 2.10). The states of Washington, California and Oregon are the top three producers of renewable energy. Colorado in contrast produces very little renewable energy.

If the carbon intensity of energy supply is to reduce in Europe and the USA then renewable energy capacity needs to be drastically increased. However, in order for renewable energy to be an acceptable alternative some issues need to be overcome including: resistance within the energy industry to the use of non-fossil fuels (created by powerful vested interests), technological and network inefficiencies, intermittency, the spatial variation in the avail-

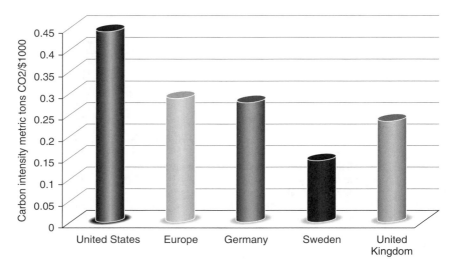

Figure 2.6 Carbon intensity of energy supply.

Source: Energy Information Administration, 2010.

ability of resources, connecting to the grid, and the sheer scale of energy demand.

Some of these problems can be overcome through technological advancement (e.g. technological and network inefficiencies) regulatory changes (quota systems, easing connection to the grid) and fiscal incentives (subsidies, taxation, carbon trading, etc). Intermittency and spatial variation in availability of resources can be tackled by improving storage systems or expanding existing grids. However, demand management is also important. It is more difficult for heavily industrialised countries or those with large urban populations to generate enough renewable energy (at least domestically) to sustain themselves. Managing demand through technological fixes, fiscal instruments, educational tools and regulation is very important.

Storage

Energy storage can help to tackle a number of issues within the electricity system (Figure 2.11). Storage can help to increase the stability of the energy supply, by broadening the energy base (increasing the inclusion of renewable sources) and reducing system losses. This helps to tackle the volatility of energy prices and increases energy security. Storage can increase the efficiencies of large power generation by enabling the storage of energy produced during off-peak periods. It can prevent congestion in the transmission

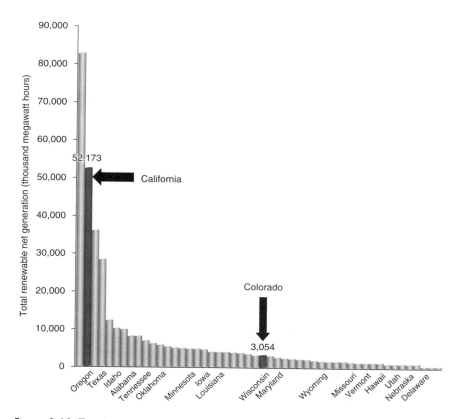

Figure 2.10 Total net renewable generation across the USA, 2007.

Source: Energy Information Administration, 2010.

network by storing energy produced locally until the transmission system can accommodate it. It can also enable the integration of more intermittent, low carbon energy sources into the power grid. The more efficient use of power generated in combination with an increase in power generated from low carbon sources all helps to decarbonise the energy supply.

Energy storage has a critical role to play in the growth of renewable energy generation. Storage options help to synchronise renewable energy supply with periods of peak consumer demand. Also electricity generated from renewable sources during times when the value is low can be 'time-shifted' so that the energy can be sold when its value is high (Electricity Storage Association, 2010). This means that renewable energy is used more efficiently and that it becomes more economically competitive with traditional sources of energy.

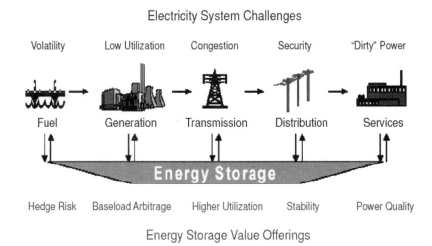

Figure 2.11 The benefits of energy storage.

Source: Tinkler, 2009.

There are numerous storage options available: pumped hydro storage, compressed air storage, fuel cells, batteries (flow, NAS, metal-air, lead-acid, Ni-Ca, Li-ion), thermal energy storage, flywheel storage, superconducting energy storage and energy storage in super capacitors. The most competitive for the storage of renewable energy appear to be pumped hydro, compressed-air, hydrogen fuel cells and some batteries (Figure 2.12). The suitability of each depends on the system power ratings.

Currently, pumped hydro storage (PHS) and compressed air storage (CAS) are the most often used for large-scale storage, often in combination with large-scale wind power. The conversion efficiency in both instances is relatively good (65–80% pumped hydro and 70% compressed air storage). Both are relatively low cost. However both are constrained to certain locations by geography or geology (Table 2.6). Batteries (flow, NAS and metal-air batteries) are also a popular form of storage for smaller amounts of renewable energy (for example, that produced from concentrated solar plants). The hydrogen fuel cell offers a storage option for power systems ranging in size from 1kW to 10MW. However, this is a new and very expensive technology, with very low energy efficiency.

A study (Ibrahim et al, 2008) suggests that for small- and large-scale systems in isolated areas relying on intermittent renewable energy the lead battery remains the best option in terms of cost and performance. Alternative solutions are either less efficient or too expensive: compressed air (self-

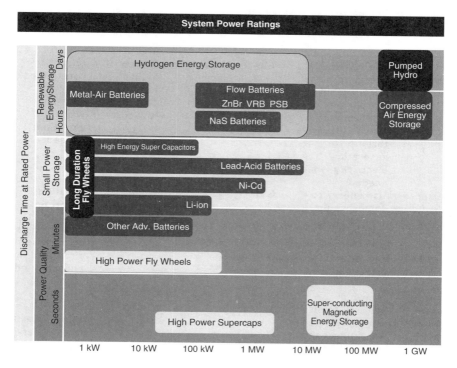

Figure 2.12 Comparison of competitive energy storage technologies.

Source: Electricity Storage Association, 2010.

discharge problems), fuel cells (expensive and low energy efficiency), and flow batteries (high maintenance costs). However, in less isolated locations pumped hydro and thermal energy storage are suited to large-scale storage of renewable energy and superconducting magnetic energy storage provides a shorter-term storage option. It is expected that new storage technologies will emerge and existing technologies may become more cost-effective in time.

Ultimately another way of addressing the CO_2 emissions from the energy supply is to move towards a system based on hydrogen (Figure 2.13). Here renewable energy will be used to generate hydrogen which can then be stored. Fuel cells can then be used convert hydrogen back into energy. Eventually they could replace combustion plants. This energy can then be used by communities. Of course the hydrogen can also be used to power vehicles with fuel cells. Hydrogen storage can be used to match intermittent renewable energy supply with demand. It can enable renewable energy to be used for base load power eliminating high cost and CO_2 emitting power plants. It can also enable load profiling including grid optimisation and peak shaving

Table 2.6 Comparison of storage options

Storage type	Description	Power rating	Efficiency	Advantages	Disadvantages
Pumped-hydro storage	Use renewable energy to pump water up hill and store in reservoir to be released to drive turbine generating electricity when needed	I GW	Conversion efficiency 65–80%	Readily available, high capacity, low cost	Location constrained– site with different water elevations needed
Compressed air energy storage	Use energy to compress air. To produce energy air allowed to expand and drives turbines	I GW	70%	High capacity and low cost	Location constrained– geology important as compressed air stored in underground chambers[1]
Thermal energy storage	Heat bulk material (molten salt/pressurised water) heat then recovered to produce water vapour that drives turbo-alternator system.	Small/ medium	–	–	For the option using water – large water-tight systems buried in rock needed – subject to geological constraints
	Heat storage with turbine		60%	Stores very large quantities of energy	
				Not subject to geological constraints Investment costs low	
Energy storage using flow batteries	Energy stored in chemical compounds and released by electrolyte.	100 kW –10 MW	70%	High capacity, independent power and energy ratings	Low energy density, high maintenance costs

Super-conduc-ting energy storage	Store energy in the magnetic field created by the flow of direct current in a superconducting coil where energy can be stored indefinitely. By discharging the coil the stored energy can be released back to the network.		95%	Ideal for regulating network stability; high efficiency; short-term storage	Refrigeration system is costly; at large-scale must bury coil underground because of large magnetic forces
Fuel cells	Off-peak energy used to generate hydrogen which is then used to power a fuel cell during peak load.	1 kW–10 MW[2]	35–70%[3]	Very flexible can be used in a variety of situations.	Low efficiency, the investment costs are prohibitive and life expectancy is very limited, especially for power network applications

Source: Generated using information from Ibrahim, Ilincaa and Perron (2007) and Electricity Storage Association, 2010.

Notes
1 However air could be compressed and stored in underground, high pressure piping (20–100 bars). This method would eliminate the geological criteria and make the system easier to operate.
2 Fuel cells can be used in decentralized production (particularly low-power stations – residential, emergency, etc.), spontaneous supply related or not to the network, mid-power cogeneration (a few 100 kW), and centralized electricity production without heat upgrading. They can also represent a solution for isolated areas where the installation of power lines is too difficult or expensive (mountain locations, etc.).
3 Combining an electrolyser and a fuel cell for electrical energy storage is a low-efficiency solution (at best 70% for the electrolyser and 50% for the fuel cell, and 35% for the electrolyser with fuel cell)

opportunities. However, this option is still very expensive, the technologies are still relatively inefficient in terms of energy consumed in the production of hydrogen and there are also potential problems with leakage.

A super-grid

A super-grid could enable the redistribution of renewable energy from areas of production to areas of consumption. Generally the most populated urban

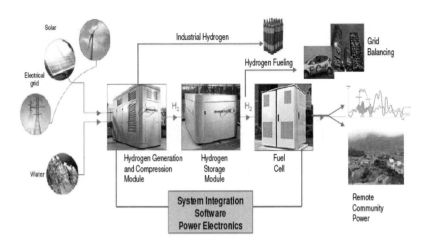

Figure 2.13 Hydrogen storage system

Source: www.hydrogenics.com.

areas are not where energy is produced. It can also enable the transmission
of energy from areas of surplus to areas of deficit. A super-grid could expand
the existing energy resource base thus increasing the reliability and stability
of supply. It could also be used to send renewable energy to locations to be
stored until it is needed.

Currently there is some discussion about a European super-grid. The
North Sea grid is already under development. It will connect nine countries
in Europe: Germany, France, Belgium, the Netherlands, Luxembourg, Denmark, Sweden and Ireland and the UK. It will link European energy consumers to wind farms in Germany, Denmark and the UK; hydro-power in France
and Sweden; wave power in the UK, Belgium and Denmark; solar arrays in
Germany. It could also link into Norwegian pumped hydro systems, which in
turn could act as an energy storage facility for Europe. Already a power grid
between the Scandinavian countries exists which could be incorporated into
the new North Sea grid and form part of the wider European super-grid.

Eventually the European super-grid could be expanded to include the
Middle East and North Africa to maximise use of the solar capacity demonstrated in these regions (Figure 2.14, see colour plates). The Desertec project
aims to provide 15% of Europe's electricity by 2050 or earlier via solar
power. The scheme brings together three regions to cooperate in the production of electricity and desalinated water using concentrated solar thermal
power plants and wind turbines in the desert. The electrical power generated can be transmitted via high voltage direct current (HVDC) transmission
lines to Europe (with overall transmission losses of about 10–15%).

The economic viability of a super-grid grows as renewable energy capacity in Europe expands (Figure 2.15). Since 2000 there has been a significant increase in wind energy in Europe as well as more measured increases in solar power, hydro-power and biomass. More than 100GW of offshore wind projects are under development, equivalent to around 10% of the Europe's electricity demand. The actual cost of a North Sea grid has not yet been calculated, but studies suggest the costs to be between €15bn (Greenpeace, 2008) and €30bn (EWEA, 2010).

However, there are concerns that geo-political barriers may interfere with the establishment and operation of a super-grid. Many decisions concerning strategic energy policy (particularly investment in future supplies and infrastructure) are made at a national level rather than a continental level, leading to difficulties in ensuring a coordinated European approach to energy policy. This could result in multiple and conflicting objectives. Thus, developing a super-grid is likely to be a slow process for a whole range of reasons including the cost, long lead times for projects, cross-border agreements and issues of energy security.

A more coordinated regional approach is starting to be adopted in Europe. The European Renewable Energy Directive sets targets for each member state and each state is required to produce an action plan setting out how its target is to be achieved (i.e. the types of policy instruments that will be used to encourage an expansion in generating capacity). Each member state is free to decide how it plans to achieve these targets (depending on what resources

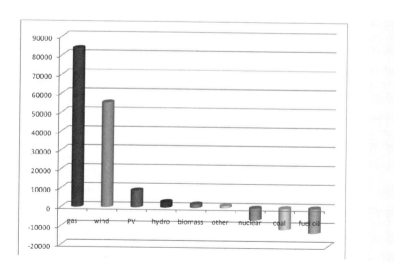

Figure 2.15 Net increase in power capacity in Europe 2000–2008.

Source: Based on EWEA data, 2009.

are available). The European Union is also coordinating the development of a Europe-wide electricity grid and requiring that member states alter regulations to enable renewable generators to connect into the grid. Ultimately it is likely that large-scale renewable energy projects linked by a super-grid will play a key role in providing a sustainable low carbon energy supply in Europe in the future, but it will take some time.

Of course there would be scope for a similar approach in the USA where variation in geology, vegetation and climate offers great potential for developing a diverse renewable energy mix and potentially some degree of self-sufficiency. Currently there is an equivalent grid planned for the USA – the unified national smart grid – although it is not based purely on renewable energy. The proposal is for a national interconnected network linking all the nation's local electrical networks that have been upgraded to smart grids.

Currently the US grid is a series of independently operating regional grids. Its limitations and vulnerability to failure reportedly cost the nation $80 billion to $188 billion per year in losses due to grid-related power outages and power quality issues. Also areas rich in renewable resources are currently not well served and thus have no infrastructure available to move power outputs to the markets where power is needed. A unified national smart grid could monitor and balance the load, accommodating distributed energy from local areas.

Decentralised energy

A decentralised approach to energy provision could as much as halve CO_2 emissions from the power sector (Greenpeace, 2005). There are two key facets of a decentralised energy system: a local distribution network for heat/power and local power generators. In decentralised systems buildings (including homes) and communities can become power generators. A whole range of technologies can be used by individual households, neighbourhoods or districts to generate low carbon heat and or electricity including: PV cells, solar collectors, biomass boilers, wind turbines, heat-pumps, micro-CHP, fuel cells and anaerobic digesters. The local distribution networks can then be used to redistribute the surplus energy produced to local customers (district heating/cooling) or alternatively feed-back into the grid (electricity).

The benefits of decentralised systems are four-fold. Firstly, the introduction of a decentralised system lowers transmission and distribution losses found in most centralised systems (although efficiency of a centralised system could be improved with the introduction of a smart grid technologies). Secondly, research (Devine-Wright, 2006; Dobbyn and Thomas, 2005; Farhar, 2006; Faiers and Neame, 2006) suggests that the inclusion of micro-technologies in homes has a positive impact on overall energy demand and raises awareness of energy consumption patterns amongst consumers. It also enables households to become co-providers of energy. Thirdly, having a large number of small generators in a system can help to increase energy security. Fourthly, the diffusion of micro-generation technologies into the wider community helps to increase renewable energy capacity, and thus decarbonisation of the grid.

It is difficult to estimate the scale of the CO_2 savings that can be made through the use of these technologies since this varies widely. The incumbent energy system and resource availability (influenced by various geographical variables – i.e. solar radiation, geology, hydrology, relief, etc) affects base-line CO_2 emissions which in turn impacts on CO_2 savings calculations. Of course the variation in local energy resources also impacts on the operational effectiveness of the technologies. For example micro-wind is very ineffective in urban areas where buildings interrupt air flow (Figure 2.16).

Micro-generating technologies producing electricity can be 'grid-tied', part of a 'micro-grid' or 'off-grid'. Grid-tied technologies are the most common. Energy produced is fed back into the grid. This has the benefit of not requiring any form of storage. However, the success of this model depends on grid connection, technological viability and financial feasibility. The introduction of smart grid technology and production subsidies (e.g. feed-in tariff) can be used to support the 'grid-tied' technologies. Micro-grids are semi-autonomous systems that have the capability of operating separately from the main network. Micro-grids offer greater supply security to the consumers on the grid. However, micro-grids also suffer from technological,

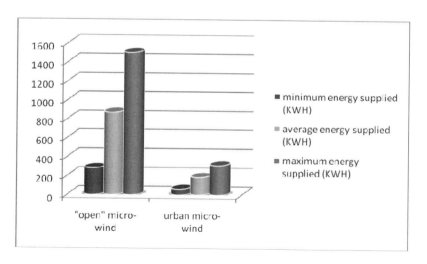

Figure 2.16 Energy supplied by micro-generators to the point of use (estimated).

Source: Allen et al, 2008.

legislative and safety issues. Off-grid generators utilise all the energy they generate (i.e. households become autonomous energy systems in the best case scenarios). The viability of this option is improved by the introduction of storage capacity (batteries/fuel cells) which enable surplus energy to be stored for peak demand periods. However, the introduction of storage capacity significantly increases the cost of a system and requires more space in the home.

Heat can also be produced and distributed locally. The efficiencies of the technologies and sources of energy used to power district heating systems affect the carbon intensities of the heat supply (Figure 2.17, see colour plates). For example in the UK[14] a medium CCGT natural gas CHP produces lower CO_2 emissions (2300 kg/annum savings) than a small (less powerful) CCGT natural gas CHP system (2000 kg/annum savings). A community boiler fuelled by biomass compared with one fuelled by natural gas makes an additional 2600 kg/annum saving (*Pöyry*, Faber Maunsell (AECOM), 2009). Small-scale anaerobic digestion (with CHP) offers the greatest potential CO_2 savings, whilst community boilers powered by natural gas offer the least. Biomass-fuelled heating systems produce greater CO_2 savings than gas-fuelled heating systems. Low carbon district heating technologies compete favourably with stand-alone technologies including heat-pumps and solar thermal heat.

The degree to which district heating systems are already established varies greatly between countries. District heating systems have been deployed in the UK since the 1950s but still only supply 2% of heat demand. This contrasts with Sweden, Germany and Denmark where a significant proportion of heating demand (40%, 40% and 60% respectively) is met by district heating systems. The district heating system was first developed in the USA and implemented in Philadelphia by Benjamin Franklin in the eighteenth century. Due to lack of data it is difficult to estimate the coverage of district heating systems in the USA. The main explanation for low penetration rates in the UK is the high installation cost of a district heating system when compared with traditional gas and electricity heating systems.

Providing a local heat supply network is expensive (*Pöyry*, Faber Maunsell (AECOM), 2009). The capital cost of the infrastructure and of retrofitting networks into existing communities can be high. The capital cost of setting up a district heating system can be a major barrier to deployment. Perceived risk associated with projects in combination with high capital costs makes it difficult to secure investment. Lack of knowledge and experience of district heating systems amongst providers and consumer groups increases the risk to investors. The variability of supply, revenue and difficulties predicting output further impacts on investors' willingness to invest. In addition, the potential redundancy of the network if alternative technologies (for example heating from decarbonised electricity) were to become more competitive also reduces willingness to invest.

For a district heating system to be economically viable during operation, sufficient local demand for heat is required. This demand must be spread across a 24-hour period; thus a variety of customers are needed (from domestic, commercial and industrial sectors) with variable peak-loads. The more proximate the customers to the power plant, the lower the emission losses from the system and the lower the cost of the infrastructure (i.e. it limits pipe-work). Thus, ideal locations for district heating systems are high-density, mixed-use areas – i.e. high heat density areas. In lower density areas other sources of heat – solar collectors and heat-pumps – are likely to be more economically viable.

The consistency and reliability of heat supply is also instrumental in gaining customer confidence and securing investment. An assessment of the reliability of potential heat sources is crucial to ensuring a consistent supply. Where cheap sources of heat (i.e. waste heat from power plants) can be found and electrical heating systems are replaced, district heating systems can become very economically competitive (*Pöyry*, Faber Maunsell (AECOM), 2009).

The provision of a local energy distribution network may enable new small-scale generators to emerge: energy service companies (ESCOs) community energy cooperatives, industries, businesses, local authorities and individual households. Of course access to the networks will be dependent on the standards set out by those owning or regulating it. If new small-scale generators have access to the network this creates huge potential for utilising waste heat more effectively but also for the growth of small-scale generators of low carbon heat and electricity, particularly if a market is guaranteed and operational subsidies are available. Access to the local supply network and a guaranteed financial return is crucial in facilitating decentralised energy generation.

The ownership and management arrangements can seriously affect generators ability to access the supply network. Networks owned by a single generator are the least likely to offer good access to the supply network for other smaller generators. The generator who owns the network will wish to maximise profits and reduce competition. Thus access to other generators is likely to be restricted. This favours a more centralised approach to generation and is likely to drive up the cost of energy (since there is no competition) unless regulators can keep the network owner in check. Currently no regulation exists governing competition for heat supply in Europe (unlike that for electricity supply) which can result in monopolies particularly if the generator model is adopted. In America power monopolies also exist where single energy companies own and operate the entire network.

If the network is owned by an independent body greater competition and access to the network is facilitated. However, it may be more difficult to raise private finance to set the network up initially. In some parts of Europe this was overcome for heating through major public investment (by municipalities) in local heat distribution networks. In this instance networks are controlled and owned by the municipality. This model allows a variety of generators to supply heat to the local consumers. It also generates revenue for the municipality. But it does involve significant up-front costs for the public sector. Finding private finance for a network without guaranteed returns is likely to be more difficult, particularly in countries where a market for district heating/cooling has yet to be proved.

The ongoing management and maintenance of the district heating system, private wires and low carbon technologies are also very important. Experience in the UK suggests that neither house-builders nor households are keen to be involved in the ongoing management and maintenance of these low carbon energy systems (Williams, 2008a and 2010). In other countries (for example Germany, Denmark, Austria) these processes are often overseen by ESCOs. There are three broad models: facilities management model, community model and household model (Watson et al, 2006). The latter two are most relevant to housing (Table 2.7).

In the case of the community model, ESCOs manage the design, build, finance and operate low carbon energy systems. ESCOs are generally formed through partnerships between a private sector energy company and a local authority. However, in large new housing developments partner-

Table 2.7 Models for energy service provision

	A community model	A domestic energy supplier Model
Service offered too	Large new build developments or existing homes	Existing and new homes
Body offering energy services	ESCO (part of the utility, partnerships between energy service provider, municipality, housing developer)	Utility/installers
Services offered	Usually includes design and build, finance and operation	A range of options: 1. Utility may install, maintain and operate technologies and rent space from household. 2. Utility may install technologies and buy back energy from household. 3. Installers may install technologies and utilities buy back energy from household.

Source: Compiled from UKERC and Sustainable Development Commission, 2006.

ships between energy providers and house-builders, or energy providers and residents might also be possible. The ESCO (however it is formed) then has exclusive responsibility for the operation, maintenance and energy supply to the community for a defined period. The ESCO will be responsible for the whole energy system which may include district heating systems and/ or micro-technologies for individual households (e.g. solar collectors, micro-CHP, fuel cells, etc).

The ESCO can design and manage the assets to achieve least life-cycle costs. In new developments, the cost of energy efficiency, district heating systems and micro-generation is a marginal cost over and above the technologies that would be routinely installed (e.g. individual gas boilers and gas network). New systems can be integrated in a building from the start (e.g. metering and generation systems). The capital cost of installing technologies in new build projects is lower than in retrofit situations. Economies of scale can also be achieved in larger developments or by ESCOs who have a contract for several housing projects.

In new developments, an electrical network has to be installed to each home. This is usually given to the distribution network operator to manage because it is seen as a liability by house-builders. If this is designed and installed by an ESCO it can be retained and used to sell surplus electricity by private wire back to the grid, thus increasing revenue. Equally, surplus heat can be piped back into the district heating system. An ESCO could also be a facilitator of more general energy saving services in a community to tackle household energy consumption (for example linked with mobility or perhaps the rebound effect of living in more energy efficient accommodation). Thus there are several areas in which ESCOs could generate revenue and improve energy efficiency.

The second model – domestic energy supplier model – can be applied to both new and existing stock at a variety of scales. It is more commonly used than the community model. This involves the utility (or possibly the technology installer) offering additional energy services to households, for example the installation of energy-saving devices or micro-technologies, low carbon infrastructure maintenance services and buying back the energy generated by households. Utilities may take a rather hands-off approach and merely install technologies and buy back the energy produced from households. At the opposite end of the spectrum utilities could install, operate and maintain technologies on people's homes and merely pay households for the use of their roof space. In some instances installers of low carbon technologies have also begun to offer similar services where incentives are available.

Concluding remarks

This is the toolbox of technological solutions which may be used to achieve the zero carbon standard. The technologies can be combined in a number of ways to achieve the same outcome. In all instances a rather complex techno-logical system results. The manner in which these technologies are combined to provide a zero carbon energy system is likely to vary enormously with the physical, demographic, socio-economic, technological and cultural characteristics of the local system in which they operate. In addition the political and regulatory context in which systems operate is likely to influence the viability of different systems. It seems that being very prescriptive about a blue-print for achieving zero carbon homes could be foolish; this a hypothesis to be tested and discussed in the book.

These technological solutions might be deployed in a number of ways, via housing programmes (Chapter 3), changes to energy infrastructure (Chapter 4) or perhaps through the creation of more holistic zero carbon neighbourhoods (Chapter 5). A variety of examples from Germany, UK, Sweden and the USA will be presented in the book. This will provide a brief overview of possible technological and policy options which is by no means exhaustive. However, the case studies chosen do represent the state of the art in technological terms at the time of writing this book. These case studies will demonstrate the degree of variation in response to the zero carbon agenda and issues surrounding deployment.

Part II

Chapter 3

Innovative housing programmes

Introduction

One approach to the deployment of zero carbon homes (and their constituent technical systems) might be through strategic housing programmes. Various attempts have been made to address the energy efficiency and /or CO_2 emissions from housing through strategic programmes. In this chapter we discuss four from the case study countries: the Zero Carbon Homes programme (UK); California Solar programme (USA); Miljonprogrammet (Sweden); and the German Energetic programme (Table 3.1). These programmes have been used to encourage the deployment of a range of LZC technical systems (low energy, passive, zero carbon and solar houses).

Each housing programme has been motivated by a diversity of factors ranging from addressing energy security to improving living standards. Some programmes purely focus on new housing, whilst others tackle existing stock. The impact of each programme also varies significantly. For example a quarter of the Swedish national housing stock has been influenced by the Miljonprogrammet housing programme, whilst in the UK only a few demonstration projects have been built to date as part of the zero carbon homes programme. These examples provide insight into the array of policy instruments which could be used to encourage the deployment of zero carbon homes. They also offer some appreciation of the kind of changes needed in industry to produce zero carbon homes.

Zero carbon Programme

Of the four examples outlined presented in this chapter, the UK zero carbon homes programme was the only one which aimed to produce housing stock from which there would be no net CO_2 emissions. The zero carbon homes policy was first introduced in the United Kingdom in 2007. The Government set a target to achieve zero carbon emissions from all new housing by 2016. This was the most ambitious target set for new housing globally. It was introduced as part of a wider push to achieve a reduction in carbon emissions from the domestic sector. Tackling emissions from new housing was seen as

Table 3.1 Summary of innovative housing programmes

	Zero Carbon homes programme	Solar homes programme	Miljonprogrammet	German energetic programme
Technical systems	Complex[1]	Energy efficiency and solar technologies	Energy efficiency	Energy efficiency
Motivation	Targets for CO_2 reduction, energy security, industrial innovation	Energy security, growth of new industry, lower energy prices	Comfort, cold climate, energy security	Targets for CO_2 reduction, energy security, industrial innovation
New/existing stock	New (and major refurbishments)	Both	New	Both
Deployment	A few demonstration projects	8,000 homes	25% of current housing stock	Over 600,000 since 2006
Policy instruments of deployment	New housing programme, targets, building code, subsidies[2], planning	New housing programme, targets, subsidies[3], training programmes, expedited planning process	New housing programme, building code, subsidised loans	Building code, subsidised loans, training programmes, accreditation schemes
Impact on industry	Very significant for energy and house-building industries	Very limited – similar model but develop supply chains	Significant change supply chains & construction process	Limited – similar model but develop supply chains

Source: Author's own.
1 includes energy efficiency, on-site generation (micro-technologies and district heating systems), off-site generation from LZC sources.
2 capital and operational costs.
3 capital and operational costs.

a 'low-hanging fruit' by the UK Government, easier to tackle than emissions from existing building stock, car travel or aviation. It was hoped that the target could significantly reduce domestic CO_2 emissions without major public subsidy.

When the policy was introduced it was envisaged that new housing would be needed to accommodate the predicted increase in households in the UK from 18 million currently to 24.4 million in 2050. Thus the government introduced a house-building programme in 2006, to develop 2 million new homes by 2016 (3 million new homes by 2020)[1]. It was anticipated that the house-building programme would provide a test-bed for low or zero carbon (LZC) technologies and drive the changes required within the house-building and energy industries to deliver zero carbon homes from 2016 and be more competitive in future environmentally aware markets. Various factors inspired the programme, the most influential being the statutory CO_2 reduction targets; EU energy performance standards for buildings; national targets for renewable energy production; and the need for greater national energy security.

The UK Government produced a definition of what constituted a zero carbon home to give some clarity and guidance to the house-building industry. The definition stated that a zero carbon home should produce zero-net emissions of carbon dioxide from all energy use during operation (regulated and unregulated[2] emissions). The definition excluded emissions generated from the fabrication, transportation, construction or demolition processes[3]. The government also produced a hierarchy of measures[4] for meeting the zero carbon standard in new build housing (Figure 3.1).

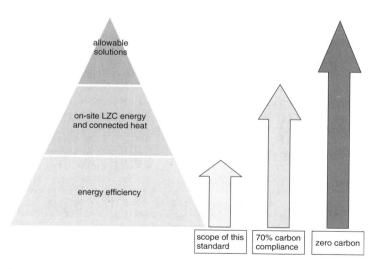

Figure 3.1 Zero carbon hierarchy

Source: zerocarbonhub.org.

The hierarchy required that the bulk of the carbon savings would be made through improvements in the energy efficiency of new housing. Seventy per cent of the remaining emissions would be tackled on-site (called 'carbon compliance') through installation of LZC heating systems or microgenerating technologies, or connection to LZC heat supply off-site. The remaining 30% of emissions would be dealt with off-site (called 'allowable solutions'), largely through various off-setting mechanisms which would result in the reduction of CO_2 emissions in the wider community.

A variety of technical solutions resulted (Table 3.2). Although the zero carbon programme essentially affects new housing, the use of 'allowable solutions' meant that emissions from existing stock could also be tackled (at least partially) in the process directly (through the energetic renovation, the installation of LZC heating systems or generating technologies in communities surrounding the development) or indirectly (via an energy infrastructure fund).

Deployment of zero carbon homes

To date very few zero carbon homes have been built in the United Kingdom. Various attempts have been made by the Government to support the devel-

Table 3.2 Technical systems to achieve zero carbon standard

	Definition	Technical systems
Energy efficiency	Energy efficiency of the dwelling unit[1]	1. Insulation 2. Airtight shell 3. Passive solar technologies
Carbon compliance	Carbon compliance – a 70% reduction in CO_2 emission required on-site and/or through direct connection to LZC heat.	1. Microgenerating technologies in the fabric of the building 2. CHP system 3. Direct connection to a near-site LZC heat network
Allowable solutions	Residual emissions (i.e. the remaining 30%) can be dealt with either by off-site solutions or by house-builders contributing to a buy-out fund – allowable solutions[2].	1. Energy efficiency technology off-site 2. Microgenerating technology off-site 3. LZC heat network feeding off-site properties. 4. LZC electricity supply linked by private wire to homes.

1 Minimum building fabric energy efficiency standard equals 39 kWh/m2/year for apartments and mid terrace homes; 46 kWh/m2/year for end terrace, semi detached and detached homes. The minimum energy efficiency standard equates to an approximate 20–25% reduction in CO_2 emissions compared with current regulations for a gas heated home.
2 Options include: LZC heat exported to existing properties surrounding the site that were previously heated by fossil fuels; retrofit existing buildings surrounding the development with LZC technologies to improve energy efficiency or for microgeneration; connect by private wire to a LZC energy source off-site; contribute to an energy infrastructure fund.

opment of low energy housing in one-off demonstration projects, in the hope that it would help the house-building industry to increase its capacity to deliver and to generate demand for low energy housing. The largest of these – Greenwich Millennium Village[5] (GMV) – was funded through the Millennium Communities Programme. The programme used financial incentives to encourage house-builders to deliver higher design standards (including energy efficiency) in new build developments. The GMV project was successful in that it was significantly more energy efficient than standard housing[6]. It offered a resource efficient but conventionally designed housing model to the market (Williams, 2006 and 2008). However, due to various post-occupancy problems and limited consumer interest in environmental features the house-builder was not enthusiastic about scaling-up the model (Williams, 2008a).

Meanwhile another more ambitious zero carbon development was being built in the London suburbs called BedZED (Chapter 5). BedZED not only sought to tackle CO_2 emissions from the home but from the household too. Thus attempts were made to tackle CO_2 emissions from heating, use of household appliances, travel, use of water and waste disposal in the development in a number of ways[7]. Although BedZED drew a great deal of attention particularly amongst the media, built environment professionals, the green movement and policy-makers, it was not seen by mainstream house-builders as a commercially viable model for new housing.

Although other prototype housing projects have been built since 2002, it has not seemed to greatly increase interest amongst the public in low energy homes. Nor have the lessons learnt from these projects appeared to filter back to the house-building industry. As a result the projects did seem to tail off towards 2007. However, the zero carbon agenda for new housing and eco-towns introduced in 2007 appeared to revive interest at least amongst the house-building industry. This was reinforced by discussions at a European level about new building energy performance requirements. For some time it seemed the European Union would require all new build development to achieve passive house standard by 2015 and zero carbon standard by 2019. However, this was watered down and the zero-net energy target for 2020 was adopted by the European Union in 2010 (Energy Performance in Buildings Directive 2010/31/EU). Nevertheless the target requires that new buildings are connected to a renewable energy supply, district heating system and use cogeneration as a minimum.

The UK 2016 zero carbon target resulted in some pioneering speculative house-builders testing a range of zero carbon housing models, utilising district heating with CHP and LZC technologies, working with a range of energy providers (Table 3.3). However, the global economic recession that began in 2008 has resulted in a significant drop in new housing being built in the United Kingdom by speculative house-builders. In 2007–8, 216,700 units were completed in the UK, but by 2009–10 that had dropped to 147,060 units, over a 30% reduction (Department of Communities and Local

Table 3.3 Zero carbon homes projects in the United Kingdom

Project	Tarmac Homes	Miller Homes	Creo House	One Brighton (new England quarter)	Barratt Green House
CO_2 emissions reduction (over part L 2006)	150%	148%	131%	Ecohomes excellent rating	133%
Developer	Tarmac	Miller Homes Ltd	CreoProkoncept	Crest Nicholson and Bioregional Quintain LLP	Barratt Developments Plc
Construction Architect	Lovell Partnership ZedFactory	Fraser Brown MacKenna	MJP Architects	Fielden Clegg Bradley	Gaunt Francis Architects
Completion	August 2009	May/June 2009	May 2009	First Phase June 2009	May 2008
Location	University Nottingham	Basingstoke	Watford	Brighton	Watford
Dwelling emission rate	159%	148%	N/A	0 kg/m2/yr	133%
Building fabric (heat loss parameter)	0.73[1]	0.79[2]	N/A[3]	22.83% improvement in average u-value	0.72[4]
Internal lighting	Low emission	Energy efficient	Energy efficient	–	Energy efficient
Drying space	Yes	Yes	Yes	–	Yes
Energy white-labelled goods	All A+ rated	Some A and some A+	Mix A+ and A rated	Eco-labelled goods	B and A+ mix

External lighting	Low energy and light sensors	Low energy and light sensors	Energy efficient	Low energy and sensors	Energy efficient
LZC technologies	Heat recovery and microgeneration[5]	Heat recovery and microgeneration[6]	ASHP, MVHR and PV	Biomass boiler, PV, RE sourced off-site	ASHP, MVHR, PV and solar thermal array.
Reduction in carbon emission from LZC technology (%)	99.6%	68%	N/A	N/A	109%
Cycle storage	Yes	Yes	Yes	–	Yes
Home office	Yes	Yes	Yes	–	Yes

Source: Compiled using Zero Carbon Hub database.

1 Masonary fabric with lightweight plaster, argon filled double glazing, insulation.
2 Prefabricated concrete strips – air tight envelope and high thermal mass – with triple glazing.
3 Insulated concrete framework system with high thermal mass and air tightness and triple glazing.
4 Uses medium density concrete construction to provide thermal mass and passive cooling and highly airtight, super-insulated envelope with minimum thermal bridges to minimise heat losses.
5 Biomass boiler, PV, solar thermal array, passive wind cowl to deliver heat, power and ventilation.
6 Biomass boiler, PV array and mechanical ventilation/heat recovery.

Government, 2010). However, the number of housing units built by housing associations and local authorities rose slightly.

Some believed this would a be a period of reflection for speculative house-builders, a time when they could restructure, reorganise and build their capacity to deliver zero carbon homes. Certainly some speculative builders decided to rise to the challenge, whilst others lobbied hard against the policy. It was expected that larger house-building companies would be more likely to innovate, because they had the resources available to support the changes needed. Interestingly it seems that housing associations produced the most innovative low-carbon projects during the earlier phases of the programme. This has been driven by higher energetic standards placed on all publicly funded development (including social housing) by the Government. Some speculative developers are now beginning to catch up (e.g. Barratt Homes). They are currently testing a range of models that can be scaled-up for a growing market.

Thus progress so far has been limited in the UK; however, there appears to be growing interest amongst speculative and social housing providers. But still only very few completed projects exist and most are single buildings. The Carbon Challenge (a programme run by the Homes and Communities Agency) was recently introduced to subsidise the construction of four larger, mixed use, mixed tenure, zero carbon housing schemes in the UK. The first to go on site is Hanham Hall (in rural South Gloucestershire).

Hanham Hall will be the largest zero carbon housing development in the UK once complete. Thus, the United Kingdom is in the very early stages of the deployment of zero carbon homes. It is still in the pioneering phase when different technology combinations and housing models (in terms of tenure, management and partnerships) are being trialled. Some demonstration projects exist but as yet are far removed from what is being provided by the mainstream. The process of market transformation has not yet begun.

The removal of stamp duty for zero carbon homes and introduction of green mortgages was supposed to provide sufficient incentive for the market. However, thus far the market has proved conservative in its housing preferences and uninterested in zero carbon homes. This appears to stem from a combination of factors including:

- relatively low energy price (Williams, 2010; Waters, 2007; Jones and Leach, 2000; WWF, 2003);
- higher capital cost of zero carbon homes (Waters, 2007; Williams, 2008a; Townshend, 2005; ICARO, 2009);
- limited public environmental concern (ICARO, 2009);
- public concern about the reliability of an LZC system, particularly when renewable energy is integrated into it (Williams, 2007; ICARO, 2009);
- concerns about the degree of resident involvement required to operate and maintain LZC technical systems (Williams, 2007; ICARO, 2009);
- concerns about impact on households, quality of life (ICARO, 2009).

Thus, it appears that significant Government support (regulatory, fiscal, educational instruments, etc) will be needed during the early phases of deployment to assist in the processes of market and industrial transformation.

Policy instruments

Initially the UK Government's market approach to zero carbon housing appeared to rely on the private sector (house-building and energy industries) to deliver zero carbon homes, with very little regulation or financial support (for the period 2007–10). Green mortgages and stamp duty exemption for those buying zero carbon homes were supposed to offer sufficient incentive for the market to drive production. Unfortunately, neither generated significant demand, partly because of the greatly reduced construction rates in the recession, and partly because the public were unaware of what a zero carbon house was, what it looked like, its costs and benefits. Thus, there was no market demand for zero carbon homes and no incentive for producers to build them.

In the early stages of deployment (2007–10), the responsibility for delivery fell on the shoulders of pioneering local authorities and more specifically on their planning departments.

A great deal of pressure was placed on the land use planning system to deliver zero carbon homes through the development plan and granting of planning permissions (Williams, 2008a, 2010). However, the planning system was not found to be an adequate tool to encourage the wholesale changes in industry required to deliver zero carbon homes at scale, nor was it a tool applied systematically across the country (Williams, 2010). Consequently zero carbon projects were ad hoc and very slow to emerge.

As time progresses more regulation and fiscal incentives are being introduced to improve the energy efficiency of buildings and decarbonise the fuel supply in the United Kingdom (Figure 3.2). Energy efficiency requirements for buildings have been steadily ratcheted-up though the building regulations. Previously a house built in the UK had a primary energy load of 200 kwh/m²/year (Part L Building Regulations, 2006). Targets were introduced in 2010 to improve energy efficiency of buildings by 25% (i.e. primary energy load of 150 kwh/m²/year) compared to 2006 regulations and it is intended to increase to this target to 44% (i.e. 112 kwh /m²/year – similar to passive house standard 120 kwh/m²/year) by 2013. Initial estimates are that these measures will save 1.1–1.2 MtC/year by 2020 (Ko and Fenner, 2007). Thus, building regulations are driving the transformation in the house-building industry.

Changes are also required in the energy industry to deliver zero carbon homes. The emissions trading system in Europe has been the main driver for change within the energy industry and encouraged some growth in renewable energy generating capacity in the UK. This has been further reinforced by

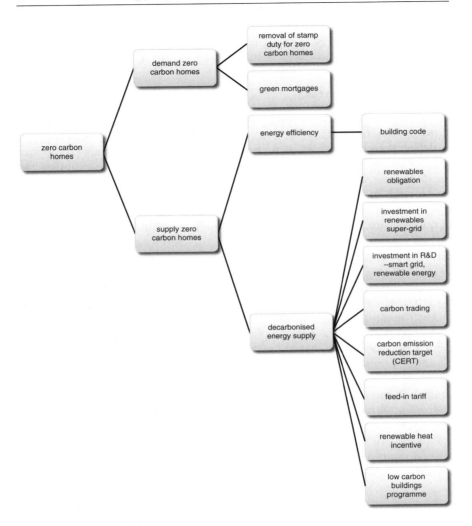

Figure 3.2 Policy instruments for encouraging deployment of zero carbon homes.
Source: Author's own.

domestic instruments (Carbon Emissions Reduction Target[8] and Renewable Obligations[9]) that require a minimum percentage of energy to be sourced from renewables (or utilities are penalised). Direct public funding for the deployment of centralised renewable energy infrastructure remains limited (Williams, 2010), although some public funding will be used to develop the European Super Grid which will help to enable the transfer and storage of energy produced from renewable sources and encourage wider deployment.

Capital subsidies for households wishing to install microgenerating technologies (Low Carbon Buildings Programme[10] and previously the Clear Skies Programme) have been available in the UK for some time. However, these funds have been limited and difficult to access. There are no capital subsidies available for house-builders and the subsidies available to households keep changing. Operational subsidies, the feed-in tariff[11] and renewable heat incentive have more recently been introduced in the UK to assist in the decarbonisation of the energy supply. These are particularly aimed at encouraging the development of a decentralised LZC energy system, by offering incentives to smaller energy producers and ESCOs. These subsidies are critical for the successful delivery of zero carbon homes in the UK and will affect the technological systems adopted. The British Government also hopes to develop a 'smart grid' which will facilitate the effective and safe operation of a decentralised energy system based on LZC sources of energy.

Thus the Government steadily introduced instruments designed to raise energetic standards in the new building stock and decarbonise heat and electricity supplies. Using these instruments in combination could provide a more robust framework for delivering zero carbon homes, but only if there is long-term consistency in approach, adequate funding to support R&D and the earlier stages of deployment (Williams, 2010).

Industrial transformation

The house-building and energy industries in the UK are conservative, being orientated towards minimising risk. Thus, innovation remains an unattractive option to both industries. The new policy framework recently introduced in the UK to encourage the decarbonisation of the energy supply, the development of more energy efficient buildings and in time the production of zero carbon homes are beginning to encourage a degree of change in both industries, but the transformation is slow.

For the UK energy industry the scale of change required to deliver zero carbon energy in terms of technology, culture, structure and practice is phenomenal. Currently only 2.25% of the UK energy supply is sourced from renewable energy and 7.6% from nuclear power (DECC, 2010). The majority of the energy consumed is sourced from fossil fuels and supplied through centralised distribution networks. There is significant resistance in the energy industry towards renewable energy and decentralised energy systems, created by technical, cultural and structural barriers. Thus carbon intensity of the existing system is high.

The energy industry tends to focus on supply rather than the management of energy, particularly on maximising consumption to maximise profit (although this is beginning to change with the introduction of CERT and carbon trading). It is also dominated by a few large utilities and access to funding and the grid for smaller operators is very restricted (Williams, 2010).

Thus there is a lack of small-scale generators to supply renewable energy to the grid and ESCOs to manage energy consumption. Limited consumer demand for zero carbon energy or even energy management services has further restricted structural and cultural change within the industry (Williams, 2010).

Path dependencies and cultural inertia in the house-building industry have largely prevented innovation in housing to date. The parochial nature of the UK house-building industry has created difficulties in establishing supply chains for new LZC technologies and developing appropriate expertise for delivering zero carbon homes. However, the scale of change required in the UK house-building industry to deliver zero carbon although large, is somewhat less than for the energy industry.

Already the house-building industry has learnt to build progressively more energy efficient houses. This has required changes to supply chains, design and construction practices. Nevertheless capacity (expertise and supply chains) will need to be built in the industry if passive house and eventually zero carbon standards are to be reached. Barriers do exist, for example, lack of stable supply chains for LZC technologies; the additional cost of construction; the apparent lack of demand for zero carbon homes; as well as limited relevant skills and expertise within the house-building industry.

The zero carbon homes programme requires the transformation of both the house-building and energy industry. However, it also requires that both industries works in partnership to achieve the zero carbon target. There is evidence that some pioneering house-builders and utilities have begun to work together. For example, Barratt Homes (a major volume house-builder in the UK) is in the process of developing a variety of zero carbon housing models with various energy providers (Utilicom, E-ON and EDF). The models vary in terms of technologies used, financing, management, operation and ownership arrangements for the LZC energy systems. However, there limited examples.

In practice there seem to be significant tensions between the approaches taken by utilities/ESCOs to the provision of energy systems and services (i.e. long-term approach) and house-builders towards the construction of homes (i.e. short-term approach). This difference in approaches , particularly in terms of culture and practice, creates problems in implementation of joint projects (Woodward, 2009). Poor design of the LZC energy network in a new housing development can have a major impact on energy losses and the carbon intensity of a project. Thus it is very important for networks to be designed and assembled with this in mind. In the models developed to date, the house-builder's role is to contract a team to provide the infrastructure to connect to the LZC energy system. It is also their role to oversee the design and assembly of the infrastructure. The house-builder often lacks the skills to oversee this part of a development project (Woodward, 2009). This has led to the creation of poorly designed and inefficient systems (Woodward, 2009).

One way to overcome this problem might be to involve an ESCO, in partnership, from the start of a new housing project, which manages the housebuilder and ensures that the LZC energy system installed in the development is effective. Alternatively, house-builders themselves will need to develop the skills required to deliver an effective LZC energy system in-house (driven by regulation, funding, etc). The former arrangement appears to be more popular amongst house-builders in the UK. Most do not want a long-term commitment to a project, but prefer to leave the site when construction is complete. Certainly house-builders interviewed in the UK, Sweden and Germany showed no interest in offering energy management services or becoming generators of LZC energy. All preferred to work in tandem with the energy companies.

For private energy companies (utilities or ESCOs) to invest in expensive LZC energy systems there must be sufficient economic return. They can profit through the generation of energy, management of energy supply or controlling access to the supply network. However, under current competition laws (at least for electricity in the European Union) the customer has the right to choose their electricity supplier. This can create problems for those providing LZC energy systems in new developments in terms of how they can recoup their costs (Woodward, 2009). Simply managing energy consumption within a community is unlikely to produce adequate economic return (Woodward, 2009). Thus, models tend to focus on generating LZC electricity which can be fed back in to the grid (encouraged by the introduction of the feed-in tariff) and community heating systems, which are currently not subject to the same competition laws (also supported by the renewable heat incentive).

The Californian Go Solar programme

The energy crisis and black-outs suffered in California in 2000 and 2001 have greatly shaken the public's trust in the existing energy system. Households are looking to increase their energy security whilst policy-makers want to diversify energy supply, increase energy security and reduce CO_2 emissions. New housing construction is seen as an opportunity to introduce new LZC technologies into the state, which can help to achieve these aims. California benefits from high levels of solar radiation between 7 and 8.5 kWh/day (Figure 3.3, see colour plates). Thus, deploying solar technologies on new homes was seen as good solution to the problems outlined. The Go Solar programme was introduced in California to encourage the deployment of new solar homes across the state.

Solar homes offer a way to tackle the problem of energy security in California whilst addressing CO_2 emissions from the domestic sector. Solar homes (or zero-net energy homes) combine highly energy efficient housing units with solar technologies (solar collectors – to heat water and photovoltaic cells – to produce electricity for lights and appliance use). The surplus electricity produced by solar homes can be fed back into the grid and thus can help to decarbonise the wider energy supply.

Deployment of solar homes

Solar homes are becoming more popular in California. By 2008 over 8,000 new homes with PV systems had been approved, capable of producing 18.28 megawatts of energy. However, although at least 64 solar home projects have now been built in California (focused geographically in San Diego, Los Angeles, Fresno, San Francisco and Sacramento), the rapid deployment envisaged by the state has yet to occur.

This is because of the slow replacement of housing stock (NHAB, 2006), path dependencies within the industry (Navigant Consulting, 2008) and limited market interest (Farhar et al, 2004; Navigant Consulting, 2008). Although solar technologies are ready for early market penetration they are not currently economically viable without financial incentives (NHAB, 2006). The economic issues (capital cost), technical issues (need for new equipment, techniques and system integration), regulatory issues, and organisational issues (the supply chains and partnerships that must be in place for a successful business model) all create barriers to delivering solar homes.

The California case study is particularly interesting because a considerable amount of research has been conducted to determine how wider deployment of solar homes can be encouraged. Of course the lessons learnt here could be transferable to zero carbon homes. This is particularly important when market models for deployment are preferred. The research suggests that for solar homes to succeed the benefits to the home-owner, house-builder and utility will need to be more apparent. House-builders believe that solar homes offer no added value (no market) and create additional investment risk (construction and planning delays which increase overall construction costs). Home-owners see only limited value (short-term view), whilst utilities believe PV to be too unreliable (Navigant Consulting, 2008).

However, other research based on the Shea Homes project in San Diego provided a more optimistic picture (Farhar et al, 2004). It found that demand for solar technologies increased once residents had experienced living in a solar home and benefitted from the financial reward. The research showed that the integration of solar technologies into the fabric of the building increased marketability. Simplifying connection to the grid was essential if solar technologies were to be acceptable to residents. House-purchasers did not want to be involved in the decision to include solar technologies in new developments. They preferred house-builders to make that decision and just include the most efficient solar technologies in all new homes. Thus, there did appear to be a potential market for passive models which limit residents' involvement in the decision-making and operational process.

A further initiative – the PIER programme – was set up to develop market ready business models for solar homes in California. These models not only addressed the cost barrier but also persistent barriers to market growth, including connection to the grid, integration of technologies into the building fabric, management and maintenance of the technologies and streamlining the construction process so as to reduce developers' costs. These improved business models can complement current government policies, to accelerate the rate at which solar homes can become fully commercialised and competitive in the marketplace.

The three business models offering a range of benefits to the household, house-builder and utility/ESCO are currently being trialled in California are:

- affordable multi-family housing with communal PV on the roof financed, maintained and managed by an ESCO;
- utility-focused models – where a customer owns a PV array subsidised by the utility, or a utility owns PV array and the customer leases it, or a utility owns PV and pays the customer to the rent roof space;
- powerlight homes – the aesthetically attractive, maintenance-free PV array is integrated into the roof and provides insulation. It is a turn-key solution and sold to single and multi-family home-owners. The cost is financed by a third party, the product delivery channel is streamlined between the builder and manufacturer, there are builder entitlements and streamlining of the city permits system.

Adopting these models may accelerate the deployment of solar homes in California. However, the key to solar homes becoming economically competitive[12] with conventional homes is including the utility operational costs in the cost of home-ownership. Part of the problem lies in the residential appraisal and lending process itself. One barrier to the rapid adoption of technology is its valuation. Solar technologies will typically add to the initial cost of a home, but reduce its operational cost.

House-builders are reticent to adopt technologies that increase the cost of their product and reduce their market. Home-buyers are often unwilling to purchase technologies that are not reflected in the appraised value of the home, thus forcing the purchaser to cover the cost upfront in the down payment rather than financing the technology over the life of a mortgage. Lenders are unwilling to provide financing for structures where the value of the property is unknown in the event of foreclosure (NAHB, 2006). This problem is systemic and needs to be addressed by raising awareness in the property market and increasing the receptivity of lenders and investors to green mortgages. In the meantime the subsidies offered by the federal, state and city governments to bridge the gap in California must suffice.

The antithesis of this argument is that supply will drive demand. The early deployment of solar homes in California will not be based on increasing demand, but on increasing supply. In this scenario the early adopters are the house-building and energy industries. They produce a supply of solar homes which ultimately leads to an increase in market demand a theory supported by Farhar and Coborn, 2006).

Policy instruments

Currently there is no mandatory zero-net energy target for housing in California. The deployment of solar homes has been encouraged by non-mandatory targets, financial incentives and training programmes. The State of California has introduced a target for all new build housing to be zero-net energy by 2020. It is expected that in most instances this will be achieved by a combination of LZC technologies, most likely using energy efficiency measures and solar power. Although this target is not yet mandatory it provides a clear guide to house-builders as to the standards expected by the state by 2020.

The Go Solar programme is a joint venture by the California Energy Commission and California Public Utilities Commission to encourage the deployment of solar technologies in the state. The goals are to encourage Californians to install 3,000 megawatts of solar energy systems on homes and businesses by the end of 2016 and to install 585 million therms of gas-displacing solar hot water systems by the end of 2017. The programme aims to establish a self-sufficient solar industry in which solar energy systems are a viable mainstream option in 10 years (Table 3.4). The programme offers various financial incentives for the deployment of solar technologies.

The California Energy Commission (CEC) introduced the New Solar Homes Partnership (NSHP) in 2007. It is a 10-year, $400 million program to encourage the use of solar technologies in new homes. The NSHP specifically targets market-rate and affordable housing, single-family and multi-family sectors. The goal is to achieve 360 MW of installed solar electric capacity in new homes, and to have solar electric systems on 50% of all new homes built in California by the end of 2016. The NSHP program offers capital subsidies to those building solar homes. Along with the financial incentive, the NSHP provides non-financial support services, offering marketing and technical assistance to builders, as well as training to building officials and sales people. This is very different from the UK where financial incentives were focused on consumers rather than producers. Such an approach recognises the need to encourage producers (house-builders) to become early adopters of the new solar technologies.

The California Energy Commission also provides a performance-based incentive (a feed-in tariff) for systems over 50KW. The feed-in tariffs (introduced in 2008) provide a 10, 15 or 20-year fixed-price, non-negotiable contract to participating small renewable generators sized up to 1.5 MW. Customers can sell renewable power under the feed-in tariff terms to a range

Table 3.4 Components of Go Solar programme

Program authority	California Public Utilities Commission	California Energy Commission	Publicly Owned Utilities (POUs)	Total
Program name	California Solar Initiative (CSI) (including CSI-Thermal)	New Solar Homes Partnership	Various program names	Go Solar California!
Budget	$2,167 million (Electric) $250 million (Gas)	$400 million	$784 million	$3,351 million (Electric) $250 Million (Gas)
Solar goals	1,940 MW (Electric) 585 million therms (Gas)	360 MW	700 MW	3,000 MW (Electric) 585 million therms (Gas)
Scope	All solar systems in large IOU areas except new homes	Solar systems on new homes in large IOU areas	All solar systems in POU areas	All of California

Source: Go Solar website (accessed 2010).
Note
The electric budgets are for 2007–2016, and the gas budgets are for 2010–2017.

of utilities[13]. This provides households with a guaranteed financial return for the surplus energy they sell back to the grid. Utilities may offer additional incentives and utility credits to local generators, driven by the renewable portfolio standard, which required that energy providers find 20% of their energy supply from renewable sources by 2010. Thus the installation of PV cells may also produce a revenue stream for households, making the technologies more attractive.

Federal incentives to encourage the deployment of zero net energy homes (including solar homes) across the USA are also available, including federal tax credits (for house-builders and households), green mortgages[14] and training programmes. Federal tax credits reduce the capital cost of LZC technologies to house-builders or households. Green mortgages offer lower interest payments for solar homes which make them more attractive to house purchasers. Training for professionals involved in the construction, operation, maintenance and marketing of zero-net energy homes will increase industrial capacity to deliver new technologies more widely and encourage deployment. Solar home owners and providers in California can tap into these federal resources.

Local initiatives have also emerged which have helped to encourage the deployment of solar homes. For example, San Diego has a target to install

50 MW renewable energy[15] in the city over the next decade (Green Power Purchase Resolution). Solar housing can contribute to this target and therefore is encouraged by the municipality. San Diego has a rather innovative approach to increasing the deployment of solar homes. The municipality has reduced the length of the planning process for any development that generates its own energy from renewable sources.

Residential projects that qualify for consideration in San Diego must provide at least 50% of their projected total energy use from renewable energy sources in order to expedite the ministerial process. This cuts the length of the planning process from 24 months to 6–9 months, which saves developers finance charges on loans. A reduced charge is also paid to make the application. Thus, the additional cost of the LZC technologies is recouped by the developer through these cost savings. Local incentives also operate in Los Angeles, Fresno, San Francisco and Sacramento. Thus, solar homes tend to congregate in locations where the economic advantage to the house-builder is clear.

Industrial transformation

The American house-building industry has been building to higher energy efficiency standards for some time. Regulated American energy efficiency standards reached the Swedish standard in 1989 (Nassen and Holmberg, 2005). The introduction of two voluntary labelling systems – EPA Energy Star and Leadership in Energy and Environmental Design (LEED) Green Building rating systems – encouraged further improvement. By 2006 around 12% of new housing was EPA rated and 14,000 projects were LEED rated. Thus, there is already capacity within the industry to deliver highly energy efficient dwellings.

However, capacity does need to be built in the industry to deliver solar homes to a mass market. New partnerships between house-builders and solar technology suppliers and installers will be needed and supply chains altered. House-builders will have to work closely with utilities to ensure that solar homes are connected to the grid and that households are remunerated for the energy they produce. Thus, new partnerships and supply chains are needed.

House-builders will take on a more facilitative role, which may require the development of new expertise and certainly the reallocation of resources. Increasingly house-builders will become educators, explaining new technologies and their benefits to prospective house purchasers. This has been shown to be essential for encouraging the formation of markets, increasing customer satisfaction and ensuring new technologies are used effectively (Farhar and Coborn, 2006). However, (as in the UK) there is no evidence to suggest that house-builders want to be involved in the long-term operation of these technologies. The operation and maintenance of technologies will be the responsibility of the householder, technology installer or utility. Thus, delivering solar homes will require limited innovation in the house-building industry.

In contrast, the energy industry will need to adapt to a more decentralised approach to energy generation. This will require that technical, cultural and structural challenges are overcome (similar to those encountered in the UK). The introduction of the smart grid (as planned for the whole of the USA) and the emergence of energy service companies would help to support this transition.

Miljonprogrammet – the Swedish house-building programme

Currently housing in Sweden is the most energy efficient in the world. This energy efficiency standard was first achieved almost forty years ago, as a result of a major publicly subsidised housing programme – Miljonprogrammet. Technically the standard was achieved using insulation, reducing the permeability of the built shell and the number of air changes in a house (Table 3.5). These factors combined to reduced heat loss from housing, thereby lowering primary energy consumption.

Table 3.5 Comparison of Swedish Building Standards (1975) and UK standards (2006).

	Sweden 1975	UK 2006
Insulation	U-values: Walls toward ambient air 0.3 W/(m²K) Window (frame and glass) 2 W/(m²K) Roof 0.2 W/(m²K) Floor (slab) 0.3 W/(m²K)	Area-averaged U-values: Walls 0.35 W/(m²K) Windows, roof windows, roof lights and doors (where >50% glass) 2.2 W/(m²K) Roof 0.25 W/(m²K) Floor 0.25 W/(m²K)
Permeability	1–2 storeys: through walls 0.4m3/(h m2) through roof 0.2m3/(h m2) 3–8 storeys: through walls 0.2m3/(h m2) through roof 0.1m3/(h m2)	10 m³/(h m2) at 50Pa
Ventilation	Natural ventilation allowed. Minimum outside air flow rate of 0.35 l/s per m² floor area	Mechanical ventilation to meet performance limits (2.0 l/(s W) for balanced systems, 66% heat recovery efficiency)
Primary energy load	110–130 KWh/m²/year	200 KWh/m²/year

Source: Ko and Fenner, 2007.

Deployment of energy efficient homes

The Miljonprogrammet was an ambitious housing programme implemented in Sweden between 1965 and 1974 by the governing Swedish Social Democratic Party. The aim of the programme was to build a million affordable new dwellings in a 10-year period. The accommodation was to be built to tackle the post-war housing shortage and increasing demand for housing (generated by population growth and rising affluence). The programme also sought to raise living standards through significant improvements in the design standards of accommodation. A large proportion of the older un-modernised housing stock was demolished to make way for new development. Approximately 1,006,000 new dwellings were built[16], constituting 25% of Sweden's current stock.

Sweden was hit by the 1973 global oil crisis and the impact was severe. Sweden's high oil dependency and cold climate combined to create a serious problem for the Government. This crisis led to a change in energy policy moving the country away from oil dependency by diversification of energy supply, use of district heating systems and improving the energy efficiency of building stock. Thus high energy efficiency standards were imposed on the new housing being built as part of the Million Programme (Miljonprogrammet).

There was considerable demand for new, spacious accommodation particularly within cities in Sweden. There was also demand for warm and comfortable accommodation. Thus, the energy efficient housing produced by the programme appealed to the market and its production was driven by the energy standards imposed by the Government. The grants and subsidised government loans made available to house-builders and access to government-owned sites encouraged house-builders, rather than households, to become the early adopters of the energy efficiency measures required by the Swedish government. Thus, the deployment of new energy efficient technologies and designs was facilitated by the house-builders involved in the construction programme.

Policy instruments

Three key elements underpinned the success of the programme in achieving higher energy efficiency standards. Firstly, the programme provided some certainty to those investing in the construction of new energy efficient housing. It guaranteed a market for the end product. Secondly, the government subsidised the additional cost of building to higher energy efficiency standards through grants, subsidised loans and the provision of state-owned sites. Thirdly, the Government sign-posted its intention to make high energy efficiency standards part of the standard building requirement for all new construction after the programme was completed. Thus house-builders realised it was sensible to build their capacity to deliver energy efficient homes, whilst subsidies were being offered in order that they could compete effectively once the programme was finished.

The scale of demand for new housing during this period drove innovation on the supply side. The size of the housing programme generated economies of scale for house-builders. It enabled them to test new designs, technologies and construction practices whilst demand for the units built was assured. Rising affluence amongst potential households also increased demand for higher quality units. Households wanted comfortable, healthy and warm living environments. The demand for these energy efficient units was secure. This reduced investment risk for the house-builders.

Public subsidy[17] also helped to reduce the investment risk. Through subsidies (subsidised loans and grants) and the provision of low cost, state-owned land the additional cost of building to higher standards was off-set. This enabled the house-building industry to invest in building its capacity (skills, supply chains, developing its construction practices) to deliver energy efficient homes. The Government controlled the quality of the homes built by only offering loans, grants or access to land to those housing companies achieving the required energy efficiency standard.

Finally, the long-term plans to incorporate higher energy efficiency standards into building regulations further reduced the investment risk for house-builders. The energy efficiency standard adopted by the Miljonpro-grammet was incorporated into the Swedish Building Standards in 1975. Miljonprogrammet offers a very interesting approach to encouraging innovation in the house-building industry. It suggests that a publicly-subsidised, large-scale housing programme could generate enough certainty amongst house-builders to enable wholesale innovation within the industry.

It also demonstrates that such a programme can be effectively used as an opportunity for trialling new technologies, supply systems and construction practices. This enables a more comprehensive assessment of the likely impacts of regulatory change before it is introduced. This ensures that changes within the industry needed to support the mass-production of new housing forms are in place and that the new energy standards set in the regulation are achievable.

Industrial transformation

To deliver more energy efficient homes necessitated significant changes in the Swedish construction industry. New technologies were required which demanded the formation of new supply chains. Producers (i.e. architects, developers, builders and tradesman) had to develop suitable skills and expertise to design and install these new technologies. Networks for collaboration and organizational learning also evolved (Nässén et al, 2008). Thus, Miljonprogrammet helped to build the capacity in the Swedish construction industry needed to deliver more energy efficient homes.

The construction process itself altered, becoming more industrialised, relying heavily on prefabrication. Much of the prefabrication was completed in temporary factories built on site. Prefabrication enabled rapid innovation and reduced the cost of production. This resulted from the economies of scale of mass producing building components and reducing transaction costs by shortening the supply chain. Prefabrication also lowered the risk of the supply chains collapsing, a problem commonly associated with more innovative forms of housing (Jakob, 2006). It allowed the quality of the components to be more easily monitored and higher energy efficiency standards to be enforced in factories rather than on site by building control officers (Ko and Fenner, 2007). Prefabrication has a high potential for exploiting economies of scale and learning, both in terms of manufacturing and installation (Jakob, 2006). Thus the industrialisation of the construction process helped to deliver more energy efficient homes.

The changes that occurred within the construction industry during this period were extensive and produced the most energy efficient houses globally. Today, Sweden still has the lowest U-values in the world. In fact some claim that passive house standard is already economic in Sweden (Fiest, 2001) because similar technologies, expertise and construction techniques are already utilised by the industry. Miljonprogrammet provides a good example of how a national housing programme could be used to drive major changes within the house-building industry leading to the development of more energy efficient homes.

The German Energy Programme

The building sector in Germany accounts for about half of national energy consumption (48%) and is consequently the biggest CO_2 emitter. Currently the housing sector consumes nearly 26% of the energy consumed by Germany as a whole. The emissions from the housing sector are declining (162 mt in 1990 to 86 mt in 2007), but still account for 11.4% of all emissions. The German Government has set testing targets for CO_2 emission reductions, driven by its Kyoto commitments. This provides the motivation at least in part for the energetic programme. The programme is also part of a wider initiative to reduce fuel imports and increase future energy security in the country.

New housing provides one opportunity to reduce future CO_2 emissions in Germany. However, current construction rates are very low. This is for two reasons: the high cost of new build construction (resulting from more demanding building regulations) and low economic returns (owing to the removal of government subsidies[18] and low rental costs[19]). Since 2005 only 235,000 housing units have been built in Germany, thus majority of housing stock is old (Bukowski, 2009). Out of 40 million housing units (total in Germany) 31 million were constructed before 1984 of which 7 million have been rehabilitated (Bukowski, 2009). Thus the focus for energetic programme has tended to be on existing stock rather than new houses. Unlike the other programmes mentioned so far, energetic improvement in housing in Germany is not being driven by a new construction programme.

Various regulations and incentives (federal and local) have been introduced to increase the energetic standard of new and existing stock to low-energy and passive house standard. In 2009 new housing built in Germany consumed 130 kwh/m²/year whilst the average unit consumes 225 kwh/m²/year (Passivhaus Kompendium, 2007). Low energy housing standards have been defined as part of a national publicly subsidised loans system, designed to encourage the energetic improvement of housing (KfW loans programme). The definition used by the loans programme uses the latest energy ordinance, which specifies mandatory energetic targets for new build and refurbishments, as the baseline standard. New low energy homes must consume 30–45% less energy than the baseline identified by the ordinance. Existing stock must achieve the baseline energetic standard set out in the ordinance. The technical systems adopted differ depending on the energy efficiency standard (Table 3.6).

Deployment of energetic technologies

The growth in low energy units can be approximately measured by the number of units qualifying for KfW loans. Currently one third of new units built reach the low energy standard[20] (Bukowski, 2009). The energetic rehabilitation rate of existing stock has increased from 1.4% in 1994 to 2.2% in 2006 (Bukowski, 2009). In the past three years approximately 188,672

Table 3.6 KfW Standards (Post Energy Ordinance 2009)

		Energy reduction (% reduction in comparison with latest ordinance)	Technical system required
KfW 55	Passive house	45	Equivalent to passive house standard: airtight, thick insulation, triple glazing, use of passive solar gain, heating from renewable source.
KfW 70	Low energy house	30	Thick insulation and usually renewable energy used.
KfW100 (refurb)	Low energy refurbishment	0	Refurbish to the current energy standard set out the energy ordinance.

Source: Author's own.

new housing units have been built to a low energy standard, whilst 411,346 units (Bukowski, 2009) have been energetically refurbished in Germany (Figure 3.4, see colour plates). Although the German energetic programme has to date not effected housing stock to the extent the Miljonprogrammet did, it has been more effective than either the zero carbon homes or go-solar programmes in terms of deployment.

Low energy refurbishments and new dwellings increased significantly from 2006–2009. This was encouraged by an increase in subsidised government loans. However, with the introduction of new, more testing, energetic standards in 2009 the number of housing companies and private households accessing the loans slowed dramatically (Bukowski, 2009). The new energetic standards required the use of more expensive technologies which render properties uncompetitive in the market. Whilst demand for new technologies remains low, supply chains cannot develop and prices are likely to remain high, a 'Catch 22' situation (Bukowski, 2009).

In existing stock there are also issues in terms of the technical feasibility of improving energetic standards. The stock that was easy to tackle has been refurbished, leaving older stock which is likely to be more difficult to refurbish (Bukowski, 2009). Many of the key players in the German housing industry have said that it would be more cost-effective to demolish the stock that remains in Germany and build new units to the higher energetic standards (Bukowski, 2009). Thus the programme appears to have entered

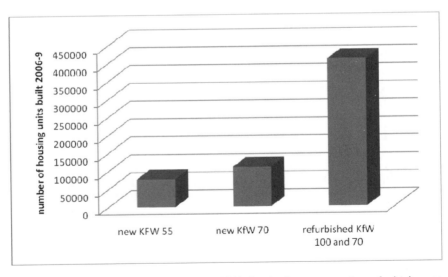

Figure 3.4 Housing units obtaining KfW funds for energetic refurbishment, 2006–2009

Source: Based on KfW data.

a period of stagnation. No doubt once the technologies and expertise needed to achieve the new standards become available and prices reduce the energetic programme will resume.

However, demand for low energy houses appears to be limited (Bukowski, 2009; Vogler, 2009). It was imagined that the introduction of the energy certificate in Germany for new and existing stock would drive demand for low energy units. However, energy cost is still a minor factor in the purchase decision, which is based on location, size of property and amenities (Schnieders and Hermelink, 2006). The real problem is that household expenditure on energy is low when compared to overall expenditure. This is compounded by the fact that tenants are charged for energy based on the size of their unit, not on the energy consumed. Thus, there is no real incentive to reduce energy consumption. Interest in energy efficiency is greater amongst those living in single-family housing, as they have both the incentive to reduce consumption and the ability to install the technologies to achieve this (Vogler, 2009).

Affordability also limits the market. The cost of building or refurbishing to higher energetic standards limits potential markets. In some regions households simply cannot afford higher rents, due to high levels of unemployment and declining net incomes (Vogler, 2009). This is particularly a problem for multi-family houses. Long-term construction costs might be recouped through energy savings, but consumers appear to base their decisions on short-term horizons and immediate concerns. In addition, those benefiting from improvements are not always those who pay for them ('split incentive dilemma'). To further confuse the issue there also appears to be some concern amongst housing companies that building to passive house standard may even increase long-term operational costs (due to increased maintenance and electricity costs). Overall there needs to be greater financial incentive to housing companies and households to invest in low energy/passive houses.

Policy instruments

Regulation, fiscal instruments and educational programmes have been used to achieve improvements in the energetic standard of new and existing homes. The energy saving ordinance (the most current being EnEV, 2009) is the most effective tool for increasing energy standards in new and existing stock. The ordinance sets mandatory energy standards (increased over time) for new buildings and refurbishments. It requires that energy certificates are provided for all new and refurbished stock.

The EEWärmeG (Renewable Energies Heat Act 2009) also influences the technological systems adopted in new and refurbished stock. It too is mandatory and requires the inclusion of renewable energy generating technologies[21], links to district heating systems or use of CHP in units. The construction industry is concerned that these mandatory requirements will slow new construction and refurbishment (Grahl, 2009; Vogler, 2009). Both will increase construction costs, and the market will not pay these higher prices. Yet more accommodation is desperately needed in larger urban areas. Housing companies argue for greater subsidy, at least until technologies become commercially viable.

The first energy efficiency loans were launched by the Kreditanstalt für Wiederaufbau[22] in 1996. Gradually loans for low energy housing were introduced. The KfW bank has provided subsidised loans[23] (with very low rates of interest) for low-energy and passive houses since 2005. After only a year of the loans being available, the number of passive houses more than doubled from 549 units (2005) to 1246 units (2006)[24] (Bukowski, 2009). However, the major change came in 2006 when the government started to make more funds available (Bukowski, 2009). For new build units subsidised interest loans are available up to a maximum of €50,000/unit (€75,000/unit for refurbishments). For refurbishments grants are also available for up to €13,125/ unit. The loan system has been critical to implementing increasingly demanding energetic standards in building stock. However, loans are not available to speculative developers[25].

Ecological tax reform in Germany increased tax on fuel oils, natural gas and electricity across all sectors, including the domestic sector. It was designed to reduce energy consumption. It also increased public interest in energy efficiency measures. Thus the eco-tax offers motivation for living in energy efficient homes. More recent reform has meant that most of the electricity generated from renewable sources is exempt from the eco tax[26], resulting in the growth of supply and demand for renewable energy. The eco tax is reinvested in energy efficiency and renewable energy projects which provides further leverage for decarbonisation of the German energy supply and building stock.

Local loans and grants for passive house are also available in some municipalities (e.g. Frankfurt, Hannover and Freiburg). This reduces the capital cost of building to passive house standard and shortens the pay-back time for new technologies. This has helped to increase interest in passive houses amongst the public and housing companies to build or refurbish to passive house standard. However, accelerated market penetration of passive house also depends upon local actors. Some cities including Frankfurt, Freiburg and Hannover have adopted instruments to promote the deployment of passive houses. Some offer low interest loans and grants to housing companies, cooperatives and private individuals wishing to build passive houses (e.g. Frankfurt and Hannover). In some instances local plans have been used to set higher energy efficiency standards for new developments (e.g. Freiburg). In other instances municipalities have required that housing built on municipally owned land is built to passive house standard or have even given preference in selling land to developers willing to build passive houses (e.g. Hannover, Freiburg).

Policies to raise energy efficiency awareness amongst producers and consumers have also been introduced in Germany. For example, various building energy labelling systems have been used in Germany (e.g. sustainability building certificate, 'energieeffizienzhaus', 3-litre house, passivhaus, energie-plus house, etc) to raise consumer awareness of the energy efficiency of their home. More recently an energy certification scheme for all new and refurbished housing has been introduced (as required by the European Energy Performance in Buildings Directive). None of these 'labelling/certification' systems have really created a palpable increase in demand for low energy homes, but in combination with increased fuel prices this could change.

Professional bodies and housing organisations in Germany have run training courses for members offering technical and financial advice for building to higher energetic standards. Some municipalities (e.g. Hannover) have introduced passive house training programmes for professionals, particularly planners, working with house-builders on new projects. Others have supported the creation of networks, offering information and training, to assist housing companies in the financing and construction of passive housing (e.g. Frankfurt and Hannover).

Certification of both producers of passive housing and the product itself coordinated by the Passivhaus Institute has assisted in wider deployment. The introduction of a certification system for passive houses in 1997 along with a computer package to make the crucial energy calculations also helped. More recently training and accreditation for house-builders, planners and architects in passive house design, technologies, financing and construction has further facilitated deployment. Providing producers and consumers with information has proven to be valuable when in combination with fiscal incentives (Vogler, 2009).

Industrial transformation

Generally the materials and construction methods currently used by the house-building industry in Germany have to alter little to achieve low energy standards (Grahl, 2009; Vogler, 2009). Similarly current construction methods do not need to transform to reach passive house standard, although the materials used will alter particularly in multi-family units. For single-family dwellings it's a different story. Many new single-family dwellings (40%) are built by the prefabrication industry. Thus, they are built to very high levels of energy efficiency, with passive ventilation systems and wooden frames, allowing for more insulation (Vogler, 2009).

Problems have been encountered in establishing reliable supply chains for new materials. For example in 2006 the energy price rises in combination with the introduction of a 1% loan for energetic modernisation (offered by KfW), encouraged many housing companies to energetically refurbish properties. Insulation suppliers didn't believe the increased demand would be a long-term trend so they didn't increase capacity. By the autumn housing companies were unable to buy insulation material and insulation prices rose up to 260% higher than the original price (Vogler, 2009). In this instance demand had outstripped supply, and thus prices rocketed.

Slowly new suppliers emerged on to the market and the prices decreased within a year (Vogler, 2009). Longer lead times and greater certainty for suppliers could help to overcome these problems. In addition, larger house-builders have worked closely with their suppliers to discuss the new technologies and technical systems required and develop effective responses to rising energetic standards (Grahl, 2009). This has offered greater certainty to suppliers and enabled them to innovate.

Accreditation of pioneering technical systems and materials is another problem. Many of the more advanced technologies used in prototype projects take a long time to become accredited. Without accreditation, new systems and products cannot be used in mainstream construction. Many innovative single technologies have been accredited and released to the construction industry; however the effectiveness of the whole technical system once assembled is often poor. More accredited whole systems are needed. The whole-system accreditation for passive house was developed in Germany to try to solve this problem.

Lack of expertise within the construction industry is often quoted as a barrier to innovation. Yet house-builders in Germany do appear (certainly within the larger companies) to have the capacity to adapt to the new requirements being placed on them and have developed their expertise accordingly. In part this has been facilitated by educational programmes run by the Government and industry. However, a great deal has been learnt within companies through demonstration projects. Effective models appear to differ significantly depending on the house-builder, the consumer and often the location of the development. Thus in some respects although educational programmes provide a useful basis for discussing ideas and experiences, there is no standard formula.

Companies specialising in prefabricated housing and those with ongoing residential energy management commitments seem to be particularly interested in passive housing (Vogler, 2009; Bukowski, 2009; Grahl, 2009). Prefabricated housing companies see a niche market to be exploited with passive houses that utilises their expertise, construction techniques, technologies and supply chains effectively. Housing or energy companies who benefit financially from lowering household energy demand (for example if the rental price of a unit includes the cost of energy consumed) are also interested in energy saving technologies. Overall there is capacity in the system to deliver more energy efficient housing in Germany. However, the cost of technologies needs to reduce or customers' willingness to pay a higher premium for energy efficient properties needs to increase if industry is to adapt.

Themes to be explored

Housing programmes have proven to be a useful vehicle for encouraging the deployment of new LZC technologies both in new and existing stock. Of course some programmes have been more successful in terms of deployment and transformation of industry than others. Some common themes have emerged from the case studies in terms of the deployment of LZC technologies. Policy instruments for encouraging deployment and industrial transformation will be explored in more depth later in the book.

All four housing programmes offer valuable lessons. The British, German and American examples indicate limited demand for zero carbon and low energy housing in the western world. They reveal similar barriers to deployment in Europe and the States. These include relatively low energy prices to date, the relatively high cost of LZC technologies, and unwillingness of consumers to pay the higher capital cost (particularly when technologies aren't valued in the appraisal of properties). Consumer concerns about the reliability of LZC systems, how they impact on their quality of life and the level of consumer involvement required in the operation of the system have also limited deployment.

The Pier programme (USA) has begun to explore 'market ready' models for zero-net energy homes. It has highlighted several factors that should be addressed to encourage the more widespread deployment of zero-net energy homes, which can also be applied to zero carbon homes. Lowering the capital cost of zero carbon homes (or at least including the LZC technologies in the valuation of the property) is critical. Ensuring that technologies are integrated into the fabric of the building and operate effectively with very limited resident involvement is also important. The availability of zero carbon homes to the market is essential if consumer demand is to grow. Just providing consumers with the opportunity to experience the benefits of living in a zero carbon home will help to generate demand. The lessons learnt from the Pier programme are particularly useful where state intervention is limited and there is reliance on the market to drive deployment and transformation of industry.

The case studies also begin to suggest that producers, rather than consumers, should be the early adopters of LZC technologies. Thus policy instruments should focus on producers, certainly in the earlier stages. Long-term policy approaches are needed to give confidence to investors (developers, sub-contractors, suppliers, etc) to innovate and invest in building requisite capacity to deliver zero carbon homes. A combination of long-term mandatory targets (for example to build zero carbon homes), coupled with short-term subsidies (to bridge the cost gap whilst capacity is being built in the house-building and energy industry to deliver zero carbon homes at scale) appears to be most successful.

Large-scale housing programmes are useful because they generate sufficient demand to reduce supply chain problems, reduce the cost of

Table 3.7 Possible lessons from housing programmes

Markets/deployment	Policy instruments	Industrial transformation
Barriers to deployment – low energy price; expensive LZC technologies; concerns about system reliability, resident involvement, impact on quality of life; limited market interest in energy efficiency or zero carbon homes	Policy instruments seem to be more effective if focused on producers in early stages of deployment	Inertia to change in industry (house-building and energy industries). Inertia to change in culture, structure and practices. Powerful vested interests prevent change
Encourage deployment – opportunity to test drive, limited resident input, lower cost, integrate technologies into building, include value of technologies in value appraisal of properties	Long-term policy approaches needed to give confidence to investors to innovate and invest in building requisite capacity	Need for networks for collaboration and organisational learning to implement innovative housing forms
Focus on producers rather than consumers as early adopters of LZC technologies	Combination of long-term mandatory targets with shorter term subsidies appears to be successful	Prefabrication lowers costs and enable innovation. Also easier to test technical system in factory
	Large-scale housing programmes generate sufficient demand to reduce supply chain problems, reduce the cost of technologies, provide certainty for investors	Supply chains and expertise lacking but can be developed with sufficient incentives
	Educational tools and accreditation schemes can be useful for developing appropriate expertise for delivery	Partnership approach will be needed to produce zero carbon – tensions between partners partly because of cultural and practice differences
	Role of planning varies considerably. It can be a useful tool in combination with others to deliver zero carbon homes, but is insufficient on its own	
	Subsidised loan systems provide a cost-effective mechanism for energetic refurbishment	

Source: Author's own.

technologies and provide certainty for investors. There may be problems during the early stages of the programme when capacity is being built. This is when subsidies will be needed to build capacity and provide security for investors. Educational tools and accreditation schemes can of course be useful for developing appropriate expertise for successful delivery at this stage and creating stable supply chains. The role of planning in the deployment of LZC technologies varies considerably between case studies. However, they demonstrate that planning can be a useful regulatory tool in combination with other regulatory, fiscal, educational tools to deliver zero carbon homes.

The housing programmes demonstrate the resistance to change in industry (house-building and energy industries). Powerful vested interests within the house-building and energy industries, rail against changes in culture, structure and practices. There is a tendency to blame lack of market demand and difficulties in building capacity within the house-building industry. However, experience in Sweden suggests that it is perfectly possible for the house-building industry to transform given the right incentives. Changes to construction processes and supply chains, networks for collaboration and organisational learning will be needed to produce zero carbon homes. The transformation required within the energy industry to deliver zero carbon homes is far more extensive and likely to be a painful process. Partnerships between the house-builders and energy providers are critical for the successful delivery of zero carbon homes. Already tensions between industrial partners, largely because of cultural and practice differences, have already become apparent in the UK zero carbon homes programme. Models for working effectively in partnership will need to develop.

Chapter 4

Low/zero carbon energy systems

Introduction

A decarbonised energy supply is an essential facet of a zero carbon home. A variety of models may be adopted (Chapter 2). Low carbon energy generating, distribution and storage technologies may be integrated into new housing developments so that they become largely self-sufficient, or even produce LZC energy that can be fed back into the wider system. New developments might be linked into existing, local, low carbon energy systems (e.g. city-wide district heating systems or closed-loop systems). These systems may operate using a mixture of renewable energy and waste products. Equally new developments might be fed electricity from a decarbonised national grid system. This chapter presents a range of approaches to delivering a decarbonised energy supply to households (Table 4.1).

The Swedish case study – the Hammarby model – is an integrated, holistic, resource efficient, closed-loop system, a highly engineered solution that can operate at the neighbourhood or city scale. The closed-loop system maximises the efficient use of all types of waste (i.e. waste heat, solid waste, sewage) to generate energy. Closed-loop systems have great potential in urban areas, where the supply of waste products from urban processes is sufficient to operate the system effectively. Urban densities and land-use mix also enhance the effectiveness of this type of system. The use of waste products is also essential in urban systems where local access to alternative energy sources may be restricted.

The German case study focuses on an ad hoc, grass roots approach taken towards the decarbonisation of energy supply in Freiburg. This regional system utilises a variety of LZC energy sources, and is made up of many different components operated by a variety of players. The regional energy company – Badenova – invests in its own LZC infrastructure (wind, hydro, solar and biomass) for generating heat and electricity. There is a city-wide district heating system (now operated by Badenova) fuelled by a variety of locally available low-carbon energy sources. Several groups – the municipality, residents, businesses and farmers – generate electricity from low-carbon energy sources. PV panels on new housing, community wind farms, large-scale PV arrays on

Table 4.1 LZC energy systems comparison

	Hammarby Model	Freiburg grass-roots system	Boulder smart grid	Decarbonisation of UK national grid
Location	Sweden	Germany	Colorado USA	United Kingdom
Size of population (2010)	1,642,095	217,547	100,160	61,792,000
Technologies	Closed-loop system (eco-cycle system)	Various	Smart grid	Renewables, nuclear, super-grid, smart grid
Energy source	Waste (waste heat, solid waste)	Solar, wind, biomass and hydro-power	Solar, wind, geothermal and hydro-power	Nuclear, wind, other renewables
Key stakeholders	Stockholm energy and municipality	Badenova, residents, farmers, businesses and municipality	Xcel energy, Accenture, Current Group, Gridpoint, OSIsoft, Schweitzer Engineering, Smart Sync and Ventyx	Private energy companies (and possibly house-builders)
Public – private partnership	public-private	public-private	private	private
Collaboration with local planning officers	yes	yes	no	no
Carbon dioxide savings	29–37% reduction CO_2 emissions	400,000 tonnes CO_2/annum	5–15% reduction CO_2 emissions	49,148,347 tonnes CO_2/annum (resulting from wind energy)

Source: Author's own.

the local football stadium, biomass cogeneration plants run by local farmers, small-scale hydropower schemes financed and operated by housing cooperatives all help to decarbonise the energy supply.

Another approach is the smart grid system being developed in Boulder (Colorado). Like Freiburg, Boulder has access to a diverse and rich supply of renewable energy sources (solar, wind, geothermal and hydropower in particular). Unlike Freiburg, Boulder does not have a district heating/ cooling system. However, it is in the process of introducing a smart grid, the first in the United States. The smart grid increases the efficient use of electricity. It also enables the connection of many small-scale generators of LZC energy to the grid. Thus it can help to decarbonise the city's energy supply. There is heavy reliance on private actors (households, house-builders and privately owned utilities) to invest in LZC technologies, incentivised by various subsidies and regulations. The climate change plan tax – a carbon tax – levied on households, businesses and industry in Boulder is being used to encourage a market transformation for energy efficiency and renewable energy products and services. This tax is the first of its kind in the United States.

The British approach to achieving a LZC energy supply starkly contrasts with these localised solutions. Although the United Kingdom is encouraging decentralised production of LZC heat and electricity (through the zero carbon homes programme, the introduction of the feed-in tariff and renewable heat incentive), its main focus is on decarbonising the electricity supply through centralised generation and supply models. The UK Government plans to use the expansion of nuclear and wind energy to reduce the carbon intensity of the electricity supply, whilst other sources of LZC electricity (i.e. wave and tidal power) are developed. They will use this as an opportunity to develop the nuclear and wind industries in the UK, to replace the coal and oil industries. Public funding is extremely limited, so the emphasis is being placed on international and national economic incentives (EU carbon trading system and UK Renewables Obligation) to encourage the energy industry to deliver the new infrastructure and services.

The Hammarby closed-loop system

Stockholm is the capital of Sweden. It currently has a population of around 1 million. Environmental problems have been a concern in Stockholm for many decades. In the 1920s the city suffered from many environmental problems, particularly air and water pollution. The reaction to this was for the city to provide the sewerage and energy infrastructure needed to ameliorate these problems. Thus the city has been investing in energy infrastructure over a long period. The first part of the district heating system in Stockholm was installed in 1953. Waste incineration has been the main source of heat since 1971, although this is beginning to shift towards biomass as a result of new national incentives and the introduction of the carbon tax.

Stockholm aims to become a fossil-free city by 2050. It has already reduced CO_2 emissions by 25% compared to the 1990 levels. Emissions are now less than 4 tonnes CO_2 per capita (half the national Swedish average). The majority of households in Stockholm (69% of all households) have access to district heating. Nearly 70% of the heat used by the system comes from renewable energy sources. Stockholm also has the second largest cooling system in the world. Until 2002 the district heating / cooling systems were owned, managed, maintained and planned by the municipal company Stockholm Energi. In 2002 this was taken over by Fortum[1]. Now both the heating and cooling systems are being operated on a commercial basis by Fortum.

The Hammarby system is an integrated energy-waste-water system operating in the city of Stockholm. The system is conceptually based on a closed-loop (or eco-cycle) model, where waste products from urban processes are used as a source of energy. The system is complemented by a low carbon electricity supply from the national grid and by embedded LZC technologies (PV cells and wind turbines) in the eco-district of Hammarby Sjöstad. The closed-loop system was initially developed by Stockholm Energi, Stockholm Water Company and the Stockholm Waste Management Administration. It utilises a range of LZC energy sources including: solid waste, biofuel, biogas and waste heat (Figure 4.1, see colour plates).

Biofuel is used by Stockholm's CHP plant, thermal power station and by municipal vehicles. Organic waste produced by households is used to fertilise the biofuel crops outside Stockholm. Household waste water is also processed to produce biogas, which is used to power vehicles and provide gas for cooking in Hammarby Sjöstad. The heat produced from the process of purifying domestic waste water is used by the thermal power station. The aim of the closed-loop system was to double energy efficiencies. In fact the environmental assessment tool developed by the City of Stockholm, Royal Institute of Technology, and the consultancy firm Grontmij AB shows a 28–42% reduction in non-renewable energy use and a 29–37% reduction in CO_2 emissions resulting from the closed-loop system, when compared with the average for Stockholm. The system also reduces water consumption by around 41–46% and waste going to landfill by 90%.

This model is unique in that it integrates four systems (energy waste water transport) creating one integrated closed-loop system. It also effectively combines energy systems operating at a number of different scales:

- LZC energy from the electricity grid (national),
- district heating system powered by waste and biofuel (city-level),
- biogas and heat produced by water treatment plant (neighbourhood level),
- embedded micro-generating technologies – PV, solar collectors, etc (individual buildings).

The integration of energy systems has various benefits. It increases the stability of energy supply, enabling the storage of energy generated locally in the strategic infrastructure (i.e. the grid or district heating system). Connecting localised and more strategic energy systems helps to spread peak load. The integration of systems can also assist in the decarbonisation of supply if individual producers of low-carbon energy can connect to the strategic supply networks. Thus integration of systems operating at different scales is important.

The Hammarby system is likely to be a more effective model for delivering LZC energy to homes in urban areas. It is reliant on waste from urban processes. Thus the waste streams must be sufficient to operate the closed-loop system. The larger the waste streams the greater the size of the population that can be supported. However, the system will never produce enough energy for a city to be entirely self-sufficient, but the shortfall can be provided for through an external LZC energy supply. In the case of Stockholm this is supplied by the Swedish national grid.

This type of system will also work best where land uses are mixed (which spreads the peak load) and densities are high (to reduce transmission losses). Both increase the efficiencies of the system. New housing developments can be added incrementally to the closed loop system as long as there are adequate processing plants, power stations, waste-water treatment plants and so on to support the additional consumers and producers. However, the density of the new development, its impact on the wider land use mix and the implications of this for the operation of the closed-loop system need to be considered.

Demand and deployment

The beauty of the closed-loop system is that it is fully integrated into the built environment. It is a complex system, but is not complicated at the user – system interface. Thus, most users are probably barely aware of using it. Culturally it is very acceptable system, because it demands limited user – technology interaction. Greatest interest in the system tends to come from those providing energy services (utilities, ESCOs or municipalities) rather than consumers (households, businesses, etc) who are less aware of its advantages.

The 'Hammarby model' has international appeal and is being exported to Russia (the Baltic Pearl Project), Ireland (Cork South Docklands Master Plan), Canada (Toronto Waterfront Revitalization Project), South Africa (Buffalo City) and China (Caofeidian International Deep Green EcoCity, Tianjin Gangdong Conceptual Master Plan, Hohhot and Wuhai Green City Projects, Inner Mongolia, Dongli Lake Project, Luodian Town in Shanghai). Similar closed-loop systems are also being designed for new cities in the Middle East.

The deployment of the closed-loop model is restricted by built form. It is more suited to higher density and mixed use environments, as it is reliant on waste from urban processes, efficiencies created by proximity and a smoothed peak load over a 24 hour period. Closed-loop systems can be expensive and disruptive to retrofit, however in new developments the infrastructure can easily be integrated. The key barrier to the deployment of the closed-loop systems is institutional.

The culture, structure and practices of the energy industry are less compatible with the closed-loop system. The system is reliant on waste and renewable energy sources, adopts a decentralised approach and requires the coordination of several infrastructural systems, which is less appealing to single-interest energy companies. Of course this could be tackled through the carbon markets and mandatory carbon reduction targets for energy companies.

This inertia in the energy industry creates problems in raising finance for closed-loop systems. Often a large amount of public investment is required to put the infrastructure in place, which restricts deployment. The involvement of municipalities (or other multi-interest organisations e.g. MUSCOs[2]) in coordinating several infrastructure systems (energy, water, waste and transport) is essential. In addition the coordination of these urban systems with development is central to successful delivery. Thus, multi-interest organisations are needed to plan, coordinate, manage and operate a closed loop system. Such bodies need to have the capacity and motivation to be involved in this process.

Approach to delivery

The Swedes have a long history of integrating these larger environmental systems into their built environment. They have achieved this through interventionist approaches, whereby municipalities design, fund and operate new infrastructure. Historically it has been easier for Swedish municipalities to achieve this degree of integration and coordination as they controlled the local utilities (i.e. waste, energy and water were dealt with in-house), some vehicle fleets and the development process. They also raise a significant amount of revenue through a local taxation system which enables them to invest in infrastructural projects.

As energy providers, municipalities were able to fund new energy infrastructure from the revenue generated by energy sales. Thus they had the power to plan and implement new 'greener' visions for energy provision. Public ownership of the supply network also meant municipal control over access to the network and pricing. Thus, the 'municipal model' appeared to be a very effective way to deliver equitable, accessible and more environmentally friendly energy systems.

For many Swedish municipalities these services (and associated infrastructure) have now been privatised. This has happened in Stockholm and has reduced municipal control over delivering a 'greener vision'. Although Stockholm can continue to plan eco-neighbourhoods, the municipality is now reliant on the private sector (construction industry and energy companies) to deliver the infrastructure. The municipality now has to negotiate with the private energy company (Fortum) in all aspects of energy provision.

Some degree of coordination between plans for development and energy provision is needed. Of course this process is more complicated and time-consuming than when all operations were dealt with by the municipality in-house. The private ownership of the energy supply network has already created problems of access and pricing for small generators, thus reducing the potential to decarbonise.

Planning of course plays a key role in the successful delivery of these big infrastructural systems, especially where the municipality has lost its other powers. In Stockholm, environmental infrastructural systems are planned alongside new developments. New development is also planned with existing energy infrastructure in mind. For example the municipality is planning to increase densities within metropolitan Stockholm, in part to utilise the existing infrastructures (including the district heating system) more effectively. Connection to the city's district heating system is often prescribed by the municipality through the planning system. However there is no legislation to support this, although it is widely practised. Stockholm also has an energy plan outlining future targets and strategies for increasing energy supply and using LZC energy sources in the city. This plan is developed in conjunction with the private energy company.

Industrial transformation

The closed-loop system challenges the culture, structure and practices of the energy industry. It doesn't use fossil fuels, is a decentralised system and requires the energy utility to work with multiple partners for successful delivery. Sweden has several advantages over other countries in this respect. Firstly the introduction of the carbon tax[3] and subsidies for various forms of renewable energy (including biofuels) has made LZC energy systems more competitive in Sweden.

Secondly, decentralised district heating systems have been operating in Sweden since the 1950s. Thus, district heating infrastructure already exists. There is also considerable national expertise in terms of the design, construction, operation and maintenance of these systems. Urban areas have also been designed and developed to support district heating systems.

Thirdly, the historic involvement of municipalities in the provision of all utilities means that they can help the private utility companies to coordinate their operations and deliver closed-loop systems. The municipality still plays a central role in delivering innovative energy systems, although it involves a great deal of awareness raising and negotiation as well as its more familiar role as a coordinator.

Nevertheless there are several barriers to industrial transformation which could prevent the wider adoption of closed-loop systems even in Sweden. For the energy industry the implementation of innovative energy systems must be weighed against their profitability. The operational costs of the closed-loop system are kept low because waste products are used as the source of energy. However, capital costs for researching, engineering and installing these bespoke systems are likely to be high. Of course fiscal incentives (capital subsidies) can be used to increase the economic viability of systems in the short term.

Difficulties in coordinating several systems could also form another significant industrial barrier. MUSCOs could provide an industrial solution to this problem, however few currently exist. Most utilities and transport providers are single-interest organisations and do not have the in-house vision or expertise to coordinate and operate several systems effectively. Thus, significant transformation is likely to be required amongst utilities to deliver closed-loop systems.

Effective delivery will also be dependent on the cooperation of municipalities. MUSCOs will rely on municipalities procuring the resources and services they produce to be economically viable. As major consumers of energy, water, waste and transport services municipalities will be important customers for the MUSCO. In addition, MUSCOs will rely on municipalities managing urban form so that development patterns support the closed-loop systems. Thus, strong partnerships between MUSCOs and municipalities are needed.

Lifestyle changes

The consumer – technology interface for the closed-loop system is not significantly different from standard energy, waste and water systems. In fact, with the exception of the waste system, where residents do have to sort their waste and put it into vacuum chutes outside their houses, the user – technology interface is exactly the same. Thus residents can use utilities as they always have and they remain passive consumers.

Evidence from Hammarby suggests the energy literacy of the consumer was not improved through contact with the closed-loop system. Thus, household consumption of energy was higher than expected. The introduction of metering or smart technologies alongside the closed-loop system could help to rectify this problem. This would provide residents with more information about their consumption patterns, which could help to inform their decision-making processes. Certainly the municipality intends that all new residential developments in Stockholm will have metering systems installed to ensure greater energy literacy and more efficient use of energy (Stoll, 2009).

Freiburg energy system

Freiburg is a town in Southern Germany, home to 200,000 people. It is situated by the Black Forest and is one of the larger towns in the region. Over a period of several decades Freiburg (and the surrounding region) has begun to develop a LZC energy system, based on increasing efficiency and use of LZC energy sources. The city region has developed its LZC generating capacity, utilising locally available sources, supported by federal subsidies.

Freiburg is surrounded by forest, mountains and agricultural land. Several rivers also cross the region. The city benefits from the most hours of sunshine in Germany (1,746 hours/annum) and solar radiation (1,117 kWh/m²/annum). Geothermal energy sources are also present in the city (150 m below the surface). The regional topography and climate means that the hills around the city provide an excellent vantage point for wind turbines. Thus, Freiburg is well endowed with LZC sources of energy. The regional energy company and the municipality are keen to develop LZC energy systems in Freiburg, and have done so subsidised by various federal programmes (the feed-in tariff, 100,000 solar roofs programme, etc) and the green tariff (Regiostrom). However, it is the residents of Freiburg who seem to have invested most in the transition towards a low carbon city.

Demand and deployment

Investment in renewable energy in Freiburg has successfully increased capacity over the past few decades. Since the introduction of the solar plan in 1986, there has been an increase in the generation of solar energy, the emergence of solar neighbourhoods (e.g. Vauban) and large solar infrastructural projects (e.g. football stadium and expressway) in Freiburg. Currently the installed capacity of PV cells in Freiburg amounts to 10MW of energy for an investment of €50 million (Figure 4.2).

Wind also has potential in Freiburg. Currently there are six wind turbines with an installed capacity of 12MW for an investment of €15 million. There is scope for wind power to be expanded as it is a lot less expensive than solar power and produces a great deal more energy. It also complements solar energy in terms of peaks and troughs in supply. But historically there has been political resistance to wind farms and surrounding region of Baden Wuttenburg. This has severely limited the production of renewable energy in the region and the city itself. Due to recent political changes in the region, the election of the green party in Baden Wuttenburg, opposition to renewable energy is likely to diminish. Currently the supply of wind energy in Freiburg reduces carbon emissions by 20,000 tonnes annually.

Biomass and biogas are also sources of energy for the city. Freiburg has 7.4 megawatts of installed biomass capacity. The Black Forest provides a good source of biomass (e.g. wood and maize) which can be used by the

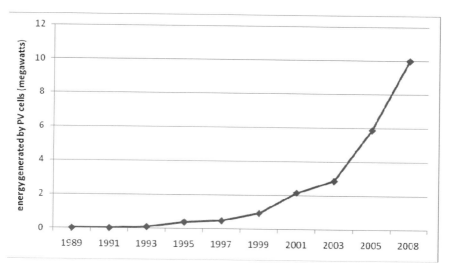

Figure 4.2 Installed PV capacity in Freiburg.
Source: Innovation Academy, 2009.

city and surrounding regions to produce heat and electricity. It also provides revenue for the farmers of the Black Forest. Various biomass facilities have been set up at a variety of scales including: a bio-oil cogeneration plant at the Solar-Fabrik, wood cogeneration plant in Vauban and various wood pellet boilers. Freiburg is moving towards having one fifth of the local grid supplied from biogas. A large cogeneration biogas plant has recently been constructed 30 km outside the city. An experimental geothermal plant has also been constructed in Freiburg to determine its economic viability as a LZC energy source. The plant produces 4–10 MW of electricity and 23–40 MW of heat. However, the problem with geothermal plants is the high investment (€50 million for this project) and drilling costs. Thus the cost-effectiveness of geothermal energy in Freiburg currently is in doubt.

Freiburg has 1.4MW of installed hydro-power capacity (Figure 4.3). These systems have largely been financed and operated by community groups. However, the figure only includes hydro-power plants within the urban area and not the big scale hydro-power plants on the nearby great river Rhine. Hydro-power generates around 10–12% of the Baden-Württemberg region's electricity. The Baden-Württemberg region leads the way in Germany when it comes to hydro-power. There are plans to expand the capacity of hydro-power plants in the greater urban area of Freiburg.

Currently there is only 31.6 MW of installed renewable energy in Freiburg, which is disappointingly low. The market for a green energy tariff is also surprisingly low, considering that Freiburg is the birthplace of the environmental

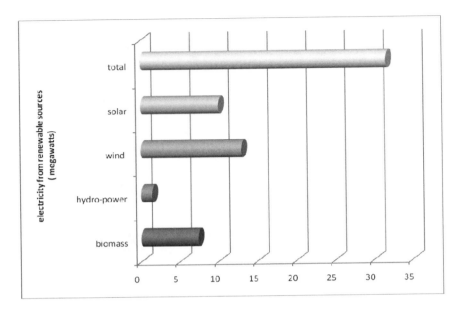

Figure 4.3 Installed renewable energy capacity in Freiburg.

Source: Badenova, 2008.

movement in Germany. However, only a mere 10% of residents have opted for the Regiostrom tariff, which supports new investment in renewable energy. However, there is a great deal of interest within the community in generating renewable energy and investing in energy efficient measures.

The Baden-Württemberg region is a prime location for companies special-ising in hydro-power, wind-power and other renewable energies. Important hydro-power firms, such as VA Tech Hydro, Voith Siemens Hydro Power Generation and Alstom Power Generation, are located in the region. It is also home to ABB, a large manufacturer of electrical equipment and genera-tors for wind farms. The company has supplied electrical equipment for a quarter of the world's installed wind turbines and been involved in the plan-ning and implementation of major wind-power projects across the globe. Important research institutions working in the field of renewable energy are also located in the region and thus there should be sufficient capacity to deliver more LZC energy locally.

Approach to delivery

The Freiburg model has evolved largely through a joint venture between the community, local utility (Badenova) and municipality. It is largely sup-ported by federal government subsidies and regulation. The Freiburg model is marketed internationally as an extremely successful model for decarbonising energy supply, even though very little of Freiburg's electricity supply is from renewable sources. This statistic suggests that it is Freiburg's marketing strategy (based on its status as a 'renewable region' or 'solar city') that is truly remarkable.

Several private energy utilities offer services to energy customers in Freiburg. Badenova is the only public-private utility operating in the region. It is made up of approximately 40 municipal energy companies from Freiburg and surrounding towns in the region. The public sector owns 53%[4] of its shares whilst the private sector owns the remainder. It is an ecologically orientated company whose goal is to reduce carbon-dioxide emissions through increasing efficiency and using LZC energy sources. Badenova has played a role in the decarbonisation of Freiburg's energy supply.

Badenova invests in new renewable energy capacity with the revenue generated by Regiostrom. Around 10% of Badenova's customers have chosen to switch to the Regiostrom tariff in order to support new investment in renewable energy. Badenova invests all of the additional income from the higher rate tariff into new capacity. To date 89 renewable energy projects have been funded by the Regiostrom tariff. Direct subsidies are also provided to customers who wish to install solar photovoltaic panels. Badenova claims that the annual carbon savings generated by this fund are approximately 400,000 tonnes CO_2/annum (Badenova, 2009).

The municipality has also played its role in the growth of renewable energy capacity in Freiburg. The leadership of a few key players in the municipality (including the green mayor and officers in several of the key municipal departments) has been critical for the delivery of the 'green vision'. The municipality supports the deployment of renewable energy technologies in a variety of ways. It has set up demonstration projects in municipal buildings and encouraged the development of LZC districts. It rents roof space on municipal buildings to others for the generation of solar energy. It provides a guaranteed market for LZC energy in the city and promotes Freiburg as an international centre of excellence for renewable energy.

The municipality has a target to reduce CO_2 emissions by 40% (from 1992 levels) by 2030. It intends to achieve this through development planning, the energetic refurbishment of municipal buildings and facilities, using waste more effectively in the district heating systems, encouraging non-motorised transport, mass transit and so on. As part of this remit Badenova now collaborates with the municipality in devising the energy strategy which informs the spatial plan for the city.

Badenova advises the municipal planning department on potential low energy solutions for new developments and refurbishments. The planning department cooperates with Badenova on the development of new renewable energy projects – acquiring land, obtaining planning permission, identifying possible sites/roofs available for projects and so on. This more proactive approach to energy planning is crucial for coordinating development with LZC energy solutions.

The community is also actively engaged in developing their capacity to generate renewable energy. Local community groups have funded small-scale hydro-power schemes in various neighbourhoods in Freiburg. All six of the wind turbines in Freiburg were subsidised by community groups at a cost of €12 million. Solar arrays throughout the city have been financed by housing associations, individual households and businesses, church groups and the Freiburg football supporters club subsidised the large PV array on the roof of the stadium. The community has probably been the most important player in decarbonisation of the energy supply in Freiburg, although their may explain why progress has been slow. Community action has been enabled by federal subsidies and regulations.

The Federal Government in Germany has provided a huge amount of support for the creation of LZC energy systems through regulation and fiscal incentives. The key source of funding for the deployment renewable energy technologies in the region has come from federal capital subsidies (e.g. solar roofs programme[5]) and operational subsidies (feed-in tariff[6]). These subsidies have played a crucial role in the expansion of renewable energy capacity in Freiburg, and enabled a number of new actors to become involved in infrastructural provision including households, farmers, businesses.

Regulation has also played a fundamental role in terms of deployment. The feed-in law (introduced 1990) which introduced both the feed-in tariff and required grid access for all generators of renewable energy, has guaranteed a financial return on energy produced from renewable sources over a period of twenty years. It offers security to the investor and increases the economic viability of generating energy from renewable sources, before the technologies become commercially viable. This law and the subsequent renewable energies acts (in 2000 and 2004) have been central to the adoption of a LZC energy system in Freiburg (and the rest of Germany).

Industrial transformation

Germany has experienced the most rapid increase in electricity generated from renewable sources globally, during the last decade. Share of electricity generated from renewable energy sources increased from 6.3% in 2000 to 14% in 2007. The renewable energy sector provided a revenue €8.2 billion and 120,000 jobs in 2001 (Wüstenhagen and Bilharz, 2006). Today Germany is the world's largest user of wind power (Runci, 2005). It also has the most technical knowledge about wind power globally (Runci, 2005). Germany is one of the world's largest producers of PV electricity (39% of world capacity).

Nevertheless it should be noted even with the introduction of the feed-in law (and later the renewable energy acts) and with significant public investment in the renewable industry (in 2006 more than €9 billion was invested in renewable energy systems for generating electricity in Germany (AGEE-Stat/ BMU)), the German energy supply is still rather carbon intensive (0.28 tons of CO_2/\$1000) and heavily dependent on imported fossil fuels. According to Runci (2005) 62% of the energy consumed in Germany is imported (EU average is 50%). Yet again the power of the vested interests in the energy industry and their desire to retain the current fossil fuel based regime is apparent.

At a regional and local level innovation hubs for renewable energy industries have begun to form in Germany. Freiburg provides a good example. Freiburg is now home to a large number of specialist energy institutions and enterprises including: the Kiepenheuer-institut für Solarenergie, the Fraunhofer-institut für Solare Energiesysteme, the International Solar Energy Society, the Öko-Institut and the Solarfabrik. These form the basis of the solar competencies in the city.

There is also an extensive network of local technical expertise and financing bodies (offering cheap loans for LZC technologies) established in Freiburg, which support the installation and operation of LZC technologies assisting in their deployment. There are approximately 1,500 environmental companies now situated in Freiburg, and 80 are in the solar industry. This has enabled the creation of an innovation hub, which has attracted those in the renewable energy industry from around the world to locate in Freiburg (e.g. the International Solar Energy Society).

Meanwhile farmers within the region, encouraged by low financial returns on crop yields, have begun to diversify and offer energy solutions for the rural towns surrounding Freiburg (biomass district heating systems) or supplying developments in Freiburg itself with biomass. Local citizens and small businesses have begun to invest in renewable energy projects. A number of innovative 'green' projects have been introduced in Freiburg, which has generated a great deal of international interest. This further reinforces the importance of the visibility of renewable energy in the city. It may well be the reliance of the local economy on all things 'green' that will ensure the longevity of the local politicians' resolve to support green policies and renewable energy regardless of political change at a local and federal level.

Interestingly at a regional level political support for larger scale renewable energy projects, particularly wind farms, has been lacking. Thus, planning applications for wind farms have often been declined. This has slowed deployment of renewable technologies in the wider region. It accounts for the surprisingly low generation capacity in and around Freiburg, despite the existence of the industries and research institutions which support the development and deployment of renewable energy technologies.

Approximately 9,400 people work in the environmental 'cross-sector' in the Freiburg Region, which constitutes 3% of all employees. Around 1,500 of the region's companies participate in adding value to the environmental sector, which is worth €500 million per year (Lutzky, 2004). The economy of the Freiburg Region is dominated by the service and environmental industries. Growth areas include eco-tourism, ecological construction, specialist university courses, energy and environmental consultancies, organic agriculture and production of renewable energy.

The inherent strengths of Freiburg under-pinning growth in these industries (particularly the renewable energy industry) are based on local natural resources, continued support from the municipality and the development of local technical competencies (an innovation hub). Growth in global demand for green products and services[7] in the future suggests long-term export opportunities for the environmental sector (Lutzky, 2004). However, current reliance on federal subsidies, a restricted manufacturing sector and competition from other countries, cities and regions all pose a potential threat to the continued success of the renewable energy industry and other green industries in Freiburg (Lutzky, 2004: Table 4.2).

Lifestyle changes

Growth in support for renewable energy in Freiburg began in 1973. The city-region was threatened with a major nuclear expansion programme[8].

Table 4.2 Strengths, weaknesses, opportunities and risks for the Freiburg green economy

Strengths	Opportunities
• political priorities/civic involvement know-how and creativity • innovation, production and user skills • institutions and networks • Freiburg regional centre • image as an 'environmental and solar capital' • climate and ecology	• growth markets • regional market potential/districts • tri-regional market potential • regional innovation and value-added chains • competence advantage • communication • 'Freiburg mix'

Weaknesses	Risks
• manufacturing sector • commercial exploitation of R&E • limited regional market • non-central location within Germany • limited subsidies by the federal state	• volatile markets: dependence on subsidies, integration of environmental technology • concentration at the expense of regional SMEs • international supplier competition , e.g. from Japan, the US and Switzerland • competition from other regions, eg. Lower Saxony, Bavaria, Switzerland • image competition, e.g. Ulm, Berlin

Source: Lutzky, 2004.

This was initially opposed by the regional wine-growers (a powerful lobby) who were convinced that the cooling towers needed for nuclear power plants would affect the local climate and produce fogs that would impact negatively on wine-growing. The wine-growers were soon joined by local people in non-violent resistance to the development of nuclear power stations.

Eventually the strength of opposition encouraged the politicians to reconsider their plan for nuclear power stations. The anti-nuclear movement wanted to find an alternative to nuclear energy. Various individuals within the movement (i.e. academics, engineers, environmental scientists, architects, etc) had the technical expertise to create and test alternatives. Small renewable energy demonstration projects began to appear in and around Freiburg. This drew others with similar technical and research interests to Freiburg and over time related research institutes developed (e.g. the Fraunhofer and Öko institutes).

After the 1986 Chernobyl disaster the city of Freiburg drew up a strategy for moving away from nuclear energy which focused on energy saving, cogeneration and solar energy. Freiburg was one of the first German local authorities to establish an urban energy plan in collaboration with the municipal utility[9]. A municipal solar development programme was also introduced to increase the deployment of solar technologies (solar collectors and PV cells). As renewable energy schemes began to develop in Freiburg, a growing number of residents have been employed in related industries, which has generated more local support for renewable energy. Increasingly residents have invested in renewable energy, both in terms of one-off projects (e.g. community-owned wind turbines, solar collectors on the roof of individual dwellings, etc) and opting for the 'green tariff'. This has been under-pinned by capital and operational subsidies (both federal and local).

It is said that the German green movement began in Freiburg. Thus it is hardly surprising that public awareness of energy and environmental problems as well as involvement in decision-making processes is strong and well established. Environmental industries are an important part of Freiburg's economy, thus many residents are employed in 'green jobs'. Nevertheless demand for the green tariff and installed renewable energy capacity remains low. This begs the question – what has created such a gap between rhetoric and reality?

The Boulder Smart Grid

Boulder (Colorado, USA) has a population of approximately 100,000 citizens. Currently each citizen produces approximately 13.5 tonnes CO_2 equivalent/capita/ annum, three times that of an average citizen in Stockholm. Increasing population and 'per-capita carbon intensity'[10] have combined to drive Boulder's carbon inventory upward over the period 1990–2007. Boulder's residential sector creates 27% of the city's GHG emissions and is expected to contribute to 31% of the reduction by 2012. The introduction of a smart grid to the city of Boulder could potentially help to reduce emissions from the sector.

Research conducted in Colorado showed that the greatest CO_2 reductions could be achieved with the introduction of a smart grid with high penetration of wind. By moving the load to renewable generation, the smart grid increases the renewable energy which can be taken into the system and decreases total carbon emissions. For one scenario in which 50% of the energy supplied to the grid was from wind, the smart grid element contributed up to 23% reduction in CO_2 emissions. The second biggest contributor to CO_2 reductions from the smart grid was found to be energy efficiency in general. Smart grid changes consumer behaviour using price signals and feedback. However, the research also suggested that a perfect demand–response system (without renewable energy) is likely to reduce operating costs by 2% but increase CO_2 emissions by at least 1% because it would reduce energy prices and therefore increase consumption (Johnson, 2010).

In 2010, it became a federal policy to support the deployment of smart grids across the USA. Boulder will be the first city in the USA to have a smart grid. The Boulder smart grid will use real-time, two-way information to determine the most efficient distribution of electricity throughout the city supply network, thus potentially reducing CO_2 emissions. Smart homes, with smart appliances, smart meters, plug-in hybrid electric vehicles and microgenerating technologies will be connected to the grid. Smart meters, smart appliances and online monitoring systems will enable households to manage their energy consumption and the utility to manage supply effectively.

The monitoring system helps the consumer to manage consumption. Households with PV cells can also monitor the energy fed back to the grid. The system also enables the consumer to determine the quantity of energy, the type of energy and when the energy is consumed. Alternatively the consumer can opt for a tariff and the utility determines how the energy supply is managed according to the tariff. The utility can even control the smart appliances remotely if the consumer prefers.

Plug-in hybrid electric vehicles can be used to store energy during periods of low demand and feed back into the grid during periods of peak demand (as long as they aren't being driven). This is particularly useful in Colorado as the wind tends to blow in the evenings. Thus, the energy produced by the wind farms overnight can be stored in the electric vehicles (or used by household appliances) in addition to using pumped-hydro and compressed air storage options. The smart grid will enable the energy system to cope better with changing patterns of demand and supply. It will also allow producers of renewable energy (large and small scale) to connect to the grid, which will help to decarbonise supply further.

Colorado is fortunate to be one of the richest states in renewable energy resources in the USA. It is the eleventh windiest state, the sixth sunniest state and ranked high in geothermal potential. Most of these resources are spread throughout Colorado, offering the benefits of renewable generation to most communities in the state. According to the Governor's Energy Office the renewable portfolio standard[11] (RPS) will lead to the development of over 5 gigawatts of renewable energy capacity.

There are many new opportunities for developing the renewable energy capacity of Colorado: affordable PV cells[12], wind power[13] with hydrogen storage, concentrated solar power[14], geothermal energy[15] and hydro-power[16]. Thus Colorado intends to build its LZC energy generating capacity both at a strategic and local level through public-private partnerships. Expansion in LZC energy supply and demand-side management (through energy efficiency measures) will be delivered by the investor-owned utilities (e.g. Xcel), municipal utility companies and rural electric cooperatives. The Boulder smart grid will enable the integration of renewable energy from all sources (from wind farms to PV cells on individual homes) into the local energy supply.

Boulder City is the test-bed for the smart grid. Multiple partners[17] are involved in the project being headed up by Xcel energy (the only investor-owned utility operating in Boulder city). A partner-based co-investment[18] model is being used to fund the smart grid, predicted to cost around $100 million ($142 million has already spent). The smart grid provides an opportunity to test a range of new technologies as part of a holistic system. The partners in the venture will of course benefit from their involvement in this ground-breaking project as long as similar systems are eventually rolled out across the USA (and internationally). Another impetus for developing the smart grid has come from new policy priorities outlined at federal (the federal stimulus bill) and state level (the state governor's new energy economy initiative) to tackle carbon emissions.

Boulder city was chosen to pilot the smart grid for a number of reasons. First, the municipality offered the political and regulatory support needed to introduce the smart grid. Second, Boulder is home to environmentally conscious consumers. Third, Boulder city is an operationally well defined, geographically concentrated, medium-sized metropolitan area. Fourth, it contains or has access to the components necessary to implement and validate the smart grid concept. Fifth, the city will potentially demand additional green infrastructure and services associated with the smart grid. Finally, it is a very 'visible' community which provides a marketing opportunity for all those involved in developing the smart grid.

Demand and deployment

The deployment of smart grid in Boulder is not based on a growing demand for energy efficiency or renewable energy amongst the public. The smart grid is being deployed because of Xcel Energy's desire to:

- increase the efficiency of energy supply and economic return;
- develop a commercially viable smart grid which can be replicated elsewhere – i.e. commercial potential;
- comply with state and local CO_2 reduction and renewable energy generation targets;
- access various federal, state and local subsidies.

It is also being driven by the consortium's desire to become leaders in the deployment of smart grid technologies. Thus the producers are driving the deployment of the smart grid, not consumers. Of course it is difficult to determine public demand for a technical system which doesn't currently exist. However, research has been conducted in Boulder to determine the factors that may influence public demand for smart grid technologies and consumers' willingness to connect to the smart grid (Farhar, 2009). The research suggests that there are various practical, altruistic, technical and moralistic motivations for connecting to the smart grid amongst potential consumers (Figure 4.4).

Practical motivations concentrate on saving energy and money. Altruistic motivations focus on environmental concerns. Those who were technically motivated were intrigued by the smart grid because of their technical and professional interests. Some were curious about the technologies used. Others were interested in how the information generated by smart grid could help their businesses. The 'moralists' took a judgemental and punitive view of those consuming energy to excess. They were concerned with the principle of inter-generational equity[19] and wanted to impose controls on the behaviour of wider society for the good of future generations. They suggest

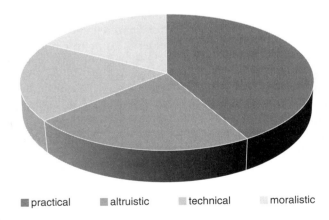

■ practical   ■ altruistic   ■ technical   ■ moralistic

Figure 4.4 Reasons given for volunteering to link into smart grid in Boulder.
Source: Farhar, 2009.

that smart technologies could help to identify those consuming energy excessively and that this information could be used punitively to impose fines on excessive consumption. These motivational drivers – practical, altruistic, technical and moralistic – were not found to be mutually exclusive, although those with moralistic motivations did tend to be a group apart from the rest (Farhar, 2010).

According to those researchers working with the smart grid (Farhar, 2010 and Reed, 2010) concerns were raised about the intrusive nature of the technologies and the privacy of personal data generated by the system. The smart system would generate a lot of very sensitive data, providing information about ownership of appliances and occupancy. There were concerns about who would have access to and indeed own this data. The public were anxious about the level of control they would have over their own energy supply and smart appliances. Would energy companies be switching off appliances during periods of peak demand? Many were also apprehensive about the level of involvement required in managing their own energy supply and additional smart technologies. They were unconvinced of their ability to operate such a potentially complicated system effectively. Others felt that the smart grid would actually increase energy consumption and for this reason would not be connected to the grid. Thus, there appears to be many potential market barriers to the deployment of the smart grid in Boulder.

Approach to delivery

The commercial potential of smart grid is largely responsible for driving the investment decision. The Boulder smart grid is largely financed by six private sector partners, in return for a share of the intellectual property rights and a share in the creation of new products and services. For the energy provider the smart grid will also increase the efficiency of operation which has obvious economic advantages. However, a raft of federal, state and city-level incentives (targets, regulations and subsidies) also support the implementation of the smart grid in Boulder (Figure 4.5).

The Federal Government has set aside $15.5 billion to provide stimulus funding for smart grid and demonstration programmes. Carbon targets have been set at the state and city level. Colorado has set a target to reduce greenhouse gas emissions by 20% from 2005 levels by 2020. Reaching this goal would curb Colorado's emissions to 94 MMTCO2e by 2020. In May 2002, the Boulder City Council passed Resolution 906[20] setting the goal of reducing community greenhouse gas emissions to 7% below 1990 levels by 2012. Both are supportive policy instruments but specific mandatory carbon reduction targets for energy generators/suppliers are likely to have more effect. Currently these do not exist at national, state or local level.

The renewable portfolio standard has been used to encourage utilities to build their renewable energy portfolio in Colorado. It has been particularly

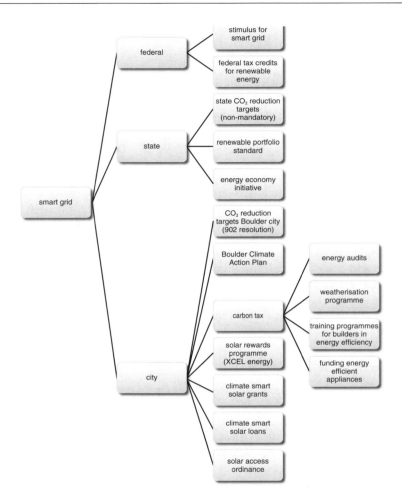

Figure 4.5 Policy instruments supporting the introduction of smart grid.

Source: Author's own.

helpful in deploying wind energy. Xcel energy is required by the RPS to source 10% of its retail sales from renewable energy by 2015. Most of Xcel's 'green electricity' is currently sourced from wind power[21]. However, with the introduction of a new state regulation[22] 4% of retail sales now need to be sourced from solar energy. Thus Xcel is keen to encourage builders and householders to install solar technologies by offering incentives through its solar reward programme[23]. This energy can be fed into the smart grid and help decarbonise the power supply.

Boulder has produced a Climate Action Plan (CAP) to tackle emissions from all sectors. The plan outlines programmes to increase energy efficiency, increase renewable energy use and reduce emissions from motor vehicles. The overarching vision of the Plan is to develop a sustainable energy future for Boulder. The CAP provides a framework to compare and analyse alternative strategies and policies, in order to facilitate the Council's decision-making process. The city's primary role to date has been to act as a facilitator and educator, and to promote market transformation for energy efficiency and renewable energy products and services.

In the residential sector the CAP has funded audits (residential energy audit and multi-family unit energy audit), grants for energy efficient lighting, weatherisation for low income households, and training programmes for builders in energy efficiency[24]. In order to finance a programme like this across all sectors the city needed to raise funds. Initially finance was raised from the 'trash tax' but more recently by the Climate Action Plan tax (also dubbed the Boulder 'carbon tax').

The Boulder climate action plan tax (CAP tax) was the first of its kind in the USA and globally. In November 2006 the majority[25] of Boulder's citizens (60%) voted to approve the CAP tax. This authorised the city to levy and collect an excise tax from residential, commercial and industrial electricity customers for the purpose of funding the city's climate action plan programme. The initial tax rate was set at $0.0002/kWh for all residential customers[26], with the average household paying $1.33/month[27] thus generating $1,000,000/year. The tax proved unpopular amongst the business community[28]. To date it has been largely ineffective in reducing energy consumption and carbon emissions from the residential sector in Boulder city[29]. However, it could be used to support the deployment of LZC technologies in the city.

Various financial incentives have been used in Boulder to encourage the incorporation of LZC technologies in new and existing buildings. These technologies may be linked into the smart grid. A solar sales and use tax rebate for photovoltaic (PV) and solar water heating installations was introduced in the city of Boulder in 2006. This enabled solar system owners to receive a rebate (essentially a tax refund) drawn from the unrestricted tax revenues collected from solar energy sales. The city estimated that the refund equated to approximately 1% of 'average' PV system costs[30]. The remaining 65% of the unrestricted revenues are used to finance the Climate Smart Solar Grant Fund. These grants are given for PV and solar water heating installations on housing for low to moderate income persons in single and multi-family homes and on the facilities of site-based non-profit entities operating in Boulder. To date the scheme has had very limited success[31].

Boulder city also operates a loan scheme[32] for energy efficiency and renewable energy projects – the Climate Smart Loan Program. Individuals or businesses can use the loans to invest in LZC technology for existing and new buildings. The climate smart loan is attached to a property rather than an individual. These loans are paid back through an incremental increase in the property tax at the sites where the LZC technologies have been implemented. During the first round in 2009, $6.6 million worth of loans were approved county-wide, all in the residential sector. Within Boulder $1.67 million of loan proceeds were invested in energy efficiency, $1.04 million in solar photovoltaics, and $0.19 million in solar water heaters.

A preliminary analysis[33] estimates that the projects generated by these loans will account for 1,700 tCO2e of annual GHG reductions for Boulder's residential sector. When the additional $21.4 million currently available for the residential sector is loaned out in 2010, annual GHG reductions will increase to 7,200 tCO2e. This is roughly 8% of the reductions required for the residential sector to hit its nominal target in 2012. The loans, tax rebates and grants offered by Boulder City may be useful in encouraging house-builders and households to integrate LZC technology in new homes, but so far the impact seems to have been limited.

Boulder has also implemented a solar access ordinance (not to be confused with the Colorado solar ordinance[34]) which guarantees access to sunlight for homeowners and renters in the city. This is achieved by setting limits on the amount of permitted shading by new construction. A solar access permit is available to those who have installed or who plan to install a solar energy system and need more protection than is provided by the ordinance. For new developments, all units which are not planned to incorporate solar features must be sited to provide good solar access and not shade adjacent structures. The climate smart loans and solar access ordinance in particular could help to support the development of solar power to feed into the smart grid.

Although there appear to be various instruments that could support elements of the smart grid (particularly encouraging the generation of renewable energy), and a federal fund to help finance the development of smart grids, there appears to be nothing to ensure that the CO_2 emissions from the smart grid are minimised. Right now because there are no effective (mandatory) targets for utilities to reduce greenhouse gas emissions in the USA (or even in Colorado specifically) the utility has no incentive to reduce its carbon emissions at all.

Paradoxically, smart grid could help the utility to reduce its costs without reducing CO_2 emissions (Reed, 2010 and Johnson, 2010). Mandatory CO_2 reduction targets are essential for encouraging utilities to use smart grids in a pro-environmental way. Such targets might also encourage the utility to think more about how to reduce overall consumption. If utilities are compensated for encouraging individuals to reduce their carbon footprint this will help to encourage them to work in that direction. The way smart grid regulations are currently developing in Colorado, all the focus is on cost reduction. Only the environmental benefits that are incidental to cost reduction will occur.

Industrial transformation

The culture, structure and practices of the energy industry may mean that the introduction of the smart grid could in fact increase energy consumption and associated CO_2 emissions. The energy industry (if unchecked by regulation or fiscal instruments) aims to maximise consumption and the efficiency of supply. It doesn't aim to reduce consumption or CO_2 emissions. Public policy instruments (mandatory carbon targets or a carbon tax) will be needed to keep this tendency in check. In the case of Colorado a protected monopoly further exacerbates the problem.

In theory a utility's renewable energy portfolio will grow in response to market demand. Today 850 utilities in the USA offer green power tariffs. Green power sales increased in 2008 by 20% when compared to 2007 and accounted for over 5% of the electricity sales. Currently around 6,500 residential customers in Boulder are sourcing their electricity supply from renewable energy (8% of the sectors electricity load – slightly above the national average). According to an NREL survey XCEL ranks third in the USA in terms of renewable energy sales (KWH/annum).

Yet even in Boulder, where the population is made up of people who are more pre-disposed to buying and investing in green energy, only 8% of electricity sales are sourced from renewable supply. The reason why Boulder doesn't have a higher market penetration rate for renewable energy is because XCEL energy has chosen not to expand its renewable portfolio in Colorado. It is a vertically integrated utility and its base-load is reliant on coal. XCEL operates a protected monopoly and thus there is no retail competition in Boulder. This lack of competition in the state means that Boulder consumers don't have the choice to opt for green tariffs.

Colorado is a traditionally regulated state which means in every service territory in which electricity is sold one company owns all the generation, transmission and distribution assets which includes all smart grid components. In Boulder the grid is owned by XCEL. This restricts who can connect to the grid and sell smart grid technologies to consumers in Boulder. There has been talk of edge service providers being able to sell components directly to consumers to allow them to monitor their energy use, but that has not been borne out in any of the business models as yet (Reed, 2010). Right now the utility is buying many of the components direct from the manufacturers. The utility owns the technologies, installs them and maintains them in residents' homes. Thus the utility retains ownership and control over all the components of the smart grid

Until very recently it was very difficult to sell electricity back to the grid from any kind of on-home system, because essentially the utility was the sole service provider. However, recent legislation in Colorado (2007) has required utilities to have net metering, so that households generating energy can be credited for it (Reed, 2010). However, in 2009 this was scaled back to restrict the number of kilowatt hours that XCEL had to credit (Reed, 2010). So they limited the size of the energy generation system that could be put on a home in line with the demand of the home. This was because people had been putting on larger systems in order to make a profit. Now residents can only have a system that provides 120% of their yearly energy needs. The industrial monopoly operating in Boulder seems to be limiting innovation. It is certainly restricting the development of a larger renewable energy portfolio.

The movement of utilities away from generators and suppliers of electricity to managers of electricity is being discussed in the USA. However, the major barrier to this is the utilities themselves. They are populated by staff uninterested in testing new business models (Reed, 2010). Utilities aim to minimise risk, thus, to get them to innovate is difficult (Reed, 2010). However, if the utilities don't have a change in leadership, vision and priorities towards these energy management questions soon, it is likely there will be a big space for edge of service providers (ESPs) to enter the market place. This will have to occur with the public utilities commission (PUC) approval because the ESPs will be dealing with utility infrastructure and customer data. It is likely that the PUC will see the value in doing this particularly if the utilities don't rise to the challenge. Most utilities have shown little interest in addressing energy management issues and CO_2 emissions to date. In traditionally regulated states, like Colorado, there will be a great deal of resistance to industrial transformation.

Lifestyle changes

Essentially the introduction of smart grid technologies can significantly increase consumer involvement in the process of energy management (and in some instances energy storage and generation). At a minimum the consumer will monitor their energy consumption at home, online and choose tariffs. At a maximum the consumer will be managing their energy supply, producing energy, selling it back to the grid and storing it. This requires significantly more interaction with the energy system than is required with the conventional grid system. Thus, residents connected to a smart grid will transform from being passive consumers to active energy citizens. This could potentially help to increase energy literacy, reduce energy consumption and encourage the substitution of fossil fuels with LZC energy sources.

However, the complex nature of smart systems, the time commitment and expertise needed to operate smart technologies effectively may well be off-putting for many households and limit demand. Households connected to the smart grid interact with metering systems in the home and complicated online energy management systems. They have to make all sorts of decisions for example what energy sources to use; when to consume and store energy;

which appliances to use, to switch off and when. Households connected to the smart grid may also produce renewable energy which they then feedback into the grid. The energy produced must be monitored and managed by the household. However, in Boulder renewable energy technologies are generally maintained by the utility (if provided by the utility).

Plug-in hybrid vehicles can be used by households to store energy as well as transport them to a variety of destinations. Households have to judge how best to utilise these vehicles to manage energy most effectively. The household will need to make decisions about when to store energy, when to release it to the grid and when a vehicle is actually needed for transportation. Operating and managing all of these smart technologies effectively is likely to be very complicated and time consuming.

Certainly some of these energy management decisions can be made by utilities operating smart grids, based on a few preferences indicated by households. However, some concern has been expressed by households about lack of individual control over energy systems in these circumstances. A significant cultural change will be required in most instances for households to become involved actively in the management of energy. It is likely that such a change in the short term at least will need to be incentivised, perhaps through a tariff system or even personal carbon quotas.

The British system: decarbonising the national grid

The United Kingdom opted to take a two-pronged approach to decarbonising its energy system, to some extent based on the centralised generation of energy from low carbon sources (i.e. renewable and nuclear energy)[35], whilst also encouraging the introduction of decentralised LZC energy systems (encouraged by incentives including the feed-in tariff and renewable heat incentive as described in Chapter 3). This chapter concentrates on the former[36]. The UK planned two major new programmes for decarbonising the national grid focused on nuclear and offshore wind energy.

Currently the carbon intensity of the UK's energy supply is slightly higher than average for Europe[37]. In the UK the electricity supply is more carbon intensive than gas[38]. It is argued that in the near future space heating will consume less energy than appliances and water heating in British homes (Lowe, 2007). This is because of the significant improvement in the energy efficiency[39] of building stock (Figure 4.6, see colour plates). Water heating and appliance use is largely reliant on electricity (rather than gas). Thus it will become increasingly important to tackle the carbon intensity of the electricity supply (Lowe, 2007).

It seems that the carbon intensity of electricity has declined steadily since the 1950s. This is partly due to a change in fuel mix, the movement away from carbon intensive sources (coal and oil) to lower carbon energy sources

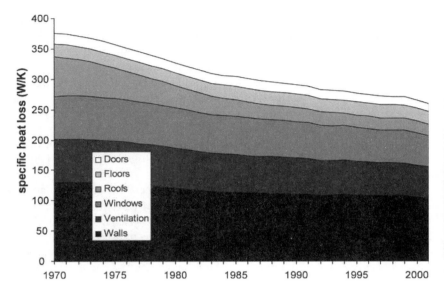

Figure 4.6 Heat loss of average dwelling in Britain.

Source: Shorrock and Utley, 2003.

(gas, nuclear and renewable). It is also due to increased efficiencies in electricity generation through the use of CHP (Figure 4.7).

Decarbonising the national electricity supply is central to delivering low carbon energy to both new and existing stock. The United Kingdom is very urbanised. This restricts the potential for decentralised generation of electricity (Chapter 2). For example wind turbines in urban areas generate approximately a fifth of the power of those situated in rural areas (Allen et al, 2008).

The network of district heating systems is also under-developed in the UK. District heating systems only supply 2% of heat demand in the UK. To retrofit district heating systems into existing urban areas will be an expensive and disruptive option. In addition, if Lowe is correct in his assumption that space heating will consume progressively less of the household energy budget, there seems limited point in introducing more district heating systems. Thus, for new housing developments in urban areas (without existing district heating systems) it might make more sense to connect to a centralised source of LZC electricity.

Currently 6.7% of electricity generated in the UK is from renewable sources and 13.5% from nuclear energy (statistics from 2010). By 2050 virtually all electricity will need to come from low carbon energy sources

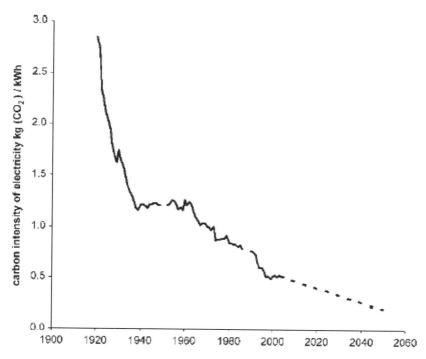

Figure 4.7 The carbon intensity of UK electricity from 1920 to 2004 with a projection to 2050.

Source: Lowe, 2007.[40]

(renewable, nuclear sources or fossil fuels with carbon capture) if the United Kingdom is to achieve its carbon reduction target, which will require rapid deployment of renewable technologies and nuclear facilities.

Demand and deployment

Public demand for renewable energy is limited. Only 340,000 customers have green tariffs in the UK, constituting about 1.5% of the customer base (Diaz-Rainey and Ashton, 2008). The price of fossil fuels remains comparatively low and there is little economic incentive to purchase renewable energy or to generate it. Thus, stimulus for energy companies to increase their renewable generating capacity from the market has been lacking. The introduction of the EU carbon emission trading system, Renewable Obligation Certificates and carbon emission reduction targets (CERT) has provided more motivation for the industry to try to innovate and this is now beginning to filter through.

There has been growth in electricity generation from renewable resources between 1990 and 2008 of nearly 4% (from 1.8 to 5.5%: Figure 4.8, see colour plates). Initially, the bulk was produced from hydro-power, but increasingly wind power and biofuel are playing a more significant role (Figure 4.8). There was an increase in the installed generating capacity of renewable sources in 2008[41], mainly as a result of growth in wind power[42]. There was also an increase in electricity generated from large scale hydro[43] sources and fuelled by waste combustion[44].

Wind

There has been a significant increase in wind-generating capacity offshore and onshore since 2000. By 2009 the UK had reached nearly 4GW operating capacity (BWEA, 2009). This could supply 2,161,674 homes with their entire energy requirement[45] and produce carbon savings of 4,368,742 tonnes[46] (BWEA, 2009). Currently the UK is the fifth largest wind energy generator in Europe (including on and offshore generation). However, the UK leads the market for offshore wind development (Figure 4.9, see colour plates), with just under 700MW operational, over 1,000MW under

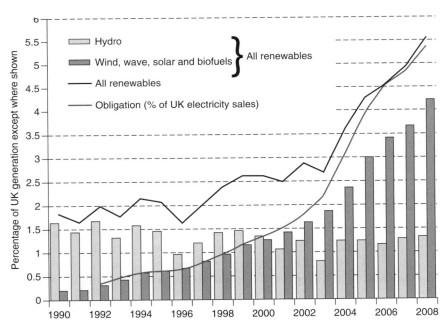

Figure 4.8 Percentage electricity generated from renewable sources 1990–2008.
Source: UK Energy Digest, 2009.

construction and a further 3500MW consented (BWEA, 2009). Three phases of deployment have been planned for offshore generation, eventually providing 45GW capacity, producing carbon savings of 49,148,347 tonnes (BWEA, 2010).

However, there have been various obstacles to offshore deployment including a lack of grid connections, rising production costs and limited existing supply chain capacity. The UK Government decided to develop a new offshore transmission network to manage grid connections. Large sections of the UK grid require replacement. Two-thirds will have to be upgraded or entirely replaced in the next 5–10 years. This creates an opportunity to rebuild the grid system which can accommodate decentralised energy production and a new offshore grid network. In the short term the National Grid can manage with a much larger proportion of wind energy with little or no adjustment. However, with the increase in wind energy predicted more active management will be required. Demand control can be facilitated by the use of a smart grid and variation in generation can be overcome through large-scale grid connection with the rest of Europe (via the 'super-grid' – Chapter 2).

Production costs for offshore wind have doubled since the first phase of deployment, rising from £1.5 million per megawatt (MW) to £3.1 million/ MW. This has been driven by the falling exchange rate (for sterling), historically high commodity prices and a lack of competition between manufacturers. Lack of manufacturing capacity for turbines[47] and cables combined with a shortage of installation vessels will in the short term restrict delivery. However, the dramatic increase in market size represented by the deployment programme is likely to attract new players into the market and reduce prices. The Government aims to encourage the development of a British-based supply chain, to bring jobs to the UK and reduce technology costs (by limiting import costs). The creation of coastal manufacturing hubs – or 'offshore wind ports' – is critical for future investment, as well as providing companies with the space and quay facilities they need (Figure 4.10). This approach has been taken in Germany and proved very successful.

Onshore wind will also play a key role in decarbonising the UK's electricity supply. However, progress in onshore wind is limited by the relatively small number of larger sites. Activity in the UK onshore construction market remains stable. However, the industry is not seeing growth in either the number or capacity of consents coming through the planning system. Seemingly the planning process itself (or at least public opposition) is the main barrier to the deployment of onshore wind farms. In 2009 many schemes were held in the planning system[48] (Figure 4.11).

However, despite poor decision making at Section 36[49] and local level, developer interest has continued to be consistently high in the UK onshore wind market, with a sustained supply of projects being fed into the planning system. However, when all the larger projects have been identified and a

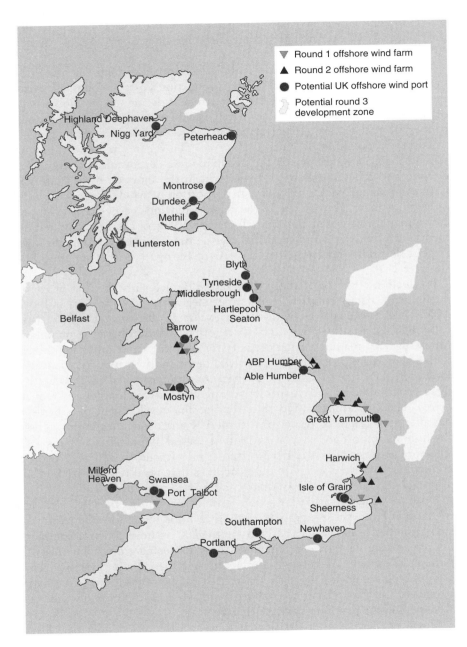

Legend:
▼ Round 1 offshore wind farm
▲ Round 2 offshore wind farm
● Potential UK offshore wind port
Potential round 3 development zone

Highland Deephaven
Nigg Yard
Peterhead
Montrose
Dundee
Methil
Hunterston
Blyth
Tyneside
Middlesbrough
Hartlepool
Seaton
Belfast
Barrow
ABP Humber
Able Humber
Mostyn
Great Yarmouth
Harwich
Milford Heaven
Swansea
Port Talbot
Isle of Grain
Sheerness
Southampton
Newhaven
Portland

Figure 4.10 Offshore wind deployment, Phases 1–3.
Source: DECC, 2009.

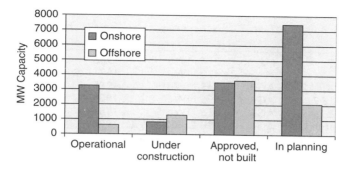

Figure 4.11 Status of UK energy capacity in 2009.
Source: BWEA.

greater number of smaller projects are targeted, it is likely that more pressure will be placed on the planning system with increasing public opposition.

Nuclear

The Government argued that nuclear power was needed to fill the energy gap left by fossil fuels. Nuclear power was seen to be more reliable than renewable energy currently and also produced less CO_2 emissions than fossil fuels[50]. Government ministers and advisers believed 40%[51] of the United Kingdom's energy supply should be sourced from nuclear power, although the government did not go beyond replacement as their policy target, which equated to around 20% (DECC, 2008).

In 2006 nuclear power provided approximately 19% of the electricity generated in the United Kingdom (69 billion kWh of some 380 billion kWh net); by 2007 this declined to 15% (57.5 TWh) and in 2008 it dropped still further to 13.5% (52.5 TWh). In 2010, 19 nuclear power stations (totalling 11 GWe capacity) operated in the UK, but all will be retired by 2023 (Table 4.3). The Government intends to replace all the existing power stations by 2025.

Problems of disposing of nuclear waste, the potential for nuclear accidents or even nuclear terrorism have made nuclear energy historically very unpopular with the green lobby and the general public. In 2001 only 20% of the public supported the development of new nuclear reactors in the UK. Public opposition to nuclear power has certainly limited deployment in the past. However, a survey conducted in 2009 found that most of the British public were in favour of nuclear power.

Of those questioned 67% said that nuclear was needed as part of the UK's energy mix, 43% said that old nuclear power stations should be replaced with new ones and 40% would like to see an increased role for nuclear

Table 4.3 Reactors operating in the United Kingdom, 2010

Reactors	Type	Net capacity each	Start operation	Expected shutdown
Oldbury 1&2	Magnox	217 MWe	1968	Dec 2010
Wylfa 1&2	Magnox	490 MWe	1971–72	Dec 2010
Dungeness B 1&2	AGR	545 MWe	1985–6	2018
Hartlepool 1&2	AGR	595 MWe	1984–5	2014 (2019?)
Heysham 1&2	AGR	615 MWe	1985–6	2014 (2019?)
Hinkley Point B 1&2	AGR	620 & 600 MWe	1976–8	2016
Hunterston B 1&2	AGR	610 & 605 MWE	1976–7	2016
Torness 1&2	AGR	625 MWe	1988–9	2023
Sizewell B	PWR	1196 MWe	1995	2035
Total (19)		11,035 MWe		

Source: WNA, 2010.

power in the UK (IPSOS / Moray, 2010). Thus, public opposition appears to no longer be a major barrier to deployment. However, opposition to the general principle of having nuclear power compared with having a nuclear power plant or waste dump situated in close proximity to one's home tends to elicit very different responses.

The cost of waste disposal has limited deployment of nuclear power stations. Burying waste deep underground could cost as much as £10 billion, according to the UK's Committee on Radioactive Waste Management. The high cost of decommissioning nuclear power plants, approximately £75 billion, also limits deployment (Nuclear Decommissioning Authority, 2010). Nuclear companies have expressed doubt over whether they could afford the full waste and decommissioning costs of power plants. The private sector argues that it needs a limited liability guarantee, and would support a scheme which required only limited contributions to decommissioning costs for new plants.

The restricted availability of uranium could also limit deployment of nuclear power and threatens the long-term sustainability of nuclear power as an option for the UK. Uranium depletion affects the stability of supply. Since the UK doesn't have a sufficient local source it will need to import uranium, which of course impacts on carbon intensity of nuclear power. Importing uranium can present long-term fuel security issues, as with other finite resources.

Approach to delivery

The Government decided to take a regulated market approach to the delivery of both wind and nuclear energy[52]. This approach relies on the private sector delivering new nuclear power stations and wind farms with very limited public subsidy. Various mechanisms currently in place including the EU carbon trading system (EU ETS), the renewables obligation (RO) and the environmental transformation fund (ETF) should provide some incentive to encourage the development of LZC power in the UK. The EU Emissions Trading Scheme puts a cap on the CO_2 emitted by business and creates a market and price for carbon allowances. This increases the economic viability of investing in LZC energy sources. The Renewables Obligation requires electricity suppliers to source a proportion of their supply from renewable generators[53]. This offers stakeholder incentive and should stimulate production and innovation within the renewable energy industry.

The environmental transformation fund can be used to speed up the commercial use of low-carbon energy and energy efficiency technologies in the UK, raising their profile in the energy market. It has a budget of £400 million to be spent from 2008 to 2011, which is a rather small budget considering the deployment costs for wind and nuclear energy. The ETF replaces a large number of other low carbon technology investment programmes[54], which actually reduces the funds available for LZC energy. It also reinforces the competition for funds between renewable and nuclear energy.

There are still significant hidden subsidies for nuclear. There is limited liability for nuclear operators in the case of an accident. The costs of the pre-construction safety analysis are covered by the Nuclear Installations Inspectorate. The Office of Civil Nuclear Security pays towards the security of nuclear facilities and materials in transit. The Government pays the costs of the UK's membership of the EU nuclear agency, Euratom and the International Atomic Energy Agency, both of which do promotional and safety work for nuclear power. The UK Government is also paying for research into so-called 'Generation 4' reactor designs.

Lack of public funding has historically limited the growth of renewable energy in the UK. Historically there has been significantly more public investment in nuclear energy. However, in countries where there has been greater public investment (e.g. Germany's investment in renewable energy and France's in nuclear energy) in renewable and nuclear power, industries have grown significantly[55]. The British approach has already been met with a great deal of scepticism from the large energy companies who expect subsidies, guaranteed prices or supply contracts to incentivise the development of nuclear power stations or wind farms. Of course both nuclear and wind energy will become more competitive as the price of carbon increases.

However, the costs of decommissioning nuclear power stations and the disposal of nuclear waste make it an expensive business. In real terms the legacy costs of dealing with radioactive waste and decommissioning existing reactors are far greater than the capital cost of construction. They are also far greater than the combined capital and operational cost of wind farms. The Government is keen to avoid these costs in future nuclear programmes. Overall a stable, long-term policy framework supporting LZC energy and a robust carbon pricing system is the minimum required to ensure investment in wind and nuclear energy in the UK.

Attempts have also been made to streamline the planning process to reduce the current inertia towards large energy infrastructure projects (renewable and nuclear energy). The Government set up a single body (previously the Infrastructure Planning Commission in 2010, now the Major Infrastructure Unit) to review applications for major energy infrastructure projects. This body has the power to grant permission for development. This should speed up the application, consultation and decision-making processes and provide greater certainty for investors. This in turn will reduce development costs for investors and increase the commercial viability of wind farms and nuclear reactors. It should also result in the better strategic coordination of major energy infrastructure projects. However, it lessens community involvement in decision-making processes and is likely to create friction in the long term.

Industrial transformation

The benefit of adopting a centralised generation and supply model is that it enables a more rapid decarbonisation of the energy supply. It is also more acceptable to the energy industry. Adopting this approach utilises existing supply networks. It enables economies of scale to operate in terms of production and supply and reinforces the existing hierarchies. It assumes the deficit model, that households are passive consumers rather than actively involved in the production or management of energy. This model doesn't fundamentally change the current culture, structure or practices of the energy industry. Thus, it does not threaten the powerful vested interests that constitute it.

The energy industry in the UK has shown itself very resistant to change particularly in terms of adoption of renewable energy generation as part of a supply strategy. Frequent changes in renewable energy policy in the UK have resulted in a lack of price and market security for investors (Lipp 2007; Ragwitz and Held, 2006). Long-term, chronic under-investment in the renewable energy industry[56] has meant that research, development and deployment of technologies have lagged behind other European countries. This has been further exacerbated by problems accessing the grid, particularly for smaller generators, and planning constraints (Lipp 2007; Ragwitz and Held, 2006). This combination has resulted in higher costs for producing renewable energy and a lack of diversity in supply (Lipp 2007; Ragwitz and Held, 2006).

The market for renewable energy in the UK has been distorted as the real cost, including the environmental cost, of using fossil fuels has not been internalised into the calculation of the worth of renewable energy. The price of fossil fuels has remained comparatively low. The energy sector is monopolised by existing utilities and to gain access requires considerable investment. A lack of information about renewable markets and high transaction costs have been limited the number of smaller energy providers entering the market (Painuly, 2001).

The capital costs of investing in renewable technologies are high and there is a lack of support for projects from financial institutions (Painuly, 2001; DTI, 2006). Historically lack of certainty in the absence of a clear political lead or robust regulatory framework for promoting renewable energy has reinforced the concern amongst investors in the security of renewable energy projects for long-term investment (Painuly, 2001; Reiche 2002). These problems persist. Long pay-back periods and low demand for these technologies further frustrate the market (Painuly, 2001; DTI, 2006). Government investment provides an alternative solution; however, funding for deployment, research and development of new technologies has been very limited in the UK to date (Painuly, 2001; Reiche 2002).

The nuclear industry has been more heavily subsidised, which has resulted in it growing more quickly than the renewable energy industry. However, decommissioning and waste disposal costs, combined with limited stocks of uranium, make it a less attractive long-term option, particularly when combined with the removal of subsidies. The key to encouraging growth in the use of LZC energy is for the full environmental cost of using fossil fuels to be reflected in their price, using carbon taxation or through the carbon trading system.

Another issue appears to be that the UK is likely to experience an energy gap (i.e. when demand will outstrip supply) within the next 15 years if existing capacity is not increased. It is likely that the deficit will be addressed through energy imports, largely fossil fuels. However, with the construction of the Super-grid the UK could in fact potentially import renewable energy, rather than fossil fuels to top up supply. Of course this will be in conjunction with expanding existing capacity.

Lifestyle change

This centralised approach to decarbonisation of the energy supply adopted by the UK should result in no real changes in lifestyle. In some respects this makes it a very attractive option for policy-makers since it would be easily accepted by the public. They would continue to be passive consumers, driven by maximising personal utility and minimising their involvement in the management or production of energy. However, there is a problem with this approach. It does not address the underlying problem of increasing energy consumption. For the system described to be effective long term, energy consumption will need to reduce. Nuclear and renewable energy sources will not be able to feed a continual increase in energy consumption as is being experienced currently.

Thus, people need to become more energy literate. This can be enabled through the introduction of smart meters in homes and businesses or, at the other end of the spectrum, a full range of smart technologies. Energy literacy can of course be increased through resident involvement in the management and production of energy. However, isolating residents from both processes means that they remain energy illiterate and passive consumers. The UK Government's intention to introduce a national smart grid should help to overcome this problem.

Themes to be explored

The four case studies offer very different systems approaches to delivering LZC energy at different scales. The appropriateness of each system will be dependent on the context (physical, political, cultural, institutional and economic) in which it operates. For all their diversity the systems highlight four important issues which will affect the successful delivery of a decarbonised energy supply in the future.

The first of these themes relates to markets and deployment. It becomes apparent from the case studies that there is still limited demand for LZC energy amongst the public. However, in at least one instance lack of availability had also restricted the market (Boulder, Colorado). Consumers will not drive sufficient changes needed within industry to deliver LZC energy systems. Transformation will require that energy producers rather than consumers become the early adopters of new LZC energy systems, encouraged by a range of policy instruments.

However, there is huge resistance to industrial transformation within the energy industry. The use of non-fossil fuels, decentralisation of energy systems and the management of energy consumption lack credibility within the industry. Yet in the long term all three will be needed to secure a sustainable low carbon energy supply. Changes in culture, structure and practices will be needed to deliver LZC energy systems and a mixture of regulation and fiscal policy will be needed to ensure this transformation.

Purely market-based approaches are unlikely to be effective in these circumstances because of the resistance to change demonstrated by the energy industry. A more interventionist approach would involve regulation to limit the use of fossil fuels and carbon emissions, enable competition, allow new entrants into the market (ESCOs, ESPs, etc) and ensure access to the distribution network and so on, all of which are essential for the transformation. It is equally essential that the full costs of fossil fuel are factored into its price or quota systems are used to limit extraction or consumption.

However, it is not only the energy industry that will need to transform. Culturally most people are used to the centralised (deficit) model of energy generation and supply and as such act as passive consumers, largely divorced from the process of energy management and production. This does not help to raise energy literacy amongst consumers. Yet raising awareness is essential if the underlying consumption problem is to be fully addressed. To become more engaged in these processes will require a significant cultural shift that could be incentivised through tariffs or personal carbon quota systems. These themes will be picked up again later in the book.

Chapter 5

Low/zero carbon neighbourhoods

Some very interesting demonstration projects that combine LZC energy systems with energy efficient buildings and low carbon lifestyles have been developed in Europe and the USA. These low-zero carbon (LZC) neighbourhoods utilise a range of technical systems and demonstrate a variety of approaches to the financing, planning, production and operation of LZC neighbourhoods. They also provide examples of industrial innovation, although in some instances this has not led to long-term changes in industrial practice. Some of the case studies chosen require active involvement of residents in their design and operation; in others residents have a passive role. In all cases the future demand for LZC neighbourhoods, particularly amongst the wider community, is questioned.

The LZC neighbourhoods (Table 5.1) presented in this chapter are:

- B001 Western Harbour (Malmö, Sweden);
- Hammarby Sjöstad (Stockholm, Sweden);
- Vauban (Freiburg, Germany);
- GEOS (Arvada, Colorado);
- BedZED (London, UK).

The energy efficiency of housing built in each development varies significantly from a primary energy demand of 105 kWh/m² to energy- plus houses (Vauban and GEOS). In some instances the neighbourhoods are linked to a city-wide energy system (BedZED and B001) and in others the energy systems are more localised (Hammarby, GEOS and Vauban). An array of renewable technologies has been adopted in the neighbourhoods including: solar thermal, solar PV, biomass, biogas, wind, geothermal, waste heat and waste incineration. Thus the physical energy infrastructure varies between neighbourhoods.

The neighbourhoods also vary considerably in terms of age, scale, location, density and CO_2 emissions. B001 has been existence for longest (nine years) whilst GEOS is currently being built. The neighbourhoods vary in size from 262 units (GEOS) to 9,000 units (Hammarby). A variety of locations are represented both urban (Hammarby, B001 and GEOS) and

Table 5.1 Comparing the LZC neighbourhood case studies

	Hammarby Sjöstad	BOO1 Western Harbour	Vauban	GEOS	BedZED
Population neighbourhood	20,000 residents (9,000 units)	2,000 residential units completed in the first phase	5,000 residents	Approx 680 residents (262 units)	244 residents (82 dwellings)
Population urban area	1,000,000 (Stockholm)	290,000 (Malmö)	217,000 (Freiburg)	107,361 (Arvada) 2,357,404 (Denver met area) Started summer	7,556,900 (Greater London)
First phase completion	2004	2001	2007	2009	2002
Household characteristics	Affluent	Young and affluent	Families (variety of incomes)	Mixed (but generally affluent	Mixed
Country	Stockholm, Sweden	Malmö, Sweden	Freiburg, Germany	Arvada, Colorado (USA)	London, UK
Location	Urban waterfront (former industrial site) – prime development site	Urban waterfront (former industrial site) – prime development site	Suburban (former industrial site)	Urban	Suburban
Land use mix	Mixed	Mixed	Mixed	Mixed	Mixed
Density	High (50 units/hectare)	High (57 units/hectare)	Medium	Low (2.32 units/acre)	High (50 units/hectare)
District heating systems	See Hammarby closed-loop model	Malmö district heating system.	Local biomass fuelled CHP plant	Geothermal heating loop	Biofuel CHP – changed to gas CHP

	60 kWh/m²/year	105 kWh/m²/year	LEH, (65kWh/m²/year) PH and Energy-plus standard	Zero-net energy house	82 kWh/m²/year
Buildings energy efficiency (primary energy demand) or standard	60 kWh/m²/year	105 kWh/m²/year	LEH, (65kWh/m²/year) PH and Energy-plus standard	Zero-net energy house	82 kWh/m²/year
Energy sources	PV, waste water treatment, biofuel, waste incineration, groundwater heating/cooling	Wind, PV, solar collectors, ground water heating/cooling, waste heat, waste incineration, biofuel	PV and solar collectors, biofeul, biogas, hydro-power, wind	PV, solar collectors, geothermal loop	PV, biofuel CHP (now gas CHP)
CO_2 production in neighbourhood (tonnes/capital annum)	2.5–3.0	N/A[1]	0.5	N/A	0.51
CO_2 production in city (tonnes/capital annum)	4	4.4	8.5	N/A	9.85
City target for CO_2 reduction	Fossil free by 2050	100% renewables by 2040	Reduce CO_2 by 40% (from 1990 levels) by 2030	None set for Arvada as yet	National target for zero carbon new build by 2016. Local target for all zero carbon buildings by 2025

Note

1 Reduced CO_2 emissions by 315 tonnes/annum

Source: Author's own.

suburban (BedZED, and Vauban), ranging from high (Hammarby, BedZED and B001) to low density (GEOS). Energy consumption and CO_2 emissions also differ between neighbourhoods.

Hammarby Sjöstad

Hammarby Sjöstad is a pioneering eco-district on a site just outside the centre of Stockholm. It is in a prime, waterfront location (Figure 5.1). The site covers 200 hectares and was municipally owned. It was contaminated[1] and had poor access to the city centre. The site was decontaminated as part of the redevelopment programme and a neighbourhood tram system was introduced, which significantly increased access from Hammarby to all parts of the city. Thus proximity and access to the city centre, combined with its waterfront location has meant that Hammarby is a popular (and expensive) district to live in.

When complete the eco-district will house 20,000 residents in 10,000 units (Figure 5.2, see colour plates). The first phase was completed in 2004. It accommodates a number of uses (residential, commercial, leisure, industrial and retail) and is built at densities similar to the old town of Stockholm (50 units/hectare). The aim was to reduce CO_2 emissions in the district so that each resident produced between 2.5 and 3.0 tonnes CO_2/capita/annum (compared to 4 tonnes CO_2/capita/annum on average for Stockholm). To achieve this goal the buildings have been built to higher energetic standards (60 kWh/m² primary energy demand) in some cases with embedded microgenerating technologies (PV cells and solar collectors). All units are also connected to the closed-loop energy system (Chapter 4).

At the heart of the community is an environmental advice centre which provides information to local residents about leading low impact lifestyles, however, there are no household energy monitoring schemes operating in the district.

Approach to delivery

Stockholm's bid for the 2004 Olympics was the primary stimulus for the development of Hammarby. Although the Olympic bid wasn't successful it brought together key stakeholders in the city to discuss a vision for the site. The networks of communication, concepts and organisational structures developed for the bid provided the basis on which the district was eventually planned and built.

The city formed a project group for Hammarby with its own budget, a chief executive officer and an environmental unit (a team of professionals from the city council with relevant technical expertise). The group applied for national[2] and local[3] funds to subsidise the development of the eco-district.

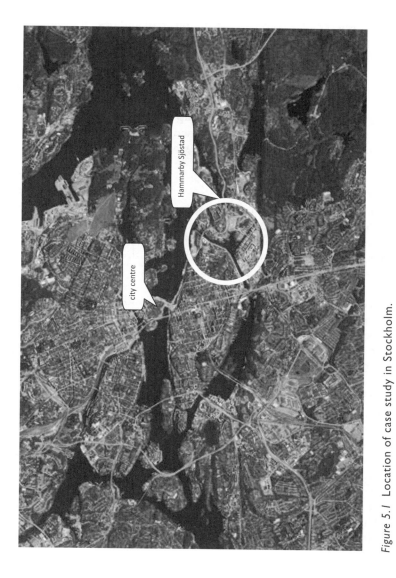

Figure 5.1 Location of case study in Stockholm.

Source: Jonas Risén.

The planners in the city environmental unit facilitated the development process, acting as project managers. This was an iterative, dynamic and collaborative process which brought developers into discussions at the earliest possible stage in the planning process. It enabled developers to work alongside the environmental unit and those delivering the environmental infrastructure on site, to discuss possible technological and design solutions, as well as logistical problems (for example the connection of units to the closed-loop system and how to achieve high levels of energy efficiency in buildings).

After these initial discussions open meetings with all the developers putting in proposals for the site were held. Developers presented their projects every couple of months to their peer group and the environment unit. This enabled the transfer of information, generation of knowledge within the industry and encouraged greater competitiveness between development companies. Eventually the winning projects were identified by the Hammarby project group. This highly collaborative planning process became known as the 'Stockholm process'.

There was a very strong vision for the project to become an eco-district (seen as key to winning the Olympic bid). From the beginning, the city set out an environmental quality programme for the development, which stated that emissions and energy use should be half the environmental load for 'normal construction'. Any developer wishing to build on the site had to commit itself to these stringent environmental goals. At least initially the fact that the municipality owned the site reinforced this position.

Technical competitions between developers were encouraged to try and achieve the best possible environmental design standards. This level of competition encouraged significant improvements. Developers were also aware of the high-quality environmental infrastructure being provided in the development and realised that the building stock would have to reflect this quality. Thus the environmental programme set out to encourage the development of very energy efficient buildings (60 kWh/m2[4]) linked to the closed-loop energy system.

The closed-loop system was wholly funded and planned by the municipality and utilities. Developers were not expected to contribute funding or to the planning of this infrastructure[5], only to connect to it. Developers were expected to deliver very energy efficient buildings. In some instances buildings also incorporated LZC technologies for generating energy. The additional cost of these technologies was largely borne by the residents (those living in Hammarby tend to be affluent, Exploateringskontoret, 2005).

However, the energy efficiency standards set by the programme weren't achieved. The residential units were larger than average and oversized in relation to functional requirements. This increased the amount of energy needed for space heating and cooling. The units also had oversized windows, which increased heat loss during the winter and contributed to over-heating in the summer. The technologies used weren't as high a standard as promised. Carbon dioxide emissions reduced by 29–37% (Brick, 2008) compared with the average dwelling (rather than 50%). Thus, the energy efficiency of the units built in Hammarby was disappointing (Stoll, 2009). Some of the developers are now beginning to replace the larger windows with smaller ones to try to reduce energy consumption.

One of the major problems encountered in delivering energy efficient buildings in Hammarby was the lack of systematic monitoring, evaluation and enforcement. The city council relied on energy modelling exercises completed by third parties on behalf of developers during the planning phase of projects. However, the energy efficiency of the units was not systematically checked after construction (Stoll, 2009). This is the system of enforcement adopted nationally in Sweden. Increasingly post-occupancy energy surveys suggest that the energetic standards modelled during the planning process are not being achieved in practice (Nässén et al, 2008). In some instances this may result from inferior materials being used in construction. However, more often it seems that the manner in which buildings are constructed is to blame for this mismatch (Linden, 2009; Svenberg, 2009).

A change in political control in Stockholm over the construction period (1998–2012) affected the environmental standards imposed on the project. When the principal decision to develop Hammarby was taken in 1995, the City of Stockholm was governed by a red-green coalition, who supported the ambitious environmental programme (Vestbro, 2002). When the blue coalition took over in 1998 it decided to convert the status of the environmental programme from being binding to a status of recommendation. Thus, municipal control over the project slackened (Vestbro, 2002). The blue coalition decided that municipally owned land should be sold to the private sector. Thus they started to sell land on the Hammarby site to private housing and construction companies. They argued that land lease contracts could include clauses about environmental standards, but the reality was that selling the land made implementation of the environmental programme much more difficult (Stoll, 2009; Vestbro, 2002).

Lifestyles

LZC technologies are well integrated into the Hammarby development. The approach taken adopts a deficit model which limits household involvement in the management of energy. Thus, households in Hammarby tend to be passive consumers. This has not helped to raise energy literacy or reduce energy consumption amongst households living in Hammarby. Nor has it encouraged other pro-environmental behaviours. However, a few households do have micro-generating technologies and some have metering systems, which have helped to increase energy literacy and alter consumption patterns.

It was implicitly assumed by those designing Hammarby that by providing residents with integrated environmental infrastructure (the closed-loop system, public transport system, etc) and environmental information (provided by the GlasHut information centre) they would adopt less consumerist lifestyles (Vestbro, 2002). However, this assumption proved to be misguided. Residents moved to Hammarby Sjöstad not because of its environmental technologies or their green credentials, but because of its location, aesthetic quality and services.

Residents appreciated the environmental profile of Hammarby, but they were not prepared to make changes to their lifestyles and habits to achieve environmental goals (Axelsson et al, 2001; Magnuson 2004[6]). Hammarby residents were also generally affluent[7]; they could afford to be more profligate with energy. It has been recognised that introducing metering at least to properties in Hammarby would be beneficial. Stockholm city council is now looking at ICT (e.g. metering) and costing solutions to tackle energy consumption amongst households in Hammarby (Stoll, 2009).

Industrial innovation

The closed-loop energy system was the only real example of industrial innovation in the Hammarby Sjöstad project (discussed in Chapter 4). The targets set for energy efficiency in the housing were not sufficient to drive any real innovation in the house-building industry.

Demand and deployment

The demand for units in Hammarby was not driven by its environmental design and LZC technologies. It was driven by other issues including location, affordability, access to services and facilities, aesthetic attractiveness, good public transport connections, design of individual units, and access to open space and water (Figure 5.3, see colour plates). The environmental qualities of the development were considered but were of secondary importance in the residents' decision to settle in the area. The technical aspects of the LZC neighbourhood will not sell it to the mass market, but the location, affordability and design will.

To some extent designing the development on the basis of a deficit model (i.e. one in which the household is a passive consumer) is likely to produce this outcome. If the technical system had been designed to require greater household involvement in operation, then the presence of LZC systems would have become more influential in the residents' decision to settle in Hammarby. However, it is possible that such an approach could have put off potential purchasers. Passive systems, although less likely to increase energy literacy, do tackle CO_2 emissions to an extent, whilst appealing to the mass market.

The Hammarby model has provided an international showcase for good practice in low carbon development. International visitors (policy-makers, urban professionals, the house-building and energy industries) have flocked to the development. The Hammarby model has informed new development and regeneration projects in China, Russia, South Africa, Canada and the UK (Chapter 4). It is also influencing the development of new urban quarters locally.

The largest of these is Stockholm Royal Seaport[8]. An ambitious environmental programme has been adopted for the seaport development. An integrated LZC energy system is planned for the new eco-district fuelled by the Fortum CHP[9] plant (run on biofuel). Interestingly the more complex closed-loop model is not being adopted.

As in Hammarby, a higher energetic standard for housing units has been set at 55kWh/m²/annum primary energy demand (half that required by national regulation and close to passive house standard) for the first phase of the development. All units will also be fitted with metering systems, a lesson learnt from Hammarby, or other more innovative technologies[10] which encourage a reduction in energy consumption. The energetic standard of new units will change for the second phase of the development to track technological progress. Stockholm City Council are hoping to increase the standard to passive house or zero-energy standard during the second phase of the development.

Stockholm's involvement in the 'Clinton Climate initiatives' means that the city will be pushing for energy-plus housing in the future stages of development (i.e. within the next five years). The developers involved in the project are aware of this intended progression which has created a framework for long-term innovation and offers security for investment in building capacity to reach these standards.

The role of the municipality now in the development of new eco-districts in Stockholm is largely one of strategic planning, negotiation and governance. In addition, the municipality also provides technical information to potential developers. It can act as the coordinator of a procurement approach for new LZC technologies (i.e. the municipality can buy LZC technologies at scale to reduce costs to developers). The municipality also offers subsidies for the introduction of LZC technologies into new developments. In this way the municipality may be able to encourage the deployment LZC technologies in future developments.

B001 Western Harbour

B001 is an eco-district built in the Western Harbour in Malmö (southern Sweden). The eco-district is mixed-use (including retail, commercial and leisure uses) and built at high densities. The first phase of the B001 project provided 2,000 residential units. Once all phases are complete the entire development will comprise 20,000 residential units. The housing built in the eco-district was constructed to a high energetic standard (105 kWh/m²) and connected to a bespoke LZC energy system (Figure 5.4, see colour plates). Higher efficiency standards were achieved by using space efficient layouts, avoiding thermal bridges, creating air-tight shells and installing passive heating / ventilation systems.

The energy system uses local renewable energy sources (Figure 5.5, see colour plates). A large wind turbine (2 MW) is positioned in the harbour 3 km from the development. It produces 6,300,000 kWh/annum providing enough electricity to power 2,000 residential units, heat pumps and recharging station for electric vehicles. Photovoltaic cells (120 m²) are embedded into the development producing 12,000 kWh/year, enough to supply electricity to only five dwelling units. Solar collectors (4400 m²) have been placed on ten buildings in Western Harbour to provide hot water. These produced an average of 375 kWh/m²/annum.

A heating and cooling system has also been developed. Heat is extracted from a local aquifer using a large heat pump. The aquifer provides 3,000 MW of heat for 2.4 MW power. This heat can be directly fed into buildings in Western Harbour or into the city-wide district heating system. Most has ended up in the city-wide system. The aquifer has enabled seasonal storage of energy for heating and cooling. The heat produced in the summer is saved for the winter when it is made available to the city-wide district heating system. Cold water from the winter is saved and used by the district cooling system during summer.

All LZC technologies are managed and maintained by E-ON (the energy company for the city). However, in future projects the energy company are not proposing to manage and maintain any building integrated technologies (e.g. PV cells, solar collectors, etc), because of the issue of ownership. Thus the owners of the buildings with the integrated LZC technologies will be responsible for operating and maintaining these technologies and feeding the energy produced back into the wider energy system.

Like Hammarby, the B001 eco-district has been built in a popular location. It is very close to the city centre and in a prime waterfront location. The site was municipally owned and was formerly used for industrial purposes and thus needed to be decontaminated (Figure 5.6, see colour plates).

Approach to delivery

Structural changes to industry in Malmö led to the loss of 35,000 jobs. By the late 1990s the city was in desperate need of rebranding and regenerating. The Öresund link connecting Malmö to Copenhagen (and its international airport) looked as if it could bring new employment opportunities to the area and attract residents from Copenhagen, but only if significant infrastructural improvements were made. The municipality believed that developing a model for a sustainable district in Malmö for Housing Expo 2000, could help attract much needed investment and promote the area.

During the same period the local energy company – Sydkraft – had to close a coal-fired power station and replace its generating capacity. For some time Sydkraft had been associated with nuclear energy which had not been good for public relations since the Chernobyl disaster in the mid-1980s. Sydkraft was looking to develop a new state-of-the-art energy system that was efficient and used renewable energy sources. Thus, designing a sustainable district with a LZC energy system for the EXPO 2000 provided the municipality and the utility with a great opportunity. In 1996 Malmo won the bid for EXPO 2000 and work began.

As with Hammarby, the B001 eco-district was the product of a highly collaborative planning process. The municipality, energy company and developers began discussions about the project at a pre-planning stage. The environmental programme (including energetic standards and LZC energy system) was one of the key issues discussed to test the market viability of various infrastructural options. These discussions also continued throughout the planning stage and were supplemented with educational seminars (about new technologies, processes, funding mechanisms, etc) and peer-review of project proposals. Thus, a method very akin to the 'Stockholm process' was adopted.

The municipality set up a special unit – the sustainability unit – to identify and apply for potential sources of funding for the project. B001 received substantial support from public subsidies[12]. The unit also acted to attract private investment into Western Harbour. Under EU rules support for investment in competitive activities (i.e. by developers, utilities etc) was limited to 30%, whilst those undertaken by municipalities could receive 50–100%. Thus, the municipality was responsible for public spaces and strategic technical infrastructure on the site. The energy company was responsible for delivering the localised LZC energy system and developers were responsible for connecting to the system and ensuring buildings were as energy efficient as possible.

In addition to raising funds to leverage innovative projects, the sustainability unit assisted in creating networks, enabling communication and negotiation between key players involved in the implementation process. The unit worked alongside the planning department to assist in the implementation of the planners' vision for Western Harbour. The unit also acted as a conduit for the dissemination of knowledge gleaned from innovative projects, which it used to raise the profile of the city and attract further investment. Thus the sustainability unit played (and continues to play) an integral role in the delivery of innovative projects in Malmö and Western Harbour.

The energetic standard set for new housing units was 105 kWh/m².[13] This standard was identified in the quality programme prepared by Malmö City

Council (MCC) and housing expo architects. Several mechanisms were used by the municipality to enforce higher energetic standards. The municipality owned the site and would not release plots to developers unless they agreed to comply with the energetic standard. Because MCC owned a significant amount of land in the city this provided an incentive for the developers to build to higher standards. Subsidies from the EU and the Swedish Government were used in part to finance the capital cost of the new technologies used in the units. The subsidies were also used to assist developers in building their capacity (i.e. knowledge, expertise, supply chains, etc) to deliver low-energy homes.

An educational process was established in which developers could learn about the technologies and design solutions available for achieving low energy housing at organised seminars or through consultation exercises with the city planners. Developers were invited to present and discuss their design solutions with their peer group and the energy company which also helped to further facilitate the learning process. Developers were involved in the discussions for setting the energetic standards and refused the more stringent standards suggested by MCC (the developers felt these standards were uneconomic). The district cooling system was also abandoned in all but two houses because developers did not think it would be cost-effective. Consequently the standards set were not very taxing. They did not test technological boundaries and limited innovation.

Even so the units built in the first phase of the Western Harbour development did not achieve the energy standard set. There was quite a difference between energy consumption estimated by the energy model[14] used by developers and actual consumption data (Figure 5.7). Energy consumption was monitored for ten different properties. It was found that estimated energy consumption values were considerably lower than actual energy consumption[15] values. A similar analysis was completed for district heat consumption. Again estimated heat consumption values were below actual values (Figure 5.8). Of the ten properties investigated none reached the 105 kWh/m² standard set by the environmental programme.

Currently enforcement of energetic standards in new development (in B001, Malmö and Sweden as a whole) appears to be insufficient and sporadic. There is heavy reliance on energetic modelling (commissioned by the developer) and generally no monitoring post-construction. Even when buildings are monitored post-construction the penalties are limited. The most effective weapon in the municipality's armoury appears to be land ownership. Many municipalities (certainly Malmö and Stockholm) own land which they release for development. The municipality can refuse applications from developers if they have failed to achieve the environmental programme standards in previous projects. This provides some incentive for developers to achieve the standards set, but only if post-construction monitoring is carried out effectively. The B001 example underpins the need

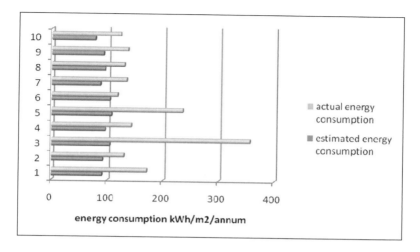

Figure 5.7 Energy consumed by B001 buildings (estimated and actual).
Source: Nilsson and Elmroth, 2009.

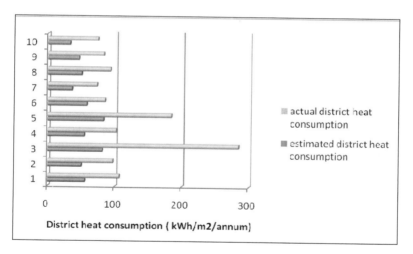

Figure 5.8 District heat consumed by B001 buildings (estimated and actual).
Source: Nilsson and Elmroth, 2009.

for more reliable energy models, or a switch to improved monitoring and enforcement post-construction.

There have been major changes in Malmö over past ten years (since the inception of the B001 project). When B001 started there was a great deal of resistance from developers to the energetic standard set and in real terms most of the developers did not deliver the standard. However, after a lot of work the energetic standard has finally been reached in Phase 1 (through improvements to the shell in most instances), but it has taken nearly ten years to get there.

The phasing of the Western Harbour development provides an opportunity to study the impact of different approaches to delivery. For the first phase of development a more interventionist approach was adopted by the municipality. For the second phase a market-led approach was adopted. This has produced very different development outcomes. During the first phase of development where there was significant intervention (in the form of public subsidies, the quality programme and so on) the energetic building standard was low, but this was partially off-set by some localised low carbon energy generating capacity (i.e. from the on-site wind turbine, PV cells and solar collectors).

For the second phase of development, there was limited public subsidy available for the capacity building process rather than the physical infrastructure. The focus was on raising awareness and increasing the knowledge base within the house-building industry to deliver low-energy and passive houses. The municipality financed workshops for the developers to discuss issues surrounding the delivery of sustainable residential areas. Ideas were generated from the workshops and were communicated to other developers. In some cases the workshops have also led to developers conducting their own research into new products.

In contrast to the first phase of development, passive houses have been built on commercial grounds in the second phase by two house-builders (for rental), which is slightly surprising since there has been less intervention. There appears to be two key drivers that have produced this outcome. Firstly, both house-builders believe that there is now market demand for low-energy or passive houses in Sweden. Secondly, the house-building industry has increased its capacity to deliver low-energy or passive houses, by establishing supply chains and developing appropriate technical expertise.

Both have helped to increase confidence amongst house-builders in building energy efficient homes. However, the majority are building to far lower energy standards on phase two than for the first phase of the development (Graham, 2009). Thus the success of the market-led approach in delivering higher energetic standards (and thus lower CO_2 emissions from buildings) is very limited, unless there is a market advantage to the developer. In this instance developers with a long-term interest in the development could see financial reward for ensuring the accommodation was very energy efficient.

The market-led approach has also meant that there is no localised LZC energy system installed in the second phase of the development. Without subsidy the energy company suggests that it would be uneconomic to provide a localised LZC energy system similar to that installed for the first phase of the harbour development (Rosén, 2009). This is at least in part because of the limited interest shown by developers and householders in the previously developed LZC energy system (Rosén, 2009). It is also reinforced by various technical problems that were encountered with the aquifer system and the limited quantity of energy generated by solar technologies (Rosén, 2009). Thus cost, technological difficulties, inefficiencies and lack of consumer demand suggest that a new approach to energy supply may be needed in the second phase of the harbour development. The energy company favours a more centralised municipal system based on waste heat, waste incineration, biofuel, biogas and possibly wind, partly supported by national subsidies and the carbon tax.

Thus, there is a clear distinction in the LZC technical systems provided in the first and second phases of development. This is in part because of the technical difficulties encountered, but it is largely because there is no market for LZC systems. This might be overcome if there was some economic advantage gained through the installation of LZC energy systems. This could perhaps be delivered through carbon pricing, carbon reduction targets for energy providers, subsidies for LZC energy and passive houses, building code or the long-term involvement of house-builders in the operation of buildings (to overcome the split incentive[16] problem).

Lifestyles

A deficit technical model has been chosen for the B001 eco-district (similar to that in Hammarby). Households are passive consumers and generally uninterested in energy usage. Energy consumption amongst households living in B001 was significantly higher than expected. This could be because the residents are generally very affluent, so their energy use is likely to be higher than average. However, their behaviour could also explain some of the discrepancy between real and predicted energy consumption in the B001 development. Household behaviour particularly influences energy consumed by electrical appliances and water-heating in the home.

Information was given to residents in the B001 development about their energy consumption via metering and annual information pamphlets produced by the energy company.It is important to introduce educational programmes to tackle household energy consumption alongside the introduction of new LZC infrastructure in order that households operate systems effectively. However, according to the energy company, this approach appears to have had limited impact on consumption to date (Rosén, 2009).

Industrial innovation

The B001 eco-district provides an interesting case study in innovation. Some lessons have been learnt by the energy companies and house-builders involved in the project which may inform their future practice. However, this is only likely to occur if appropriate regulatory or fiscal incentives are introduced. When a non-interventionist approach to delivery is taken there appears to be very limited willingness, particularly amongst house-builders, to innovate and adopt higher energy efficiency standards or LZC technologies in new homes, unless there is a proven market for them.

The innovators in the house-building industry tend to be those with a long-term interest in the operational cost of the buildings. However, some innovators have emerged from related industries and are now building to higher energy efficiency standards. For example a steel-making company has started building passive houses in the second phase of development in the harbour.

Previously the company had fabricated steel for house-builders but saw some market advantage in delivering the end product themselves, so they have undergone a transformation process to facilitate this switch. The company see building their capacity now to deliver passive houses as a worthwhile investment, because of EU legislation (the energy performance in buildings directive is requiring new buildings to be built to passive house standard by 2015). This legislative framework guarantees a future market for their product.

There are also some construction companies building housing in Western Harbour (e.g. NCC, Skanska). These companies have a national and international presence in terms of house-building. Thus, one would expect that the lessons learnt from bespoke projects might transfer between regions in Sweden and to other countries where the companies operate. Indeed in many companies there are processes and systems set up to ensure the internal transfer of this information (Hellman, 2009).

However, the extent to which the innovations learnt in one bespoke development are transferred to another appears to be limited. Partly this seems to be that there is a great deal of regional variation (let alone international variation) in the resources (materials, technologies, skills, expertise, subcontractors) available for delivering projects and construction processes (Hellman, 2009). There is also an issue in terms of variation in individual project managers' approach to site assembly as well as their priorities (Hellman, 2009; Svennson, 2009; Graham, 2009).

Although the energy company in Western Harbour has chosen not to adopt many of the technical systems used in the first phase of the project, it is looking to develop alternative low carbon energy systems for the second phase. The technical system used for the first phase of the project was expensive, suffered technical problems and there was limited demand for the energy produced.

The company intends to develop a more efficient and economic system, which can be easily managed and maintained (Rosén, 2009). It intends to enlarge the existing district heating system to encompass the new development, and decarbonise the entire energy supply of Malmö using LZC heat (Rosén, 2009). This technical solution has entirely been driven by economies of scale, national subsidies for biofuel and the carbon tax (Rosén, 2009).

The company also has an international exchange programme. This allows employees to visit or work in Malmö and learn from the bespoke project. Unfortunately there is very little evidence to suggest that these ideas are being adopted elsewhere. There is some evidence to suggest that international transference is hampered by different physical, political, economic and cultural contexts. This in itself is an interesting finding because it suggests that bespoke energy systems may not be particularly transferable, particularly between nations.

The municipality has set up a sustainability unit. The unit is an innovation that has proved rather successful in its promotion of the city. The sustainability unit operationalises the vision of the planning department by finding funding for projects, liaising and negotiating with developers. This is a new model in Sweden. The unit currently generates 100 kr for every 1 kr the city invests (Graham, 2009). Thus it significantly increases the economic viability of projects without a huge commitment from the city. However, it is important to tap into some good funding streams to provide this kind of leverage for innovation (Graham, 2009).

The sustainable innovation unit are using the B001 project to attract innovative green industries and businesses to Malmö (Graham, 2009). The municipality is supporting local companies and innovators as well as attracting international business that want to locate in Malmö for its environmental benefits or because they have products they want to test (Graham, 2009). Thus, sustainable innovation is being used to support the local economy in Malmö and enable regeneration.

Demand and deployment

As with Hammarby Sjöstad, B001 is located in an excellent position. It is close to the attractive historic city centre of Malmö, on the waterfront and adjacent to transport connections to Copenhagen (20 minutes by train). It is an attractive development (Figure 5.9, see colour plates) with good access to a range of services and amenities. Consequently there has been significant demand for properties. Only the more affluent can afford to live in the development.

Residents living in B001 were not motivated to do so by its environmental credentials. The environmental performance of the buildings and energy system are of secondary importance. The passive model adopted allows for this and some energetic savings are made regardless of residents' involvement in the process. However, as was suggested earlier, in the case of Hammarby, greater engagement could help to make greater energy savings.

Nevertheless, it should be noted that it was market demand for non-nuclear and non-fossil fuel energy which drove Sydkraft to try to develop a bespoke LZC energy system initially in the B001 project. It should also be noted that the municipalities' interest in environmental sustainability was driven by public support for local green politicians. These supporters of environmental ideals may not now be living in B001, but they certainly played a role in the creation of the project.

Vauban

Increasing demand for housing in recent years in Freiburg and lack of supply led to a migration of young people (particularly young families) from the city. Many of these people still worked in Freiburg but commuted. This was obviously not sustainable, so new housing was needed. New areas for development were identified in Rieselfeld (an old sewage plant) and Vauban (an old army barracks).

The Vauban district is not far from the centre of Freiburg but is suburban in character (i.e. lower density and largely residential – Figure 5.10, see colour plates). Five thousand residents live in the district; the majority are families from a variety of income groups. The development has a mixture of tenures (offering both rental and ownership options) and involved a range of developers (*Baugruppen/Baugemeinschaften*[17], municipal housing companies, private housing companies) in its construction. In addition to supplying accommodation for young families, Vauban was expected to provide a test-bed for new LZC technologies and to showcase low-carbon living (Figure 5.11, see colour plates).

When compared with a standard German development energy consumption in the Vauban district reduced by 7.8 MWh/annum translating into a reduction in CO_2 output by 2,087 tonnes/annum (Antonoff, 2007). The average Vauban resident produces 0.5 tonnes of CO_2/capita/annum (Act Planning, 2010) compared to an average resident of Freiburg who produces 8.5 tonnes of CO_2/capita/annum (ICLEI, 2008). Vauban combines energy efficient housing with LZC energy systems. The development has a cogeneration plant linked to 2,000 low-energy units via a district heating system. The plant is fed on woodchip from the Black Forest (wood consumption 20,000 sM³/a) and generates 12,000 MWh/annum of heat and 1,000 MWh/annum electricity (Preiser, 2009). Some of the units in the development use solar energy to provide heat (solar collectors) and power (PV cells). The cogeneration plant in conjunction with the PV cells provides 25% of the electricity for the area (Preiser, 2009).

A variety of houses were built to a range of energetic standards in the development including low-energy, passive (200 units) and energy-plus units (Figure 5.12, see colour plates).

The low-energy housing units in Vauban cost around 2% more to construct than a standard housing unit. Energy consumption in a low energy unit falls by up to 80% compared to existing building stock and CO_2 emissions are reduced by 30%, whilst around 2,100 tonnes CO_2 are saved in the passive housing development. The consumption of oil for heating in low energy units is reduced from 12–15 litres to 6.5 litres per square metre heated. Low-energy housing is cost-effective, particularly with rising energy prices. Low energy units in Vauban save residents more than €1,000 a year per dwelling (C40 cities, 2011).

The 'solar settlement' in the Vauban district (seen in yellow on the diagram) consists of 59 energy-plus houses (which are CO_2-neutral) and a solar garage designed by Rolf Disch Architects. The energy-plus houses have been designed to passive house standard and generate energy. They each produced more than €4,000 each year in solar energy profits (Disch Architects, 2011). Thus they quickly pay back the original capital cost of the LZC technologies. The urban design of the 'solar settlement' also applies ecological and social contact design principles to encourage more sustainable behaviour and a sense of community amongst residents. These energy-plus (solar) homes provide an excellent model for zero carbon housing particularly in suburban and rural areas, where densities are lower and district heating systems are uneconomic.

Approach to delivery

The municipality bought the land on which Vauban is built when the French army moved from the site, and the plan was to build a low carbon neighbourhood. Municipal ownership of the site provided the city council with leverage to demand higher environmental standards in Vauban. Limited sites in Freiburg meant that competition amongst developers for the site was fierce. Housing companies and cooperatives competed against each other for the land. When deciding on which projects got the go-ahead the municipality prioritised energy efficiency. Thus higher energetic standards were achieved in Vauban.

The municipality imposed stringent energetic requirements on Vauban. When the LZC neighbourhood was planned the federal building code (2002) required that new homes had a space heating standard of 100kWh/m²/annum. In Freiburg the land use plan required that on municipally owned land the minimum energetic standard was 65kWh/m²/annum (the low energy standard – Figure 5.13).

All units in Vauban achieved the low-energy standard as a minimum. However, some exceeded this standard. The passive house units achieved a space heating standard of 15kwh/m²/annum and the units built to the revised building standard achieved 40kwh/m²/annum. The LZC neighbourhood has acted as test-bed for these higher energetic standards, which are now being used to inform the latest zoning plan for Freiburg[18].

The 2010 plan requires much higher energetic standards in new development on both municipal and privately owned-sites (Figure 5.13). Thus Vauban has led the way towards higher energy standards in the rest of the city.

Various subsidies are available at a federal and local level in Germany to support improvements in energy efficiency and/or the installation and operation of LZC technologies in new developments. Housing companies and cooperatives can access subsidised federal loans (KfW loans) for construct-

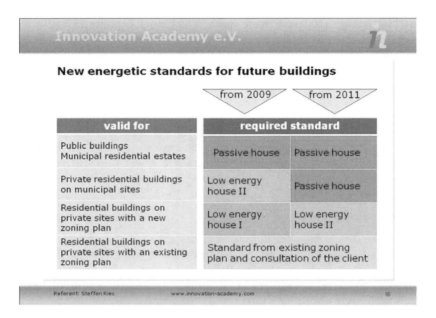

Figure 5.13 Energetic requirements of new build development in Freiburg.[19]
Source: Freiburg City Council, 2009.

ing more energy efficient buildings. Operational subsidies (e.g. feed-in tariff) and capital subsidies (e.g. solar roofs programme) are also available from the federal government for LZC technologies.

Local funds are also available from the regional energy company (Badenova) in Freiburg for local low carbon energy projects. The revenue from Regiostrom is used to subsidise the installation and production of energy from LZC technologies locally. Funds were obtained from federal and local sources to subsidise the capital and operational cost of incorporating LZC technologies into the Vauban development. Now housing companies are even retro-fitting solar panels on the roofs of their developments in Vauban, in order to maximise their economic return from the projects. This will become more common with the introduction of the new federal law requiring that 20% of all energy consumed by a building comes from renewable sources[20].

The long-term commitment of those designing the community to its successful operation, provided significant leverage for features that in the short term increased capital cost but in the long-term reduced operational cost. Residents, housing companies and cooperatives all have long-term interest in energy efficiency since they manage and maintain units post-construction.

Thus, lowering energy consumption could in fact increase the profit margin of the housing companies or reduce energy cost to residents in cooperatives. This long-term involvement in Vauban helped to overcome the perennial principal-agent problem or split incentive encountered in speculative housing developments. Thus the housing companies and cooperatives investing in the LZC technologies also benefitted from the financial savings produced by reducing energy consumption.

Vauban was conceptualised through a highly participative planning process with residents, planners, housing companies, *Baugemeinschaften/Baugruppen,* utilities all working together to achieve a sustainable neighbourhood. Three key groups were involved in the planning of Vauban: Project Group Vauban[21], City Council Vauban Committee[22] and Forum Vauban[23]. A host of other actors also had the opportunity to feed into the planning process (Figure 5.14).

Citizen involvement in building accommodation in Vauban has been with the emergence of *Baugemeinschaften* (also known as *Baugruppen).* These individuals or groups needed support from expert planners, architects, financiers, builders, engineers and so on to design, build and manage their new accommodation. Thus an additional role for Forum Vauban, in conjunction with the municipal planning department, was to provide access to expert support to those building the community.

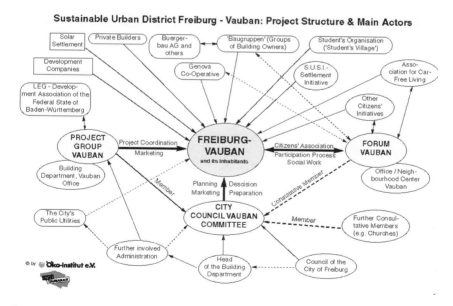

Figure 5.14 Actors involved in the participative planning of Vauban.

Source: Brohman, B. et al (2002).

This level of involvement and cooperation helped to ensure that all those involved had a vested interest in the outcome of the process and the future operation of the community. A variety of views and requirements were taken on board. Conflicts were dealt with and resolved at an early stage in the planning process. This consensual approach was at least in part responsible for the successful implementation of the project and its operation.

Lifestyles

The prioritisation of green issues by residents in Vauban underlies its success. Around 60–70% of Vauban residents vote green. This also translates into green actions, for example only 16% of inhabitants in Vauban own a car, whilst 35% of inhabitants in Freiburg and 65% in Germany own a car. Thus, those people moving into Vauban were generally motivated to do so at least in part by ethical concern. This contrasts with the two Swedish eco-districts. A surfeit model has been adopted for Vauban. This means that residents are actively involved in decision-making processes and the delivery of services in the community, rather than merely acting as passive consumers as with the deficit model. Vauban residents have been heavily involved in the design and planning of the community (as described above). They decided to adopt LZC technologies and thus have been supportive of these technologies from a very early stage in the process and active in their effective use.

Many of the residents are now involved in the management of their building through residents associations/cooperatives. They are also involved in the management of energy for their buildings. This raises their awareness of actual energy consumption in the community and enables residents to make expenditure decisions based on that information. Thus it increases their energy literacy and control over decisions regarding their energy supply and management. Residents associations can decide whether to invest in LZC technologies for the community. Some residents in Vauban actually produce energy. Overall residents in Vauban are prepared to be more actively involved in tackling their energy consumption and carbon footprint. Of course it is unlikely that most people will want to be so proactive. However, some of the more active models employed in Vauban – co-design, co-management or co-production – may have wider appeal.

Industrial innovation

Freiburg is an innovation hub for sustainable living and renewable energy (see Chapter 4). The city's economy relies on eco-tourism, which in turn is dependent on showcasing examples of green innovation. The Vauban neighbourhood is integral to this. The ideas developed in Freiburg and the surrounding region have been presented to an international audience, and filtered into projects in the wider global community.

Two key innovations have been used in Vauban which set it apart from the Swedish case studies. The first innovation is the extent of involvement of residents in the planning and operation of the community. Residents are involved in key decision-making processes, managing the community and its resources and in some instances generating energy. Residents are no longer passive consumers but are active participants, completely engaged in the process, which has helped to raise their energy literacy. This surfeit model requires significant support from energy and housing providers, built environment professionals and the municipality.

The second innovation is the long-term involvement of housing companies and *Baugemeinschaften/Baugruppen* in the operation of the community. Unlike speculative house-builders, this group has long-term management interests in the communities they build. They invest in the LZC technologies and are rewarded with a financial return from energy efficiency savings and energy generation. This long-term approach nullifies the 'split incentive' problem found in speculative developments.

Vauban also showed the importance of using demonstration projects to test new instruments for delivery. Introducing higher energetic standards in Vauban, demonstrated the industrial capability to achieve the standards. It enabled the municipality to set standards more widely in the city, confident in the knowledge that the there was sufficient capacity in the construction industry to deliver them. Testing innovative policy instruments locally can be an excellent way to assess outcomes and implementation problems.

Demand and deployment

Demand for housing in Vauban came from a much more diverse audience than for either of the Swedish case studies. A mixture of household types (families, couples, one-person households) representing a range of income groups and ages are living in the neighbourhood. The common characteristics that bind the residents together appear to be their prioritisation of environmental values and their willingness to be active participants in their community. This in itself makes them unusual by today's standards. It may also restrict the market for this model at least in the short term. However, with rising energy prices this could well change.

The provision of mixed tenure units in Vauban has made it possible for this diversity of residents to live there. It has allowed a wider range of people to test new LZC technical systems and ultimately may broaden markets for LZC development. One example of this is the solar settlement in Vauban. A group of investors (the solar fund) have funded some of the energy-plus houses in the development which they rent out. This creates mixed tenure and provides the opportunity for people to try living in energy-plus houses, a key mechanism for encouraging future deployment. 'Trialability' is known to be helpful in encouraging the deployment of new technologies, as demonstrated by the experience with solar homes in California (Chapter 3).

Many policy-makers visit Freiburg and Vauban every year from all over the world with the intention of developing similar eco-districts in their own countries and cities. The variety of technical systems and models for delivery in the district make it impossible to track the extent to which the model in its entirety has been adopted elsewhere (unlike the closed-loop model which is more easily recognisable as a complete system). However there appears to have been particular interest in the energy-plus houses and the processes through which citizens become more engaged and active in decision-making, delivery and operation of the neighbourhood.

GEOS

The GEOS neighbourhood will be the largest zero-net energy, urban mixed-use project in the United States. It is currently under construction in the city of Arvada, just west of Denver Colorado. This area benefits from sufficient solar radiation and geothermal energy for the neighbourhood to be entirely powered by zero carbon energy sources. Thus no fossil fuels will be provided to the site, which covers 25.2 acres. A mixture of uses will be provided on the site including 282 residential units (built at a net density of 23.2 dwelling units/acre) and 12,000 sq ft of commercial space. The development will include a mixture of housing (live-work units, condominiums, duplexes, town houses, single-family homes, intergenerational and senior cohousing) to attract a range of residents. (Figure 5.15, see colour plates)

The GEOS neighbourhood will generate enough renewable energy to off-set its annual energy needs. The neighbourhood incorporates on-site solar and geothermal systems that are designed to supply all of the community's energy needs, and work in conjunction with energy consumption patterns that are considerably lower than those found in the nation's average homes. All homes have PV cells (5 KW per household) generating electrical energy which is fed back into the grid but off-sets all electricity consumed by a household (Figure 5.16, see colour plates). Ground source heat is provided through a horizontal loop. Units which are too far from the geothermal loop will use solar thermal collectors to generate heat. All units are built to passive house standard[24] and thus the energy requirement (particularly for space heating and cooling) is very low. The layout of the development, in terms of orientation[25], staggering and density, optimises solar gain and mini-mises heat loss from transmission in the geothermal heating system. New design and technological solutions are being used in this development which set it apart from the European case studies.

This technical system was chosen because it suited the local climatic conditions (300 days of sunshine a year) and geology. The choice was also based on economic cost. Initially the team did consider using solar heating systems. However they were found to be too expensive (both at an individual building and community level). Instead a geothermal heating system was chosen. Financial incentives were being offered to households by Xcel energy for installation of PV cells, which made PV more economic. Thus the system chosen was cost-effective and suited local resource availability.

The most appropriate scale at which to install a heating system was considered by the GEOS team. Initially a district heating system for the whole development was the preferred option. However, due to the way in which the development had to be financed, it was not cost-effective to build the system in one for all 250 units. Thus smaller scale heating systems serving around 5–6 units have been developed. As the development grows heating systems will be built alongside new units. Again the economics affect the choice of technical system.

Approach to development

In contrast to the German and Swedish examples, the development of GEOS is being driven by a developer (rather than the municipality). The developer's motivations are partly altruistic and partly pragmatic. The developer has a significant personal interest in sustainability (Stenftenagel and Klebl, 2010). He is a pioneer in this field in America and wanted to produce a zero-net energy development that was affordable, by transferring lessons learnt in Europe (e.g. regarding passive house, district heating systems, geothermal energy, etc) to the American situation (Stenftenagel and Klebl, 2010). The developer sees potential future markets as energy prices rise and people become more environmentally aware (Stenftenagel and Klebl, 2010). Colorado is a state that already demonstrates market interest in green issues and green products including housing. Thus, there are also commercial reasons for pioneering the first zero-net energy neighbourhood in the state (Stenftenagel and Klebl, 2010).

Local, state and federal support for the GEOS project has been very limited (Stenftenagel and Klebl, 2010). Energy efficiency requirements in the building code are minimal for Arvada City. No land zoning classifications for mixed-use zero-net energy developments existed. The GEOS team produced the first detailed design code for zero-net energy mixed-use development, which the city used to approve the project (Stenftenagel and Klebl, 2010). This code is now being refined by the city for future development. Thus, there was no real regulatory framework to support the higher energy standards adopted by the GEOS project.

Similarly there were very limited financial incentives to support the delivery of GEOS (Stenftenagel and Klebl, 2010). Capital subsidies are available from Xcel energy (via the Solar Rewards Programme) for the installation of PV cells on new houses. Tax credits for generating renewable energy and green mortgages are available to households. However, incentives for developers are very limited. Financing the new service infrastructure (including energy systems) in a development of this nature is problematic (Stenftenagel and Klebl, 2010).

Getting finance for any new housing development currently in the USA is of course very problematic particularly because of the current economic/ financing crisis. Obviously, this is a problem which is not peculiar to zero-net energy housing. However, there is a significant problem with raising finance for new service infrastructure (like the bespoke energy system) which is peculiar to zero-net energy projects (Stenftenagel and Klebl, 2010). The market value of the system is difficult to calculate and thus is a risky investment. This situation needs to be addressed if zero-net energy developments are to be deployed more widely.

For the GEOS project the developer has financed all the planning stages of the development (Stenftenagel and Klebl, 2010). This has cost over $1.5 million (Stenftenagel and Klebl, 2010). The project is also being built on land owned by the developer. The municipality was very accommodating and supportive of the project. However, this did not translate into any regulatory or financial support. It is a testimony to the enthusiasm and tenaciousness of the developer and the GEOS team that the development is being built at all.

The municipality could have provided a more supportive regulatory framework, which required zero-net energy development or at least the inclusion of LZC infrastructure in future new developments. This would have encouraged investors to support zero-net projects and helped the house-building industry to build capacity to deliver them. The municipality could also have offered subsidies for zero-net energy projects to developers (rather than households) as in the Go Solar programme in California, and /or waive the service connection charge for zero-net projects. This developer-led approach of course reduces the degree of state intervention needed to build zero-net projects. However, it is unlikely that market demand will increase very rapidly, thus providing developers with the impetus to do so.

Lifestyles

GEOS will adopt a surfeit model, in which residents are actively engaged in the design, decision-making and operation of the community. One of the key aims of the project is to foster environmental stewardship in the community. Residents will be encouraged to take an active role in managing their resources and environment (including energy consumption). Prospective residents have been involved in discussions with the development team about how they might manage resources in the community and adopt greener lifestyles. There has been a great deal of interest in edible landscapes (growing their own food) and vehicle pools (Stenftenagel and Klebl, 2010).

Overall, residents opting to live in GEOS are likely to already be predisposed towards environmental behaviour (Stenftenagel and Klebl 2010). The physical infrastructure provided in GEOS will simply provide an environment in which it is possible to consume less resources, produce less waste and adopt more sustainable lifestyles (Stenftenagel and Klebl 2010). Monitoring of energy and water consumption through metering should further reinforce pro-environmental behaviour. Metering will help to raise energy literacy amongst residents, critical to behavioural change and better management of energy consumption. Strong social networks built in the community can act as conduits through which relevant knowledge is passed (peer learning) which will also help to encourage changes in behaviour.

Industrial innovation

Producing GEOS has meant significant innovation in existing supply chains and the construction process. The supply chain for GEOS development had to be totally rebuilt with new suppliers and installers. The GEOS team had to source ideas for new technologies and then arrange production with local suppliers (e.g. highly energy efficient windows). The team negotiated with existing suppliers to reduce the costs of bespoke technologies (e.g. insulated prefabricated panels) and installers to reduce the cost of installation (e.g. PV installation was more expensive than the panels themselves). The team also worked to rationalise the supply chain where possible. For example they negotiated with a supplier to deliver all energy efficient appliances for the development.

So far planning and setting up the GEOS development has taken around three years. A large proportion of this time has been used establishing new supply chains, which has been extremely time-consuming, and makes it very unappealing. For a bespoke development to become main-stream the new supply chains established have to be scaled up. According to the GEOS team all of the examples given above (with the possible exception of the insulated panels) could be scaled up, but this takes time.

Building to the zero-net energy standard has also had a significant impact on the construction process; new technologies, new designs, new methods for assembly and so on. Thus, more training for contractors and sub-contractors is needed. This also lengthens the time-line for development and increases construction costs.

A further innovation is that the developer is setting up a contract with installers to maintain the new LZC technologies integrated into GEOS for a period after the developer has left the site. The contract will be between installers and the home-owners association (HOA). The HOA will be free to negotiate a different agreement at the end of the contractual period, but the contract does provide some guarantee that the new LZC systems will be adequately maintained at least in the short term.

There is no system for ensuring LZC systems are retained once the developer has left site. However, the residents moving into GEOS are likely to be motivated by environmental objectives and thus are unlikely to want to reduce their capacity to be energy efficient or generate low-carbon energy, at least according to the developer. In reality, long-term design integrity can be an issue in these bespoke developments (Williams, 2006, 2008).

The lessons learnt by the GEOS team are being disseminated through the usual channels (i.e. publications, lectures, workshops, seminars, etc) to the wider house-building industry. However, the GEOS team will also be offering detailed consultancy advice throughout the design and planning phases to those developers interested in replicating the GEOS model in other locations. This provides consultancy opportunities for the GEOS team and enables the GEOS model to be deployed more widely. It also means that other house-builders do not have to build capacity in-house for the delivery of zero-net energy homes, providing efficiencies at least in the short-term.

Demand and deployment

For a developer-led model (i.e. non-assisted), market demand is essential for its success. GEOS is being built very close to Boulder, where there is a cluster of green consumers. This provides some guarantee that there will be a market for the zero-net energy houses built in Avarda. Initial market research suggests that those buying into GEOS are a diverse group, which bodes well for future deployment. The common characteristic amongst those buying into the development is that they are well-educated (Glavis, 2010). Other characteristics are not important (affluence, age, gender and household type). There appears to be interest in GEOS from families, 'empty nesters', 'DINKS' (duel income no kids) in fact virtually every segment of the market in every age group (Glavis, 2010).

GEOS appeals to households for a range of reasons, according to the market research (Glavis, 2010). It is attractive to those who are interested in establishing their green credentials, those looking for high technological performance (usually men) and those looking for safe and healthy living environments (usually women). It is a concept which is of interest to a wide audience. Some people just like to have the newest and best homes. Others want to live in a green community surrounded by those with similar values to themselves (Glavis, 2010). Some people are buying into this type of development because of the potential financial implications of rising energy costs. They want to buy a home which is insulated against rising energy costs.

The price range for units in GEOS is also rather broad. It starts at the lower end of the market ($225,000) rising to the higher end of the market ($600,000). This represents the average range of purchase price in which most people are buying homes in the state. Providing units in this price range helps to maximise market potential. The aim is also to make zero-net homes cost neutral (i.e. a zero-net house will cost the same as a standard house of similar dimensions). The GEOS team have projected that the cost of building to a zero-net specification will add $285 to monthly mortgage repayments. However energy savings of approximately $200/month can be made. Also the resident can get tax savings on mortgage interest of $85/month. This means that the LZC technologies in effect cost nothing. This can help significantly in generating demand for LZC technologies. It also shifts the cost burden onto residents (and away from the house-builder), thus overcoming the spilt incentive issue which always arise with speculative housing developments. Once the cost of zero-net properties is the same as that for a standard property, the only real barrier to the market is the lack of awareness.

Market research in Colorado (Glavis, 2010) suggests that the public is unaware of the opportunities afforded by zero-net homes. It also shows that realtors don't understand these more sophisticated types of development. There are a lot of 'green agents' who don't understand how new LZC technologies work. Nor do they understand the 'green cultural creative' that might want to live in a zero-net energy property – what motivates them for example. It is very important that realtors understand the building science and the potential consumers of the zero-net energy property. If realtors are better educated then consumers will also become more aware of the benefits of living in zero-net energy properties. Ecobroker offers training to realtors in understanding and marketing green buildings in the USA.

GEOS will act as a blue-print for future development in Colorado, since the climatic conditions and the financial incentives which largely govern the technical system adopted in the Arvada development, remain fairly constant across the state. Elsewhere different solutions may be needed to suit climate, local regulations and fiscal incentives. New projects might be built by the GEOS team, or the team may provide advice to other developers.

The wider deployment of the GEOS model depends on supply and demand. On the supply-side it seems that it will take time and resources for most house-builders to form the supply chains and expertise needed to deliver zero-net energy projects. However, if the cost of zero-net energy housing is similar to traditional units and they are marketed more successfully by those in the property industry, demand should be able to drive the changes in industry needed to increase supply.

Beddington Zero Energy Development

Beddington Zero Energy Development (BedZED) is a LZC neighbourhood, situated in the South London suburbs (London Borough of Sutton). It is located close to a rail station connecting the site to the city centre and has good access to all public transport services operating in the locality. The site covers 1.7 hectares, accommodating 82 dwellings and 2369m² of work/commercial space (BRE, 2002). It is a high density (50 units/hectare), mixed-use development, which accommodates 244 residents offering a mix of tenures (BRE, 2002); social housing (25%), shared ownership (24%), private rented and private owned (51%). BedZED is the smallest of the case studies presented. It was the first zero carbon development in the UK fully completed in 2002 (Figure 5.17, see colour plates).

BedZED seeks to reduce CO_2 emissions produced by a variety of household activities (including travel, consumption of food and production of waste), not simply by those produced by thermal demand and electricity consumption in the home. It aims to do this using technological and design solutions. It has also adopted some more progressive solutions which encourage residents to share resources (e.g. the car pool), use locally sourced materials (e.g. woodchip to power a CHP system) or work locally (e.g. live-work units).

Various LZC technologies were incorporated into BedZED to reduce fossil fuel consumption. PV cells were integrated into the building fabric to generate electricity[26] (BRE, 2002). A prototype woodchip CHP system designed to serve the electrical and heat demand of the community was also installed. The generator engine was fuelled by a combustible mix of hydrogen, carbon monoxide and methane gases, produced from woodchips by an on-site gasifier[27] (BRE, 2002).

Triple-glazed windows[28], super insulation[29], thermal mass, energy efficient appliances, passive ventilation with heat-recovery systems and visible hot water meters have been used in homes to reduce energy consumption (BRE, 2002). Triple-glazed, argon-filled windows with low emissivity glass, large panes and timber frames reduce heat loss. Well-sealed windows and doors, together with the concrete construction, ensure air-tightness. Heat exchangers in the passive, wind-driven ventilation systems recover up to 70% of the heat from outgoing stale air (Figure 5.18). These technologies are central to reducing energy consumption and operational CO_2 emissions.

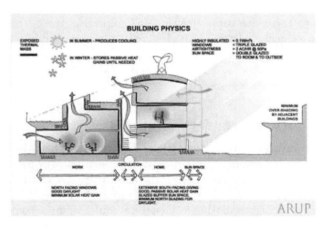

Figure 5.18 The BedZED technical system.

Source: Arup.

Urban design has also played a key role in reducing carbon emissions from the development. The buildings have been orientated and staggered to maximise solar gain[30] and reduce over-shadowing, which has increased potential for using PV cells, reduced the need for heating and lighting in homes. High densities have increased insulation between units and buildings and reduced the cost of district heating system infrastructure. The mixture of uses in the development has enabled peak energy loads to be spread throughout the day.

The carbon footprint of the average resident of BedZED is 0.51 tonnes co_2/capita/annum compared with 9.85 tonnes co_2/capita/annum for an average London citizen. Apart from producing no net CO_2 emissions from energy use, BedZED meets targets across a range of sustainability objectives. For example water saving, reusing and recycling materials, reducing car travel, increasing biodiversity, improving access to a range of services locally, reducing living costs, offering affordable accommodation, a strong sense of community and so on. It was recognised that to attract a diversity of people to live in BedZED a more holistic approach offering a range of benefits across the environmental, social and economic spectrum was required.

Approach to development

The BedZED concept was developed by a design team – Zed Architects, Bioregional (sustainability consultant), Ove Arup (engineering) and Gardiner and Theobald (quantity surveyors). The team sought to find a willing developer and suitable site for the project. The London Borough of Sutton (the local council /municipality) was committed to sustainability, and was interested in promoting a model for energy conscious development. Bioregional discussed the BedZED model with the municipality, which generated a great deal of interest amongst officers and councillors.

A developer – the Peabody Trust (social housing provider) – joined forces with the design team (Bioregional and Zed Architects) to build the zero carbon model. The Peabody Trust's long-term commitment to innovation in construction, providing high-quality affordable housing and minimising fuel poverty meant it was keen to be involved in the project and prepared to take the financial risk.

In 1998 a site owned by the Sutton Council was put on the market along with a planning brief for its development[31]. The brief did not address energetic standards or carbon emissions in the new development. The BedZED development team submitted an offer for the Sutton site which was lower than that of other competitors, but the local council chose it anyway.

The council based its decision on the added value it believed the BedZED proposal offered over and above its competitors. The carbon savings[32], employment opportunities, marketing potential, reduced waste and educational value of the project outweighed the higher prices offered for the site by other developers. The land sale was agreed in 1999. The council required the development team to produce a scheme specification summarising the main environmental targets for the development, alongside a green travel plan. Thus sale and planning agreements were ultimately used to ensure that high environmental standards were maintained. In return the team managed to secure the site at lower than market rate, which helped to off-set the additional technology costs.

Thus, there were four key catalysts for the development. First, the dynamism of the design team which generated the concept and sold it to the municipality. Second, finding a developer willing to take a risk investing in the prototype development (the Peabody Trust). Third, the local support for the project (particularly from the London Borough of Sutton) which enabled the team to successfully bid for the site well below the market value. Finally, including a range of stakeholders in early project discussions also helped to encourage interest and support for the BedZED project.

Lifestyles

BedZED adopts a surfeit model, where residents are actively engaged (at least in part) in the management and production of resources in their community. They play a more limited role than in the Vauban example (they were not involved in visioning and design process), but are far more involved in energy management and production than residents living in either Swedish eco-district.

BedZED was designed to be carbon neutral, to generate as much or more renewable energy on-site than was used in the buildings for heating, hot water and electrical appliances. The key operational aims of BedZED in terms of energy use and related CO_2 emissions were as follows:

- to reduce electricity consumption compared to the UK average by 33%;
- to reduce space heating needs compared to the UK average by 90%;
- to eliminate carbon emissions due to energy consumption;
- wider aims to tackle CO_2 emissions from travel were also included in the brief, but are not considered here.

The post-occupancy evaluation (Bioregional, 2009) of BedZED revealed that households use 2,579 kWh of electricity per year which is 45% lower than the average in Sutton. The average BedZED resident consumes 3.4 kWh/person/day compared to the average Sutton resident who consumes 5.5 kWh/person/day (Bioregional, 2009). The average BedZED resident produces 1.4 kg CO_2/person/day whilst each dwelling produces 1079 kg CO_2/dwelling/year (Bioregional, 2009). Thus the original target set for electricity consumption was exceeded.

However, most of the savings have been made through energy efficiency measures in the dwellings, rather than the generation of low-carbon electricity on site (Bioregional, 2009). Currently most of the electricity consumed by BedZED is supplied from the national grid with a proportion (around 20%) of low-carbon electricity being generated on-site by photovoltaic panels. This electricity is used in the home and not to power electric vehicles as originally envisaged[33] (Bioregional, 2009). The surplus electricity generated is fed back into the grid. It is estimated that 13959.48 kWh is exported to the grid from BedZED annually (Bioregional, 2009).

The average heat consumption (for space heating and hot water) was found to be 5.2 kWh/person/day or 3526 kWh/dwelling/year (Bioregional, 2009) for those living in BedZED (81% less than the average in Sutton). The heat demand for units in BedZED is high (48 kwh/m²/year) compared with passive houses (i.e. 15 kwh/m²/year) but considerably lower than average for new build housing in the UK (i.e. 231.8 kwh/m²/year – Bioregional, 2009). CO_2 emissions produced by heating were also considerably lower (i.e. 9.3 CO_2/m²/year compared with the UK average of 45 CO_2/m²/year- Bioregional, 2009). This was despite the fact that the original heating system – a biomass CHP plant – was replaced in 2005 by a gas powered district heating system and gas condensing boilers.

The biomass CHP plant was replaced due to various technical problems[34] (Bioregional, 2009). The plant was designed to minimise maintenance costs[35] but, in practice it required full-time manning with frequent downtime for equipment modifications. The plant never consistently reached the agreed outputs of 120 kW of electricity and 250 kW of heat (it regularly operated at 80–90 kWe – 30% below the target – Bioregional, 2009). This placed considerable pressure on the resources of Exus Energy (who operated the CHP system on a turn-key contract) and eventually led to the company's demise[36]. The scheme was just too small scale to justify the maintenance needed to keep it operating. LZC heating technology has advanced considerably since 2005 and Peabody is searching for a zero carbon alternative to the current system.

Resident behaviour has also influenced the effectiveness of the LZC design. One explanation for the higher temperatures in units in the summer is that residents do not use the windows and sunspace to cool units[37], as they are designed to do (Bioregional, 2009). This appears to be due to their concern about security when leaving windows open. In contrast the replacement of energy efficient appliances or fittings with less efficient alternatives has not been a problem in BedZED, unlike other low carbon housing schemes in the UK (Williams, 2006 and 2008). Overall 13% of households have replaced energy efficient fixtures and appliances over the period until 2007 and of those only one did not specifically choose an equally efficient replacement (Bioregional, 2009).

More generally it is hard to say whether living in BedZED has impacted on residents' behaviour in terms of efficiency and environmentally awareness. It is very likely that those opting to live in the neighbourhood were already of the 'green' persuasion. However, many BedZED residents have adopted a 'greenish' lifestyle (for example 86% buy organic food, 39% grow their own food and 60% recycle waste). Paradoxically they also fly more often than the average resident of Sutton.

Energy consumption and associated CO_2 emissions in the home appear to be governed more by the technologies, distribution systems and management services operating in the community than resident behaviour. In some instances residents cannot easily reduce their consumption because of the manner in which the system is set up. For example even with visible metering residents cannot reduce their energy consumption without individual controls built into the system. This demonstrates how actively engaged citizens can be hampered by passive technical systems that are difficult to engage with.

Most of the BedZED residents appreciated the sustainability features of the development, including the energy saving devices (Figure 5.19). Reduced living cost – particularly energy bills – were also welcomed. Residents were unhappy about the management and maintenance of the energy system, complaining particularly about the CHP system and hot water supply. The

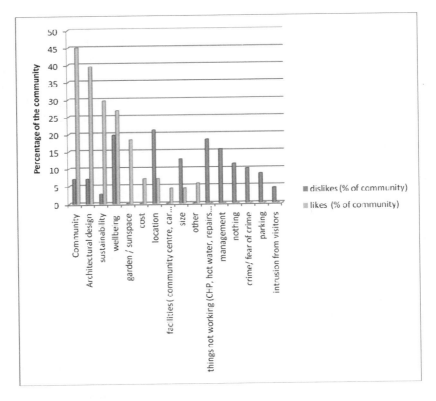

Figure 5.19 BedZED residents' likes and dislikes.

Source: Created using data from Bioregional, 2009.

case study again flags up the importance of considering comfort, convenience and cost when determining the most appropriate energy system for a LZC neighbourhood.

Industrial innovation

BedZED was a prototype, the first low carbon development built in the UK. New design principles and technologies were adopted for the project. This required that new supply chains were established and that capacity was built amongst the sub-contractors to construct the project. Sustainable supply chains for new technologies were difficult to create. The expertise and skills required amongst the sub-contractors to assemble BedZED developed 'on the job'. New technologies were expensive and unreliable. Some also required specialist on-going maintenance.

At the time BedZED was built there was limited appetite amongst speculative and social housing developers to replicate the model. This was largely blamed on a lack of public interest. However, the cost of LZC technologies also made it an unattractive option, particularly when consumers were demanding affordable accommodation. A limited supplier base and lack of appropriate skills and expertise within the construction industry meant that to produce this type of bespoke housing would be expensive. The need for developer involvement in operational issues, particularly the maintenance of LZC technologies, was also off-putting to most speculative house-builders.

Demand and deployment

Adopting a similar model for commercial housing developments did not seem viable at the time the project was built, nor was it something the all BedZED team aspired to. Even the more conformist Greenwich Millenium Village development was not deemed to be a commercially viable model by its creator when it was built (Williams, 2008a). However, several years on, the price of LZC technologies has fallen somewhat and the Government has introduced a zero carbon policy for all new housing development. In these circumstances building to the zero carbon standard not only becomes more economically viable, it is also essential.

Since the completion of BedZED the key players involved in the development have gone their separate ways. ZED Architects are designing zero energy developments all over the world (Grande Synthe, France; Tongshan, Beijing and Changsha, China) and in the UK (Upton Square, Bow, Andover and Leicester). They have developed a tool-kit for delivering zero carbon communities. The tool-kit considers a series of system elements covering buildings, transport, energy systems and food. The tool-kit ensures low embodied carbon in new developments. Zed architects use a replicable design methodology which can be applied in a range of contexts and scaled up. Their designs range from those for urban neighbourhoods to city master-plans. The experience of Zed Architects in China suggests that the volume production of LZC technologies is the key to scaling up the production of zero carbon homes and ultimately the delivery of zero carbon urbanism.

Bioregional has teamed up with a volume house-builder (Quintain) and is now trying to bring 'BedZED style' developments to the mass market. Bioregional Quintain Ltd has recently managed to build to 'zero carbon' standard within the normal range of build costs – the One Brighton sustainable community. There are other similar developments planned for Middlesborough, London, Surrey and Thames Gateway. Bioregional Quintain is now developing new models for facilities management and community management as part of a new One Brighton housing project. This should help to bring the zero carbon concept to a wider audience.

There is no doubt that BedZED's existence and success has played a key role in the emergence of the zero carbon homes policy. It demonstrated the feasibility of building communities to a low carbon standard. It has inspired the London Borough of Sutton to set a target to make all buildings 'zero carbon' within its boundaries by 2025. However, to date the deployment of zero carbon homes in the UK and market demand continues to be limited (Chapter 3).

Themes to be explored

Some clear lessons begin to emerge from these case studies that will be developed in later chapters. Both deficit (Hammarby and B001) and surfeit (Vauban, BedZED and GEOS) models have been illustrated by the case studies which will create passive energy consumers or active energy citizens. The case studies suggest that the latter model (surfeit model) is likely to create the greatest lifestyle changes, in the long term reducing energy consumption and CO_2 production. However, the former model (deficit model) is likely to be more acceptable to the mass market, as consumers are accustomed to passive systems. Thus, the deficit model is likely to be deployed more widely, more quickly and will produce carbon savings. This presents a conundrum as to which is the best model (deficit or surfeit) for delivering zero carbon homes and lowering CO_2 emissions from households.

The case studies demonstrate that successful approaches to delivering zero carbon homes are likely to require strong leadership from the municipality and the developer. The municipality will need to encourage zero carbon development through political support, regulatory controls and financial incentives. The developer will need to build capacity amongst sub-contractors (including suppliers) to construct zero carbon housing and ensure that developments have been assembled correctly. The developer will undoubtedly have to form new relationships with energy sub-contractors for LZC energy systems to operate effectively. For zero carbon communities to be successful long-term, greater involvement from key stakeholders in all stages of the process, from visioning to operation, will be needed. This will provide a more systematic and holistic approach to the delivery of a complex system and ensure that all parties have a vested interest in the system working effectively.

House-builders and energy companies will need to be the first adopters of LZC technologies, not consumers, and will act as the innovators in this process. However, the case studies demonstrate significant resistance to innovation within both industries. The problem is that the national and international landscape (political, cultural, economic, institutional, physical and social context) in which both industrial regimes operate creates many barriers to the development of zero carbon homes (and communities) but provides little in the way of incentives.

Considering the extent to which most of these developments have been marketed, it is surprising how few projects they have spawned. These bespoke projects tend to remain isolated examples. This can largely be explained by the local 'landscape' in which these projects are set. In all instances the local landscape has been manipulated to enable the delivery of the project. The problem is that this is not then replicated in the wider national and international landscape. Thus the concepts adopted in these innovative developments tend not to diffuse out into the wider world.

Part III

Chapter 6

Markets for zero carbon homes

Introduction

Determining markets for zero carbon homes is rather difficult, since currently few examples exist. However there are a variety of low carbon housing models that do exist internationally that approximate to this standard including solar homes, passive houses, zero-net energy houses, energy-plus houses and low energy houses. Perhaps we can learn about factors influencing markets for zero carbon homes from the experience of other low carbon housing forms (i.e. zero-net energy, solar, passive, energy-plus houses).

Smart technologies (metering systems, smart appliances, remote energy management and electric vehicles), low carbon energy systems (district heating systems and microgeneration based on non-fossil fuels) and low carbon energy are all potential components of the technical system constituting a zero carbon home. Thus, we can also learn more about the factors that may influence demand for zero carbon homes from the markets for smart technologies, low carbon energy systems and low carbon energy.

The complexity of the zero carbon home as a technical system means that a wide diversity of models are possible. Of course each technical system is likely to have different deployment rates. Some technical systems will be more compatible with the existing landscape (i.e. the technological, economic, environmental, social, institutional and cultural context) in which they are embedded than others. This will influence market demand and rate of deployment. It will also influence the technical systems adopted by producers.

In this chapter, the current markets for innovative forms of low carbon housing, smart technologies, low carbon energy systems and low carbon energy are investigated. An analysis of the potential barriers to the wider deployment of zero carbon home is presented. Solutions for encouraging wider deployment in the future are discussed.

Current markets

Adoption rates provide some idea of the extent to which LZC technologies

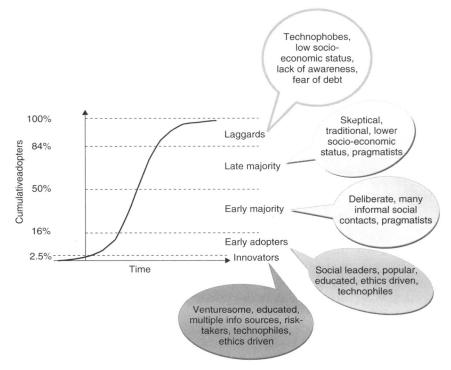

Figure 6.1 Technology diffusion S-curve with adopter categories.

Source: Adapted from Rogers, 1983.

and products have penetrated the market (Figure 6.1). By analysing cumulative adoptions (as a percentage of the total population) one can determine whether the technology has been taken up by the innovators and early adopters (i.e. less than 16% of the population) or reached the majority of the market.

The different categories of users are defined by several characteristics:

- their motivation for adopting technologies;
- knowledge and expertise;
- the networks through which they receive information about the technologies;
- position in the networks;
- affluence.

During the early stages of market transformation, the pioneers are driven by ethical concern and their interest in technological solutions to adopt new technologies. They tend to have developed their knowledge and expertise of both environmental issues and technological solutions through their formal education. They are generally very well educated. Their networks are often within the academic, scientific and industrial communities. However, they will not necessarily be very active within their local community.

Early adopters tend to be local leaders (i.e. politicians, teachers, health professionals, civil servants, etc) well integrated into local social networks. Thus, they can encourage others to adopt new technologies. This group too tend to be well educated, although do not necessarily possess the degree of technical knowledge demonstrated by the innovators. They will receive their information from technical experts. Similarly to the innovators, early adopters are driven to adopt LZC technologies because of ethical concern. Both innovators and early adopters tend to be affluent which enables them to take the risk of adopting new technologies which may be unreliable and expensive.

The majority of the population will be motivated to adopt LZC technologies for pragmatic reasons (e.g. reduction of operating costs, improvement in quality of life). They are not risk takers and thus are not inclined to adopt new technologies until the benefits have been proven. The early majority have many informal contacts and this is the mechanism through which they obtain feed-back on the performance of new technologies. Equally this is the network through which they inform others. Their knowledge and expertise will tend to be built through social networks, rather than formal education. The late majority tend to be more sceptical about new technologies. They tend also to be less affluent and less able to take risks with new technologies. Their social networks may be more restricted and their outlook more traditional, both of which may create barriers to the adoption of new LZC technologies.

Finally the laggards are the hardest to reach group. They tend to be the least affluent and not inclined to take risks. Their awareness of new technologies is restricted by limited formal education and social networks. This combination really prevents many of those in this group adopting new technologies.

Overall adoption data for LZC technologies is rather patchy. There is some data available for adopters of single micro-technologies (e.g. PV cells), green tariffs and innovative forms of low carbon housing. However, there is limited data available for the adoption rates of smart technologies and localised low carbon energy systems. Overall demand for low carbon energy, homes and infrastructure in Europe and the USA appears to be limited (Figure 6.2).

Statistics suggest that 1.5% of the population in the UK (innovators) and 5% of the population in the USA (early adopters and innovators) have opted for a green energy tariff. Of course demand is higher in some locations populated by innovators and early adopters (for example adoption rates in

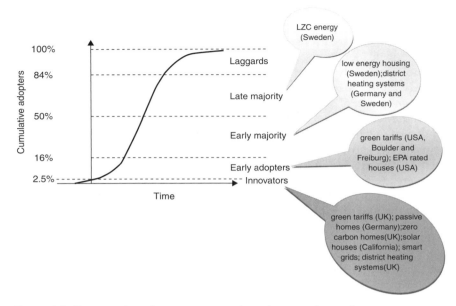

Figure 6.2 Degree of market penetration based on numbers adopting systems.

Source: Adapted from Rogers, 1983.

Boulder and Freiburg are 8% and 10% respectively). Green tariffs appear to have reached the innovators and early adopters in UK, Germany and USA. In Sweden consumption of low carbon energy is much more widespread. Here over 50% of the energy consumed by the population is from LZC energy sources. However, consumers are not involved in deciding the type of energy they will consume. The industry makes this decision (based on resource availability, demand, regulation and financial incentives) and supplies it to the consumer. Thus, consumers in this case are 'passive' adopters.

Statistics for the adoption/deployment of innovative forms of low carbon housing are difficult to obtain. However, it seems from the data that is available adoption rates have been very low. Only 0.05% of the population in Germany is living in a passive house, whilst 0.06% of households in California live in a solar home. It should be noted that those living in solar homes in California are doing so largely for pragmatic reasons. In this instance the degree of market penetration does not reflect the characteristics of those adopting the technological system (i.e. doesn't conform with Roger's definitions). In the UK pitifully few zero carbon homes have been built to date outside of BedZED. These figures suggest that current markets for innovative forms of low carbon housing are very limited. In contrast EPA rated home sales in the USA experienced enormous growth, going from zero in 1995 to 130,000 in 2004, with up to 40% penetration into some markets (NAHB, 2006).

Most of the LZC technical systems discussed have only reached the very early stages of market penetration and have been adopted by innovators and early adopters. However, in some instances where energy or housing providers have been required and/or encouraged to produce low carbon alternatives (driven by regulation and or fiscal incentives), LZC technologies and products have permeated more widely (e.g. low energy housing in Sweden, district heating in Sweden and Germany, low carbon energy in Sweden) or have been adopted by those with characteristics of the early majority (e.g. solar homes in California).

A brief discussion of the factors influencing the deployment of innovative low carbon housing forms, smart grids, LZC community energy systems and green tariffs now follows.

Zero carbon homes

Zero carbon housing has yet to penetrate UK markets. Currently a few demonstration projects exist (Chapter 3). The UK is in the very early stages[1] of market development although BedZED has been in existence since 2002. Wider deployment has been very limited since that time, according to house-builders this is because there has been no demand for zero carbon homes.

Market research suggests that consumers buy homes for practical reasons (Zero Carbon Hub, 2010). Very few will make the decision to purchase a house based on ethical reasons. Evidence suggests a focus on zero carbon can polarise the market. It can be off-putting to some consumers who do not wish to be associated with this particular set of values, it will attract others, but overall for the majority of consumers it will not play a fundamental role in their purchase decision.

Labelling a house 'zero carbon' provides no information about the other benefits it might offer to the consumer, for example a comfortable lifestyle, lower operating costs, good design, access to a range of services and facilities. This is the information that sells homes and without it demand is limited. In existing zero carbon homes, residents are interested in liveability issues not technologies and thus, marketing material should focus on these if it is to be successful. Complicated LZC technologies that are poorly understood by consumers can act as a deterrent. If LZC technologies are unreliable this can also be off-putting for consumers.

This problem is amplified by the additional expense of buying a unit with LZC technologies installed. In the UK the average construction cost premium for constructing zero carbon homes entirely within a development site could be between 17% to 24% higher than current build costs (CLG, 2008). However, by 2016 this would decline as systems for production and assembly of the new technical systems are scaled up and costs correspondingly fall. In the short-term these additional costs will be passed on the house purchaser, as will annual fuel bill savings which could be up to £387 per dwelling (CLG, 2008) and rising given the likely future price increases.

Unfortunately it appears that house purchasers tend to focus more on short-term rather than long-term rewards. Thus, focusing on the operational cost savings made through the inclusion of LZC technologies in a home to the exclusion of other short-term gains will limit demand. However, as one of many benefits advertised the long-term cost savings resulting from the inclusion of LZC technologies in a home is likely to have a positive effect, particularly in combination with tax incentives (removal of stamp duty for zero carbon homes) and the inclusion of operational cost savings in the valuation of the property (via green mortgages).

Currently there is no proven market value for zero carbon. Until more zero carbon homes have been built and systematic post-occupancy studies completed there will be a lack of information to support the higher capital costs of construction. Post-occupancy studies can be used to determine resale values and the operational cost savings made through living in a zero carbon home. This will help to determine market value and increase the popularity of zero carbon homes.

Information campaigns can be used to generate markets. The research suggested that currently most British consumers lack an understanding of the benefits of living in a zero carbon home; how it works; how to use the systems provided; the difference between zero carbon and other homes; the appearance and costs associated with a zero carbon home. This kind of practical information could help to reduce consumer concerns and generate greater interest in zero carbon homes.

According to house-builders highlighting their eco-credentials as a differentiator in the UK housing market can often be counter-productive. It can reduce their market share as house purchasers view their products as potentially more expensive and complex options. Thus, there appears to be a major challenge to normalise zero carbon features. This can only be achieved if the housing industry as whole is moving in the same direction with a common vision that the consumer can buy into. House-builders suggest that there is a need to develop a clear, consistent, generic, pan-industry marketing message about zero carbon homes.

Some argue that there is in fact latent demand for zero carbon homes amongst consumers, which is ignored by house-builders who wish to maximise their profits by minimising their build costs and financial risks. They argue that it is in fact a lack of supply that is limiting demand. The problem for zero carbon housing appears to be in a 'catch-22' type situation, whereby house-builders are unwilling to build zero carbon homes without a proven market (and by this they mean a proven market amongst the majority of consumers, not innovators or early adopters). Yet market demand cannot be generated without examples on the ground that consumers can experience. This creates a negative feed-back loop. Without some house-builders taking a risk and building zero carbon homes the British public will continue to be ignorant of the benefits.

Low energy housing

Currently, a growing interest in low energy housing amongst the European and American consumers is reported (Bienert et al, 2007; Eichholtz and Kok, 2009). Nevertheless energy efficiency still appears to be a minor factor influencing the purchase or rental decision, even with rising energy prices (Vogler, 2009; Grahl, 2009; Waters, 2007; Williams, 2008b). In Europe those involved in marketing property suggest the introduction of energy certificates for all properties (bought in by the Energy Performance in Buildings Directive) have had very limited impact on purchase or rental decisions. Yet in the USA, others report higher resale values for low energy homes (Glavis, 2010; Farhar and Coborn, 2006), thus suggesting that the positive experience of living in a low energy home can generate future market demand. The transparency of data surrounding capital, operational costs and resale values could help to address current lack of awareness amongst house purchasers.

Capital cost is the key factor affecting the market for low energy homes. Additional costs for low energy buildings cannot be predicted with precision, as costs are dependent on specific local conditions. However, in Europe a maximum of 10% extra capital investment costs are reported, although this figure is reducing as the house-building industry scales-up its operations. The transferability of cost estimations from one country to another is questionable, as building code requirements, energy prices, labour cost, skills and expertise and construction processes differ significantly. In particular, it seems misleading to try to transfer the price estimations from countries where the market is better developed (e.g. in Germany, Sweden) to other countries where low energy buildings are less common.

Generally the additional investment in a low energy building will be in the range of €100/m² (Lenormand and Rialhe, 2006) with a pay-back period of less than 20 years (Passive-on, 2010) offering considerable savings in energy bills over their lifetime, as they only use 15–25 % of the energy required for a conventional unit (Passive-on, 2010). As before, potential adopters are more influenced by capital rather than operational costs. No doubt as the price of energy rises low energy homes will become increasingly popular although this could take some time.

The alternative is to adopt a more interventionist approach. In some countries the deployment of energy efficient housing has been more widespread, driven by regulatory frameworks and public investment programmes (e.g. Miljonprogrammet in Sweden), not consumers. Thanks to the Miljonprogrammet, more than a quarter of current housing stock in Sweden is built to a very energy efficient standard. The programme enabled the house-building industry to develop the capacity to build low energy homes at scale with very limited risk. The house-builders were the innovators and adopters of new LZC technologies in this case.

Passive houses

European construction data for passive houses suggests increasing market penetration (Figure 6.3, see colour plates). Certainly the graphic presented below suggests that passive house will be moving towards the 'take-off' phase imminently. The figure shows that in Europe growth has been particularly strong in Germany and Austria, where various policy instruments have been used to support their deployment (Chapter 8). However, actual numbers of passive housing units are still very small compared to national housing stock. For example in Germany only 0.05% of stock is built to passive house standard (even with the various incentives offered to build passive housing or refurbish to passive house standard at a local and national level).

Even in Germany, where market penetration is greatest, passive house has only been adopted by the 'innovators' (i.e. the first 2.5% of the market), both home-owners and housing companies. For home-owners and housing companies the energy savings that can be made (and associated reduction in operational cost) are attractive, although this is only if the housing company is charging a 'warm rent'[2]). However, pay-back times are still relatively long as technologies are expensive. Housing companies also build passive houses for a number of other reasons, both ethical (to reduce energy consumption and environmental impact) and commercial (to be market leaders).

In Sweden, market penetration of passive house has been far slower than in Germany. This is in spite of the climatic conditions which increases the economic viability of passive houses, particularly in less densely developed areas where there are no district heating systems to connect to. Consumer demand for passive houses in Sweden has been limited by concerns largely about mould, damp and related health issues. The introduction of the more stringent prescriptive building code in the 1970s was critical to improvements in energy efficiency in housing. But unfortunately lots of problems with ventilation and air exchange resulted from greater airtightness, which created problems with moisture and mould. The public now associate airtight houses with these problems and this is a major cultural barrier to overcome with passive house (Sven Berg, 2009).

Concerns surrounding difficulties in maintaining sufficient indoor temperatures have also been voiced, particularly for those living alone or out at work all day (Linden, 2009; Sven Berg, 2009). Issues surrounding the effective use of passive systems have also been highlighted. The compatibility of passive houses with district heating systems is also an issue in Sweden. Passive houses are not compatible with district heating systems. Essentially this is because district heating systems provide an oversupply of heat to passive houses which only require a very limited top-up facility. Yet over 40% of

Swedish heat demand is supplied through district heating systems. Nonetheless passive houses are a suitable technical option where there are no district heating systems, particularly in lower density areas.

Lethargy on the part of the Swedish construction industry has slowed deployment of passive houses (Sven Berg, 2009). Swedish house-builders and politicians have become complacent as they have led the world in terms of building energy efficiency for decades. The Swedish building code is no longer visionary. Nor does it provide any indication of where Sweden wants to be in terms of building energy efficiency in the future. This doesn't provide any direction for house-builders. Nor does it provide them with any certainty, which means that innovation is far more risky.

The additional capital cost of passive houses has been highlighted as a concern more widely for the market. Yet in Germany and Sweden it is now possible to construct passive houses for costs that are no longer significantly higher than for normal. The extra cost of construction is generally indicated to be in the range of 4–6% more than for the standard. However, the build cost for passive houses varies significantly across Europe (Figure 6.4).

In terms of construction cost, building to passive house standard (specific energy requirement of 15 kwh/m²/year) can actually produce savings, since passive houses do not require central heating systems (Figure 6.5). This cost saving can be passed on to the consumer and used to help generate markets for passive house.

Over its lifetime the passive house will of course make significant energy savings (the value of which will be dependent on the price of energy) which

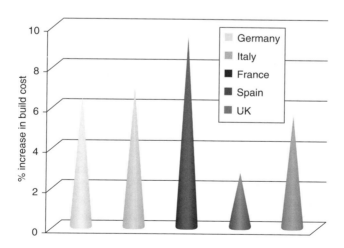

Figure 6.4 Variation in build cost for passive house across Europe.

Source: PASS-NET, 2009.

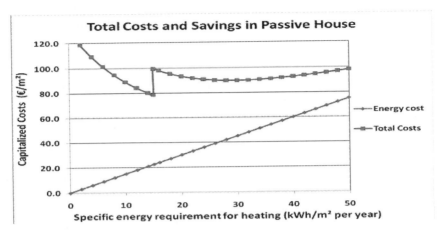

Figure 6.5 Total costs and savings in passive house.

Source: Laustsen, 2008.

translate into cost savings. However, there does appear to be some additional costs associated with systems maintenance. As with low energy housing the market value of passive house is difficult to discern, and this limits wider deployment. However, methods are being sought for linking property valuation with energy efficiency (e.g. the EU Immovalue project).

Solar homes / zero-net energy homes

Market interest in solar homes has also been limited (Farhar et al 2004; CEC, 2008). In California the Go Solar Programme has so far not been very successful. A mere 0.06% of the housing stock in California are solar units, which suggests solar homes are in the very early stages of market penetration. Thus it would be reasonable to assume that demand currently comes wholly from 'innovators'.

However, the characteristics of those living in solar homes in California do not necessarily match the profile of the 'innovator' (i.e. pioneering, well-educated, risk taking, affluent, technophile motivated to buy solar homes by ethical concern and technological excellence). In fact those living in solar homes demonstrate the characteristics of the 'majority' motivated in their purchase decisions by pragmatic reasons.

Research showed that the decision to purchase a solar home in the first instance was driven by location, affordability, aesthetic attractiveness of properties and access to services (Farhar et al, 2004): in fact all the usual factors influencing a house purchase decision. Low energy costs and energy security were of secondary importance to consumers. This suggests that by focusing on standard market attractors (i.e. affordability, location, etc) rather than technical systems, it is possible to generate demand for solar homes amongst the early majority.

Interestingly, having lived in solar homes the majority of households were impressed by the energy savings made and the resulting reduction in operational costs (Farhar and Coborn, 2006). Most households reported they would like to live in a solar home again if they moved and many were prepared to pay above the market rate to do so (Farhar and Coborn, 2006). Thus providing the opportunity for people to be able to test new technologies will help to create a market for solar homes.

The early adopters of solar technologies in California were the house-builders (encouraged by local incentives), rather than consumers. They increased access to solar homes, enabling households to experience the benefits. This in turn generated secondary markets. Experience from the west coast of America suggests that the best way to increase market demand is to deploy the solar homes more widely so that the pragmatic benefits can be experienced by a larger section of the population (NAHB, 2005). In this way solar homes may become attractive to the majority. As more solar homes are deployed they become familiar and readily accepted by all parties in the property transaction process. However, more data is needed to demonstrate the value placed on solar homes by the market.

The cost of solar homes has been subsidised in California. However, without the subsidies solar homes are likely to cost more than standard units. Of course there are savings made whilst in operation created by energy efficiency measures and the energy generated by the solar technologies. There are also issues surrounding grid connection and long-term maintenance of technologies, which has restricted markets and supply. However, in California these problems are being addressed by house-builders and energy companies. In addition new edge-of-service providers have emerged to maintain the LZC technologies used in solar homes. The aesthetics of solar technologies also appear to be a potential barrier to deployment. The more integrated the technologies the greater the market demand.

Solar homes are more easily incorporated into the mainstream residential construction industry in California than in other US states. Generally, the solar resource in California is considered much greater than other states in the USA. Innovative practices are more readily embraced by producers and consumers in the sunshine state. The subsidies offered by the state and federal government also reduce the cost of a solar home (where the cost of the solar and energy efficiency upgrades may only be from 3 to 10% of the cost of the home, NAHB 2006), yet deployment has still been relatively slow.

Market penetration of highly efficient homes with solar energy systems has already begun, and will continue in selected markets in America. PV system costs have continued to decline while production continues to increase by nearly 30% annually (NAHB, 2006). However, it is not economically viable at this time to build solar homes without financial incentives. In order for solar homes to succeed in the market, a coordinated effort is needed to reduce the cost of LZC technologies and to facilitate transformation of the new homes market (NAHB, 2006).

Smart grids

Smart technologies are in their infancy in both Europe and the USA. However, both the UK and USA have signalled their intention to use smart technologies to address energy demand. In both countries the energy industry will act as the innovators and early adopters of this technology. Currently 'smart grids' are limited to a few demonstration projects but feedback suggests there is interest amongst the public in smart grid technologies (ICARO, 2009; Farhar, 2010), particularly if issues of privacy and individual control can be overcome.

The difference with smart grids and other technologies discussed so far is that the energy providers are keen to implement them. This is because smart technologies help with supply management, increase efficiencies and reduce operational costs for the energy provider. Although the capital cost for energy providers installing and operating smart grids are high, this expenditure can be recouped reasonably rapidly through increased efficiencies in the system (for example reducing system-spinning capacity, reducing time-lines for fixing faults in supply network, managing supply and demand more effectively). The consumer's reaction to smart technologies and their effective use of these technologies will however affect whether the energy provider continues to operate smart grids.

The research conducted in Boulder (Farhar, 2010) suggested that there were various practical, altruistic, technical and moral motivations for adopting smart technologies amongst potential consumers (Chapter 4). Of course practical motivations concentrate on saving energy and money. Altruistic motivations focus on environmental concerns. Some residents were intrigued by the smart grid because of their technical and professional interests. Some were curious about the technologies used. Others were interested in how the information generated by smart grid could help their businesses. The 'moralists' were concerned with the principle of inter-generational equity[3] and wanted to impose controls on the behaviour of wider society for the good of future generations and felt that the smart grid would help in this process. These motivational drivers – practical, altruistic, technical and moral - were not found to be mutually exclusive, although those with moral motivations did tend to be a group apart from the rest (Farhar, 2010).

Various issues were raised by the research which could limit market demand for the smart grid in Boulder. Personal privacy was a key concern, in terms of who would have access to the sensitive data generated by the system. The security of online management systems was a great cause for concern. The ownership of the personal data produced by the system was a further issue. If the utility owned the data would they pass that information onto others? Many of the respondents wanted individual control over their energy systems and didn't welcome potential interference from the utility. However, others were concerned about the degree of consumer involvement in energy management and their capacity to deal with such a complex system. Thus, there was a clear demand for different approaches to be taken towards those who wished to be passive consumers and those who preferred to be actively engaged energy citizens.

The research in the UK suggests that consumer interest in smart grids seems to be largely based on economic rationality and utility functions (ICARO, 2009). British consumers were interested in being given more information about their consumption habits (via smart meters) in order that they could manage their energy consumption and expenditure more effectively. According to a survey (ICARO, 2009) 83% of respondents gave a positive response to the installation of smart meters in homes. They were also attracted by having a central in-home 'hub', which could be programmed by the consumer to switch appliances on and off when not in use, or to 'power down' the house when absent. Again the majority of respondents (81%) gave a positive response to an in-home hub.

However, those interviewed were less supportive of any form of external control of energy systems in the home, even at a relatively minor level or for short periods of time. This was seen as an invasion of privacy. UK consumers seemed to prefer systems offering individual control, personal choice and privacy reflecting the same concerns raised by those interviewed in Boulder. However, there is overall a lack of collective experience of smart grids. Thus issues surrounding demand for and use of smart technologies are as yet largely unknown.

Community LZC infrastructure

The majority of consumers prefer energy systems which are reliable, cost effective and require little input from the user. Centralised, fossil-fuelled systems (based on the deficit model) have successfully delivered a cheap and reliable electricity supply for many decades in Europe and the USA. These systems limit consumer involvement in the management or generation of energy. Thus, the current market for private wire[4] LZC electricity systems is likely to be limited.

District energy systems have also developed. Currently, 40% of heat demanded in Sweden and Germany is provided by community heating systems. The development of community heating systems has been encouraged over decades by significant public investment and supporting regulation. More recently operational subsidies have been used to encourage the decarbonisation of the heat supply (e.g. biofuel subsidy in Sweden). For most urban consumers in Germany and Sweden connection to the existing community heat networks is the simplest option.

Neighbourhood energy systems are less prevalent. Economies of scale mean that it is more cost-effective to deliver energy systems to a larger number of consumers, in areas where there is a mixture of uses. However in the UK at least, with the introduction of the zero carbon policy, feed-in tariff and renewable heat incentive, there are now adequate reasons for the energy industry to start to develop models for neighbourhood energy systems.

The most popular model currently appears to be neighbourhood district heating systems in combination with PV cells linked to the national grid. Neighbourhood district heating networks appear to be popular amongst most consumers for a number of reasons. They offer security of energy supply, limited consumer involvement and provide a more energy efficient, 'greener' option (ICARO, 2009).

The technologies used in community energy systems will vary of course with the landscape (environmental, political, institutional, cultural, and economic) in which they are embedded. For example the GEOS model developed as a result of the natural resources and fiscal incentives available to the developer in that specific location. This model will incidentally be appropriate for most of the State of Colorado as incentives and access to geothermal and solar energy remain relatively constant.

Consumers are attracted to community energy systems by the potential cost savings that can be made by increased energy efficiencies. However, paradoxically they are also concerned about the fair allocation of the cost savings within the community. There appears to be a fundamental conflict between the need to provide community energy systems (rather than individual energy systems) to maximise energy efficiencies and an embedded distrust in the fairness of more communal approaches amongst households.

Consumers are also concerned about technology failures, particularly where relatively new technologies are deployed in communities. Issues surrounding the management and maintenance of community energy systems have been raised in a number of instances (ICARO, 2009; Williams, 2008b). Most households are keen to remain passive consumers. Thus systems operated by utilities, energy service companies or other property service providers tend to be preferred.

Key issues around personal control and choice emerges when discussing community energy infrastructure. This is particularly an issue for heat as local networks need to managed and maintained by and ESCO or utility. This limits consumer ability to choose suppliers. Utilities, ESCOs and consumers have highlighted this as a problem. The situation for electricity is different where for most models housing, units are connected to the national grid (thus consumers can choose their supplier) and export LZC electricity.

Currently there is no inclusion of an evaluation of LZC community energy systems in estimated property values. This creates problems for developers (house-builders and energy companies) financing community infrastructure, highlighted in the Colorado case study (Stenftenagel and Klebl, 2010) and in the UK (Woodward, 2009). It can also produce problems in obtaining adequate personal finance when buying properties in a zero carbon community.

Green tariffs

In the UK only 1.5% (Diaz-Rainey and Ashton, 2008) of the customer base for electricity is registered for a green tariff (Figure 6.6). These are the innovators in the market who are likely to base their decisions on ethical concerns rather than cost (or other more practical matters). In America 5% of the customer base for electricity is registered for a green tariff.

This suggests that green tariffs have had greater success in terms of market penetration in the USA and have now reached the early adopters in the market. Again this group will be motivated to purchase green tariffs for ethical reasons. Amongst the majority of the population the decision to purchase a particular tariff is usually based on cost and reliability of supply rather than on ethical concern. Thus, price and reliability of green energy is crucial for its wider adoption.

It should be noted that green energy tariffs provide consumers with the opportunity to contribute to energy companies environmental programmes, rather than pay directly for carbon neutral or renewable energy. This limits

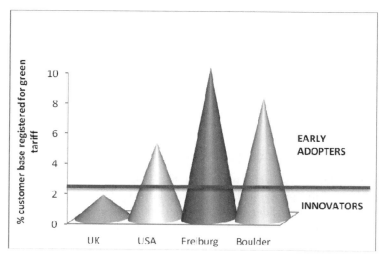

Figure 6.6 Comparison of customer base registered for green tariff.

Source: Author's own.

their value, since the payment of green tariffs doesn't directly correspond with the decarbonisation of the energy supply. It also relies on a few altruistic customers to invest in the decarbonisation programme for the benefit of the rest of society.

Unsurprisingly this has limited market appeal and will never lead to a wholesale change in energy systems: far better to require that energy companies decarbonise supply using regulation and fiscal policies. Regulation and fiscal policies can be used to alter the energy mix. Where there is better access to LZC energy, market penetration is likely to be greater.

Questions have also been raised about the extent to which energy companies invest the revenue from green tariffs on decarbonisation (or indeed wider environmental improvements). There is evidence to suggest that investment is often very limited as is transparency (Williams, 2010). This further restricts demand for green tariffs, even amongst the most altruistic.

Markets for LZC energy vary at a local level. Where there are high concentrations of innovators and early adopters demand for LZC tariffs is likely to be higher. For example in Freiburg (Germany) and Boulder (Colorado, USA), more citizens are prepared to pay a significantly higher tariff to subsidise decarbonisation (Figure 6.6). However, demand in both cities (although above the national average) is actually still rather low. These figures suggest that so far it is still only the innovators and early adopter who are buying LZC energy. If market penetration is so limited even in 'green cities' what hope is there for green tariffs to be adopted by the majority of the population?

The economic, resource and political landscape may provide motivation for more households to invest in LZC energy tariffs in the future. Increasing energy prices and supply failure will encourage households to look for energy supply alternatives that are cheaper and more secure. As fossil fuels become increasingly scarce unit price will begin to rise making non-fossil fuels more competitive. Producers will also begin to seek alternatives to fossil fuels. Thus they will invest more in LZC energy systems. The emphasis will begin to move from public funding of new systems to private funding

Summary: barriers to LZC technical systems

This review highlights several barriers to the wider deployment of LZC technical systems and energy. Table 6.1 summarises the barriers identified by the research and the wider literature for LZC homes, community energy systems, smart technologies and low carbon tariffs. For all the options considered the higher cost of the system or service restricts demand. Energy efficiency and carbon savings are not a priority amongst consumers and do not influence purchase decisions. Nor has it been demonstrated that energy savings create additional market value for properties. However, there does appear to be a section of the market that believes LZC technologies have an adverse aesthetic impact on homes. These factors in combination severely restrict the market for low carbon systems.

Limited availability of low carbon technical systems also restricts demand. Markets develop through social networks. If few people within social networks have experienced these systems, market potential is reduced. In addition, if consumers cannot access new technical systems they will become quickly frustrated and seek more easily accessible alternatives. The impact of using new technical systems on consumers' quality of life and the perceived reliability of new technologies will also influence markets. The complexity of a system (particularly at the user-technology interface) will also affect demand. The more simplistic the interface the greater consumer demand. Options also need to be compatible with existing technical systems and culture if they are to have wide appeal.

Trust issues also create market barriers. For smart technologies there are 'trust concerns' surrounding privacy of personal data and degree of personal control over energy systems. For community energy systems there are 'trust concerns' relating to maintenance (who will maintain community infrastructure) and equitable division of financial rewards. For green tariffs there are 'trust concerns' surrounding the transparency of the energy providers' real environmental contribution.

Low carbon tariffs appear to have the fewest reported market barriers, which is unsurprising since tariffs challenge the technical, cultural,

Table 6.1 Barriers to growth in markets for LZC technical systems

Barriers	LZC homes	Smart technologies	LZC community energy systems	Low carbon tariffs
Cost	☑	☑	☑	☑
Energy not a priority	☑	☑	☑	
Market value of property	☑		☑	
Availability	☑	☑	☑	
Awareness/lack of collective experience	☑	☑	☑	
Impact on quality of life[1]	☑	☑	☑	
Lack of trust		☑	☑	☑
Reliability	☑		☑	
Compatibility	☑		☑	
System complexity	☑	☑		
Negative aesthetic impact	☑			

Source: Author's own.

Notes

1 Convenience, individual control, privacy, comfort, health impacts, disruption, etc.

institutional and political context the least. However, they are the most limited in terms of encouraging the transformation of industry and technical systems.

The market for LZC homes appears to face the greatest number of barriers. Essentially consumers do not choose homes (or value them) on the basis of energy efficiency or carbon emissions (whereas for the other energy systems both can be a consideration). Nor do they believe that LZC homes will improve their quality of life. Thus, the additional costs for LZC technologies are unwelcome. The aesthetic impact of LZC technologies in the home (private space rather than in communal or public space) also limits demand, partly as consumers believe it could potentially de-value the property.

Consumers also assume they will have to be more involved with technical systems in the home, whilst they believe service providers will operate (manage and maintain) energy systems in the community. Thus consumers seem to prefer the latter because it limits their involvement or interaction with technical systems. Lack of technical expertise and the potential complexity of the system also limit demand. Of course there are some consumers who want to be more actively engaged in the operation of systems, but the majority appear to prefer a passive role.

Creating markets for zero carbon homes

The diffusion of zero carbon homes throughout the social system is influenced by several factors: relative advantage, compatibility, complexity, trialability and observability (Rogers, 1983). Relative advantage is the degree to which the new technical system (a zero carbon home) is perceived as better than the one it replaces (a standard home). The degree of relative advantage may be measured in economic terms, social prestige factors, convenience and satisfaction. The greater the relative advantage of a technical system, the more rapid its rate of adoption.

To ensure the wider deployment there needs to be parity between zero carbon and standard homes in terms of convenience (i.e. use of passive systems, management companies to operate, manage and maintain systems), life satisfaction, economic cost and the social prestige they offer. However, zero carbon homes also need to advertise their additional advantages including: lower energy bills and carbon emissions; benefits for future generation; greater autonomy; and energy security.

For zero carbon homes to diffuse more widely they need to be compatible with the landscape (environmental, institutional, cultural, economic and political context) in which they are embedded. Of course some models are more compatible than others. These are the ones that are more likely to diffuse. However, the biggest compatibility barrier to the diffusion of zero carbon homes is institutional. The key to encouraging speedier diffusion of zero carbon homes is to tackle the institutional inertia in the energy industry which creates resistance to zero carbon energy systems. If this problem isn't tackled zero carbon communities are unlikely to scale up.

Technical systems constituting a zero carbon home also need to reflect cultural norms. It is essential that a zero carbon homes is perceived as being consistent with existing values, past experiences and the needs of potential adopters if it is to be successful in the market place. Thus, trying to introduce a model which requires the active involvement of adopters in its operation is likely to alienate large sections of the market in more passive cultures. Here deficit models (e.g. green tariffs or LZC energy systems managed by service providers) are likely to be more successful.

Experience shows that the more complex a technical system, the slower its rate of diffusion through a social system. Complex zero carbon models, those perceived as difficult to understand, engage with and operate, will deploy only to a very limited extent. If the complexity of a zero carbon home as a technical system can be reduced through the use of passive technologies and the introduction of service providers to manage and maintain the systems, deployment is likely to increase. Complex systems like smart grid, which require a great deal of consumer-technology interaction and incorporate a number of technical sub-systems are likely to be less attractive to the market. However, complex systems can be simplified for the user to increase market demand. For example, smart grid users can opt for tariffs which allow the utility to make all decisions concerning the management of their energy supply based on the tariff they opt for. This means that their level of involvement in decision-making and operation is minimised.

Trialability is also critical to speeding up the process of diffusion. Trialability is the degree to which a technical system may be experimented with on a limited basis. A zero carbon home that is 'trialable' represents less uncertainty to the individual considering adoption. For example rental units in zero carbon communities could provide a means by which more people could test the system before buying into it (e.g. solar settlement in Vauban district). However, most of the bespoke zero carbon developments presented in this book do not offer rental options. Of course those living in zero carbon developments can stimulate market interest informally through their existing social networks, or formally acting on the behalf of the developer. Certainly both approaches have worked well for stimulating markets for other innovative housing forms (Williams, 2008b).

Observability is the degree to which a technical system is visible to others. The easier it is for potential adoptees to see the advantages of a technical system, the more likely they are to adopt it and the faster the diffusion rate. The problem is that the key benefits of zero carbon housing are not visible. In some instances even the physical technologies and infrastructure are so well integrated into the building and urban fabric they are not visible. In fact this is also necessary in order that the technical systems are acceptable. Post-occupancy surveys that monitor the financial, environmental and social benefits of zero carbon living might be helpful in highlighting advantages to a wider audience. The property industry also needs to be more active in marketing zero carbon properties. The evidence suggests that existing capacity needs to be built within the property industry to enable this to happen.

This analysis provides us with some insight into how to generate demand for zero carbon homes and encourage wider deployment. First it is important to publicise the relative advantages of living in zero carbon homes through post-occupancy surveys, via the property industry and social networks. Second it is important to increase the availability of zero carbon homes, using policy instruments to stimulate supply (discussed in Chapter 7). Increasing public access to zero carbon homes will raise public awareness and broaden the collective experience. This may help to overcome some of the public's concerns particularly in terms of the operational complexity, reliability and aesthetic impact of zero carbon systems.

Areas in which zero carbon homes are potentially at a disadvantage also need to be addressed. More cost-effective zero carbon housing models and systems for valuing LZC infrastructure are needed. The negative impacts of LZC systems on quality of life need to be addressed (discussed in Chapter 11). The complexity of models should also be tackled, as the simpler is the system is to operate, the more numerous are potential adopters. The models will also need to be compatible with the local context in which they are embedded (discussed in Chapter 10).

Strategies for increasing demand

There are three critical issues currently limiting the market for zero carbon homes: poor marketing and publicity; high price and limited valuation models; and lack of available examples. If these issues are tackled the rate of deployment of zero carbon homes is likely to increase.

Marketing and publicity

A variety of marketing strategies are needed to generate interest in zero carbon homes amongst a range of groups, with different motivations. In Sweden, Germany, UK and USA, at least four consumer groups have particularly shown themselves to be interested in zero carbon housing forms for a range of reasons (Table 6.2). Green consumers are attracted to living in zero carbon communities because it provides the opportunity to live in accordance with their values and with other like-minded individuals. Technophiles are fascinated by the technical systems. Conservationists focus on the cost and energy savings that can be made by living in zero carbon homes. Concerned parents are influenced by ethical concern for future generations and a healthier living environment for their family. Thus targeted

Table 6.2 Marketing strategies for zero carbon homes

Group category	Group characteristics	Motivations influencing house purchase/rental	Marketing strategies
Green consumer	Affluent, educated	Environmental ethics and social opportunities	Focus on energy/emission savings and being part of a green community where there are shared values.
Technophile	Male, affluent, educated	Interest in technologies	Focus on the efficiencies of technologies.
Conservationists	Retired and mid-low income groups	Efficient use of resources	Focus on energy efficiency and operational cost savings.
Concerned parents	Families, affluent, educated	Safety, security, health, futurity	Focus on the benefits for children and future generations. Also focus on the healthy and secure living environment

Source: Author's own.

marketing which highlights these dimensions of zero carbon housing could help to generate greater market demand amongst these groups.

The lesson from the America is that there is already a growing latent demand (although still limited) for communities which offer low carbon lifestyles and infrastructure. As the cost of energy increases and energy security declines there is likely to be an increase in those searching for energy efficient dwellings, as well as a cheaper and more secure source of energy. Thus, the market is likely to expand for pragmatic reasons. If a variety of housing options are provided in new zero carbon communities, for a range of prices, the customer base is likely to grow and become increasingly diverse.

In the short term, whilst energy is still relatively cheap and available, a more traditional approach to marketing is required. Such an approach should focus on the wider attributes of a development including affordability, good location, re-sale value and design. Of course the energy efficiency of units is important, but should be viewed as only one of many advantages. In this way the development is more likely to appeal to a wider audience. This approach alienates nobody and it focuses on the factors which currently influence house purchase decisions. Thus it should attract the early and late majority.

Currently a dearth of expertise amongst those selling and buying zero carbon properties is also limiting the market. Consumers have given poor feedback on the attempts of developers and property agents to talk through the

LZC features of their new homes. Equally, those selling zero carbon homes (or similar) have complained that it is very difficult to find property agents with the appropriate expertise to promote their homes successfully. Thus, developers and property agents who are experts in zero carbon property are needed to offer advice to consumers and to market homes appropriately. This requires that training programmes (for example the programme offered by Eco-broker in America) are introduced for those selling properties to build capacity in this area.

A further problem relates to the way in which both those buying and selling properties identify the property agent they will use. Many people base their decision on word of mouth recommendation or local advertisement. Existing agents with appropriate expertise are under-utilised because buyers and sellers are not aware of their existence. Thus it is important that zero carbon property agents use local communication networks to effectively build a client base.

Those who have experienced living in zero carbon properties provide an excellent marketing resource. This group are best placed to highlight both the problems and benefits of living in a zero carbon community to prospective adopters. They can answer questions about how living in a zero carbon community can impact on lifestyle and practical questions concerning the operation and maintenance of LZC technologies in homes. Of course this happens informally to an extent through social networks. However, it could also be formalised as part of the marketing process.

This technique was found to be a useful strategy for marketing cohousing developments (Williams, 2008b). Cohousing is similar to zero carbon housing in that it is an innovative form of accommodation, which has been experienced by a relatively small proportion of the population. Open days and social events held in cohousing communities provided interested consumers with the opportunity to discuss these questions with residents. In some instances developers used existing residents to recruit newcomers to communities in the formal marketing process. Both strategies were found to be successful.

Post-occupancy monitoring can provide essential information – energy efficiency, cost savings and resale values - which can be used for marketing zero carbon homes. Cost savings and resale values are particularly important for marketing. If the claims made for significant cost savings and /or higher resale values can be substantiated the market for zero carbon homes will grow. These are two key motivators influencing the purchase decision for the majority of the population and could help zero carbon homes move into the mainstream.

Post-occupancy monitoring can also be used to identify the types of consumer buying into zero carbon development and their reasons for doing so. This information could help to develop the targeted marketing strategies. It can also begin to identify gaps in the market and help to inform developers of facets that could be introduced into zero carbon housing to broaden market appeal.

Cost and valuation

Cost is fundamental in house purchase decisions. As has been demonstrated zero carbon homes are likely to be more expensive to purchase at least during the early stages of deployment. However, this additional cost can be recouped over time, although there are concerns amongst consumers about the pay-back periods for these technologies. In fast-moving markets households may move before they recoup the additional costs of LZC technologies through energy cost savings. However, if factored into the valuation of the property this is not a problem in itself.

The operational cost savings could be included in the valuation of zero carbon properties. Green mortgages factor in operational costs (including energy savings) when a property is valued. Thus, green mortgages can be used to promote zero carbon homes. The valuation of LZC technologies in private units is relatively simple to calculate on the basis of energy (cost) savings. However, the valuation of community LZC infrastructure has proven more difficult.

This has created problems for some developers, preventing them from raising finance to provide community LZC infrastructure. For demand to grow, the energy cost savings produced by LZC technical systems (integrated into or linked to a property) should be included in the market valuation of zero carbon homes.

Lack of availability

The limited supply of zero carbon homes and component systems severely inhibits markets. Most importantly those innovators and early adopters wishing to buy or rent zero carbon homes cannot do so, because there are none available in appropriate locations. Lack of availability also increases price which further restricts markets.

By limiting the number of households who can experience living in zero carbon homes it is more difficult to change existing attitudes towards them or to establish zero carbon homes as a social norm. It also limits the potential for post-occupancy evaluation. The collective experience of zero carbon housing remains undeveloped. Thus opportunities for marketing through social networks are impeded.

In order for markets to grow, the supply of zero carbon units must increase. This will improve access to units. It should also drive down costs, resulting in growth in market demand. It will help to increase awareness of the benefits of living in zero carbon homes and dispel concerns. Thus increasing the supply of units can help to alter attitudes towards zero carbon homes and possibly establish them as a social norm. Thus, policy instruments to encourage industry to increase supply are needed urgently (Chapters 7, 8 and 9).

It seems that house-builders and energy companies need to be the early adopters of these new technologies rather than households, if markets are to develop. However, there appears to be significant industrial resistance towards increasing the supply of LZC technical systems without demand being demonstrated. In the next chapters the causes of this industrial inertia will be investigated and appropriate solutions for encouraging an increase in supply of zero carbon homes will be explored.

Chapter 7

Transformation of the house-building industry

Introduction

The demonstration projects discussed in earlier chapters are not being replicated at scale or within regions. Nor do lessons learnt from the projects appear to be adopted by industry. Often these demonstration projects appear to remain exactly that. They attract a huge amount of media attention and attract large numbers of international visitors. However, this seems to translate into very few additional projects on the ground. The question is what mechanisms within the current system are preventing wider deployment from occurring?

In the previous chapter it became apparent that one barrier to deployment is the current lack of market demand and it was suggested that one of the key methods for addressing this problem would be to increase supply. However, there appears to be some inertia concerning this on the part of the house-building and energy industries. In the next two chapters we investigate what causes is resistance to transformation in both industries and explore possible solutions.

The delivery of zero carbon homes will be dependent on the transformation of both the house-building and energy industries. Transition theory suggests this transformation might be driven by the wider context in which industries are set (i.e. at the macro-level) or result from the development of innovative projects by a few actors in industry (i.e. at the micro-level). The structure, culture and practices of both the energy and house-building industries encourage conservativeness. There is a tendency in both industries to focus on optimisation rather than innovation, which creates great internal resistance to the kind of radical transformation required to deliver zero carbon homes.

A transition can be seen as a long-term systemic shift which changes systems infrastructure and dominant culture as well as the behaviour of actors (Rotmans et al, 2001). There can be technical transitions (Geels, 2005) and societal transitions (Rotmans et al, 2001). The former looks at new technologies and surrounding institutions (including industry). The latter looks at shifts in behaviour and societal functions. The delivery of zero carbon homes is likely to demand both technical and societal transitions.

Transition theory highlights the interdependency of institutions and infrastructure constituting societal systems and subsystems. These societal systems comprise inter-locking social, cultural, economic, infrastructural and regulative subsystems (Geels, 2005), which are associated with a range of groups (e.g. house-builders and energy providers) and result in various types of lock-in that stifle innovation (Smith et al, 2005). The stability and cohesion of societal systems is established and reinforced through cognitive, normative and regulative institutions which can be represented by the concept of a regime.

A regime is a set of practices, rules and shared assumptions which dominate a system of actors (Rotmans et al, 2001). The house-building and energy industries both have regimes. Regimes tend to focus on system optimisation rather than system innovation, because habits, existing competencies, past investment, regulation, prevailing norms, world views and so on act to lock in patterns of behaviour and result in path dependencies for technological and social development (Smith et al, 2005; Geels, 2005). The house-building and energy industries demonstrate this tendency.

The multi-level concept (Figure 7.1) subdivides areas where innovation and transformation might occur into three levels - macro-level, meso-level and micro-level (Kemp and Rip, 1998; Rotmans et al, 2001). At a macro-level world views and paradigms, the macro-economy, material infrastructure, natural environment and demographic trends, regulation, policy instruments and institutions all influence the potential for industrial transformation.

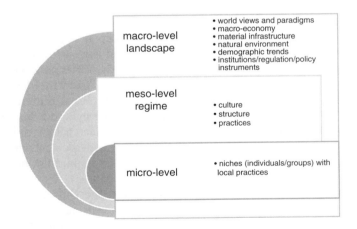

Figure 7.1 Multi-level concept of transition theory.

Source: Adapted from Bergmann et al, 2008.

At the meso-level (i.e within industries themselves) there are also factors (i.e. culture, structure and practices) which influence potential for regime transformation (Bergmann et al, 2008). Sometimes the stimulus for industrial transformation may also come from the micro-level, instigated by the formation and strength of empowered niches (Bergmann et al, 2008). Thus grass-roots innovation may eventually inform, or even radically alter industry, if conditions at a macro-level are conducive.

To move towards zero carbon homes will require substantial change within both the house-building and energy industries. To deliver zero carbon homes will require that housing is built to extremely high energy efficiency standards and that the energy supply is decarbonised. It will also require that both industries work together in optimising the production and operation of systems. In this chapter we will explore the degree of transformation required in the house-building industry, barriers to transformation and the drivers for change.

The housing landscape

At a macro-level (i.e. the landscape in which the house-building industry is embedded) there are various factors currently influencing the construction of housing and the adoption of LZC technical systems in the case study countries. Demographic trends (at least in Europe and the USA) are leading to a reduction in household size, an increase in household numbers and demand for new homes. Reduction in household size is also resulting in an increase in energy consumed and CO_2 produced by households per capita (Williams, 2006). However, this has not as yet driven the industry to develop more energy efficient, low carbon alternatives for smaller households.

Increase in affluence, popularity of home-ownership, second homes and buy-to let properties has fuelled an increase in demand for new homes (particularly in the UK). However, certainly for buy-to-let properties and second homes energy efficiency is low priority. For the former there is a split incentive which limits landlords' willingness to invest in energy efficiency technologies. In the latter low occupancy limits owners' willingness to invest in energy saving measures or energy generating technologies.

Migration from rural to urban locations has resulted in a growth in demand for new properties in urban areas (e.g. Germany and Sweden). As urban locations become more popular, land values have risen and the cost of development increased. In Germany, those moving to urban areas tend to be the young, who require affordable accommodation. This limits housing companies' willingness to invest in expensive low carbon systems in urban areas, unless they also manage the properties and charge 'warm rents'.

Housing construction rates in all case study countries are currently very low, which reduces the potential for industrial transformation. The macro-economy of course impacts on housing markets and construction rates. The global economic crisis has severely affected housing markets in Europe and the USA. Difficulties in obtaining credit has led to a rapid decline in the demand for housing. House-builders tend to build fewer, standardised units, to reduce the risk of any remaining unsold. Thus, economic slumps can slow the rate of development and make house-builders more risk averse. Neither is conducive to technical innovation.

Economic slumps could offer a time for reflection and innovation in the house-building industry, particularly amongst those players looking for a market advantage. However, in practice technical and operational innovation in the industry appears to be very limited during these periods (Ball, 1999). When the housing market is growing and house prices are inflated there is greater willingness to innovate amongst house-builders. During these periods the additional costs of new technologies can be passed on to the customer and recouped in the value of the property.

The conservativeness of the market, the 'world-view' of a home and the value placed on specific facets of a home by the consumer limits house-builders willingness to innovate (Chapter 6). The market places value on the location, design, affordability, convenience and comfort offered by a property. The environmental impact or operational cost of a home is rarely considered by most consumers: they are more concerned with the capital cost (Williams, 2008a). Low energy costs mean household expenditure on energy is a less significant factor driving rental and purchase decisions. If energy prices rise significantly, this is likely to change and could drive innovation in the house-building industry.

The physical environment can also influence house-builders willingness to adopt LZC technologies. For example, availability of resources, access to appropriate distribution networks, climate and built form can all impact on the cost-effectiveness and appropriateness of adopting LZC technical systems. These systems have been more readily adopted in more extreme climatic environments (e.g. Sweden's low energy housing); where low carbon energy sources are particularly abundant (e.g. solar homes in California and Colorado); where the supply infrastructure already exists (e.g. district heating systems in Sweden and Germany).

The institutional landscape also influences the house-building industry's ability to deliver zero carbon homes. A lack of suitable institutions to supply, construct, manage, maintain, accredit and enforce LZC technical systems will restrict the house-building industry's ability to deliver zero carbon homes successfully. Institutional landscapes certainly differ at an international level and thus scope for industrial transformation is likely to vary.

Regulatory (building codes and planning) and fiscal instruments (taxes and subsidies) have already produced significant innovations in the house-building industry. Without a regulatory and fiscal framework supporting the delivery of zero carbon homes there is very limited motivation for existing regimes to innovate to deliver a more expensive and currently less popular product. Building codes provide a statutory requirement to build zero carbon homes. Product legislation can be used to ensure that LZC technologies are available to the market. Planning can be used to encourage the deployment of LZC technical systems in new development, although it can also slow innovation too. Tax incentives to encourage households or house-builders to adopt LZC technologies have also proved successful. Various capital and operational subsidies available to households, house-builders and energy service providers have helped to encourage industrial transformation. These instruments for change will be discussed further in Chapter 9.

Culture of the house-building industry

The culture, structure and practices adopted by the house-building industry can limit innovation and transformation. In cultural terms the house-building industry tends to be conservative and risk averse. It operates within short time horizons and suffers from internal industrial inertia as regards innovation. The conservativeness of the industry is reinforced by the conservatism of the market and path dependencies existing in terms of industrial practice. However in some instances it is also reinforced by profit-making strategies.

For example, the British profit-making model limits innovation in terms of the product and construction processes, whilst the Swedish model promotes it. The British house-building industry focuses on the speculative management of land banks and the dynamics of price inflation to generate profit (Bramley et al, 1995). In contrast house-builders in Sweden profit from higher build quality[1] or increasing efficiency of construction processes (Barlow and King, 1992). This approach could reinforce the delivery of zero carbon homes, whilst the British approach undermines it. An industrial focus on build quality as a mechanism for profit generation is needed to support the delivery of zero carbon homes.

House-builders are generally risk averse, as are other players in the delivery chain including financial institutions. They are exposed to a range of risks throughout the development process including: cyclical downturns in the housing market; fluctuations in the prices of materials, land and labour; costs of complying with unanticipated changes in building codes; uncertainty over the granting of planning permission and the costs of meeting the conditions of any permissions. Building to a zero carbon standard could lead to an increase in build cost, refusal of planning permission, lengthening of the planning period, and refusal of financial institutions to invest in projects (particularly where no market demand for zero carbon homes has been established). For risk averse house-builders this creates a very significant barrier to the construction of zero carbon homes. Lack of a long-term regulatory framework for energy efficiency improvements in buildings in Sweden has led to stagnation (Sven Berg, 2009).

There are also internal organisational barriers (including internal competition for resources, conflicting priorities, institutional inertia and informal relations) in the house-building industry to innovation, that may prevent zero carbon homes from being built (Ko and Fenner, 2007). The energetic standard of housing units is likely to be low priority amongst house-builders (unless enforced through building code or markets for LZC technologies are demonstrated). Resources are spent by the industry on optimising existing housing models to generate greater profit margins rather than on technical innovation (unless technical innovation creates greater profit margins). Adding LZC technologies to a unit does not necessarily raise its value but does increase its cost, which could limit the market. In addition, the introduction of LZC technologies into a development is likely to have significant resource implications for the house-builder (with no guaranteed return). Thus, for house-builders zero carbon homes are a risky investment.

Generally, speculative house-builders have a very short-term view of the product, focused on designing, constructing and marketing. To develop the expertise and skills needed to deal with long-term operation (in particular energy management) would require additional resources. Thus, speculative house-builders prefer not to be involved in the ongoing management and maintenance of properties (Williams, 2008a). A split incentive is created resulting from the disjuncture between those investing (i.e. house-builders) in energetic efficiency and those benefitting from it (i.e. households), which is certainly an issue for the speculative house-building industry.

Structure of the house-building industry

The house building industry is a complex socio-technical system made up of many actors (developers, builders, financial institutions, suppliers, technical consultants and local authorities) who both act together and constrain each other's actions. These relationships can slow the transfer of more innovative technologies and building designs (Ko, 2007). They can also slow organisational learning. The complexity of the system encourages path dependency, since the resources required to alter existing supply and construction chains are significant. Most house-builders will attempt to retain existing suppliers and building contractors to limit build cost and disruption. Thus, complex relationships between actors in the house-building industry are likely to slow the deployment of zero carbon homes.

House-builders have to coordinate a range of functional activities some of which are dealt with in-house (Figure 7.2). The standard model is that a house-builder designs, markets, raises finance, sources land, obtains planning permission for and manages the construction of new housing projects. Sub-contractors engaged by the house-builder provide labour, materials and equipment for construction. The more functions carried out in-house, the less complicated the construction process and the greater the ability of the house-builder to enforce higher energetic standards. However, altering the construction process will have significant resource implications for the house-builder.

In most instances sub-contractors will continue to play a role in the construction process. Thus, innovation is not only influenced by the competencies of the house-builder, but also by those of the sub-contractors working on a project. Of course the skills base varies. In continental Europe the skills base is much greater than in the UK and USA (Ball, 1999), which is likely to help enable the adoption of new LZC technologies and practices. New sub-contractors may emerge with the appropriate skills for low carbon construction.

However, it can be very difficult for new, more innovative and highly skilled entrants into the market to gain a foothold. Under these circumstances there is heavy reliance on existing sub-contractors to innovate offering new skills within the workforce and new technologies. This can limit innovation. In some rare instances larger firms may offer some support (e.g. offering training) to the sub-contractors to enable them to develop the skills and expertise needed to deliver zero carbon development. For example NCC (Sweden) provides training in environmental construction for sub-contractors and offers guidance on new LZC technologies for existing suppliers.

House-builders will also have to work with an additional group of players – the energy service providers – who can design, install, manage and

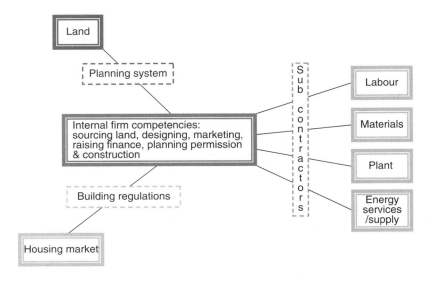

Figure 7.2 House-builders' functional activities.

Source: Adapted from Ball, 1999.

maintain LZC technological systems for zero carbon homes. New partnerships will help to overcome the skills deficit in this area amongst housebuilders. In the UK some concern has been expressed by energy service providers about house-builders' willingness and ability to effectively design, install and link up LZC technologies in individual units to wider community energy systems (Chapter 3). This again raises a whole set of new problems in terms of coordination and division of responsibilities between the housebuilder and the energy service companies.

The size of house-builder may also influence its ability to innovate. Larger house-builders may be at an advantage in delivering zero carbon homes. They have the resources to develop the energy modelling and design expertise in-house needed to deliver zero carbon homes. They can afford to trial more innovative construction techniques and technologies in model developments as well as provide training programmes to sub-contractors to raise their skills base. Larger house-builders can offer stability to suppliers through large-scale procurement, thus guaranteeing markets for new LZC technologies. Relationships with energy service providers may be easier to establish for large house-builders as they work on large or multiple projects. The economies of scale offered by large house-builders may give them the edge in innovation.

Yet a disproportionate fraction of effective innovation has been undertaken by small house-building companies (Lowe and Oreszczyn, 2008). It seems that the learning and innovation process in smaller companies can be more rapid because the feed-back mechanism on projects is more clearly established. Smaller companies involve fewer sub-contractors in delivery and thus they also have greater control over the quality of the finished product (Clarke, 2006). Also there appears to be less internal institutional resistance to change, there are fewer key actors to convince, less competition for resources and fewer vested interests all of which may work against the delivery of zero carbon homes. Smaller companies may also be more dependent on build quality to differentiate their product in a market. Thus technical aspects of design and construction are more important to smaller firms, whilst for larger firms the focus tends to be on management and cost control (Lowe and Oreszczyn, 2008). Overall the evidence shows that both large and small house-builders are equally able to deliver zero carbon homes, but the capacity-building process could take time.

Practices in the house-building industry

Housing emerges from the complex interaction of 'engineering practices, production process technologies, product characteristics, skills and procedures, ways of handling relevant artefacts and persons, ways of defining problems; all of them embedded in institutions and infrastructures' (Geels, 2002) . These practices can create path dependencies and lock-in for various technologies. Here we consider four key practices which influence the house-builder's ability to deliver zero carbon homes.

Supply chains

House-builders have reported different levels of difficulty in establishing supply chains for low energy, zero carbon, passive house and zero-net energy houses in Europe and the USA. In Germany and Sweden supply chains for low energy houses are already established and limited changes to supply chains would be needed to deliver passive houses in Sweden and Germany (Sven Berg, 2009; Hellman, 2009; Linden, 2009; Vogler, 2009; Grahl). In contrast significant changes to supply chains in the USA and UK would be needed to deliver zero carbon and zero-net energy homes (Stenftenagel and Klebl, 2010; Fox, 2010). In the UK, historically unambitious energetic standards for housing means that sustainable supply chains even for very low energy housing have not yet been established (Williams, 2008a). In America energetic standards for new housing have been significantly higher than in the UK for some time, thus supply chains for low energy housing are better established.

Both zero carbon and zero-net energy homes incorporate energy generating as well as energy efficiency technologies. This creates a significant departure from the existing supply chains. Thus, house-builders either need to help existing suppliers develop their capacity to deliver LZC technologies or establish relationships with new suppliers. Finding new suppliers of LZC technologies can be difficult due to lack of available information. Lists of accredited LZC technologies and suppliers do not currently exist. House-builders will need to allocate additional resources to develop new supply chains. Thus, developing new supply chains may be expensive and time consuming.

There is a tendency amongst house-builders to work with existing suppliers to develop new supply chains to deliver zero carbon homes. This can limit the technologies used and restrict product innovation. However, it can help suppliers to increase their capabilities and their market value, as highlighted by construction companies in Sweden and Germany (Hellman, 2009; Grahl, 2009). It may also shorten the lead time for introducing new technologies, as it removes the need for house-builders to establish new partnerships with new suppliers. Thus, retaining existing suppliers may reduce the cost of innovation.

Monopolies within supply chains or a limited number of suppliers can stifle innovation in the housing sector. For example the insulation industry held the German housing sector to ransom in 2006 after the introduction of loans for energetic refurbishment and energy price rises. The cost of insulation rose by 260%, but dropped again in 2007 as more suppliers entered the market (Vogler, 2009). Suppliers didn't believe there would be a long-term increase in demand for insulation, so didn't increase capacity. Thus supply was restricted and the price rose exponentially.

This experience clearly demonstrates that prices for LZC technologies may rise very quickly if there is a rapid move towards a mass market for zero carbon homes and a shortage of suppliers in the transition period. It also highlights the importance of providing certainty for suppliers to ensure new LZC technologies are affordable. Long-term procurement agreements can assist with this. In Sweden municipalities have supported the creation of supply chains for new LZC building technologies through procurement. They have guaranteed to buy a set number of technologies from suppliers, therefore enabling the supplier to invest in building capacity. Other approaches have been adopted in Sweden and Germany where regulation and fiscal policy have been used to increase supplier confidence (Chapter 9). Guaranteed markets for new LZC technologies, associated expertise and services can be provided by regulatory and fiscal frameworks.

Interestingly, supply chains can drive innovation within the house-building industry. In China access to cheap labour and rare earth metals means that Chinese production of PV cells and other LZC generating technologies has grown exponentially very recently. This has significantly reduced the cost of some LZC technologies. The Chinese government is now keen to deploy these technologies in the new mega-cities currently being built. Thus master-plans for new cities in China are beginning to adopt LZC design principles and technologies.

Accreditation systems and enforcement

Various accreditation systems for individual building components and some LZC technologies exist. However, LZC systems (rather than their component parts) need to be accredited. Evidence from the Swedish experience of building low energy and passive houses demonstrates this (Sven Berg, 2009; Hellman, 2009; Linden, 2009). Invariably LZC systems in Sweden have not achieved the energy efficiencies expected, because of incompatibilities between technologies or problems with assembly (Sven Berg, 2009; Hellman, 2009; Linden, 2009). The Swedish Institute for Technology has developed a system for accrediting some energy systems rather than component parts and the Swedish Passive House Institute is in the process of doing the same for passive houses.

In Germany, the component accreditation system has led to the deployment of a range of LZC technologies (e.g. solar panels, ground source heat pumps, heat recovery systems), but complete LZC systems are not effective. Combining some accredited LZC technologies has proved problematic. For example some house-builders have encountered problems when using co-generation technologies in energy efficient units

(Grahl, 2009). Combining the two technologies has led to over-heating. This highlights the need for whole system accreditation (rather than component accreditation).

It is very clear that LZC technologies are not effective in isolation. The efficiencies of the technologies used in a system; their compatibility with other technologies in the system; and how the system is assembled all influence the quantity of energy consumed and CO^2 produced by the system during operation. Accrediting individual technologies to be used in a zero carbon home therefore does not provide a good indication of how they will work together as an energy system. Thus, it is important that whole systems are accredited rather than individual technologies.

A further problem highlighted by German house-builders is that many LZC technologies used in model projects (passive and energy plus houses) are not accredited and thus cannot be used in mainstream house-building (Grahl, 2009). The accreditation process is lengthy and slows the rate of deployment. Thus, this is a major barrier to innovation. It is important that the accreditation process is speeded up to avoid delays in the deployment of new technologies. Without accreditation, regulators cannot advise or require that producers use new LZC technical systems, which slows deployment. Accreditation will also help suppliers to raise the finance to invest in expanding capacity to deliver systems to a growing market and generate demand.

The enforcement of energetic standards is also an issue in Europe and the USA. Pre-production simulation models can be used to calculate the energetic efficiencies of various systems. This is supposed to reduce problems of post-construction monitoring. Permission to build is based on these pre-production models. Unfortunately the predictions made by the models are often incorrect and energy efficiencies are significantly lower than predicted (as demonstrated by Hammarby and B001 developments). The inaccuracies in the calculations may in part emanate from the theoretical models themselves, but they also result from shortcomings in site assembly (Sven Berg, 2009; Linden, 2009) or wider contextual factors (including climate, existing infrastructure, construction technique).

On-site, post-construction monitoring also appears to be fraught with problems. For example house-builders in Sweden contract a third-party to certify their own developments. Questions have been raised about the impartiality of this approach (Sven Berg, 2009). Whilst in the UK building standards are enforced through government bodies, unfortunately most of them are lacking in the expertise needed to enforce high energetic standards (Lowe and Oreszczyn, 2008). Innovation encouraged by regulation will be introduced more effectively if systems rather than components are accredited; energetic models improve; impartial approaches to enforcement are adopted; and those enforcing the energetic standards are adequately equipped to determine compliance.

Construction processes

Construction methods vary from country to country. Levels of industrialisation in particular vary. In Germany, Sweden and the USA house-building is more industrialised than in the UK. In the UK brick and block masonry techniques have been used for centuries. This form of construction is unlikely to be conducive to achieving high energy efficiency standards. Modern methods of construction are needed to enable cost-effective technological transformation of housing. Central to this is the industrialisation of the housing industry through the process of prefabricating modules, systems, or components in factories. Once these elements have been prefabricated they are assembled on site.

Prefabrication enables greater quality control and higher energetic standards to be achieved (Ko and Fenner, 2007). Components and systems can be assembled and tested in factories before being sent out to sites. Prefabrication reduces the cost of construction, through the mass production of building components and shortening of supply chains (Jakob, 2006). It also shortens the development time-line which further reduces construction costs (Fawcett et al, 2005).

Prefabrication allowed rapid innovation and created the capacity to build low energy housing at scale in Sweden during the Miljonprogrammet. It also lowered the risk of the supply chains collapsing. Very industrialised building processes have been trialled in Sweden (e.g. Open-house, Malmo; NCC Concept Houses). Entire structures have been prefabricated. However, this method of production was not found to be cost effective The key issues were the cost of transporting large prefabricated elements and lack of adequate storage space for the elements.

In the UK industrialisation of the house-building industry has not occurred in part because of the scarcity of specialist sub-contractors able to construct prefabricated housing (Ball, 1996) and factories able to supply components/systems. House-builders in the UK are resistant to prefabricated housing for a number of reasons:

- lack of market demand for prefabricated homes,
- longevity and visual impact,
- issues with thermal mass and acoustics,
- and the risk of systemic failures (for example defects in a factory process might be reproduced in all components.

(SMARTLife, 2007)

Even in countries where the house-building process has been industrialised there have been concerns about the way components are assembled on-site. This in part is about the lack of appropriate expertise amongst sub-contractors involved in site assembly and in some cases their relaxed attitude towards assembly. For example, passive house construction is dependent on keeping construction materials dry during the construction process so as to reduce problems with moisture and mould in the finished product. Poor practice in assembling components on-site amongst sub-contractors in Sweden has led to growing problems with moisture (Sven Berg, 2009; Linden, 2009). This has led to a loss of confidence in passive houses amongst consumers, and is very damaging to the industry. It is crucial that project managers, contractors and labourers understand the importance of energetic efficiency and how to achieve it (Hellman, 2009).

In Sweden, a 'partnering model' has been developed which has helped to improve build quality (Sven Berg, 2009; Linden, 2009). The developer, project manager and sub-contractors work together in partnership on projects from the planning stage. The developer clearly conveys the objectives of the project (particularly those relating to energetic efficiency) to those working on it at an early stage and monitors implementation throughout the process. Thus, there is greater transparency during the construction process.

All the information about the construction process and materials used is available to the developer, project manager and sub-contractors. This reduces potential for the sub-contractors stinting on materials or build quality. However, the time pressure of getting to site means that the planning phase often runs parallel to the building phase, which makes it difficult to change the process once it has started (Sven Berg, 2009). Secondly the 'partnering model' relies on the developer having the expertise to indicate what is needed to the project manager and sub-contractors and to be able to ensure that it is implemented. This level of expertise is often lacking amongst developers (Sven Berg, 2009).

Partnerships between energy providers and house-builders in the construction process appear to be even more fraught with problems (Woodward, 2009). This has been demonstrated by pioneering zero carbon housing projects in the UK (Chapter 3). The key problem is that an effective energy system relies on the house-builder designing the site appropriately and building energy efficient dwellings as well as connecting to the wider energy network in an efficient manner. Yet house-builders lack the expertise to do this (Woodward, 2009).

Site assembly also influences the energy efficiency of systems. House-builders tend to focus on individual technologies rather than on how these technologies interact as a system either within the buildings or in conjunction with the wider infrastructure. House-builders often contact several different companies to install individual parts of systems, which can further undermine the effective operation of the whole system. Sub-contractors and labourers frequently lack the skills to deliver projects successfully (Woodward, 2009).

House-builders have a crucial role to play in the design and installation of energy systems, yet they don't have adequate expertise to do this successfully (Woodward, 2009). Nor in many cases do they have the motivation. The speculative house-builder tends to have a very short-term view of their responsibilities, whilst the energy provider (ESCO or utility) has a longer-term responsibility to deliver affordable energy effectively to residents (Woodward, 2009). This creates a tension between the actors and makes the partnership difficult.

Knowledge transfer and the skills gap

The house-building industry acts as a complex value chain, involving many agents and a number of different competence bases. Often the information needed to enable innovation is not communicated between these different agents which inhibits the use and development of new products and services (Halse, 2005).

One of the problems is the lack of feed back on building projects, particularly to sub-contractors and labourers working on-site. This lack of feedback is a major non-technical barrier to constructing innovative forms of housing. Information is not communicated within organisations themselves, let alone between agents in the supply and construction chains (Ørstavik et al, 2003). The creation of various positive feed-back loops between key players delivering zero carbon homes could help to improve implementation (Figure 7.3).

Strengthening the feedback between the developer, contractor and sub-contractors working on a project is essential when delivering more innovative forms of development. The developer can discuss and clarify the project objectives with the contractor to ensure that more innovative designs are produced and are effective. Contractors and sub-contractors can both feed back to the developer regarding problems they may encounter in delivering

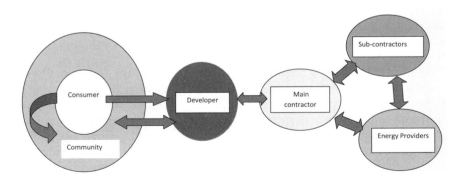

Figure 7.3 Positive feedback loops.

Source: Author's own.

more innovative projects and discuss potential solutions. Thus, feedback between contractors, sub-contractors and developers will help to determine the optimal models for delivering zero carbon homes.

Equally feedback between house-builders and energy providers working in partnership on zero carbon developments is essential. This helps both parties to determine the best designs, layouts and technological packages for delivering zero carbon developments cost effectively. Working together on projects helps developers, sub-contractors and energy providers to learn from each other as well as learn from the experience of building zero carbon projects. Creating positive feedback loops is therefore a valuable mechanism through which to learn meaningfully from innovative projects.

Feedback from the consumer to the developer and energy provider also helps to inform design and processes. Consumers are best placed to provide producers with a greater understanding of the problems encountered when living in zero carbon homes, which can help to inform future developments. This is fundamental in the processes of innovation and deployment. Consumer feedback also provides producers with information about potential markets and can help to generate local demand where projects are successful. Positive feedback loops can also be forged with the wider community.

Education levels in the industry are low (Ørstavik et al, 2003) which reduces innovation intensity. Technical innovation depends on infrastructure within the construction industry. Without the necessary skills and competence amongst those working in construction technological innovation won't break through (Halse, 2005). Programmes to encourage this transfer of knowledge between industrial actors have been operating in Sweden (organised by IVL) and Germany (organised by GdW). These are often provided by industrial organisations (e.g. GdW in Germany), government bodies (e.g. IVL in Sweden) and other organisations (e.g. passive house institutes in Sweden and Germany). However, experience shows that there are hard-to-reach groups (for example the skilled tradesman) who do not attend these programmes (Sven Berg, 2009). Experience from Germany and Sweden demonstrates a huge variation of expertise amongst companies and individuals in delivering LZC homes. This makes the dissemination of appropriate knowledge difficult. Nonetheless networks for dissemination of this sort are needed.

Various approaches to dissemination have been adopted. Larger companies adopt a more centralised approach to the dissemination of technical knowledge. More progressive companies (e.g. NCC Sweden) employ environment managers to champion environmental construction issues and co-ordinate technical training for all involved in the construction process (from project managers to labourers on-site). The environment manager involves all key players (from the construction and supply chain) in meetings to discuss new technological options for meeting energetic or carbon targets. This increases awareness of the possible LZC technologies available and raises interest in possible inclusion in the projects they are involved with. Yet even when such a proactive approach to raising awareness and developing appropriate skills within the workforce is adopted, there is still evidence that higher environmental standards aren't achieved in practice. Although the central team within larger companies may be very supportive of this approach in practice the regional offices are often less enthused. This can result in lower environmental standards being achieved on-site.

The 'partnering approach' (described earlier) allows a greater degree of feedback between those involved in the delivery of projects as well as the client and local community. These positive feedback loops enable all actors to learn from the process. This provides them with the expertise needed to replicate the model elsewhere. However, it is important that development teams stay together, or the knowledge capacity that has been built throughout the project may be lost.

Peer group learning is another approach to knowledge dissemination and training. In Sweden, municipalities facilitated knowledge transfer between peers in the construction industry (Chapter 5). Expert meetings to discuss technological and non-technological issues surrounding the delivery of innovative forms of low energy housing projects (Hammarby and B001) proved successful, as long as the focus of the discussion was a live project in which the actors were involved. However, there was limited evidence to suggest that lessons learnt from these projects were applied to future developments.

A third approach is for innovative house-builders to offer educational training or consultancy advice for developing zero carbon communities to others within the house-building industry. This approach is being adopted by the GEOS team (Chapter 5). The advantage of this model for the innovative house-builder is that it creates a revenue stream from dissemination, thus providing greater incentive for innovative developers to impart their knowledge to others. The consultancy option is also a more cost-effective approach for those house-builders without the capacity to train their staff.

Financing

There are additional costs associated with incorporating LZC technologies/infrastructure in new housing developments. These need to be financed by a house-builder or energy service provider and the additional cost passed on to the purchaser. Difficulties in house-builders securing finance for more innovative LZC energy systems in new developments have been highlighted in the UK and USA. Similar problems also face consumers trying to obtain mortgages for zero carbon homes.

For house-builders problems securing finance for LZC infrastructure appear to be due to a combination of factors. First, financial institutions are unwilling to finance infrastructure which in their experience adds no market value to properties. Second, they are concerned that house-builders will not have the skills or expertise to deliver LZC infrastructure effectively. Third, there is concern that in such a new market there is a danger of supply chains collapsing, rendering technologies obsolete and worthless. All create a risk for financial institutions and mean they are unwilling to invest in LZC infrastructure.

For the consumer it is difficult to obtain a green mortgage that values the operational cost savings of living in a zero carbon homes. Financial institutions do not incorporate operational costs into valuation of properties (NAHB, 2005). This stems from a lack of interest and appropriate expertise for valuing LZC infrastructure amongst financial institutions (NAHB, 2005). Financial institutions argue that the energy savings made by zero carbon homes are not significant enough to have a major impact on their valuation (NAHB, 2005). Of course the value placed on energy efficient and energy generating dwellings will increase as finite energy sources diminish and energy prices rise.

Financial savings can be made by providing energy systems at a community level rather than for individual units. However, financiers are resistant to investing in community energy infrastructure provided by house-builders (NAHB, 2005; Stenftenagel and Klebl, 2010). Resistance appears to be based on difficulties in evaluating the individual benefits of a community system for individual properties. Thus house-builders prefer to provide individual systems which can be appraised in terms of value for each housing unit (Fox, 2010).

Simple and accessible financing is critical for the deployment of LZC homes (Zero Carbon Hub, 2010). One solution could be for energy service companies (ESCOs) to finance, design, install, manage and maintain LZC infrastructure. ESCOs are in a better position than house-builders to provide LZC infrastructure in new developments as they have the capacity, experience and expertise required. If energy management contracts can be established for new developments, ESCOs will be able to recoup their costs from consumers and be commercially viable. Removing the link between LZC infrastructure and individual properties also enables the most cost-effective and resource-efficient community-wide LZC technologies to be introduced where these are more viable. A supportive regulatory and fiscal framework will be needed to encourage the emergence of more ESCOs.

Empowered niches

There are examples of house-builders in Europe and the USA who are adopting innovative approaches towards delivering LZC homes (Chapters 3 and 5). As yet these innovators have not created empowered niches which threaten the existing industrial regime. This is largely due to the degree of industrial resistance to change experienced in the house-building industry.

However, there is also very little at a macro-level to encourage industrial transformation.

The case studies highlight a few interesting examples that could eventually help to form empowered niches for zero carbon homes, if supported by the landscape (regulation and fiscal incentives, physical environment, institutional landscape, economic system and culture) in which they are embedded. These are the supplier model, ESCO model and the consultancy model.

Supplier model

For this model, the supplier of LZC technologies becomes the producer of zero carbon homes; thus companies that supply a key component of a zero carbon house (timber frame, steel sheeting, insulation, triple-glazed windows, PV cells, etc) become developers. This model increases demand for LZC technologies, thus increasing the value of the supply business. It also helps to guarantee demand.

Initially the supply arm of the business produces a revenue stream for the construction arm. Eventually this will reverse and the construction arm will provide guaranteed revenue for the supply arm of the business. The supplier model shortens the supply and construction chains, which could ultimately reduce build costs and barriers to knowledge transfer. It also creates a stable supply chain for key building components for zero carbon homes. Both should encourage wider deployment.

The supplier model was adopted by a couple of innovative companies in Malmö (Chapter 5). A timber company and steel manufacturer both began to build passive houses. Of course both suppliers had to expand their existing skills, which had an upfront cost. However, once the companies start to build at scale this cost can be recouped. This is more difficult in countries where new housing construction rates are low.

In contrast the potential for this model in a country where construction rates are high is far greater, for example in China. Suppliers of the component parts (e.g. PV cells) of zero carbon homes could profit greatly from becoming producers of zero carbon homes, not least because of the sheer scale of the build programme in China. This is further facilitated through a more industrial approach to house-building, an approach already adopted by the Chinese.

ESCO model

In the UK, Barratt Homes is partnering a series of energy companies (E-ON, EDF and Utilicom) in the construction of zero carbon developments (Chapter 3). The roles of both the house-builder and energy provider are clearly defined. The energy provider supplies LZC energy to a development, whilst the house-builder constructs highly energy efficient homes with connections to the LZC energy supply.

They work together to design the infrastructure needed to supply LZC energy to the development and develop the services needed for ongoing management and maintenance of this infrastructure. This approach optimises use of existing resources, experience and expertise in both industries. It also increases investor confidence in projects and reduces problems of obtaining finance.

To a large extent this model works well within the current industrial regime. It allows house-builders to retain a short-term involvement in the delivery of new communities. It passes the responsibility of the long-term operation of LZC energy systems to the energy provider and householder. The ESCO model also enables the cost of new LZC energy systems to be shared with the energy provider and house purchaser. It requires more limited expansion of skills amongst those house-builders constructing zero carbon homes and relies on the expertise of those already working within the energy industry to deliver the LZC energy systems.

The model is innovative in that house-builders have to work closely with energy providers to deliver LZC developments. However, it doesn't significantly alter the role of the house-builder or require that additional skills capacity is built. Thus a regime change is not required. However, it does require significant changes to the regime within the energy industry (Chapter 8).

The consultancy model

The GEOS development provides an example of the consultancy model. In this example, an innovative developer can create an empowered niche by offering support (providing guidance on designing, financing, project managing, constructing a zero carbon development) and training to other developers who wish to construct zero-net energy housing projects. Thus, by providing developers with the tools to build zero-net energy homes the GEOS team will assist in the wider deployment of zero-net communities.

Potential for replication and wider deployment is increased by limiting the number of technical models that are appropriate based on the local environment (built and natural), regulation and incentives. Thus, the consultant can develop technical models for a range of scenarios. However, if bespoke models are needed in each case, offering training becomes more difficult.

Dissemination and learning within peer groups has been shown to be a very successful approach to encouraging innovation. It could certainly help to encourage the deployment of zero carbon homes. However, it is unlikely to alter the regime in the house-building industry, unless regulatory (i.e. building regulations) or financial (i.e. energy prices) controls are used to provide a landscape in which zero carbon development could flourish. Market demand is still very limited currently and the transaction costs are too high.

Strategies for transformation

Overall changes are needed in the house-building industry to deliver zero carbon homes. At a macro-level the value placed on the energy efficiency of a home, reducing carbon emissions and energetic self-sufficiency by society will need to be addressed if industrial transformation is to be market driven. This could be encouraged through a significant increase in the price of carbon and fossil fuels. Equally, it could be driven by supply-side regulatory and fiscal interventions. A long-term regulatory framework is essential in order to provide industry with the security needed to invest in building the capacity to produce zero carbon homes. This framework should encourage house-builders to focus on build quality as a profit-making strategy.

The adjustments needed within the house-building industry itself to produce zero carbon homes are not revolutionary, as long as the house-builder focuses on the dwelling unit. The technological capacity is already available to build to low energy and passive house standard in a variety of climates. However, the development of appropriate expertise, alterations to supply chains, construction and accreditation processes are still needed to support the production of passive or low energy houses at scale.

It is clear that LZC technologies are not effective in isolation. The efficiencies of the technologies used in a system, their compatibility with other technologies in the system, and how the system is assembled all influence the quantity of energy consumed and CO_2 produced by the system during operation. Accrediting individual technologies to be used in a zero carbon home does not provide a good indication of how they will work together as an energy system. Thus, it is important that whole systems are accredited rather than individual technologies. This may lead to the formation of more multi-disciplinary companies.

Pre-production simulation models can be used to calculate the efficiencies of various systems. This is supposed to reduce problems of post-construction monitoring. However, there is evidence to suggest that in Europe and the USA, there are problems with model accuracy. Post-construction monitoring suggests that energy consumption and CO_2 emissions in practice are often significantly higher than predicted by the model. Of course differences in system assembly or wider contextual factors (including climate, existing infrastructure, construction techniques) may account for these disparities.

Perhaps these problems could be overcome by more accurate models (which take various contextual factors into account) and greater standardisation of assembly practices (for example ensuring passive houses are assembled in dry conditions). It is important that post-occupancy monitoring of systems is enforced initially to help to improve the accuracy of the pre-production models. It is also important that the accreditation process is speeded up to avoid delays in the deployment of new technologies. Without accreditation, regulators cannot advise or require producers to use new LZC technical systems, which slows deployment. Accreditation will also help suppliers to raise the finance to invest in expanding capacity to deliver systems to a growing market. It can also help to generate demand for new systems.

Enforcement of energetic standards by impartial, adequately skilled bodies is required. Lists of accredited systems and possibly suppliers of those systems could be helpful in establishing new supply chains. Long-term procurement agreements with low carbon systems suppliers will also provide them with the security they need to invest in production.

Adopting modern methods of construction should speed up innovation and enable higher energy efficiency standards to be achieved. Site assembly can be improved using the 'partnering model'. This also forms an excellent basis for the long-term improvement in the construction industries skills base. The 'partnering model' appears to be a more successful method for improving the skills base than non-project related training workshops and programmes.

Finally it is essential that the house-building and energy industries work in partnership to deliver zero carbon homes. The ESCO model overcomes a whole range of problems for house-builders, including their unwillingness to remain on-site post-construction, problems financing community LZC infrastructure and lack of adequate expertise to design, manage or maintain a LZC energy system.

Chapter 8

Transformation of the energy industry

Introduction

To deliver zero carbon homes it will be necessary to decarbonise the energy supply. This in turn will necessitate the transformation of the energy industry. Various technological approaches for decarbonising the energy supply have been discussed in earlier chapters. Here the macro-level factors influencing the transformation of the energy industry will be discussed. The cultural, structural and practice dimensions of the energy industry and how they affect the rate at which it can transform will be explored. The industrial regimes do vary between case study countries at least in part driven by the different contexts in which they are set. However, these differences begin to highlight the conditions needed to encourage decarbonisation. Finally, the ability of bespoke, decarbonised energy systems to scale up will be discussed.

The energy landscape

At a macro-level there is a range of factors positively and negatively influencing the decarbonisation of the energy supply. The key drivers for decarbonisation of the energy supply appear to be:

- depletion of fossil fuels (and escalating costs);
- national energy security;
- climate change;
- and the increase in the value of carbon.

These four factors in combination should eventually be sufficient to drive the radical transformation of the energy industry. However, there appears to be significant resistance to this change, which comes from within the industry, but which is also reinforced by the energy landscape.

At a macro-level growth in GDP is taken as a measure of development and advancement. Growth in GDP has been intrinsically linked with energy consumption, mainly fossil fuels. There is a degree to which some decoupling is beginning to occur between growth in GDP and energy consumption, owing to improvements in energy efficiency. However, as we become more affluent these limited savings are being off-set by an increase in individual consumption (i.e. the rebound effect). In addition, world population is growing and emerging new economies are placing increasing pressure on a dwindling fossil fuel supply. The problem with capitalism is it sets no environmental limits to economic growth and presumes an infinite supply of resources.

The low economic value placed on energy and carbon is a key barrier to industrial transformation. Energy has been relatively cheap over a prolonged period. Low energy prices have encouraged an inefficient use of energy as well as growth in consumption. This has been enabled because both nuclear and fossil fuels have been subsidised (by subsidies and tax incentives) over a prolonged period (Geller, 2003; Goldberg, 2000; GAO, 2000; Jochem, 2000). In contrast, there has been limited subsidy for renewable energy sector which has restricted its growth.

Meanwhile the European carbon trading system, designed to increase the value of carbon on world markets and assist in the decarbonisation of the energy supply in Europe, has also been less effective than expected (Convery and Redmond, 2007). Initially carbon quotas have been too generous and key carbon producing industries have not been included in the scheme. Thus, the value of carbon has risen very slowly and there has been little economic incentive to decarbonise the energy supply. Until the true cost of fossil fuel – economic, social and environmental – is internalised into its price, markets for low carbon energy will remain limited.

Increasing energy consumption can also create a significant barrier to the adoption of non-fossil fuel energy. There is currently insufficient capacity to generate adequate energy from renewable and nuclear sources to cater for global demand, although over time capacity can be developed. According to some there is sufficient solar energy potential to cater for global energy needs at least to 2100 (Rogner, 2000). Certainly Turkenburg (2000), Rogner (2000) Geller (2003) and Droege (2009) provide compelling evidence which suggests existing renewable energy sources could cater for current and future global energy needs if the infrastructure was developed. Nonetheless this should be combined with energy conservation measures.

Existing infrastructure and technologies also reinforce the use of fossil fuels (roads, cars, centralised energy supply networks and lack of storage capacity for renewable energy). Huge investment will be required to rebuild existing and build future infrastructural systems to enable the decarbonisation of the energy supply using decentralisation, substitution and co/tri-generation strategies. This creates a barrier to industrial transformation.

The local environmental context (built and natural environment) can also influence the viability of decarbonising energy systems in specific locations. Climate directly influences the quantity of energy consumed by households and it can also influence the type of energy available. The local availability of energy sources influences the energy mix. The relief and geology of an area will influence its natural storage capacity for energy produced from renewable resources. Thus the local natural environment influences the energy industry's ability to decarbonise (Chapter 10). The local built environment also influences the types of LZC energy systems that can be used. Population size, mixture of uses, density of development, height of buildings, orientation and shape of the urban area affects the integration of LZC energy systems into the urban fabric. It also influences the availability of local energy resources including solar radiation, waste and wind (Chapter 10).

The institutional landscape also affects the decarbonisation of energy supply. The powerful institutions which comprise the fossil fuel industry create this resistance to transformation (Geller, 2003). They are a well-organised and very powerful lobby. They control the entry into the market of new players, services and products. Meanwhile, the renewable energy industry remains fragmented, with limited lobbying power. There also continues to be a lack of companies offering energy management and other support services needed for decarbonisation. Some players within the fossil fuel industry are developing their renewable capability. However the mining and processing industries producing fossil are very politically powerful, and see the renewable energy industry as a future competitor. Without any controls over the rate of fossil fuel extraction this is likely to remain the situation until fossil fuel supplies are depleted.

The current regulatory and fiscal framework is insufficient to encourage the expansion of the renewable energy industry. Subsidies offered to the renewable energy industry are insignificant in contrast with the finance available for the fossil fuel and nuclear industries (Geller, 2003). Without international regulation to control the rate of fossil fuel extraction and internalisation of the environmental cost of fossil fuels into their price on the market (i.e. carbon tax, emissions trading schemes, etc), these industries will find it difficult to compete. The key to transformation would be to encourage those in the fossil fuel industry to genuinely expand their interests and investment to renewable energy.

The culture of the energy industry

There is enormous cultural inertia regarding transformation in the energy industry. The priority of energy companies is to maximise profit (the focus is on optimisation rather than innovation). In most instances that is achieved by maximising rather than managing energy consumption. Energy companies are looking for the cheapest and most reliable source of energy to supply their customers. Centralised energy systems based on fossil fuels currently offer the most cost-effective means of supply and thus are preferred by energy companies. Some may see benefits in diversifying the services they offer (for example offering energy management services); however, many suggest this is resource-intensive and risky.

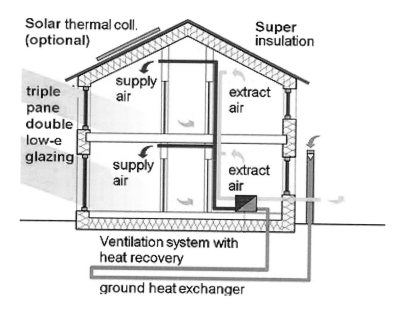

Figure 2.2 Principal features of passive house in cooler climates.

Source: Feist, Peper and Gorg, 2001.

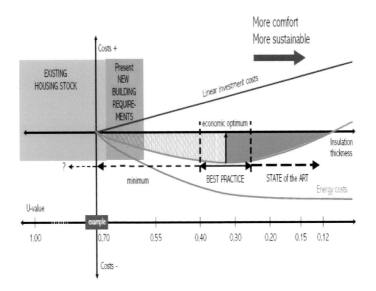

Figure 2.4 Defining the cost-optimum.

Source: Ecofys, 2006.

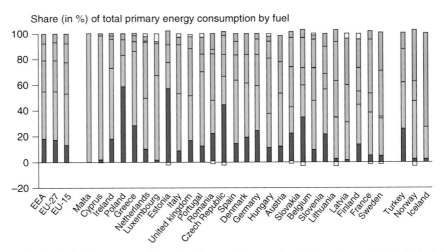

Share (in %) of total primary energy consumption by fuel

■ Coal and lignite ▫ Oil ▫ Gas ▪ Nuclear ▪ Renewables ▫ Imports-exports of electricity

Figure 2.7 Share of total primary energy consumption by fuel, by country in 2005.

Source: EEA, 2008 (based on figures from Eurostat and IEA).

Figure 5.4 View of B001.
Source: Author's photograph.

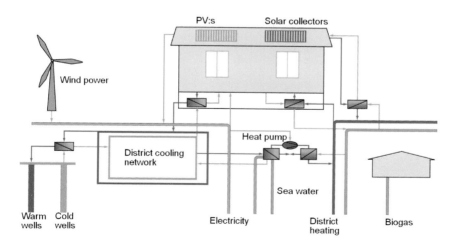

Figure 5.5 B001 energy system concept.
Source: E-ON, 2009.

Figure 5.6 Location of B001.[11]
Source: Photograph Lars Bygdemark.

Figure 5.9 Views of B001.
Source: Author's own.

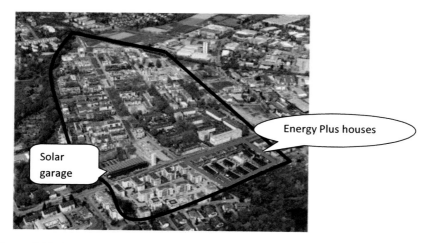

Figure 5.10 Location of Vauban district.

Source: Hans-Jörg Schwander, 2009.

Figure 5.11 Views of Vauban.

Source: Author's photograph.

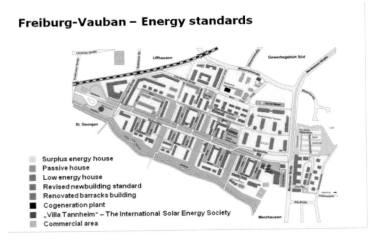

Freiburg-Vauban – Energy standards

- Surplus energy house
- Passive house
- Low energy house
- Revised newbuilding standard
- Renovated barracks building
- Cogeneration plant
- „Villa Tannheim" – The International Solar Energy Society
- Commercial area

Figure 5.12 Energetic standards in Vauban.
Source: Hans-Jörg Schwander.

Figure 5.15 GEOS Neighbourhood Plan.

Source: David Khan Associates, 2009.

Figure 5.16 Energy infrastructure in GEOS neighbourhood.

Source: David Khan Associates, 2009.

Figure 5.17 BedZED.

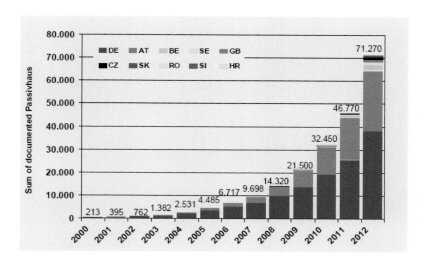

Figure 6.3 Passive house trends in 10 European countries.

Source: PASS-NET (2009) International passive house database.

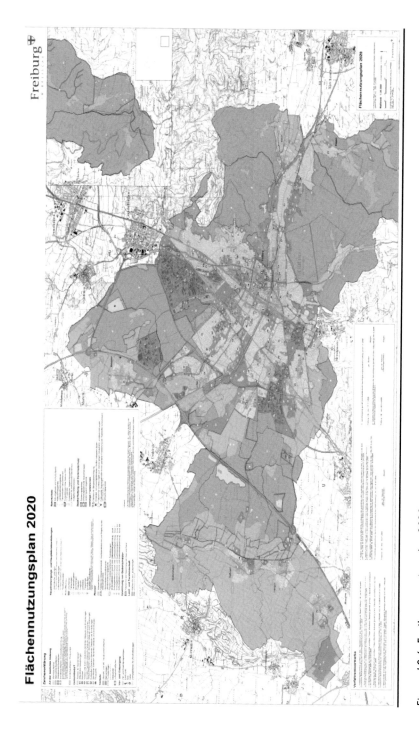

Figure 10.6 Freiburg zoning plan 2020.

Source: Freiburg's municipal planning department.

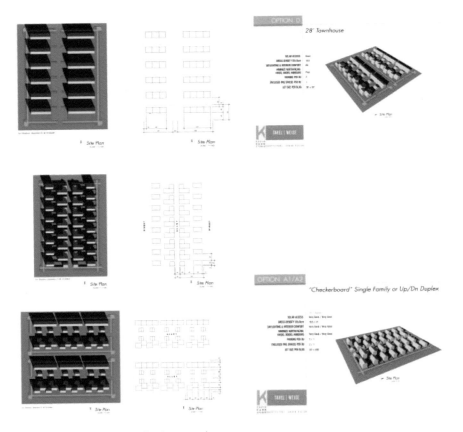

Figure 10.7 Designs to facilitate solar access.

Source: GEOS, 2010.

Four views in particular have predominated in the energy industry and have actively undermined the decarbonisation process. First, fossil fuel offers the only cost-effective and stable source of energy supply. Renewable energy is viewed as being too expensive, intermittent and unreliable. Nuclear power is expensive (particularly waste disposal and decommissioning) and publicly unpopular. Negative public opinion towards nuclear power in Germany resulted in the banning of further nuclear development for over two decades after the Chernobyl incident.

The second view held by many of those in the industry is that maximising supply is preeminent over managing energy quality and demand. Improvements in energy supply systems tend to increase consumption (and CO_2 emissions), as demonstrated by the smart grid in Colorado (Johnson, 2010). For most utilities profit is based on selling as much energy as possible. Only energy service companies (ESCOs) base their profit on minimising energy consumption. In many countries very few ESCOs currently exist. Subsidies and targets have been used to encourage energy providers to decarbonise the energy supply and offer energy efficiency measures for the home to their customers. This may eventually contribute to transforming the existing regime, but to date results are limited.

The third view is that economies of scale make centralised energy systems the most cost-effective. Decarbonising the energy supply is dependent in part on shifting towards a more decentralised system of production. This reduces transmission losses, enables the use of waste heat and the effective incorporation of many smaller LZC energy suppliers into the system. However there is resistance to this within the industry. Of course there will need to be a combination of decentralised and centralised approaches to the decarbonisation of the energy supply.

The energy industry also has a 'deficit view' of the consumer. The consumer is viewed as being ignorant, lazy, passive, disempowered, individualistic and self-interested; driven by the maximisation of personal utility and egoistic values (Devine-Wright, 2006). This means that energy systems are designed to minimise user – technology interaction. Consumers are involved only to a very limited extent in managing their energy consumption and supply. Of course with more decentralised, decarbonised energy systems there is likely to be greater consumer/citizen involvement in management of energy and possibly production. This runs counter to the current industrial culture, but is necessary to reduce energy consumption and carbon emissions long-term.

Structure of the energy industry

The structure of the energy industry is complex. The energy delivery chain breaks down into four key activities: generation, transmission, distribution and supply[1] (Figure 8.1).

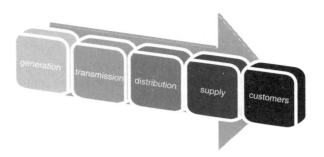

Figure 8.1 The energy delivery chain.

Source: Author's own.

The degree of centralisation in an energy system influences complexity. There are more players in decentralised energy systems and thus they are more complex. The number of players in a system will also be influenced by bundling of services and degree of monopolisation. For example where vertically integrated monopolies exist, the utility provides all business functions and there are no competitors. Here the industrial structure is simple.

In more competitive markets or where energy systems are decentralised, the structure becomes more complex. More players are involved in designing, installing and operating systems. Thus, there are a larger number of interactions and exchanges, which require greater coordination than in a centralised system operated by a single utility.

The introduction of LZC energy systems can potentially generate demand for a range of new services and spin-off industries. With the emergence of new LZC technologies (e.g. smart grid, microgenerating technologies, renewable energy storage facilities, etc) and practices (e.g. focus on energy management, decentralised energy systems, increasing consumer involvement) the institutional landscape is beginning to change and become more complex.

New players are beginning to emerge: installers of LZC and smart technologies, energy service companies, maintenance services for LZC technologies, LZC market research consultants, electric vehicle manufacturers, LZC designers, resource stewards, energy data managers and IT support services for smart grids. However, there is concern that there are not currently adequate support services to facilitate a rapid transformation of the existing energy systems.

In some countries this change in institutional landscape (and structure of the energy industry) is occurring very slowly. For example, there are very few energy service companies (ESCOs) in the UK[2]. This is creating a barrier to the introduction of district heating systems in cities and community energy systems in new housing developments. Thus new capacity within the energy industry needs to develop to support the introduction of decentralised LZC energy systems. In the UK this is being encouraged using regulation (i.e. mandatory CO_2 reduction targets, CERT) and financial incentives (i.e. heat incentive and feed-in tariff). Certainly stability in energy policy, regulation, financial incentives and significant public investment could help to encourage growth in new capacity in the energy industry.

Lack of information has also created problems in establishing supply chains for new LZC products and services. Suppliers find it difficult to obtain market information, which would enable them to assess the feasibility of investment. In some instances this is because the information has not been collected. In other instances utilities are controlling the release of that information. A major concern with the smart grid in Boulder is that the information collected by Xcel from customers about their consumption habits is not available to the wider energy industry. Without more knowledge of the markets, the LZC energy support services and technology suppliers will be slow to emerge. This will limit the adoption of LZC energy systems.

Decarbonisation can be affected by the degree of monopolisation and bundling of service functions within the energy industry. Four generic models have been postulated for the electricity industry (Table 8.1): vertically

Table 8.1 Four generic models of electricity industry infrastructure

	Vertically integrated monopoly	Unbundled monopoly	Unbundled limited competition	Unbundled full competition
Degree of utility control	The electricity utility controls and undertakes all business functions: generation, transmission, distribution, wholesale and retail energy supply and services	Generation is separated from all other functions: several generation companies serve distribution companies and, possibly, major industries	Generation is separated from natural monopoly functions: many generation companies servedistribution companies and, possibly, major industries through a competitive whole sale market	Generation, transmission and distribution functions are separated
Degree of competition	There is no competition at any level. Utilities have the obligation to serve customers within their own region	Generators and distributors maintain monopoly status: the generation company has the exclusive right to supply customers within its franchise area, and the distribution	There is competition at the wholesale level: primarily among generation companies and there may be some competition through the use of self-generation by large customers. But there is no competition at	There is competition among generators. There is complete competition at the whole sale and retail level. At the retail level, two new organisations supply electricity to

		companies have a monopoly to serve customers in their respective areas. Transmission is provided by generators, distributors, or a separate entity or entities	the retail level	end-use customers: independent retailers[1] and brokers[2]
Access to distribution/ transmission network	Controlled by monopoly	Controlled by monopoly	Generators have open access to the transmission and distribution grid	Generators have open access to the transmission and distribution grid
Regulation	Government regulates the utility to prevent monopoly abuse	Government regulates the monopolies to prevent monopoly abuse. Competition may occur at the generation level, but there is no competition at the retail level.	Government regulates the transmission and distribution system to prevent monopoly abuse	There is some regulation of the whole sale and retail markets to ensure a more efficiently operating market and to prevent abuse of market power. In addition, government regulates (or maintains ownership of) the monopoly transmission and distribution systems
Market	All customers in the region must buy energy from that utility	All customers in a region must buy energy from the retail utility which holds the franchise to their geographical area	Customers can choose supplier	Customers can choose supplier

Source: Adapted from Energy Futures Australia, 2004.

Notes
1 Independent retailers (who have no interest in the distribution 'wires' business) purchase electricity in bulk from the wholesale market and on sell to end-users.
2 Brokers provide a similar service without ever owning the electricity.

integrated monopoly, unbundled monopoly, unbundled limited competition and unbundled full competition (Energy Futures Australia, 2004). The greater the control a single company has over the transmission and distribution networks, the more control it has over the generators connecting to them. This can prevent generators of renewable energy from connecting to the grid.

This problem was encountered in Boulder, Colorado where a vertically integrated monopoly exists. Xcel energy controls and undertakes all aspects of the electricity supply process. There is no competition at any level in Boulder. The transmission and distribution networks are owned by Xcel and the company generates the energy which it supplies to households. Thus, other renewable energy companies cannot use the network to distribute their energy unless sanctioned by Xcel Energy.

For both monopolistic models regulation will be needed to encourage the creation of LZC energy systems. The Colorado state government has regulated Xcel Energy's activities using the Renewable Portfolio Standard (RPS). The RPS places requirements on Xcel to source 10% of its retail sales from renewable sources and 4% from solar energy (Amendment 47). This could encourage Xcel to allow other renewable energy generators greater access to the grid. It seems to have encouraged Xcel to build their own renewable generating capacity and to support decentralised solar energy generation by property owners/developers.

Similar problems also affected the city heating network in Malmö. A private utility now owns and controls access to the network, which has restricted access to generators of low carbon heat. In Sweden national subsidies and regulation are being used to encourage a switch to low carbon fuels for district heating systems. This should mean there is greater incentive to increase access to the heat grid for low carbon generators. However, in Malmö it has resulted in the private utility increasing its generating capacity, by building a biofuel plant.

Protected monopolies amongst utilities tend to restrict choice and innovation. In addition to restricting the connection of LZC generators to the grid, this model may also limit grid and customer information needed to co-ordinate a decentralised LZC system. Thus it excludes new players, particularly small-scale generators and edge of service providers, from entering the market.

More competitive models enable greater access to electricity and heat grids for LZC energy generators. This is essential for innovation and the decarbonisation of the energy system. For competitive models, the distribution network is provided by a third party (often government owned but could be a private company) and regulated by the government. Regulations can be used to optimise environmental (i.e. reducing carbon emissions) and social benefits (i.e. producing affordable clean energy) as well as economic return.

There are problems with the competitive models. Firstly there are technological difficulties with incorporating a large number of small, intermittent renewable energy generators into a distribution network. This can be improved through the use of smart grid technologies and by building in additional storage capacity in the system, but both are expensive. Secondly, there may be difficulties in financing distribution infrastructure. Creating new, more flexible distribution systems may be risky and will be expensive.

The municipal model adopted in Germany and Sweden has many advantages. Municipalities in both countries were originally responsible for the local supply of energy. Municipalities generated energy (particularly heat) and distributed it to households. They funded, managed and maintained the infrastructure. The revenue generated from the units sold to local residents and businesses was then used to reinvest in the energy system and the locality. One of the major benefits of this model is that social, environmental and economic objectives are balanced by a municipality, unlike a private company whose motivation is profit optimisation. Thus, a municipal energy company would be more inclined to consider using more expensive low carbon technologies to reach its environmental objectives than a private company.

Municipalities are also able to coordinate several resource systems (energy, water and waste) with development. This may help to enable the introduction of 'closed-loop' systems in new developments (e.g. Hammarby, Stockholm) thus enabling resource optimisation. Also if the energy infrastructure (i.e. the distribution network, smart grid and metering devices) is owned by the municipality, greater access for smaller energy generators to the distribution network can be facilitated and useful information (collected from the smart grid and metering devices) can be made available to edge of service providers.

Overall, the potential for innovation appears to be much greater if a municipal model is adopted. However, the capital costs for a municipality would be high. Of course these may be recouped long-term from the revenue generated by the system. However, in countries where municipalities do not have access to a large source of funds introducing this model would be problematic (for example the UK). Here partnerships between the municipality and utility to form ESCOs or even multi-utility service companies (MUSCOs) would be more appropriate (e.g. Thameswey Woking Borough Council's partnership body).

The structure of the energy industry affects its ability to transform and decarbonise. It needs to allow the entrance of new players (particularly renewable energy generators) and enable healthy competition between them. This requires that they have access to market information, distribution and transmission networks. The introduction of new technologies (i.e. smart and renewable energy technologies) in a decentralised LZC energy system will also require new support services to manage and maintain them. This will also affect the current structure of the industry. It is likely that the structure of the energy industry will become more complex and will require greater co-ordination as a result. A regulatory and fiscal framework can be used to encourage this transformation and provide some clear guidelines and certainty for new investors.

Practices in the energy industry

There are five industrial practices currently adopted by the energy sector which create barriers to the decarbonisation of the energy supply and the provision of zero carbon homes:

- the open system approach;
- focus on supply rather than managing demand;
- lack of maintenance support for decentralised energy systems;
- lack of partnerships with the house-building industry;
- the creation of the passive consumer.

Closing the loop

Ecological design demonstrates the benefits of the closed-loop approach to resource management (e.g. the Hammarby model, Stockholm). Most utility (water and energy) and waste systems are open. Thus, there are inputs into the system, processes which utilise these inputs and produce outputs. In an open system these outputs are lost as waste. Such a system is very inefficient. In a closed-loop energy system the outputs from one process become the inputs of another. The degree to which the system can be closed affects the efficient use of resources within it.

In addition to having multiple environmental benefits (Chapter 4), a closed-loop energy system should produce cost savings for utilities and waste authorities. The more efficient use of resources (water, energy and waste) reduces the operational costs for service providers. The use of waste heat and household waste to generate energy provides greater energy security and autonomy in a more volatile global fossil fuel context. It also provides comparatively cheap energy. The closed-loop system dramatically reduces the quantity of waste going to landfill, which can in turn reduce waste disposal charges (for municipalities and tax payers) and loss of valuable land for landfill. Configuring and installing closed-loop systems is likely to be fairly capital intensive (although it is hard to find data to confirm this), but the pay-back times will shorten as the value of energy, water and land increases. In the short term, closed-loop systems can also be supported through regulatory and fiscal instruments which increase the value of these resources (e.g. landfill tax, carbon tax, energy tax, mandatory carbon reduction targets, personal carbon allowances, planning, etc). An economic assessment of closed-loop systems based on whole-life costing is needed to determine cost-effectiveness.

Delivering the closed-loop system in Hammarby required the involvement of the utilities (energy and water), transport, planning and waste management authority in delivery. In Stockholm this was easy to co-ordinate because the municipality was responsible for all of these functions at the time the system was developed. In addition the municipality had the finances to invest in developing the closed-loop system. The Stockholm experience demonstrates the importance of the effective collaboration of several key actors in the delivery of the closed-loop system and the need for significant investment.

A closed-loop system would be difficult to develop through a partnership between the several private utilities. This is largely due to the fact that most utilities are single-interest organisations and do not have the expertise or the ability to coordinate resource provision across several sectors. It is also due to lack of willingness on the part of private sector to take the financial risk and innovate unless subsidised. The capital cost of a closed-loop system and difficulties coordinating actors from several industries to adopt a more holistic approach to energy, water supply, transport and waste management are likely to create barriers to the wider deployment of closed-loop systems.

However, the emergence of multi-utility service companies (MUSCOs), multi-interest organisations with a diversity of expertise and experience in service provision, could provide a suitable model to start to address this issue. In Sweden, the municipality acted as the MUSCO. However, there is no reason why a MUSCO should not be a private sector organisation working in partnership with a municipality to deliver closed-loop systems.

The scale at which systems operate effectively is a logistical issue which also deserves further study. It is unlikely that streets, neighbourhoods, or cities could produce sufficient waste (waste heat or organic waste for bio-digestion, biofuel or incineration) from their metabolic processes to be energetically self-sufficient. Greater efficiencies in these metabolic processes may be achieved with technological improvements which may assist in this. A more detailed investigation is needed to determine thresholds based on population size, socio-economic characteristics, density and mixture of uses for the successful operation of closed-loop systems.

Energy management

The introduction of decentralised energy systems, incorporation of renewable energy technologies into communities, and the need to reduce energy consumption, requires a new approach to energy provision, which focuses on managing consumption and quality of energy supplied. Energy service companies (ESCOs) are focused on the efficient delivery of local low-emission energy, offering a genuinely competitive and innovative alternative to the supply on demand model in the energy sector. ESCOs can offer a range of functions including: design, build, finance, operation and maintenance of installations in any combination.

The ESCO concept started in Europe over a century ago and moved to North America. In the last decade Europe has seen an increased interest in the provision of energy services. This has been driven by the restructuring of electricity and gas industries as well as the push to achieve sustainability targets. The market for energy efficiency services in Western Europe was estimated to be €150 million per annum in 2000, while the market potential was estimated to be €5 to €10 billion per annum (Bertoldi et al, 2003; Butson 1998). It is therefore unlikely that the market potential for ESCOs is currently being realised.

There is significant variation in the number of ESCOs in Europe and the USA. For example a survey of ESCO activity in Europe showed that there were approximately 20 ESCOs in the UK whilst in Germany there were 500–1,000 (Vine, 2003). This is largely due to the long-term financial incentives (capital grants and feed-in tariff) offered to ESCOs in Germany (Bertoldi et al, 2006). Lack of regulatory and financial support for ESCOs has stunted their growth in the UK. However, introduction of carbon reduction targets, renewable heat incentive, feed-in tariff and the emissions trading scheme should all help to create interest in the formation of ESCOs.

Maintenance and management of decentralised LZC infrastructure

One of the key concerns for consumers when considering decentralised LZC infrastructure is how it will be managed and maintained (ICARO, 2009; Williams, 2010). Utilities manage and maintain existing centralised energy systems, but the management and maintenance of decentralised energy systems (particularly LZC technologies that are embedded in buildings) is an issue for the energy industry. Various approaches have been taken: resident-led, developer-led and ESCO-led/utility-led models (Table 8.2).

Although three models have been depicted here there is of course a great deal more variation in reality. Nevertheless these three models span the key management and maintenance options. The resident-led model places the onus on households to maintain and manage their own LZC energy system. This has the benefit of aligning incentives, since residents benefit financially from the energy savings and energy produced. Their involvement in this process also raises their level of awareness of their own consumption patterns and helps to alter their energy consuming behaviour.

However, the transaction (time, money and effort) costs for many residents are too high (Williams, 2008a). They experience difficulties maintaining LZC technologies because of lack of availability in normal retail outlets and shortcomings in their own expertise (Williams, 2008a). They can also

Table 8.2 Management and maintenance models

Maintenance & management model	Description	Example	Advantages	Disadvantages
Resident-led	Resident maintains LZC technologies and manages energy consumption	Solar homes in California, Vauban in Freiburg	Aligned incentive – resident benefits financially directly from energy production and savings Resident learns from involvement in the process changing consumption behaviour	Residents lack expertise needed to maintain technologies Problems connecting to distribution networks Difficulties replacing technologies Time and effort required on part of the resident seen as a high transaction cost and limits public interest
Developer-led	Developer has an on going interest in the development - maintains LZC technologies and manages energy supply/consumption.	German housing companies	Overcomes transaction costs for residents associated with resident-led model and thus is more attractive to the market Providing management and maintenance services can generate additional revenue for the developer	Transaction costs high – operational costs, time, effort Lack expertise – need to build capacity Problems connecting to distribution networks Difficulties replacing technologies and establishing supply chains

	Description	Examples	Pros	Cons
ESCO/ utility-led	ESCO/utility manages energy supply/ consumption and maintains LZC technologies (probably designs and installs also)	Smart Grid Boulder, B001, Hammarby Model, Barratt Homes Model	In-house expertise and capacity to deliver services effectively Removes responsibility for residents and developers – increases market demand Greater investor confidence – less risky Additional revenue for ESCO/utility Help utility reach renewable energy/carbon reduction quotas	Investment risk Limits resident involvement – less potential for learning Limits customer choice of service provider Limits resident involvement – less potential for learning Additional cost for utility

experience difficulties connecting into distribution networks and obtaining payment from energy providers (Williams, 2010).

Developers are responsible for the ongoing management and maintenance of LZC infrastructure once a project is complete in a developer-led model. The developer charges residents for providing this service. In the case of the German housing company model the resident pays a 'warm rent' (i.e. the energy cost is included in the rental cost). If the housing company can increase the energy efficiency of the stock this increases their return. Thus there is an incentive to improve energy efficiency.

This model overcomes the transaction costs for residents associated with the resident-led model and thus is more attractive to consumers. Providing management and maintenance services can also generate additional revenue for the developer. However, transaction costs for the developer can be high. Also developers may lack the expertise to needed to manage and maintain LZC energy systems. Thus, delivering these services could require capacity building on the part of the developer which is expensive and time-consuming. Developers can also experience difficulties replacing technologies before supply chains are well developed. There is likely to be an investment risk involved in adopting this approach. The model also limits resident involvement in energy management, which reduces the potential for increasing energy literacy, when comparing it with the resident-led model.

The ESCO/utility-led model overcomes many of these problems. ESCOs and utilities already have the capacity to deliver energy management and LZC infrastructure maintenance services more easily than developers. It is a more popular model amongst residents and house-builders, removing the transaction costs for both groups. It produces a revenue stream for ESCOs and utilities. It can also help utilities to reach carbon reduction or renewable energy targets in situations where they are imposed. For ESCOs and utilities there is some risk associated with investment in these services without a supportive regulatory and fiscal framework. Lack of resident involvement in the case of both the developer-led and ESCO/ utility – led model is also unlikely to be as effective in improving energy literacy, without the provision of smart technologies.

Partnerships

The energy industry will need to form partnerships with other players to deliver a decarbonised energy system (Figure 8.2). The industry does not have the capacity, resources or experience to deliver all elements of a decarbonised system alone. For example energy service providers will need to work in partnership with water utilities and waste management services to deliver closed-loop energy systems (e.g. the Hammarby model). ESPs will need to team up with the IT industry and smart technology specialists to develop smart grids (e.g. Boulder smart grid). ESPs will need to work

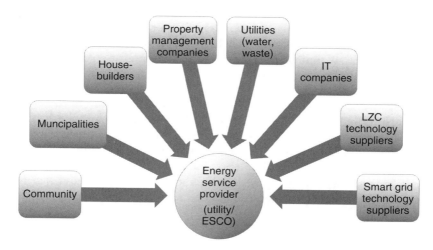

Figure 8.2 Partners for delivering low carbon energy systems.

Source: Author's own.

in partnership with house-builders (e.g. Barratt Homes), property management companies or communities to deliver zero carbon homes.

Working in partnership reduces the input required by any one organisation in delivering these complex systems. Thus experts can pool resources in delivering projects. Investment risks are reduced because the most expert organisations with experience in delivering specific products and services work in partnership rather than alone. Existing expertise and supply chains can be used more effectively, rather than building additional capacity. Markets for new products and services can also be reinforced through partnerships between key players through long-term procurement policy. Some of these partnerships are beginning to develop as demonstrated by the case studies including the Hammarby model, the Boulder smart grid model and the Barratt zero carbon home model.

Passive consumer

The energy industry currently tends to view the public as passive consumers – the deficit view. Energy systems are largely designed to minimise consumer involvement. However, some technologies which can be used to help decarbonise the energy supply (e.g. smart and micro-generating technologies) will require considerably more public involvement in their operation. For example consumers may be required to manage the quantity and quality of energy they are using. They can monitor and control their usage patterns, switch to LZC energy supplies or generate their own LZC energy.

If residents take a more proactive role in conserving and generating energy, research suggests that it raises their energy literacy and encourages pro-environmental behaviour (Chapter 11). It also helps to reduce public opposition (within the planning process) to the installation of energy systems, if residents are involved in the process of managing energy and understand the direct benefit to them.

This movement towards a more proactive role will require technological and institutional changes. User-friendly LZC technologies and the introduction of energy service companies to deal with the long term maintenance of technologies will be needed. User-friendly interfaces for managing energy consumption both online and in the home will be required. Significant cultural changes will also be required within the energy industry and society in some countries. This transition is discussed at length in Chapter 11.

Empowered niches

Various innovative examples of LZC energy systems have been developed (as demonstrated by the case studies) by a diversity of organisations, at variety of scales. Overall none as yet have challenged the current regime, but they do offer alternatives. The energy landscape does little to support the scaling-up of these innovative systems and the energy industry resists change. Thus, empowered niches have not as yet developed. However, there are various factors that have enabled innovation locally and could help to promote the wider deployment of LZC energy systems in the future.

Public involvement

Public or community ownership (or part ownership) of a utility is one factor that appears to impact on an institutions willingness to broaden its operational objectives to include environmental goals. Sydkraft[3] and Badenova[4] were/are both partially publicly owned and accordingly do not only seek to optimise profits, but to achieve environmental and social goals. This influences their willingness to take a risk developing LZC energy systems.

The closed-loop system (Hammarby model) demonstrates how the municipal model offers an extremely successful approach to delivering a LZC energy system. Municipal control over utilities and development enables better integration and coordination of infrastructure and services. The public ownership of the distribution system also offers potential for adaptation and inclusion of new energy generators. Thus, the municipal model offers great potential for more risky, innovative LZC energy systems.

From these examples we learn three things. First, the goals of the energy company are very influential in motivating innovation. Second, public involvement in an energy company (through municipal or community ownership, public ownership of shares) can broaden its objectives and operational agendas, thus enabling environmental innovation. Of course these outcomes could also be achieved through regulating private sector energy companies. However, close collaboration between service providers in the public and private sectors will be needed to deliver holistic and integrated energy systems regardless.

Commercial drivers

Commercial drivers have of course also led to innovation. It is no coincidence that innovative energy systems have tended to emerge in communities where there is greater market demand for green products and services (i.e. Stockholm, Freiburg, Boulder, etc). Under these conditions investment is less risky. It also provides a more favourable context in which companies can test new concepts and technologies before they roll them out elsewhere (as with smart grid in Boulder).

Green credentials can also help to raise the market value of energy companies. For example the systems implemented by Sydkraft, Badenova and Stockholm Energi were all developed at least partially in response to public opposition to nuclear power and fossil fuels. All three acknowledged the marketing potential of low carbon energy systems.

The new owners of these bespoke systems in Sweden (E-ON and Fortum) have recognised the marketing potential they offer, although neither appear to be keen to replicate the models elsewhere (largely for financial reasons). However, in real terms public demand for green tariffs in all case study countries appears low, yet market value of 'greener' energy companies is rising.

City marketing, regeneration and growth

Zero carbon could be used as a tool to market cities. Cities with innovative low carbon policies, infrastructure and neighbourhoods have become 'platforms for innovation' (e.g. Freiburg, Malmö, Boulder, Stockholm). These 'platforms' attract international funding, associated research institutions and industries. They also bring in those with relevant skills and expertise which helps to build capacity to deliver new infrastructure and associated services locally. Demonstration projects and conferences also draw international eco-tourists. This of course generates additional employment and revenue for cities.

For some cities becoming platforms for zero carbon innovation has helped to rebuild infrastructure and regenerate failing economies (e.g. Malmö). For others it has helped to reinforce their environmental credentials (e.g. Stockholm, Boulder), or to diversify economies through the growth of new innovative industries (e.g. Freiburg). Thus the deployment of bespoke zero carbon systems, projects and policies, could be linked to city marketing, regeneration and growth strategies.

Local links

Local links and well-developed feedback loops help to embed new socio-technical systems. Sydkraft, Stockholm Energi, Badenova and the Black Forest farmers all operate in a relatively small catchment area with strong links to the local community. This has helped to generate greater interest at a local level in the more innovative energy systems that have been developed by these providers.

The communities in each case have been able to give direct feedback to the energy providers concerning difficulties encountered when operating systems. This improves the operating efficiency of systems and ensures that they better match the context in which they are embedded and the purpose for which they have been developed. In some instances communities have in fact been involved in the design of the bespoke energy systems (e.g. Vauban, Freiburg) which has further reinforced their interest in ensuring its success.

Proximity of the consumer to the energy system increases visibility. The consumer can see and experience directly the benefits of their investment in green infrastructure, for example: lower energy costs, more comfortable living conditions, lower emissions, revenue and jobs generated by the energy systems and eco-tourism. Local social networks provide useful channels for promoting the wider adoption of zero carbon energy systems, if they are seen to be successful.

Transfer of expertise

Empowered niches may also be created through the transfer of expertise within the industry. The knowledge gained by those involved in the creation of bespoke low carbon energy systems can be transferred through training, consultancy or the transfer of personnel.

The transfer of the expert technical staff within the energy industry should help diffuse knowledge more widely. Indeed in some instances staff exchange programmes have been set up to encourage the cross-fertilisation of ideas particularly within international energy companies. However, even with specific mechanisms in place for knowledge transfer there is little evidence that it is taking place. Certainly it has not led to the wider deployment of similar systems.

This appears to be linked to inertia within the energy industry and the lack of a coherent framework promoting a shift towards decarbonised energy systems. Thus those controlling energy companies appear to have an entrenched view which perpetuates the centralised, fossil fuel-based deficit model of provision.

In some more extreme cases the bespoke low carbon energy systems bought by energy companies are being replaced with more carbon-hungry alternatives. In other instances energy companies maintain the low carbon energy systems they acquired, but almost view them as museum piece, to be used to boost their environmental credentials within the industry and amongst policy-makers.

Some innovations push against the industrial regime and energy land-scape, whilst others work within them. The latter find it easier to diffuse into mainstream practice. For example, decentralised renewable energy systems require that the regime and landscape alter for wider deployment to occur. In contrast the supply-side management of energy offered by the smart grid aligns with the industry's key focus on maximising energy consumption. Thus, the energy industry will find it easy to adopt some elements of the smart grid but not decentralised renewable energy systems.

Although thousands of people (including from the energy industry) flock to see the bespoke energy systems of Stockholm, Malmö and Freiburg every year, the existing regime has not been threatened. This is likely to remain the case until the wider landscape begins to enforce this change. This may be encouraged by a significant increase in cost of fossil fuel, mandatory car-bon targets, or an increase in the value of carbon. As with the house-build-ing industry, empowered LZC niches have not yet appeared in the energy industry.

Strategies for transformation of the energy industry

Greater changes will be required in the energy industry than the house-build-ing industry to deliver zero carbon homes, although both exhibit consider-able resistance to innovation. Currently the standard model for the energy industry is based on fossil fuels, largely centralised systems providing energy to passive consumers. In order for the industry to decarbonise it will need to move towards decentralised and centralised energy systems, based on LZC energy options, using smart grid technologies and with actively engaged consumers.

This requires fundamental changes at a macro-level (economic, infrastruc-tural, technological and cultural) and within the regime itself (in terms of culture, structure and practices). The low price of carbon, issues of infra-structural compatibility, problems with the technological reliability and lim-ited public willingness to be involved in managing energy consumption all create major barriers to transformation. To a large extent these problems could be overcome if fossil fuel extraction is limited and/ or fossil fuel price rises significantly. This would provide impetus within industry to find and fund efficient low carbon alternatives to current fossil-fuel based systems.

This would in turn require a restructuring of the energy industry and the creation of new energy service providers. Initially this may need to be under-pinned by a supportive regulatory and fiscal framework to allow the emer-gence of new players (ESCOs, MUSCOs, etc) in the industry. The underlying principles of the regime would also need to shift to focus towards energy quality and management. Fundamental changes in terms of infrastructure and delivery of services would also be required.

The regime transformation could be demand-driven, activated by public concern about environmental threats, energy security, or a rapid rise in the cost of fossil fuels. Or it could be supply-side driven by mandatory carbon targets, renewable energy targets, and or fossil fuel extraction quotas imposed on the energy industry. Currently there is no real evidence to suggest that the transformation of the energy industry will be driven from the grass-roots, through the formation of empowered niches. In fact this is highly improbable considering the current regime and landscape in which it sits. Radical policy instruments will be needed to encourage this transformation (Chapter 9).

Industrial strategies for delivering zero carbon homes

Transformation of both the energy and house-building industries will be needed to deliver zero carbon homes. The energy industry requires a wholesale change in its current regime in terms of culture, structure and practices. The changes in the house-building industry largely relate to changes in practice, although in some countries the intrinsic culture of the industry also needs to be addressed (e.g. the UK). Currently there is no evidence to suggest that empowered niches are forming in either industry which could bring about more fundamental regime changes, although isolated examples of good practice do exist.

Technical and societal transitions are needed to deliver zero carbon homes. In terms of technical transitions the adoption of modern construction methods, renewable energy, decentralised energy systems and smart grid technologies are crucial. In terms of societal transitions lack of demand for zero carbon homes and the role of the consumer in the management and generation of energy needs to be addressed. Regulatory, fiscal and educational instruments will be needed to encourage these transitions.

The degree of industrial transformation required does depend on the technological packages adopted (i.e. the combination of smart, renewable energy, energy management technologies) and the context in which the industries are set (i.e. differences in local resources, climate, infrastructure, supply chains). Generally technologies which fit within existing infrastructure and industrial cultural norms are least likely to meet with opposition (e.g. smart grids).

Context is also very important. For example if we compare the UK and Sweden we can see a huge difference in the degree of industrial transformation required in order to achieve zero carbon buildings. The Swedish energy supply is already relatively decarbonised and housing is built to very high energy efficiency standards. The modern construction techniques and materials currently used in Sweden mean that minimal changes within the industry would be needed to mass produce passive houses. The existence of decentralised heat networks and reliance on low carbon energy sources for electricity supply means that Swedish energy already has a low carbon content.

In contrast radical transformation of both the UK house-building and energy industries would be required to deliver zero carbon homes. The UK is heavily dependent on a fossil-fuelled, centralised energy system. Radical changes to the energy industry's current regime (culture, structure and practices) would be needed for a decarbonised energy system to emerge. Equally a regime change in UK house-building would be required to deliver passive house, let alone zero carbon homes.

A successful strategy for encouraging industrial transformation will need to create more certainty for investors and all those involved in the delivery of zero carbon systems (Figure 8.3). This can be achieved using a long-term regulatory and fiscal framework which supports the delivery of new technical systems, new entrants into the market, and should provide a return on investment (Chapter 9). The strategy will also need to build capacity in both industries to deliver these new technical systems. This will require that organisational learning is vastly improved, probably through the creation of effective feedback loops within industry and between industry and the

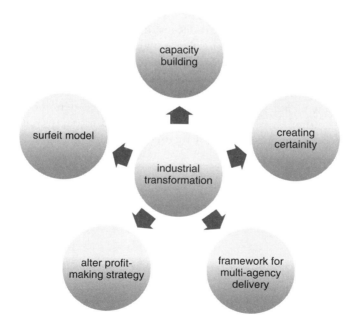

Figure 8.3 Components for industrial transformation.

Source: Author's own.

consumer. The institutional landscape will also need to better reflect the new technical systems. Partnerships between the house-building and energy industries will be important. The expansion of edge-of-service providers will also be required to install, operate, manage and maintain systems. These will need to be supported through a regulatory and fiscal framework.

The sheer complexity of this new institutional landscape required to deliver zero carbon homes will also need to be addressed. Coordination of these institutions will be essential to ensure that they work effectively together throughout the development and operational stages of the process. This could be a role for a municipality, private companies or a public-private partnership organisation. The coordination of multiple agencies for the delivery of zero carbon systems is critical for success.

The profit-making strategies of both industries will need to be modified for zero carbon homes (and zero carbon development per se) to scale up. The European model which places emphasis on the quality of housing and efficiency of the construction process provides a good example. Profit-making strategies should be based on the quality of the product or service and its wider societal benefits (i.e. environmental, social and economic) rather than on purely optimising utility. This could be encouraged through regulatory and fiscal frameworks.

Challenging both industries view of the consumer is also central to successful industrial transformation. The introduction of zero carbon homes as part of a wider decarbonised and decentralised energy system will require greater involvement of households in the maintenance of LZC technologies, management and possibly the production of energy, which challenges the deficit view of consumers held by the energy and house-building industries. Of course there are many consumers who will wish to limit their interaction with these new technical systems, however it should be incumbent on industry to deliver alternative options for those engaged, proactive citizens who are keen to be more responsible for their consumption (Chapter 11).

Chapter 9

Instruments for change

Introduction

It is apparent that zero carbon homes will not simply materialise without a supportive policy framework. Policy instruments are needed to encourage the transformation of the house-building and energy industries. Meanwhile policy instruments to encourage growth in market demand for zero carbon homes are also required. Such a framework will help to reduce risk of investing in zero carbon homes, as well as lower transaction costs for producers (house-builders and energy providers) and consumers.

Various policy instruments could be used to achieve this end. The instruments chosen will depend on the political approach adopted by those governing the system. This will for instance affect the extent to which governments rely on the private sector to instigate industrial transformation or public spending programmes. The type of policy instrument will also be determined by whether the aim is to tackle demand for or supply of zero carbon homes. This will be dependent on whether consumers or producers are expected to be those driving innovation.

The scale (i.e. international, national, or local) at which policy instruments are introduced is a further consideration. Instruments implemented at a local level offer an opportunity to test possible policy outcomes before they are rolled out more widely. They also offer tools that are more specifically designed for the context in which they are implemented. However the international nature of the environmental problems (resource depletion and global warming) and the energy industry suggests international policy instruments are also needed. The combination of instruments quotas, loans, building code, carbon tax, planning and so on used to deliver zero carbon homes is also critical.

Drawing on the experiences of the UK, USA, Germany and Sweden this chapter outlines key lessons for those designing policy instruments to encourage an increase in the demand for and supply of zero carbon homes.

A review of policy instruments

Before focusing on these lessons it would be useful to briefly review the key relevant policy instruments that have been adopted or trialled in the UK, Sweden, Germany and the USA (Table 9.1).

Carbon tax, quotas and trading systems, infrastructural levies, capital subsidies, public investment programmes, operational subsidies, product legislation, building codes and planning are all instruments that have been used to increase the carbon/energy efficiency of housing stock, decarbonise the energy supply and promote demand for zero carbon products and services.

Taxes

Carbon taxes introduced at a national level (e.g. Sweden) or local level (e.g. Boulder) can be used to internalise the economic cost of carbon into energy prices and signal the structural economic changes needed to move towards a low carbon economy. Carbon taxes can be used to encourage consumers to be more energy efficient, consume low carbon energy and live in zero carbon homes. Carbon taxes can also encourage energy producers to switch to low carbon energy sources to be competitive. For example, the Swedish carbon tax significantly increased the use of biofeul in district heating systems (Johansson, 2006).

Carbon taxes produce a revenue stream which can be used to encourage the wider deployment of LZC systems. To date the carbon tax in Boulder has been used to subsidise energy audits (residential energy audit and multi-family unit energy audit), grants for energy efficient lighting, weatherisation for low income households, and training programmes for builders in energy efficiency[1]. The revenue may also be used to help to overcome disparities created by the carbon tax. Tax revenue could be used to subsidise the construction of affordable zero carbon homes for lower income groups. For example, the Boulder Climate Smart Solar Grant Fund generated through carbon tax revenue subsidises the installation of PV and solar water heating technologies on housing for low to moderate income households.

Carbon tax as a tool for delivering zero carbon homes has strengths and weaknesses. In summary, the carbon tax assigns a value to carbon but leaves the quantity of CO_2 emissions undetermined. Thus, at first glance it may seem an inappropriate tool to attain a specified CO_2 reduction target. However, taxation produces revenue which can be reinvested in capacity building and infrastructure needed to produce carbon savings if it is hypothecated. Thus, where the short-term response to a carbon tax is relatively inelastic, recycling revenue can help to increase elasticity of the response in the longer term. Carbon taxes can be used to encourage decarbonisation through increasing energy price and thus decreasing the consumption of fossil fuels.

Table 9.1 Policy instruments overview

Tools	Scale of implementation	Change expected	Examples (from case studies)
Carbon tax	National / local	Provides consumers with incentive to consume LZC energy and homes. The revenue can be used to support the development of LZC alternatives	Sweden national carbon tax Boulder carbon tax
Infrastructure levy	Local	Development tax on new projects which can be used to develop community/regional LZC energy infrastructure where none exists	Proposed in the UK
Carbon quotas and trading for nation states	International	Encourages government to introduce policy instruments to develop LZC energy capacity – R&D, deployment programmes, etc	EU carbon quotas and carbon trading system
Fossil fuel depletion quota	International	Slows the depletion of fossil fuels and encourages extractors to invest in new energy sources	OPEC oil depletion quota
Carbon quotas for suppliers and generators of energy	International, national	Encourages the decarbonisation of energy supply – greater production and procurement of LZC energy amongst suppliers. May also encourage suppliers suppliers to form partnerships with new LZC energy producers within the community (e.g. households, businesses, etc)	EU carbon quotas for generators and suppliers; carbon emissions reduction target (CERT) UK
Renewable energy quotas	National	Encourage energy generators/suppliers to source percentage of their energy from renewable sources	UK, Swedish, Colorado quota systems
Municipal carbon quotas	Local	Increase municipal financial support for energy management services or formation of municipal ESCOs / MUSCOs.	Freiburg municipal carbon quotas; carbon reduction targets for local government in the UK; Boulder climate action plan and quotas

Table 9.1 Continued

Tools	Scale of implementation	Change expected	Examples (from case studies)
Personal carbon allowances	National	Encourages households to demand LZC homes and energy, and or to become involved in the production of LZC energy	UK trial
Capital subsidies	National, local, programmes	Encourages industry to invest in R&D, new infrastructure and technologies; reduces capital cost to consumer so can help to increase markets and encourage deployment of LZC infrastructure and homes	KfW loans (Germany); tax credits for installers of LZC technologies (USA); low carbon buildings programme and carbon challenge programme (UK); solar homes programme (California); Miljonprogrammet (Sweden);
Operational subsidies	National / local	Provides generators of LZC energy with incentive for generating	Feed-in tariff (Germany, California, UK); renewable heat incentive (UK)
Public investment programmes	National / local	Public investment in zero carbon infrastructure and LZC homes; subsidies for capacity building in industry to deliver zero carbon homes	Swedish and German district heating programmes
Legal requirement grid connection	National	Requires that all producers of renewable energy are connected to the grid	Feed-in law (Germany)
Product legislation	International	Product edit	EU legislation for energy efficient products / buildings
Zero carbon building code for new development	International and national	Removes need for market stimulus as building to zero carbon standard becomes mandatory	EU mandatory zero-net energy target for new build 2019; UK zero carbon building code 2016; zero-net energy by 2020 (California) Houses powered by non-fossil fuels by 2020 (Germany)

Ordinances	Local	Ensure the long-term resilience of an urban zero carbon system	Solar access ordinance (Boulder)
		Require the inclusion of renewable energy technology in new development or connection to LZC heat network	EEWärmeG (Germany)
Planning	Regional, local	Strategic co-ordination of resources and development, participative planning of LZC developments, zoning and codes to encourage LZC development, expediation of planning process for LZC development	Strategic co-ordination development and energy (Freiburg, Stockholm); participative planning for LZC neighbourhoods (Freiburg); Access ordinances (Colorado); fast-tracking LZC development (California)

Source: Author's own.

However, they may also stifle development if the costs of the alternative low carbon technical systems are too high. If applied to all consumers a carbon tax may also be regressive. Some provision must be made to support those who cannot afford to invest in energy efficiency measures of low carbon technologies.

Development tax can also be used to fund the creation of zero carbon systems. The UK community infrastructure levy (a development tax) requires developers to donate to a local fund for investment in community infrastructure. This can be used to support the installation of zero carbon infrastructure. The funds raised are collected by the local authority and can be invested in accordance with a local energy plan in a variety of infrastructures. A development tax could enable a more co-ordinated, local approach to the delivery of zero carbon infrastructure, potentially resulting in emission reductions from both new and existing stock.

Tax incentives can also be used to encourage the development of or demand for zero carbon homes. For example federal tax credits have been used to encourage the installation of renewable energy technologies in new and existing homes in the USA. This has encouraged existing home-owners and house-builders to install renewable technologies. In the UK stamp duty (a form of property tax) for zero carbon homes has been removed to encourage greater market interest. In LZC enterprise zones tax incentives can also be used to attract LZC producers involved in the delivery of zero carbon homes (Chapter 10).

Quota systems

Quota systems also operate at a range of scales and can be applied to energy producers and consumers. International carbon trading systems operate using quotas. The European emissions trading scheme (ETS) sets carbon quotas for producers of carbon emissions. It creates a market value for carbon and encourages producers to adopt low carbon systems. Potentially it will encourage the energy industry to decarbonise through a range of measures. It also encourages wider investment in low carbon energy alternatives. This should help to improve access to decarbonised energy systems.

Quota schemes with trading systems fix the quantity of CO_2 reductions. They are more flexible than taxation, because they allow the market to respond in a variety of ways to CO_2 emissions reduction. The quota system enables the market to find the cheapest solution for achieving targets, whilst avoiding adjustments for inflation or economic growth encountered when using taxes. The distributional consequences of quota systems can vary depending how permits for trading schemes are allocated. Over-supply of permits undermines the trading system and de-values carbon, as demonstrated by the European carbon trading system. Under-supply of tradable permits may also be damaging, as it could have significant impacts on the rate of development.

Fossil fuel depletion quotas (as described by Daly, 1974), for example OPEC oil depletion quotas, could be used to slow the rate at which fossil fuels are extracted. Introducing depletion quotas will reduce CO_2 emissions, whilst incentivising the energy industry and others to develop low carbon energy alternatives. It will encourage an increase in energy efficiency and fossil fuel substitution. Thus it should lead to a decarbonisation of the energy supply and possibly encourage the energy industry to invest in a range of zero carbon systems and products. However, it is likely to be extremely difficult to get international agreement on depletion quotas. It may also result in significant changes to the economy and the rate of development globally, unless managed effectively.

Carbon quotas specifically targeted at energy suppliers have also been introduced (e.g. carbon energy reduction targets adopted in the UK). These quotas support the decarbonisation of energy supply, by encouraging greater production and procurement of low carbon energy amongst suppliers. They shift the focus in industry towards energy management away from the maximisation of energy consumption. The quotas provide some support for the emergence of new players, particularly ESCOs, in the institutional landscape. The British experience suggests that the introduction of quotas could encourage existing suppliers to form partnerships with new low carbon energy producers within the community (e.g. households, businesses, etc). Quotas can also encourage house-builders to work with energy suppliers to develop LZC communities (e.g. Barratt Homes partnerships with E-ON, EDF and Utilicom).

Quotas to encourage the generation of renewable energy have also been introduced. The quota systems for the generation of renewable energy have operated in the UK (although recently withdrawn) and Sweden. Both countries have used this quantity-based instrument, which places obligations on suppliers to source a percentage of electricity from renewable energy sources. Parties not meeting their targets have to pay a penalty. Both British and Swedish systems have tended to support those technologies (and generators) that are closest to market maturity (Mitchell and Connor, 2004) which has limited their impact on innovation.

Municipal carbon quotas (e.g. Freiburg municipal carbon quotas, carbon reduction targets for local government in the UK, Boulder's carbon quotas) can also drive decarbonisation locally and may lead to the introduction of policies to encourage zero carbon development. Carbon quotas inform the local spatial plan, the provision of strategic infrastructure (including transport infrastructure), requirements placed on new development, policies for energetic refurbishment and planning decision-making processes. They also inform the municipal procurement policy. In some instances carbon quotas could drive the involvement of the municipality in the generation, supply and management of low carbon energy.

Personal carbon allowances (PCAs) are another form of individual quota. They have been piloted in the UK. Individuals are given a carbon allowance which can be traded between individuals depending on personal CO_2 emissions. However, the total CO_2 emissions from the population are capped. PCAs constrain in an economically efficient and fiscally progressive manner the 40–50% of UK CO_2 emitted by individuals (Roberts and Thumin, 2006). This approach works if the political system managing PCAs can maintain and tighten the cap on total emissions and individuals have access to opportunities to reduce CO_2 emissions. Early studies suggest that PCAs are more progressive than carbon tax, even if the revenue from the carbon tax is recycled to support those on lower incomes (Roberts and Thumin, 2006). PCAs could start to generate greater interest amongst the population in zero carbon homes and low carbon energy. This would help to drive markets and investment in both.

Subsidies

There are various capital and operational subsidies which have been used to encourage the decarbonisation of the energy system and building stock.

Capital subsidies – loans (e.g. KfW loans, Germany; Miljonprogrammet, Sweden) and grants (e.g. national and European subsidies to support the development of BOO1 and Hammarby; low carbon buildings programme, UK) – can be used to encourage industry to invest in research and development, capacity building or deployment of new infrastructure and technologies. They can also be introduced to reduce capital cost to the consumer of new zero carbon systems, thus increasing markets and deployment. Operational subsidies are also useful for encouraging the ongoing production of LZC energy (e.g. feed-in tariff Germany, California, UK; renewable heat incentive, UK).

Subsidies are available to the construction industry to help it to build existing capacity to enable the cost-effective provision of zero carbon technologies in new buildings (Solar Homes Programme, California; KfW loans, Germany; Carbon Challenge Programme, UK). Subsidies have been offered to households wishing to buy zero carbon homes or install and operate zero carbon technologies in their homes (e.g. Low Carbon Building Grants and removal of stamp duty for zero carbon homes in the UK). Subsidies have been made available to generators of renewable energy to help build system capacity (e.g. feed-in tariffs, renewable heat subsidies).

Subsidies facilitate behavioural change when a polluter (household, energy provider or house-builder) cannot afford to transform or if distributional issues make tax or similar measures unacceptable. Some subsidies can be expensive. For example grants (e.g. the UK Low Carbon Buildings Grants) are not directly repaid (although there may be financial benefits to the public purse resulting from these mitigation measures) and require funds to be raised through other forms of taxation. In contrast, government loans (e.g. in Germany the KfW loans programme) generate a revenue stream for government that can be re-invested into more decarbonisation projects.

Public investment programmes

There are no examples of public investment programmes for the deployment of zero carbon homes or energy systems in the case study countries. Potentially public housing and energy systems investment programmes could be used as a vehicle for the rapid deployment of zero carbon systems, a strategy currently being adopted in China. The nearest equivalent of this strategy was adopted for the deployment of urban district heating systems in Sweden and Germany.

Large-scale public investment programmes could help to overcome the market barriers encountered in the earlier stages of the deployment of LZC technical systems. However, it would be an expensive option certainly in the short term, although in the long term could significantly reduce the environmental cost of development. Public investment programmes would help to build the industrial capacity needed to deliver innovative technical systems at scale, thus reducing cost to the producer and consumer. It begins the process of large-scale infrastructural transformation that will ultimately be required as fossil fuel supplies run out.

Legislation

A legislative framework can provide certainty for producers of zero carbon products, systems and services. This helps producers to raise the finances needed to invest in innovation and deployment. It provides a road map for development. It encourages suppliers to build capacity to serve emerging markets; industry to build new supply chains, overcome path dependencies, and build appropriate skills and expertise for delivery. A legislative framework can also begin to break the stranglehold existing vested interests have over industrial production systems.

Thus, legislation can be used to change the landscape for zero carbon development and support the emergence of new industrial players to supply products, systems and services which have been hitherto restricted. For example, in Europe directives for improving the energy performance of buildings and products have been instrumental in changing industrial practices in member states. These directives have driven changes in national legislation and statutory instruments. They have led to innovation and the emergence of new players in the landscape.

International legislation is not subject to political change in the same way legislation can be in nation states. This provides greater certainty for those investing in innovation and building capacity for large-scale deployment of new systems. Of course national legislation is also important. For example national grid access laws (e.g. the German feed-in law requiring that all producers of renewable energy are connected to the grid) can also play a critical role in the decarbonisation of the energy supply. The problem with legislation is that it is absolute. It could create a problem by slowing down development when it is first introduced, at least until the industrial capacity has been built to deliver new LZC products, systems and services.

Building codes and ordinances

Building codes are a statutory instrument for delivering improvements in the performance of buildings. They may be applied at a national (e.g. UK) or state level (e.g. USA). A zero carbon building code (to be introduced in the UK in 2016) gives those in the housing and energy industries a clear target for achieving zero carbon development, thus reducing the investment risk and encouraging capacity building within the industry.

There is some discussion over whether these targets should be prescriptive or performance-based. The former provides the house-builder with a specification for zero carbon development, which could be helpful particularly in the early stages of systems development when the potential technological options are largely unknown by the industry. However, building codes of this type require constant updating as new technical systems are developed. Such an approach is also likely to be inappropriate for zero carbon systems, owing to the fact the optimal models vary greatly with the context in which they are embedded (as will be shown later in the book, Chapter 10).

The performance-based code provides some flexibility in terms of delivery, which overcomes this problem. However, it does not provide detailed information to house-builders about systems that can achieve zero carbon emissions. Thus, it requires that house-builders develop their own expertise in this area. It also necessitates that those enforcing the standard have adequate expertise or accurate models for calculating post-occupancy emissions.

In most countries building codes deal with energy performance rather than carbon emissions. There is a major issue about the fairness of imposing anything other than energy performance standards on a building, particularly when achieving zero carbon is likely to be dependent on the decarbonisation of the wider energy system. This part of the zero carbon system is something over which those constructing new buildings have very limited control. For example, the introduction of the EEWärmeG in Germany requires the inclusion of LZC technologies into new development or connection to LZC heating systems. This has been met with considerable opposition since access to LZC heat networks is limited and outside of the control of house-builders.

Local ordinances can also be used to impose restrictions on new development either to ensure the resilience of an existing low carbon system (e.g. solar access ordinance, Boulder), or to require the inclusion of certain LZC technologies into new development (e.g. solar ordinance, Barcelona). This approach is useful because it reflects the local variation required for the successful operation of a zero carbon system. Thus, requirements for solar technologies will only be placed on development in areas where it is applicable. Access ordinances are also very useful because they ensure that changes to urban form are compatible with, or enhance the performance of existing zero carbon systems (Chapter 10).

Planning

Planning is a more sophisticated and subtle tool for delivering zero carbon development. Spatial planning can be used to enable the strategic co-ordination of development with zero carbon energy systems (e.g. Freiburg and Stockholm). Participative planning can be used to help to encourage resident support for zero carbon systems (e.g. the Freiburg process) and build industrial capacity to deliver zero carbon systems (e.g. the Stockholm process). The development control process can also be manipulated to favour zero carbon development, for example by rapidly granting applications and shortening the development time-lines (e.g. fast-tracking zero-net energy development,

California). Planning is an instrument that can adapt to the context in which it operates. However, this very flexibility generates uncertainty in industry and increases risk of investing in building capacity for industrial actors. A full discussion of the role of planning in delivering zero carbon development can be found in the next chapter.

Moving from energy efficiency to zero carbon

For some time the focus of policy instruments has been on improving energy efficiency. More recently policy-makers have started to introduce instruments to encourage the decarbonisation of the energy supply. In order to move towards zero carbon homes both must be achieved. In the UK the introduction of the mandatory zero carbon homes target for 2016 has led to the implementation of a range of instruments tackling the energy efficiency of houses and the decarbonisation of the energy supply (Chapter 3). It has created some successful partnerships between house-builders and energy providers and led to innovative LZC housing models (Chapter 3). It has raised both the house-building and energy industries' awareness of the appropriate LZC technical systems available as well as approaches to constructing, integrating and managing those systems (Chapter 3). Thus it has provided the impetus within the house-building and energy industries to begin to build capacity to deliver zero carbon homes, albeit slowly.

The UK Government set the zero carbon standard during a period when the housing market was booming and it seemed entirely feasible that new zero carbon systems could be deployed as part of a major house-building programme (similar to the Miljonprogrammet). It was hoped that this approach would shift some of the cost of decarbonisation from energy companies (and their customers) to house-builders (and house-buyers and tenants). Unfortunately the global financial crisis dramatically affected house-building in the UK. It led to a virtual halt in development which in turn slowed the deployment of zero carbon homes. These circumstances have made it difficult to assess the effectiveness of the policy instruments introduced by the UK Government to support the introduction of zero carbon homes.

During its short existence the zero carbon target for housing has demonstrated several shortcomings as a policy instrument. First the definition used in the UK to describe zero carbon homes makes it a rather complex target to achieve (Chapter 3). It adopts a performance-based approach, which doesn't offer a clear and simple technological solution to delivering zero carbon homes for the house-building industry. However, it does give flexibility and enables the best technical system to be found for a particular context. It also allows for technological progress.

For suppliers this doesn't provide a clear steer about the technical systems they should invest in. For house-builders and regulators with limited expertise in this field this lack of clarity creates problems in translating, implementing and enforcing the zero carbon target in practice. Therefore introducing the target will have training, resource and supply chain implications. These are likely to significantly increase the cost of construction and enforcement in the short term. No doubt in the longer term the best technical options will become more apparent and the suppliers, house-builders and regulators will adapt accordingly.

The zero carbon target implies that it is the house-builders' responsibility to find acceptable solutions for achieving carbon neutrality. This may merely involve house-builders connecting new developments to existing LZC energy supply systems, but it many cases it will entail new developments producing LZC energy. This is rather beyond the scope of most existing house-builders, who do not have the capacity or long-term interest in generating energy, managing and maintaining systems on-site. Thus, it requires that house-builders work in partnership with utilities or ESCOs to deliver zero carbon homes (Chapters 7 and 8).

Although this has produced some very effective partnership models, there have also been conflicts between energy and house-building companies. These conflicts appear to have focused particularly around integrating systems, build quality and division of responsibilities for the on-going operation of systems (Chapter 3). No doubt these problems can be solved over the long term as a range of effective partnership models emerge from practice.

The UK zero carbon target has been without doubt the most demanding target, set globally. Using CO_2 emissions rather than kilowatt hours as a metric requires that house-builders not only consider the energy efficiency of units but also the decarbonisation of energy supply to those units when planning new developments. In contrast, house-builders in Europe and America have generally been encouraged to focus on improving the energy consumption (kilowatt hours) of new buildings (rather than reducing carbon emissions). The decarbonisation of energy supply (for which various targets have been set) is considered separately and deemed to be the responsibility of the energy industry. This separation of targets seems sensible. It assigns clearer roles to the house-building and energy industries commensurate with their expertise and capacity. It increases the technical and economic viability of tackling carbon emissions from new build development in all locations. It is also easier to enforce industry specific targets. However, it does seem to miss the opportunity to use building programmes to deploy new LZC technologies.

Setting a mandatory target to achieve zero carbon emissions in new development is technically feasible and eminently sensible, if we are serious about tackling carbon emissions. Going beyond energy efficiency measures towards generating LZC energy will be needed in order to generate adequate LZC energy for consumption needs in the future. Setting clear targets provides industry with a road map for change. It also provides security to those investing in building new capacity to deliver zero carbon development.

There will be a degree of friction whilst the most effective models for delivery are established; this may slow development for a period, but not long-term. Soon new players will emerge, new partnerships will evolve and existing suppliers will build their capacity to cater for new demand. However, the decarbonisation of the energy supply will need to be encouraged alongside a zero carbon policy for new development. This will enable new development on more marginal sites (particularly in urban areas due to financial or technical constraints for generating LZC energy on-site) and the decarbonisation of existing stock.

The importance of a combination approach

Innovation and diffusion theory suggests that a combination of regulatory and fiscal instruments is needed to successfully deploy new technologies within society (Foxon et al, 2005). A combination of statutory obligations, public investment and financial incentives are needed to encourage producers to invest in zero carbon technical systems and consumers to buy zero carbon homes (Figure 9.1). The type and mixture of policy instruments that are suitable will largely depend on how far they have penetrated the market. For example moving from demonstration projects to

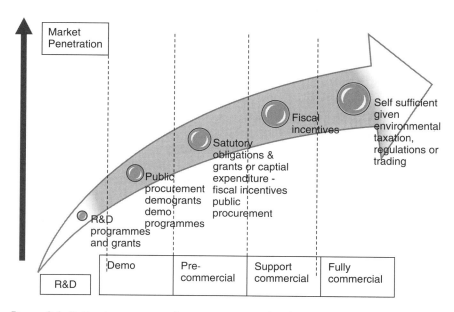

Figure 9.1 Policy instruments for encouraging the deployment of new technical systems.

Source: Foxon et al, 2005.

commercial systems will require the use of statutory obligations, fiscal incentives and public procurement. However, the phasing of these instruments is crucial.

Demonstration projects can be used to build capacity within industry to deliver zero carbon systems. These will need to be supported through grants and demonstration programmes. Demonstration projects can be used to test that zero carbon systems aren't technically flawed and are sufficiently compatible with existing technical systems, and that there is capacity within industry to produce them (at least on a small scale). To move into the precommercial phase will need the introduction of a statutory framework that requires the inclusion of zero carbon systems in new development, supported by financial subsidies. This should help producers in industry to begin to build supply chains and capacity to build at scale. Eventually, once zero carbon systems are commercially viable, the wider fiscal framework (e.g. though trading or taxation systems) could be altered to encourage the market saturation of zero carbon systems.

On the face of it a combination approach to delivering LZC housing forms has been adopted in the UK, Sweden, Germany and the USA. However, at a more detailed level each approach has been significantly different and resulted in a variation in deployment. Probably the most effective of the four approaches (in terms of the sheer number of units deployed) was that adopted in Sweden. Here the emphasis was on using statutory controls and subsidies to change the energetic standards of buildings nationally, through a demonstration programme.

The Swedish case

The Swedish Government imposed high energetic standards on new housing built during the Miljonprogrammet and offered subsidised loans to those building them to reduce their transaction costs (Chapter 3). This helped Swedish house-builders to develop their capacity to deliver units to the new energetic standard. Once the viability of new energetic systems had been tested through the Miljonprogrammet, the Swedish government introduced a new statutory obligation (through the national building code) requiring all new build development to be constructed to the same standard (without subsidy). This strategy provided house-builders with the certainty they needed, reducing investment risk, essential for encouraging change in industrial practices. The success of the Swedish approach was based on the combination and the phasing of interventions.

The German case

In Germany a similar approach towards raising the energetic standards of building stock, combining statutory obligations with subsidies, has been adopted. The mandatory energetic requirement for buildings (new and refurbished) has been steadily increased over time using the federal building code. Low interest (KfW) loans have been offered to individuals and housing companies to subsidise energetic refurbishment and low energy new build development. The Federal government also introduced an ecological tax, which helped to generate demand for more energy efficient buildings. This combination has proven rather successful (Chapter 3). However, recent increases in mandatory energetic standards (EnEV, 2009) have led to a slow-down in the take-up of the KfW loans. It seems that the economic and technical feasibility of delivering the higher energetic standards, at least currently, may be influencing the effectiveness of these instruments (Chapter 3).

The introduction of the EEWärmeG (2009) has further exacerbated the problem, by requiring that all new development incorporates renewable energy technologies or connects to a LZC heat network. Although Germany has invested in renewable energy for a long time, access to LZC heat networks is limited. Thus in most cases LZC technologies will need to be included in new buildings. Some financial support has been offered to non-commercial house-builders through the market incentive programme to deliver these new LZC technical systems, but no help for speculative house-builders is forthcomming. This has led to consternation amongst speculative builders who claim that cheap housing (demanded by consumers) cannot be delivered with so many constraints being placed on development (Chapters 3 and 7).

Subsidies could be used to encourage speculative house-builders (in addition to housing companies and individual home-owners) to include LZC technologies in new developments until capacity has been developed within the industry to deliver LZC technical systems (as with the Miljonprogrammet). The energy industry also needs to be encouraged to produce LZC heat network. This may be achieved by the introduction of the ordinance itself, since it guarentees demand for LZC heat for new development. However, it may require some addtional capital or operational susbisdies akin to those offered for LZC electricity, for example the renewable heat incentive introduced in the UK.

This case study also demonstrates the importance of a combination approach and phasing. Ideally susbisidised demonstration programmes for LZC systems are needed before statutory obligations for their inclusion are introduced. This will help industries to build their capacity to deliver LZC systems, developing technically and econmically feasible models for delivery. Fiscal incentives to stimulate this transformation in industry are likely to be needed until systems become commercially viable.

The UK case

In the UK a combination approach to the delivery of zero carbon homes was adopted. Initially there were two instruments used: the planning system and financial incentives offered to consumers to buy zero carbon homes. This combination proved largely unsuccessful (Chapter 3). There were many potential causes of the failure of this approach. There was no market awareness or demand for zero carbon homes thus offering stamp duty relief and green mortgages for a zero carbon home had limited effect. The planning system proved an ineffective tool for delivering zero carbon largely due to its low prioritisation within local planning authorities (Chapters 3 and 10).

The wider context in the UK was not conducive to the deployment of zero carbon homes. There was no LZC energy supply for new housing developments to connect to owing to a historic lack of investment in this sector. There were no incentives to support the emergence of smaller LZC energy producers or ESCOs (the feed-in tariff and renewable heat incentives were introduced much later). There were no subsidised house-building programmes to enable the house-building industry to develop its capacity to build to the zero carbon standard, or even low cost loans to reduce the build cost in the short term. Thus there were no real incentives to energy or housing producers to develop their capacity to achieve the zero carbon goal.

The statutory target set for 2016 provided a road map for innovation, but it didn't provide the practical means by which it could be achieved. To move from demonstration towards the pre-commercial phase of deployment would require greater public investment or subsidies. The focus also needed to shift from consumers towards the producers of the LZC systems since consumers could not drive the changes needed in infrastructural systems and industrial institutions needed to deliver zero carbon homes (Chapters 3 and 7). The UK example highlights the importance of public investment and subsidy when attempting to build the industrial capacity to deliver an ambitious target.

The California case

In contrast the Go Solar programme in California has relied almost entirely on fiscal incentives to encourage deployment (Chapter 3). A combination of capital subsidies (grants and tax rebates given directly to house-builders) and operational subsidy (the feed-in tariff given to households) have been used to encourage the transformation of the house-building industry and consumer demand for solar homes. In some locations planning instruments have also been used to encourage deployment in combination with fiscal incentives (e.g. San Diego). However, no statutory target to achieve zero-net energy homes has been set; only an aspirational target has been proposed for 2020.

Although the fiscal incentives have helped to generate some interest in solar homes, the market still remains very limited (Navigant Consulting, 2008). The transaction costs for the consumer and producer are still too high. Relying purely on subsidies to generate markets appears to be unrealistic. This example supports the argument that a combination approach is likely to be more successful. If the State of California set a statutory target for all new housing to be zero-net energy by 2020 (the approach adopted by Sweden), supported by existing capital and operational subsidies the producers would have more of an incentive to build their capacity to adopt new technical systems. Suppliers would have greater security when investing in new products, which would also eventually reduce the price. Producers and suppliers could operate at scale which would further reduce the cost of production and increase the affordability of zero-net energy homes. This would lead to wider deployment.

Summary

A long-term, mixed policy approach to the deployment of zero carbon systems is needed in order to reduce risks to industries investing in them. Statutory obligations are useful as they create certainty and highlight development pathways. However, if obligations are too demanding the effect may be to slow development, particularly in marginal markets. Subsidies provide some support to innovative producers of zero carbon systems in pre-commercial markets. They can be used to overcome the additional costs imposed on producers by new statutory obligations. However, subsidies alone cannot be used to deploy zero carbon systems. Supportive fiscal and legislative frameworks will be needed in combination to provide certainty for investors, producers and consumers alike.

Whom to target – the consumer or the producer?

The question as to whether policy instruments should tackle the supply (and therefore the producers) or demand (and therefore the consumers) for zero carbon homes is contested. Targeting the consumer is attractive since ultimately it is the consumer who benefits most from lower energy costs. Therefore, instruments that tackle the transaction costs facing the consumer when buying a zero carbon home improve marketability and thus their deployment.

Consumer-focused instruments

Currently in the UK and USA the transaction costs to the consumer when buying zero carbon or zero-net energy homes are high (Williams, 2010; Navigant Consulting, 2008). Both zero carbon and zero-net energy homes are more expensive in terms of capital cost (although financial savings can be made during operation). Studies repeatedly show that the additional cost of zero carbon and zero-net energy homes limits the market (Navigant Consulting, 2008; Williams, 2008a and 2010). This is the greatest barrier to deployment. Personal carbon allowances or carbon taxes could be used to drive this market by rationing individual carbon production, thereby increasing the economic value of zero carbon systems.

The pay-back periods for zero carbon systems tend to be long. This is a function of the capital cost, the financial savings made during operation and the revenue from any surplus energy generated from the zero carbon systems. Instruments which lower the capital cost, reduce the pay-back periods for the consumer and help to accelerate deployment. Capital cost can be reduced through the introduction of capital subsidies. Many options exist including grants (e.g. grants offered to consumers by the solar homes initiative California and solar roofs programme in Germany), low-cost loans (e.g. loans for energetic refurbishment and energy efficiency in new build offered by KfW Bank in Germany), tax incentives (tax credits offered to consumers installing LZC technologies in the USA and removal of stamp duty for those buying zero carbon properties in the UK). Operational subsidies (e.g. feed-in tariffs, renewable heat incentive, etc) can also be used to increase the revenue stream for those consumers producing energy in their zero carbon home. This helps to repay the capital costs of zero carbon systems more quickly.

The fluidity of the housing market contributes to wariness amongst consumers investing in zero carbon systems. The pay-back period for the system may be longer than the period of ownership in many instances. This would not be a problem if subsequent purchasers valued the benefits of living in a zero carbon home, and a higher market value could be achieved allowing the owner to recoup some or all of their costs. The problem is that property valuation does not tend to take this factor into account at the moment. Thus, new models for valuing properties that factor in the long-term financial benefits of installing zero carbon systems are needed. Attempts at this have been made in the form of green mortgages (adopted in the USA and UK).

Those living in zero carbon homes are also likely to encounter problems with connecting their zero carbon system to the grid. Problems for small producers of LZC energy connecting to the electricity grid have been highlighted in the UK[2] (Lipp, 2007; Ragwitz and Held, 2006), in Colorado (Reed, 2010) and California (Navigant Consulting, 2008). Smaller producers are often actively excluded from connecting to the grid. However, legislation can be used to require that producers are connected to the grid (as with the Feed-in law in Germany).

The planning system may also create a barrier to the installation of zero carbon systems in new and existing homes. Of course this can result in higher transaction costs for both consumers and producers. For consumers and producers tackling decisions made via the planning process can be time-consuming and expensive. This can create a significant barrier to the installation of zero carbon systems. It can be dealt with in a number of ways either by easing or removing planning restrictions for zero carbon systems (as in the UK for micro-generating technologies) or by introducing planning policies or ordinances that positively discriminate in favour of zero carbon development (Chapter 10).

Households living in zero carbon homes may also experience difficulties in maintaining and managing zero carbon systems. Lack of appropriate expertise and poor access to supply chains are the two key problems for households trying to manage zero carbon systems, as demonstrated by existing low carbon developments in the UK (Williams, 2008a). A legislative framework which encourages the emergence of energy service companies and increases the supply of zero carbon systems would help to overcome these problems. Product legislation (e.g. EU Directive for energy efficient appliances) and mandatory carbon reduction targets for energy suppliers (e.g. carbon emissions reduction targets for suppliers in the UK) would help to change the institutional and product landscape, thus delivering the technologies and services needed to support the operation of zero carbon homes.

Producer-focused instruments

Another approach is to tackle supply. In this scenario producers (i.e. housebuilders, energy companies, etc) are the innovators, rather than the consumers. Thus, producers adopt the new LZC technologies, systems and concepts, providing working models for society to experience. Producers will drive the deployment of zero carbon homes. Gradually zero carbon homes will become embedded in the technical, cultural and institutional landscape through a process of co-evolution.

The lack of willingness to instigate transformation within the energy and house-building industries means that one-off innovative projects or innovators are unlikely to form empowered niches producing a regime change (Chapters 7 and 8). The institutional resistance to this is too great. Without a supply of zero carbon homes, markets cannot develop. Thus a policy framework needs to focus on encouraging a regime change within both the energy and house-building industries (Chapters 7 and 8).

Fundamentally energy providers and house-builders see no financial advantage in providing zero carbon housing or energy supply. Transaction costs are high and profits are not guaranteed. For house-builders, designs that have been tried and tested successfully (in terms of market demand and getting smoothly through the planning process) are preferred. Product innovation will require expansion of existing capacity within companies (in terms of expertise, supply chains, etc). It will lengthen the development process and increase capital cost. Thus transaction costs are higher for zero carbon housing. In more conservative housing markets product innovation may also reduce demand, making it harder to secure investment for zero carbon developments.

One option is to offer direct subsidies to house-builders to install zero carbon technologies in new homes, to help to overcome the additional capital costs. Few examples of this exist. However, tax credits are offered to house-builders constructing zero-net energy homes in the USA. Grants are offered to house-builders in California through the solar home initiative to incorporate solar technologies and design into new housing developments (encouraging deployment of LZC technologies in 8,000 units). Subsidised loans are offered to housing companies in Germany for the construction of units built to higher energetic standards by the federally owned KfW Bank (affecting 600,000 housing units since 2006). All have demonstrated some degree of success, although deployment has been restricted.

Overall development cost for zero carbon homes can also be reduced by shortening the length of the planning process. Acceleration of the planning process for zero-net energy developments has been introduced in San Diego, with good results. An alternative to this would be to introduce differential processing period's dependent on the carbon impact of a development. Thus, applications for high carbon developments would be processed more slowly and low carbon developments more quickly.

Zoning ordinances can also be used to identify sites for zero carbon development. Thus, areas in which only zero carbon development will be accepted by the local planning authority can be identified. This provides house-builders with some certainty (although the market isn't guaranteed) as would building code. Building code has been used in Sweden to successfully increase the energy efficiency of the building stock for the past 40 years. Building code in combination with some form of financial incentive during the earlier stages of deployment is likely to be the most effective combination for delivering zero carbon homes.

To build zero carbon homes on a large scale will require the decarbonisation of the energy supply. This is more difficult to tackle and could require a combination of carbon quotas, carbon trading systems and fossil fuel extraction quotas to be introduced on a phased basis to drive the transformation of the energy industry. This combination could encourage those currently extracting or generating energy from fossil fuels to invest in alternative low carbon energy sources. This approach could bring about a rapid wholesale change in the industry and for the first time allow low carbon energy sources to compete with fossil fuels. However, it is very unlikely that international agreements which slow the rate of fossil fuel extraction for ecological reasons (rather than economic reasons as with OPEC) will be agreed.

Certainly international carbon quotas and trading systems can be used to increase the value of carbon, thus increasing the price of fossil fuels. This will encourage suppliers to seek alternative fuel supplies. Carbon quotas placed directly on suppliers (e.g. carbon emissions reduction target, UK) would also drive a change in practice. Energy suppliers would probably look for low carbon alternatives and manage customer consumption more effectively. This could also lead to the emergence of new players in the energy industry (i.e. generators of low carbon energy and energy service companies).

Subsidisation of low carbon energy sources can also increase their competitiveness against fossil fuels. Operational subsidies can be very effective. The main operational subsidies adopted are feed-in tariffs (operated in Germany, Spain, California and recently the UK) or quota systems (operated in Denmark, Sweden, USA and the UK). Feed-in tariffs in Europe have shown to be most effective in terms of increase in output for biogas and wind (Commission of the European Communities, 2008).

The feed-in tariff adopted in Germany appears have produced a rapid increase in generation of renewable energy. Since its modification in 2000 the feed-in tariff increased the share of electricity generated from renewable energy sources in Germany from 6.3% (2000) to over 14% (2007). Overall power generation from renewables grew by 141.5% in Germany, compared to 25.1% in the EU (Wüstenhagen and Bilharz, 2006). The cost of solar and wind energy declined by 30% and 60% respectively during this period (Wustenhagen and Bilharz, 2006) and Germany became the world's largest producer of PV electricity (39% of world capacity) and world's largest user of wind (AGEE-Stat/BMU).

Various studies suggest that the feed-in tariffs adopted in Spain and Germany have proved more successful than the quota systems adopted in the UK, Denmark and Sweden (Commission of the European Communities, 2008). In fact evidence from Denmark suggested that swapping from the feed-in tariff to the quota system significantly slowed growth in renewable energy generation (Lipp, 2007).

Targeting supply or demand?

Ideally a combination of approaches should be adopted to maximise deployment of zero carbon homes, mixing producer and consumer-led policies. Producer-led policies are needed to stimulate the fundamental changes needed within industry to ensure the supply of zero carbon homes. Supply needs to be established before a market can be created (Chapter 6). Consumer-led policies are needed to encourage an expansion of the market during the earlier stage of deployment, before zero carbon homes become fully commercial. They can also encourage households to use LZC technologies more effectively (Chapter 11).

The research demonstrates it is very unlikely that demand will transform supply (as tried in California with the solar homes programme).Thus consumer-led policies alone are unlikely to result in the rapid and widespread deployment of zero carbon homes. Producer-led policies could increase supply substantially and more rapidly. However, consumer-led policies are needed to tackle consumer preferences and behaviour, in order that a market for zero carbon homes develops and decentralised energy production becomes more culturally acceptable. Thus, the scale and pace of change required to deliver the carbon reductions needed to tackle climate change suggest that both producer and consumer-focused instruments are needed in combination.

At what scale?

Instruments can be applied internationally, nationally, or at a local level or indeed as part of a development programme. International or national policies or those applied to a development programme can provide a framework in which an industrial regime change can take place. However, local policy instruments can encourage the formation of industrial niches which eventually result in regime changes. A local approach can be particularly useful where other policy interventions (at an international, national programme level) have failed. The scale at which policies are most effective may vary with the scale of the problem or the scale at which the key players involved operate. The various benefits and pitfalls of introducing policy instruments at a range of scales are discussed here.

International policy instruments

The energy industry operates at an international level. Increasing carbon emissions, global warming and the depletion of fossil fuels are international problems. Thus, an international framework is needed to address the decarbonisation of the energy supply. The Kyoto Protocol did provide carbon reduction targets and quotas for those countries who are signatories. These were fed down to the nation states and translated into national policies and instruments for achieving them, tailored to the landscape in which they operated.

The Kyoto carbon reduction targets are currently being revised. Certainly there have been huge problems encountered during recent international negotiations (Copenhagen 2009 and Cancun 2010) concerning the setting of new targets (the Kyoto agreement ends in 2012). The aim of these negotiations was to ensure that more countries signed up to carbon reduction targets and that more ambitious targets were set. Indeed more countries have been included in the process, but as yet no legally binding carbon reduction targets have been reached.

The key barrier to achieving more ambitious targets appears to be a political concern that decarbonisation will result in a slowing of economic growth in both the developing and developed world. More ambitious legally binding international carbon reduction targets are essential for driving change in the energy industry, and for establishing a long-term framework for carbon pricing, but the political will to implement them is currently lacking.

International carbon pricing tools are also needed to encourage the decarbonisation of the global energy supply. Economic efficiency points to the advantages of a common global carbon price (Stern, 2006). However it will take some time for a global carbon-pricing scheme to become established (the Stern Review estimates 10–20 years). Certainly the European emissions trading scheme is beginning to raise the value of carbon, after a somewhat shaky start. Broadening the scope of trading schemes (for example to cover more sectors including aviation) will tend to lower costs and reduce volatility. Clarity and predictability about the future rules (including mandatory carbon targets) and shape of schemes will help to build confidence in a future carbon price (Stern, 2006).

International agreements for fossil fuel extraction would also help to drive a step change in the energy industry. It could encourage the energy industry to invest in fossil fuel alternatives. This would reduce the need for public investment (thus reducing the expense to the tax payer, whilst transferring the cost to the consumer) in building national renewable energy portfolios. This scale of investment should also mean that new technologies rapidly become more cost-effective. Of course the cost would be passed on to the consumer. Certainly OPEC countries have reached oil extraction agreements for economic reasons. To date similar agreements have not been established for ecological reasons. The powerful vested interests in the fossil fuel industry are unlikely to support the introduction of fossil fuel extraction quotas and it is doubtful that there would be sufficient political will in the short term to press for it, even though it would have significant environmental benefits and increase the longevity of the extraction industry.

International policy instruments are most likely to be effective in tackling global industries and global problems. Thus, international policy instruments would ideally drive the step changes needed within the energy industry to deliver a decarbonised energy supply. To apply policy instruments at this scale would hopefully avoid competition between nation states and 'race to the bottom' strategies. However difficulties in enforcing international policy instruments and in securing multi-lateral agreements, particularly for such politically unpopular agendas, means this option is unlikely to be acceptable. Unilateral attempts by nation states or international trading blocks (as in the European Union) to address decarbonisation appear to be the most feasible option currently.

National policy instruments

If the international regulatory framework is in place to encourage the decarbonisation of the energy supply and building stock, this should feed directly into national policy. The policy instruments used by a nation state to achieve the targets set at an international level will reflect the political, cultural and economic system in which they operate. Thus, a range of interventions might be adopted as demonstrated by the case studies. National policy instruments (including the carbon tax and building code introduced in Sweden; the ecological tax, feed-in tariff and feed-in law introduced in Germany) have proved very successful in encouraging the decarbonisation of energy supply and reduction in energy consumption.

Adopting policy instruments at a national level has several advantages. Firstly, where the international regulatory framework is weak, the nation state can take the lead in developing innovative policy instruments to encourage the deployment of LZC systems. Thus, nation states can act independently to create a landscape in which zero carbon systems can become commercially viable.

Secondly, it helps to ensure a more strategic and co-ordinated approach to the decarbonisation of energy supply and building stock. This has the benefit of enabling the implementation of more strategic solutions to decarbonisation. One example of this is the introduction of the federal fiscal stimuli for encouraging the development of a national smart grid in the USA (Chapter 4).

Thirdly, it reduces the problems of competition or Nimbyism created by localised policies. For example, when the planning process was used to deliver zero carbon homes in the UK it was found to be singularly unsuccessful (Chapters 3 and 10). Local areas competed with each other for development and were not inclined to place additional requirements on developers, less they lost out on opportunities for growth, provision of new community infrastructure or affordable homes.

Fourthly, national policy instruments also provide a degree of certainty for producers and investors. This produces economies of scale that cannot be achieved by applying policy instruments at a local level. Mandatory national energetic or carbon emission standards for buildings provide greater certainty for house-builders and lower the risk of investment in developing appropriate expertise and supply chains to deliver them (e.g. zero carbon standard in the UK and low energy standard in Germany). National subsidies for renewable energy (e.g. national capital and operational subsidies in Germany) have greatly increased capacity for generation (Chapters 7 and 9). Thus, national policy instruments should increase the speed at which industrial transformation takes place.

To an extent the importance of a supportive policy framework at a national level will be dependent on the size of the nation state in question. For countries the size of the UK, Germany and Sweden a national framework is appropriate. In the United States the sheer variation at a national level in climate, let alone the wider environmental, economic, cultural, political and institutional context, suggests that national policy instruments, apart from offering very strategic pointers for transformation (e.g. mandatory carbon reduction targets) would not be appropriate. However, these strategic pointers are essential if any kind of transformation is to occur, as reflected by the disparity in the energetic standards set for buildings between states in the USA.

Yet some flexibility in the standards set at a national level is crucial. Performance-based approaches allow for the variation in the local context which may influence the type of zero carbon system that is viable. However, national targets should prescribe the reduction in energy consumption or carbon emissions to be achieved by the system. Thus the most appropriate systems for a locality can be introduced, whilst the energy and carbon targets set nationally are achieved.

Imposing national standards may also prevent development in marginal markets and on marginal sites (as experienced in Germany when the Energieeinsparungsgesetz and EEWärmeG were introduced in 2009, Chapter 7), certainly in the short term before economies of scale have been established and the price of LZC systems have reduced. During this interim period subsidies for producers could be used to enable development on low-value sites and for low-value markets.

House-building programmes

House-building programmes provide a useful vehicle for the deployment of new technical systems. They can produce economies of scale, which could help the house-building industry to develop its capacity to build zero carbon homes, whilst reducing the cost of including LZC technological systems in new development. House-building programmes can also be focused in areas or during time periods when markets are buoyant. Thus embedding LZC systems in new housing should not slow development in marginal locations or markets. However, it is important that the lessons learnt from house-building programmes are used to inform future policy instruments. It is also essential that a clear framework for future technological progress is established. This provides a road map for the house-building industry and gives greater support for the process of industrial transformation.

The housing programme in Sweden certainly helped the house-building industry to innovate. It provided a risk-free opportunity for the innovators in industry to test new designs, technologies and building practices. It enabled the Swedish house-building industry to build its capacity to deliver highly energy efficient units at scale. It also provided suppliers with greater incentive to stock appropriate energy efficient technologies. The magnitude of the housing programme offered a considerable opportunity for the deployment of low energy technologies, which in turn helped to reduce the cost.

Imposing higher energetic standards on units built as part of the housing programme didn't lead to an overall reduction in construction rates. House-builders without the capacity to build low energy homes weren't prevented from building outside the programme. The programme did provide the Government with evidence that higher energetic standards were feasible. Thus, higher energetic standards were introduced into the national building code sometime later, once industrial capacity had developed sufficiently. However a clear pathway for technical progression was established. This provided the construction industry with adequate reason to transform.

Ironically, the lack of a technological road map for progression is now being blamed for the stagnation in the energy efficiency of buildings in Sweden (Chapters 3 and 7).

The solar homes programme in California highlights the perils of subsidising a housing programme, without any long-term regulatory framework to increase building standards in place (Chapters 3 and 7). The solar homes programme used public subsidies to encourage house-builders to construct solar homes. The programme helped house-builders to develop their capacity to construct solar homes. However, reports suggest that house-builders involved in the programme have faced significant transaction costs in constructing solar homes and connecting them to the grid. Certainly house-builders will not invest in solar homes without subsidy, as they are reportedly not commercially viable. However, it was demonstrated that had there been a plan to introduce a mandatory zero-net energy standard for new housing, then house-builders would of course adopt solar technologies regardless of whether they were economically viable in the short-term (NAHBRC, 2006).

Local policy instruments

Another option for policy-makers might be to introduce localised instruments to encourage the development of zero carbon homes. Policy-makers can encourage the delivery of low carbon housing or energy systems at a local level using regulation (i.e. building standards, planning control, localised carbon reduction and renewable energy generation targets), or by offering localised fiscal incentives (i.e. grants, loans or tax rebates). This approach allows policy makers to test instruments at a local level to determine their effectiveness and identify implementation issues.

The introduction of local policy instruments can help to build producer capacity to deliver zero carbon homes in a locality. However, they do not help to create economies of scale. Local instruments can also avoid the problems generated by national policy instruments of making more marginal sites redundant and slowing development in areas where demand is depressed. Local instruments allow variation in application depending on local circumstance.

Instruments focused at a local level can also be tailored to the local context. The local political system will determine which instruments are most appropriate. The willingness of local suppliers and producers to be involved in innovation and deployment will also influence the types of instruments used. Equally, the characteristics of local demand will influence the types of instrument that will be most successful in encouraging deployment. It could be argued that there is no blue-print for zero carbon housing, more a tool-box of possible technical options depending on the local context. Thus, a range of policy instruments – in fact a policy toolbox – to reflect the diversity of technical systems is needed.

Having a local focus can also benefit local communities. The introduction of zero carbon enterprise zones or even zero carbon districts could create centres of innovation. Zero carbon enterprise zones could generate new employment opportunities. They may help to attract other related industries and organisations to an area, thus creating innovation hubs (as in Freiburg). Potentially this could lead to the creation of further employment in related industries, including eco-tourism. Freiburg (Germany) and Boulder (USA) offer some interesting examples of where localised policy instruments (local building standards and local carbon tax) are being used to encourage the development of low energy, passive and zero-net energy housing.

Energetic standards in Freiburg

The City of Freiburg has been enforcing higher energetic standards in new development on municipal land or for units built by municipal housing companies for some time (Chapter 5). This has helped to inform the energetic standards set for new development by the latest zoning plan. In 2011 the city imposed passive house standard on all new housing developed by municipal housing companies or on municipal land. It imposed a low energy standard on development built on privately owned land. The city has had the courage to implement these targets because the demonstration projects built over recent decades proved it was possible. However, federal capital and operational subsidies (e.g. subsidised KfW loans; feed-in tariff; 100,000 solar roofs programme) have also helped.

Freiburg's experience has informed local instruments in other German cities (e.g. Frankfurt, Hannover, Hamburg, Munich, Ulm, etc) and nationally. Freiburg has demonstrated that building low energy, passive and energy-plus buildings is practically feasible with the right support. Nationally, the experience of these more pioneering cities has also informed federal instruments (for example the federal energy conservation ordinance).

The Freiburg case study demonstrates another important lesson. Municipal ownership of land, housing and energy companies has a very significant impact on the success of policy instruments. Cities can directly impose higher standards on new development built on municipally owned land. They can require that municipally owned construction companies build to higher energetic standards. They can compel municipally owned energy companies to decarbonise their energy supply. Thus, municipal involvement in regulating development, providing homes and energy services, gives municipalities greater leverage in delivering LZC communities.

It also enables the municipality to coordinate delivery more effectively. In this instance the introduction of municipal carbon budgets in combination with suitable planning instruments (e.g. zoning for LZC development, solar access ordinances, etc) may be sufficient to deliver zero carbon development. Of course strong (and ongoing) cross-party support for carbon reduction must be established if these more subtle instruments are to be used effectively.

When the private sector delivers housing and energy services (as is generally the case) a stricter regulatory regime is required (such as mandatory CO_2/renewable energy targets for energy producers and high energetic building standards) to deliver zero carbon homes. These regulatory instruments should be linked to financial incentives during the early stages of deployment. The municipality will act as the coordinator in the delivery of zero carbon homes, as well as the enforcer of building standards. The degree of control a municipality can exercise over a private energy company is limited unless the municipality owns the distribution infrastructure. In most instances the municipality can only exert pressure on energy companies through its role in procuring energy or controlling development.

Boulder's carbon tax

Local financial incentives – solar sales and tax rebates (Chapter 4) – have been successfully used to encourage consumers and house-builders to install solar technologies in new homes in Boulder either through direct tax rebates or climate smart solar grants. More recently, the introduction of a local carbon tax ('climate action plan tax') has increased the opportunity to raise funds for subsidising the introduction of LZC technologies into homes and businesses in Boulder.

The focus has been largely on improving the energy efficiency of existing housing stock, although climate smart loans have also encouraged the installation LZC technologies in new housing. Within Boulder $1.67 million of loan proceeds was invested in energy efficiency, $1.04 million in solar photovoltaics, and $0.19 million in solar water heaters. A preliminary analysis estimates that the projects generated by these loans will account for a significant reduction in carbon emissions annually (1,700 tonnes of CO_2) from Boulder's residential sector. Much more could be achieved if the tax levy was increased.

There has been local resistance to the 'carbon tax' particularly from businesses. They have threatened to move out of Boulder unless the tax is removed or dramatically reduced. Of course this threat concerns the municipality particularly if it affects local competitiveness. A further problem is the difficulties of enforcing and collecting the carbon tax. Boulder city doesn't have the resources to do this and has employed Xcel Energy to administer the system, which is a costly exercise. Thus, there are economic, political and administrative issues surrounding the implementation of a local carbon tax.

The subsidiarity principle

A range of policy instruments at a variety of scales are needed to deliver zero carbon homes. Ideally an international framework would provide the guidance, support and impetus for nation states to adopt suitable policy instruments to ensure the transformation of the house-building and energy industries to deliver zero carbon homes.

Nation states need to provide a policy framework that creates a clear road map for progress, whilst allowing for some local variation in how systems are delivered. Industrial capacity to deliver these new technical systems or the effectiveness of new policy instruments to produce this transformation can be tested locally or as part of new housing programmes. This limits impact on development.

However, these innovations adopted locally should be encouraged more widely through the national policy framework once demonstration programmes have proved successful. It is important that both short-term and long-term goals for development are clear, at all scales, in order to provide a road map for the energy and house-building industries.

Key lessons for policy

So what policy approach is most likely to encourage the successful and swift deployment of zero carbon homes? Various lessons can be learnt from the case studies. The need to reduce CO_2 emissions from the domestic sector is acute. The scale of industrial and market transformation required in most countries to move towards the widespread deployment of zero carbon homes is considerable and the pace of change to date has been exceedingly slow. Thus, an interventionist approach to deployment must be adopted.

A mandatory (performance-based) zero carbon target is useful for ensuring that new housing development contributes to an overall reduction in CO_2 emissions from the housing sector globally. It is technically and economically feasible to include LZC systems in new housing development and thus this target seems reasonable. However, some financial support may be needed to build capacity within the energy and house-building industries initially until cost-effective models have been established. In addition to the mandatory zero carbon target for new housing, a wider policy framework supporting improvements in the energetic efficiency of existing stock and decarbonisation of the energy supply will also be needed.

Using regulatory and fiscal instruments in combination appears to have been more successful in encouraging the deployment of LZC housing in the case study countries. Certainly providing a clear, long-term regulatory framework that progressively increases the statutory energetic/carbon reduction targets for housing and energy supply is essential. This will provide a roadmap for producers and reduce the risk associated in investing in expanding capacity to deliver new systems. The roadmap will need to be supported by fiscal instruments to transform industry and drive growth in demand for zero carbon homes in the pre-commercial phase. However, these can be phased out once models become commercially viable.

In the short term the producers (house-builders, utilities and ESCOs) must be the innovators, supplying zero carbon homes. Instruments directed at producers will be needed to encourage this innovation to occur (e.g. mandatory carbon reduction targets or renewable energy generation targets, mandatory zero carbon building standard, capital and operational subsidies). In the longer term instruments to support a growth in market demand will be needed (e.g. carbon tax, cap and trade system, capital subsidies and operational subsidies).

Ideally a regulatory and fiscal framework should be set up at an international level which encourages the decarbonisation of the energy supply (e.g. using mandatory carbon or fossil fuel extraction quotas, carbon pricing) and improvement in the carbon efficiency of the building stock (e.g. using international building code). Providing the landscape internationally which supports decarbonisation will bring about the most rapid regime changes in the house-building and energy industries. This international policy framework should feed into the national and local policy context. It should also offer the flexibility for nation states and localities to respond appropriately to the mandatory targets set, whilst reflecting the national and local context.

Without an international framework of this nature, innovative policy instruments introduced at a national, programme-based or local level will be needed to deliver a regime change. The advantage here is that progressive nation states and localities can act on reducing carbon emissions without international agreements. Many innovative policy instruments supporting decarbonisation have been introduced to date at a national or local level or as part of a development programme.

Testing policy instruments as part of development programmes or at a local level, provides an excellent opportunity to determine their likely impact and highlights practical implementation problems. This approach is useful for testing policy instruments before rolling them out nationally. However, the transferability of the results from local trials should be considered.

The contextual factors affecting the success of the policy instruments vary considerably at a local level. Thus developing policy instruments which are locally specific has its advantages. However, for widespread and speedier deployment of zero carbon systems, industrial regimes will need to be tackled at a national and international level. Otherwise as demonstrated by the case studies the impact of demonstration projects remains very limited.

There are a range of instruments which can be used to encourage deployment of zero carbon homes depending on the approach taken by policy-makers. To identify a list of the most successful policy instruments for delivering zero carbon homes (used to date) would be inappropriate. The best combination of policies will vary with context. It will also depend on the aims of the policy-maker, their general approach, the context in which they are operating and the nature of the industrial regimes they are dealing with. Thus, creating a tool box of policy instruments that can be applied in a range of circumstances is more appropriate (Chapter 12).

A spatial dimension

Introduction

Throughout history the pattern of settlement has been influenced by a variety of factors including climate, defence, access to trade and resources. Access to energy has been one of many factors affecting the geography of settlement. However, the globalisation of energy markets, the flexibility of fossil fuels and the centralisation of energy production in many countries has removed this spatial dimension. Energy is now accessible in all but the most remote locations, thus development is not inhibited by it. The scale of energy production has influenced urban form in that it has enabled cities to grow in size. The introduction of district heating systems has also influenced urban morphology. Higher development densities are maintained to ensure the economic viability of district heating systems. However, the impact of energy systems on urban morphology to date has been minimal in comparison with the impact of the automobile.

Movement towards the decarbonisation of the energy system is likely to have an impact on development patterns and urban morphology. Decarbonisation requires that we move towards the greater use of renewable energy and decentralised energy systems. Thus future development could need to locate where there is good access to a renewable energy supply and energy storage options. For example, a prime location for development might be one where there was an exceptional supply of wind and potential for pumped-hydro and compressed-air energy storage. Production of renewable energy in urban areas is likely to affect morphology. For example, cities reliant on solar energy are liable to be less dense, low rise and possibly aligned east–west, in order to maximise solar gain. Urban areas adopting closed-loop energy systems may be restricted in size by the quantity of waste they produce. Thus, if decarbonisation becomes a principle on which development is based, the geography of settlement and urban morphology are likely to change.

Spatial planning (at a national and international level) has a key role to play in the decarbonisation of the energy supply. Mapping renewable resources and potential distribution networks can help to inform both strategic resource and development plans. In the European Union renewable energy sources have been mapped and indeed some nation states have national resource as well as development plans (although by no means all). These more strategic plans can offer a framework for coordinating the development of renewable energy supplies with development. This could be very helpful when planning international infrastructure like the renewables super grid in Europe. However, the role of spatial planning in delivering a decarbonised energy supply at a national and international level is not the focus of this chapter. Instead it focuses on the role regional and local planning systems can play in delivering zero carbon homes.

At a regional and local level planning governs development patterns and urban form. Thus, planning can be used to encourage the development of renewable energy sources, the construction of low carbon development, connection of development to low carbon energy systems and identify locations for future development that can maximise the use of renewable energy sources. Development plans (local and regional) can be used to encourage the decarbonisation of energy supply and development. Planning instruments and the planning process itself can positively discriminate in favour of zero carbon development. Planners can also take a proactive role in bringing stakeholders together to discuss options and create partnerships to deliver zero carbon development and potentially innovation hubs.

The effectiveness of planning as a tool for delivering zero carbon development is contested (Williams, 2010). Issues with interpretation, competing priorities, lack of appropriate expertise amongst decision-makers and reliance on private producers to deliver innovative new development forms all impact on the ability of the planning system to effect such a major change. The role of planning in delivering zero carbon development may be enhanced in various ways, for example through the local ownership of land, energy or housing companies.

Potentially, the environmental, economic and social objectives of planning authorities can be balanced through the creation of innovation hubs. Economic growth can be based on environmental innovation. A local planning authority can offer development advantages to those planning to build zero carbon developments within their jurisdiction. Equally they can offer advantages to related zero carbon industries or businesses moving to the area (i.e. an enterprise zone for zero carbon industries/businesses). This can create jobs, develop expertise and networks within a local community which will enable local residents and businesses to be at the forefront of the zero carbon revolution in the future. Thus, planning's role in creating zero carbon innovation hubs has environmental, social and economic advantages.

A blue-print for zero carbon development doesn't exist. This is because approaches to decarbonising energy supply (and thus the technical systems) vary enormously with local context. Building code can be used effectively to deliver building-focused solutions. However, planning considers the wider local context, urban form (density, mixture of uses, orientation, relative building heights, settlement size), the energy infrastructure and resources available in the locality, and how a zero carbon development can link into this. Such an integrated approach will be essential for the delivery of zero carbon homes.

Some rudimentary planning tools are being developed to identify the best options for delivering zero carbon development given local circumstances (usually based on economic and technical variables). These tools provide a useful indicator for planners. However, they need significant development before they are sophisticated enough to provide an accurate portrayal of the range of options available. This chapter envisions the impact of achieving the 'zero carbon' principle on development patterns and urban form. It discusses the role planning can play in delivering this goal and how this role could be enhanced.

The geography of zero carbon development

Theoretically with the appropriate technologies, political support, regulatory framework and economic instruments zero carbon development could be built just about anywhere. However, in practice there is considerable spatial variation in the deployment of zero carbon technologies. This spatial variation results from the diversity of physical, economic, human capital, policy and regulatory contexts. Thus these are the factors that are likely to influence the geography of zero carbon development (Figure 10.1).

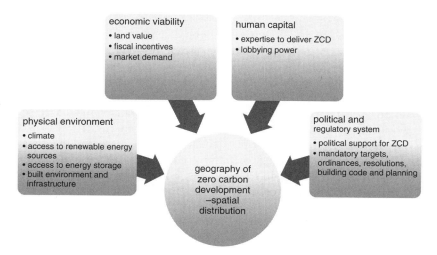

Figure 10.1 Factors influencing the geography of zero carbon development.
Source: Author's own.

The physical environment

The local climate affects the quantity of energy consumed by households. Climate varies with location. This influences the types of technical system adopted in different locations. There appears to have been earlier adoption of LZC energy systems in colder climates (e.g. Sweden) largely driven by the need to reduce energy costs and increase energy security. This has been achieved through a systemic improvement in energy efficiency (the introduction of district heating systems and higher energy efficiency standards in buildings) and the development of local renewable sources of energy. Those living in hot, dry climates are now seeking solutions to reduce energy consumption and diversify local energy supply.

The climate, topography, vegetation, relief, hydrology and geology influence the availability of LZC energy sources. Resource mapping exercises have been completed in Europe and the USA to determine areas for the future generation of renewable energy. These mapping exercises have in some instances been used to define national resource and development strategies. They have also been used to identify areas with poor access to LZC energy. Availability and access to resources will influence the technical systems adopted in any location.

For locations where there is an abundance of geothermal, tidal, wind or solar energy this will be relatively straightforward. Where the supply of renewable energy is restricted alternative technical systems will be needed. Here energy efficiency measures (passive house standard in buildings), recycling waste materials (creating closed-loop systems) and localised energy systems (district heating systems) could be used to decarbonise the energy supply without using renewable sources. Centrally generated renewable energy could provide an alternative option.

The availability of renewable energy storage options will also vary with location. The potential for using pumped-hydro and compressed air storage varies spatially. Pumped-hydro is better suited to more mountainous areas. Compressed air storage requires large underground caverns. Compressed-air and pumped-hydro storage are the most economically viable, large-scale, energy storage options. Thus, it seems for large-scale energy production, it is not only important that there is an adequate energy source but also that the local geology or relief is suited to compressed-air or pumped-hydro storage (as demonstrated in Colorado – Chapter 4). For smaller amounts of energy, other storage options (including hydrogen fuel cells and various types of battery) can also be used, which do not have a spatial restriction. However, they have various practical implementation problems[1].

The introduction of super grids (as described in Chapter 2) can help to overcome the spatial restriction created by resource and storage availability. For example, the European super grid will link the wind farms of North-western Europe and solar installations of Southern Europe and North Africa with pumped-hydro storage in Norway. This solution maximises European potential to produce and store renewable energy for the member states in the region. However, the significant geopolitical issues surrounding the formation of a super grid and the cost may limit this as an option for overcoming spatial differences. In addition, transmission losses over such a vast area would be significant.

Existing infrastructure and patterns of development also affect the implementation of LZC technical systems. In centralised electricity systems, electricity can be generated and distributed almost anywhere, as long as there is sufficient population to support the extension of a network. Essentially this means it is technically viable to deliver zero carbon electricity to all but the most remote and under-populated locations, although it may not be economically feasible.

In remote areas households can use autonomous technologies to generate electricity. In urban areas the use of autonomous technologies is limited by poor access to resources (solar and wind energy particularly) and planning restrictions (particularly in conservation areas). Here access to a LZC energy supply may be best facilitated through the existing centralised electricity system. This approach also enables significant reductions in carbon emissions from existing stock without the need for energetic refurbishment.

For many households heating is provided through a centralised, gas-based distribution system. However, decentralised heating and cooling systems are more energy efficient (Chapter 2). CO_2 reductions can be increased through the use of a low carbon energy supply (e.g. waste heat, biofuel, geothermal and solar energy). District heating/cooling systems are more economically and technically feasible in urban locations. But they are still expensive to retrofit and so heating provided by a LZC electricity supply may be more cost-effective. In low density areas passive housing, with the facility to generate electricity, provides a more economically viable option. The introduction of hydrogen fuel cells could enable zero carbon development in any location, but economic and technical issues mean that they are not currently viable.

Overall it is likely that LZC development initially will focus in locations where:

- there is some climatic, economic, or security imperative to decarbonise the energy supply and increase energy efficiency in buildings;
- there is sufficient renewable energy supply and storage capacity;
- existing infrastructure is compatible with LZC technologies.

However, future technologies such as the super grid and the hydrogen fuel cell could possibly enable zero carbon development in all regions, regardless of the attributes of the natural and built environments.

Economic viability

The economic viability of zero carbon development will also vary with location. Local variation in land value, fiscal incentives and market demand will influence the geography of zero carbon development. Land value varies geographically. Low value sites may not be able to sustain the additional costs of LZC technologies. Sites may have low value because of a lack of market demand, high remediation costs (e.g. the decontamination of brown field sites) or additional requirements placed on house-builders (e.g. to provide affordable homes as part of a development. In these circumstances the additional cost of LZC technologies may affect viability. Thus, subsidies may be needed to enable the inclusion of LZC technologies in new development on low-value sites or it may slow the pace of development.

The introduction of fiscal incentives to encourage the implementation of LZC energy systems (i.e. operational and capital subsidies, taxation, etc) can help to reduce the net construction cost and shorten pay-back periods for LZC technologies (Chapter 9). This will increase the viability of zero carbon development, particularly on low-value sites. Yet to date the introduction of fiscal incentives has resulted in pockets of innovation in the case studies examined. For example zero-net energy homes in California have focused in San Diego, Los Angeles, Fresno, San Francisco and Sacramento. Similarly clusters of passive house developments have emerged in Germany in Freiburg, Frankfurt, Hannover and Hamburg, encouraged by the introduction of a local capital subsidy.

Demand also influences the economic viability of LZC homes, which of course can vary locally depending on consumer characteristics (Chapter 6). Again there appears to be some spatial clustering of markets for LZC homes demonstrated by the case studies, particularly in Germany and the USA (California and Colorado). Clustering of affluent, educated, environmentally aware individuals in urban areas such as Boulder and Freiburg creates demand of LZC development. These are the innovators and early adopters in society and are often spatially clustered around hubs of environmental research excellence (as is the case in both Freiburg and Boulder). As zero carbon homes move into the mainstream, their spatial distribution will become more widespread.

Regulatory and political system

Local mandatory carbon reduction or renewable energy targets, resolutions and energy efficiency standards have been used to support the introduction of LZC homes and energy systems. The planning system has also been used in a variety of ways at a local level to encourage zero carbon development (discussed later in Chapter 10). Political support for LZC energy systems can also fluctuate at a local level. This influences the degree to which LZC development is supported by local planning system and the extent of local economic support for the installation of new LZC energy systems. Thus, local variation in political support and regulatory systems will also influence the geography of zero carbon development.

Human capital

Human capital (knowledge, skills and competencies) is critical to the delivery of zero carbon development. It can affect where zero carbon development locates and how quickly zero carbon systems deploy. Certainly human capital limitations in the UK have been highlighted as a key factor slowing the deployment of LZC energy systems. The lack of designers, installers, management and maintenance companies with the knowledge to deal with LZC energy systems in the UK has severely limited deployment (Brook Lyndhurst, 2004).

The human capital available to deliver zero carbon development also varies with location. Localised marketing campaigns may be used to attract those with expertise in LZC technical systems. The Californian Go Solar programme combined financial incentives, an educational programme and a marketing campaign to encourage existing installers and suppliers of solar technologies to locate in California, as well as train existing house-builders to incorporate solar technologies into new homes. This programme has helped to build the human capital needed to support the delivery of solar homes in California.

Local regulatory and fiscal incentives (under-pinned by political support) may be used to encourage the agglomeration of educational and research institutions and industries capable of delivering zero carbon development in a city or region. This agglomeration of technical expertise has been encouraged in Freiburg for example. Several important teaching and research institutions focussed on solar energy are located in Freiburg (Kiepenheuer-Institut für Solarenergie, Fraunhofer-Institut für Solare Energiesysteme, Öko-Institut) as well as the International Solar Energie Society. There are also now 1,700 green companies in Freiburg, 80 of which are in the solar industry. Currently the green sector in Freiburg generates €500,000 per annum and is growing as eco-tourism gains in popularity.

Academic institutions specialising in renewable energy have attracted linked industries and professional organisations. Educational programmes have been established in Freiburg to train the workforce for the renewable energy industry, ranging from those working in research and development to those installing renewable technologies. This has spawned products and services for both the domestic and international markets, and has led to the creation of an innovation hub in the city.

Changes to urban form

Urban form can have a significant impact on energy consumption and CO_2 emissions particularly from the transport sector and built environment. The mixture of land uses, siting in relation to the micro-climate, density, layout and orientation of development can impact on investment in energy infrastructure, energy consumed by the transport sector, energy requirements for space heating, potential for using district heating systems and renewable energy generation. There is a very comprehensive literature on this subject which has been summarised by Owens (Table 10.1)

Energy requirements for space heating (and related CO_2 emissions) can be reduced by building at high densities, as the proximity of other buildings reduces heat loss. District heating systems are also ideally suited to high density, mixed-use developments (Chapter 2). This increases energy efficiencies by reducing transmission losses and enabling a more efficient use of waste heat in urban areas. Thus insulation provided by adjacent buildings and the application of district heating systems can reduce energy consumption and CO_2 emissions in dense urban areas in cooler climates (in warmer climates it may increase the use of air conditioning, thus having a negative impact on CO_2 emissions).

As urban density increases, the heat island effect develops. This is aggravated by a lack of green space in dense urban areas. Thus increase in urban densities may generate increased demand in cities for cooling systems, particularly as the global climate warms up. Of course this will increase energy consumption and CO_2 emissions. Developing at higher densities often results in an increase in the height of buildings in urban areas. This too has implications for energy consumption. As buildings get taller more energy is needed to operate elevators, pump water up the building and so on. It may also affect the viability of some forms of renewable energy. The optimal density

Table 10.1 Energy and urban form relationships

	Density of development	Layout and orientation	Siting in relation to micro-climate
Energy investment in infrastructure	☑		
Energy requirements for space heating	☑	☑	☑
Potential for CHP/ DHS	☑	☑	
Potential for use of renewable energy sources	☑	☑	☑
Energy requirements for transport	☑		
Potential for efficient public transport system	☑		
Potential for walking and cycling	☑		

Source: Adapted from Susan Owens.

for an urban area in terms of CO_2 emissions and energy consumption has still to be determined, but it is likely to vary with locality.

The potential for using renewable energy sources is also influenced by urban form. Density, orientation, layout and siting in relation to the local micro-climate all affect the potential for using renewable energy sources in an urban area. The relative height of buildings and their arrangement relative to each other can cause overshadowing, the creation of localised wind turbulence and restrict the use of solar energy. The viability of wind as an energy source in dense urban areas is also compromised by the sheltering effect of buildings. Biofuel, biogas, waste heat and geothermal energy provide a more viable option for high density urban areas.

Layout and orientation of development also affect the quantity of energy consumed (and produced) by buildings. The orientation of buildings east–west and a staggered pattern can be used to maximise solar gain. Non-linear urban layouts are preferred for district heating systems in order to minimise transmission losses. Local micro-climate may also influence buildings space heating / cooling requirement and ability to generate renewable energy. Vegetation and water in an urban environment can be used to reduce temperature and the heat island effect.

The case studies demonstrate how the viability of four different energy systems alters with urban form (using four urban form parameters – Table 10.2). Four different energy systems were considered:

• closed-loop energy systems with a LZC energy source;
• district heating systems connected to a LZC energy source;

Table 10.2 LZC energy systems and urban form relationships

	Size	Density	Mix of uses	Layout	Example
Closed-loop energy system with LZC energy source[1]	☑	☑	☑		Hammarby Sjöstad, Stockholm
District heating system with LZC energy source[2]	☑	☑	☑	☑	B001 Malmö; Hammarby Sjöstad, Stockholm; Freiburg, Germany; BedZED, London.
Individual solar PV cells and collectors	☑	☑		☑	GEOS, Colorado; San Diego, California; Vauban, Freiburg;
Large-scale renewable energy[3]	☑				UK, Germany, Sweden, Colorado

Source: Author's own.

1 Reliance on waste products from urban system – similar to the Hammarby model.
2 For example biofuel, geothermal, solar and waste.
3 For example wind, tidal, wave, solar and hydro-power.

- individual solar systems;
- a centralised renewable energy supply.

Population size

Population size influences the quantity of energy consumed and the suitability of different energetic technical systems[2] within an area. The larger the population the more energy that needs to be generated and the more powerful the system needed for generation. Intervening variables including the operational efficiency of technologies, the local micro-climate and the consumption behaviour of households living in a locality will also influence the type of the system used. Thus it is not really possible to determine generic population thresholds for provision of different technical systems. This will need to be determined for a locality based on population size, consumption behaviour and micro-climate.

In some instances population size may also influence the quantity of energy resource available. For example, closed-loop systems are largely dependent on waste generated by the population. The larger the population, the more waste produced and the greater the potential for power generation. Again intervening variables which may affect the amount of waste produced, captured and efficiency of the system will also influence the energy output. Thus, similar difficulties in producing generic population thresholds for closed-loop systems exist. Of course the 'energy region' for a city (i.e. the area from which the energy supply to serve all citizens is sourced) will always be significantly larger than the city itself.

Density

Density influences the viability of energy systems. High densities reduce transmission losses and optimise energy efficiency in heating and electricity systems. Thus, high densities for district heating systems and closed-loop energy systems are beneficial. In contrast, high densities are not conducive to generating energy from solar or wind sources in urban areas. However, the effective application of solar technologies can be achieved in higher density neighbourhoods if the layout is such that it maximises solar gain (dependent on orientation, building heights, staggering) as demonstrated by the GEOS development (Chapter 5).

In very dense cities potential for generating LZC energy is low. Thus, strategies to reduce carbon emissions should focus on energy efficiency. This can be achieved through improving the energy efficiency of building stock, introducing a smart grid and installing collective localised energy systems (i.e. district heating/cooling systems). Connection to a LZC energy supply generated beyond the city limits may provide an alternative or subsidiary option.

In contrast, strategies to reduce carbon emission in low density neighbourhoods should focus on the production of LZC energy. Low density neighbourhoods have the space required for energy generation plants and energy storage where geography permits and also have better solar access in appropriate climatic conditions. Green space in low density neighbourhoods can also help to reduce the heat island effect. Improving the efficiency of building stock in low density neighbourhoods can dramatically reduce energy consumption (for example by building to passive house standard consumption drops to a mere 15kWh/m²/annum) thus helping households to become self-sufficient and reliant only on LZC energy sources. However, the potential for reducing energy consumption through the installation of collective localised energy systems is limited.

Mixture of uses

A mix of land uses is also very important as it helps to distribute power load more evenly, thus reducing the need for spinning reserve or storage options. Industrial and commercial premises tend to use energy during the middle of the day, whilst domestic energy loads peak during the mornings and evenings. Having a mixture of land uses in a neighbourhood ensures that the peak energy load is spread across a 24-hour period. This reduces the spinning reserve requirement in a system, which increases the efficient use of energy and results in reduction in the carbon intensity of the energy supply. It can also reduce the requirement for storage options. Using smart grid technologies energy supply and consumption in mixed use developments can be managed more effectively.

A mixture of land uses also enables potential producers of LZC energy (e.g. industries producing waste heat) to co-exist alongside potential consumers (i.e. households). The proximate nature of consumers and producers reduces transmission losses. This is particularly important for closed-loop energy systems, where efficiency within the system is essential, since the waste outputs from the system are also the energetic inputs. Thus, losses within the energy system must be minimised in order to be self-sufficient.

For decentralised LZC energy systems (reliant on localised production of renewable energy and waste) a mixture of land uses is important. These systems are reliant on many small producers of LZC energy. Mixed-use environments increase the number and diversity of potential energy producers and the proximity of producers to consumers reduce transmission losses. A mixture of land uses helps to smooth the peak load in an urban energy system, thus reducing the reserve required. Both increase the efficiency of the system making localised energy production more viable. The co-ordination of supply and demand, and integration of more variable forms of energy supply into the grid, can be facilitated through the introduction of smart technologies.

Layout

Urban layout can impact on the efficient operation of a variety of LZC technical systems – district heating systems, passive houses and solar neighbourhoods. The importance of layout can be illustrated by solar neighbourhoods, where it is extremely important for their effective operation. In addition to building individual units to a high energetic specification, it is also important to consider the surrounding urban environment and juxtaposition of buildings in a solar neighbourhood. Over-shadowing between buildings, window placement, effect of overhangs and vegetation should all be considered. If units are built along an east–west axis this maximises passive solar gain and potential for generating electricity from PV cells and heat in solar collectors.

In solar neighbourhoods, houses are designed to minimise indoor temperature variation. Thus most of the glazed area is focused on the south side of housing (with overhangs or sunshades to block the summer sun). On the east and west sides of the housing, glazing is restricted (shaded by deep porches or trees), whilst on the north side glazing is minimal (limited to what is sufficient for daylighting, comfort and cross-ventilation). To ensure solar access densities in solar neighbourhoods are generally low. However, work completed by the GEOS team in Colorado suggests that higher densities are achievable in solar neighbourhoods.

The National Energy Research Laboratory completed a detailed analysis of possible layouts to maximise solar gain in the GEOS development (based on case study examples from Latin America and Europe, Figure 10.2). A checkerboard layout was shown to be the most effective, enabling houses to be built at higher densities without compromising solar access. Buildings are spaced and staggered to maximise solar access and prevent over-shadowing (Figure 10.3).

Vegetation is used for its shading and cooling effect on the microclimate. The species, heights and placement of trees in a neighbourhood affect solar access as well as passive microclimate cooling (Figure 10.3). Deciduous trees are preferred in solar neighbourhoods, since they will only block rays from the summer sun. Trees can be placed to maximise shading during the summer rather than the spring and autumn months, and kept at an appropriate height.

Maintaining the design integrity of a solar neighbourhood long-term is not easy. The GEOS development team conceded that currently there is no system in place for the ongoing enforcement of solar design once the developer has left site. However, the developer believes that GEOS residents are motivated by green values and thus are unlikely to want to reduce their capacity to generate low-carbon energy by interfering with design integrity by for example by cutting down or growing trees in unsuitable locations. The use of solar ordinances in this case could be helpful (discussed later).

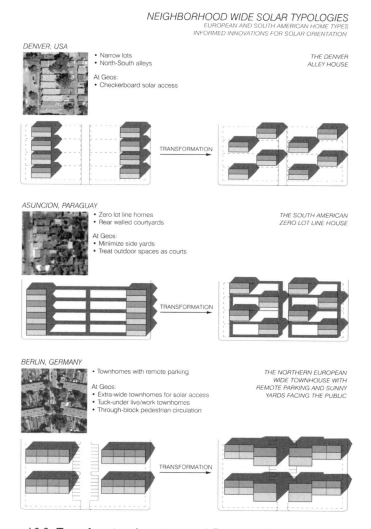

NEIGHBORHOOD WIDE SOLAR TYPOLOGIES
*EUROPEAN AND SOUTH AMERICAN HOME TYPES
INFORMED INNOVATIONS FOR SOLAR ORIENTATION*

DENVER, USA

• Narrow lots
• North-South alleys

At Geos:
• Checkerboard solar access

*THE DENVER
ALLEY HOUSE*

TRANSFORMATION

ASUNCION, PARAGUAY

• Zero lot line homes
• Rear walled courtyards

At Geos:
• Minimize side yards
• Treat outdoor spaces as courts

*THE SOUTH AMERICAN
ZERO LOT LINE HOUSE*

TRANSFORMATION

BERLIN, GERMANY

• Townhomes with remote parking

At Geos:
• Extra-wide townhomes for solar access
• Tuck-under live/work townhomes
• Through-block pedestrian circulation

*THE NORTHERN EUROPEAN
WIDE TOWNHOUSE WITH
REMOTE PARKING AND SUNNY
YARDS FACING THE PUBLIC*

TRANSFORMATION

Figure 10.2 Transforming American and European layouts to a zero-net energy layout.

Source: GEOS team, 2010.

Planning: an instrument for delivering zero carbon development?

Planning offers a spatial regulatory tool for delivering zero carbon development. It can be an extremely useful tool for:

HOMES SPACED-APART FOR WINTER PASSIVE SOLAR GAIN

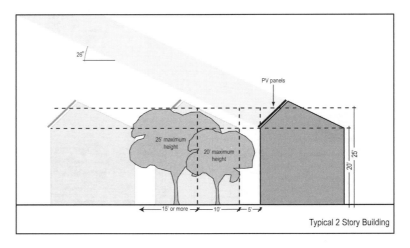

Figure 10.3 The influence of spacing of housing, placement and height of trees on solar access.

Source: GEOS team, 2010.

- coordinating resource and development strategies;
- encouraging the alterations to urban form which are appropriate for deploying LZC technologies;
- reducing the cost of zero carbon development;
- attracting appropriate human capital to design, build, manage and maintain zero carbon development;
- facilitating discussion between key players involved in delivering zero carbon development.

However, in practice the experience appears to be somewhat different. Planning is essentially a tool which can intervene in markets. It delivers development that achieves environmental, social and economic objectives. Thus, it can act as a catalyst for engendering zero carbon development, in the absence of any real market demand for it. The extent to which planning intervenes in markets depends on the political system in which it operates. Considerable emphasis can be placed on planning as a tool for delivering zero carbon development, as it was in the UK. Yet planning doesn't appear to have the teeth to deliver zero carbon development, but needs to be supplemented by wider policy and fiscal measures. In more interventionist systems, planning has been a more effective tool for delivery, although focused on a locality. Greater municipal control over resources and political support and leadership has given planning greater leverage as an instrument for enabling zero carbon development.

The rest of this chapter explores the role of planning in delivering zero carbon development. It begins by examining the weakness of planning as a tool for delivering zero carbon development, using the UK as a case study example. It goes on to illustrate the strengths of planning as a tool for delivering zero carbon development, using a range of examples of good practice. Planning's strategic role, design codes and zoning, and the planning process itself can all be used to promote and support zero carbon development. The factors which can offer greater leverage for the planning system are also considered. Finally the future role for the planning system in delivering zero carbon development, building on the examples of good practice provided by the case studies, is discussed.

The weaknesses of planning as a tool for zero carbon development

Planning was given a pivotal role in delivering zero carbon development in the UK, through the enforcement of the 'Merton rule'[3], code for sustainable homes[4], creation of energy action areas[5], low-carbon zones[6] and zero carbon projects. However, planning as a tool for intervention in the UK has been shown to be problematic for a number of reasons (Williams, 2010). Firstly, it was found to be open to a range of interpretations which reduced certainty for potential investors in zero carbon development. Secondly, planners were influenced by a range of competing demands placed on local authorities, and zero carbon development was seldom high priority. Thirdly, the decisions made throughout the planning process were influenced by the lack of environmental awareness and energy literacy amongst those dealing with the application and were subject to interference from local politicians. Fourthly, planning relied on the private sector to deliver the zero carbon infrastructure which was only effective when there was sufficient market demand (Williams, 2010).

Interpretation and implementation

Variation in the interpretation of relevant national planning guidance in the UK slowed the deployment of zero carbon development. There are several possible explanations for this. Firstly competing demands (particularly to provide affordable housing and process applications quickly for new developments) placed on planners reduced their willingness to require the delivery of zero carbon housing developments.

Secondly, guidance from Government was unclear and open to interpretation. It was unclear which of the conflicting governmental goals set for planning authorities (i.e. the inclusion of LZC energy systems in new development, the provision of affordable housing, a speedy planning process and conservation of character) were most important. Prioritisation of these goals was a matter for the local planning authorities and zero carbon tended to be low priority.

Thirdly, a lack of investment in training, tools or technical staff needed for determining zero carbon applications created a barrier to deployment. A lack of resources and appropriate expertise within planning authorities, reduced willingness amongst staff to introduce targets in the local plan which would prove difficult to enforce.

Fourthly, a lack of local political support (resulting from lack of awareness amongst councillors and significant public opposition) diminished the planners' willingness to enforce policies for zero carbon development or their inclusion in the local plan.

Even with clear guidance and strong leadership at a regional level some local authorities in the UK still implemented zero carbon policy in a very piecemeal manner largely due to competing demands, particularly for the provision of affordable housing.

Competing demands

The UK planning system is expected to deliver a number of economic, social and environmental development objectives. This makes deciding what conditions to place on permissions for new development very complicated. The decision largely rests on how the planner and local politicians prioritise the different development objectives. Reducing carbon emissions has tended to be lower on the list of priorities which is reflected in implementation.

Local planning authorities compete with each other for larger development projects. This influences their willingness to impose additional conditions on house builders to reach zero carbon standard. This problem appeared particularly acute in the more deprived areas in the UK. Here local planning authorities were reluctant to place additional conditions on house-builders to achieve a zero carbon standard, but preferred to focus on the provision of much needed affordable housing and transport infrastructure.

Finally planning approval times and the requirement for zero carbon are also in conflict. Applications for housing schemes that have included renewable energy components have taken longer to determine. This has slowed the turnover of permissions and interfered with local planning authorities' ability to achieve planning approval targets. It has also increased the cost to the house-builder as the development process lengthened considerably, making zero carbon projects unattractive.

Expertise, support and leadership amongst decision-makers

Lack of expertise amongst decision-makers (planners and politicians) has also been a barrier to the delivery of zero carbon development. Certainly tools for quickly determining the most cost-effective options for zero carbon development – for example the 'low carbon designer' (used in London, UK) and the 'renewable energy optimisation model' (developed by NREL, USA) – can speed up the decision-making process.

However, evidence from the UK suggested that lack of awareness amongst decision-makers was not the primary problem preventing zero carbon development but a lack of political support or leadership. Public opposition to some LZC technologies (usually on aesthetic grounds) and other development priorities limited political support for zero carbon schemes. Also technical problems associated with new technologies (particularly micro-wind, micro-biomass and PV cells) affecting cost, quantity and stability of energy supply also undermined support for zero carbon development.

Local planning authorities with energy champions took a more proactive approach towards zero carbon development. For example, there was a positive correlation between the adoption of the Merton rule in the local plan and the presence of an energy champion in a local authority. Those authorities without energy champions lagged behind in terms of policy. Planners working in authorities with energy champions appeared to be more motivated to deliver zero carbon development and more knowledgeable of the options for delivery. Developing renewable energy was prioritised in the local plan. Appropriate training was provided for planners and councillors to raise their awareness and technical expertise to enable implementation.

Reliance on the private sector to deliver zero carbon development

In the UK there were limited public resources available to finance the development of LZC systems. Thus, there was heavy reliance on the private sector to deliver decarbonised energy and energy efficient buildings. However, a lack of demand for zero carbon homes in the UK undermined industry's willingness to invest. Of course planning can be used as a tool to intervene in markets in order to achieve wider social and environmental goals, but the flexibility of the planning system in the UK provided no certainty to potential investors in zero carbon development and very few examples have been built. It was recognised that a clear regulatory framework would be needed to provide certainty to potential investors and producers in order for industry to build its capacity to deliver zero carbon homes. This was provided by the mandatory improvements in energy efficiency standards proposed for housing in the period 2008–2016.

The strengths of planning as a tool for delivering zero carbon development

There are also compelling arguments for the inherent suitability of planning as a catalyst for delivering zero carbon development. Planning can be used to strategically co-ordinate resources, infrastructure and development (Table 10.3). The development control function of planning can be used to enforce zero carbon standards, protect zero carbon systems once in place or discriminate in favour of zero carbon development. The planning process itself can be used to encourage discussion between key players involved in

Table 10.3 The roles of planning in delivering zero carbon development

Role of planning	Mechanism	Benefit	Examples
Strategic coordination	Combined strategic resource and development plans	Identify options for achieving zero carbon development	Freiburg and Stockholm
	Combined development, energetic and economic strategy	Identify the benefits of a low carbon economy and provides rationale for zero carbon development.	Freiburg
Development control	Zoning and design codes	Specifies sites for zero carbon development and provides indication of design standards	RMLUI, Denver; Freiburg codes
	Solar access ordinance	Perpetuates the integrity of design standards	Boulder
	Expedite planning process	Reduces overall development costs	San Diego
	Linking new development to LZC infrastructure	Reinforces the integrity and viability of existing systems	Stockholm
Facilitation	Partnerships between key players; learning and dissemination processes; community consensus building	Share expertise and risk between players; raising awareness of technical options; building community support for zero carbon development	Malmö, Stockholm

Source: Author's own.

the delivery and operation of new zero carbon systems, as well as increase acceptance of new technical systems within communities.

The strategic nature of planning is important for envisaging the most effective approach for delivering zero carbon development in any given location and context. Planning recognises the importance of the 'bigger picture' surrounding zero carbon development. Unlike building regulations (which focus on a single building) planning considers the wider community and region in which a development is set. It envisages how the zero carbon standard might be achieved in that context. For instance, the emphasis placed on energy efficiency or the generation of LZC energy within a development, a neighbourhood, city or wider city-region.

Planners can assesses the compatibility of the LZC infrastructure proposed as part of a development with the surrounding energy infrastructure, local energy sources and built environment. They can determine locations where zero carbon development is feasible and where some additional assistance may be needed. The wider benefits of zero carbon projects for regenerating local economies, developing and attracting zero carbon expertise, or building stronger local communities are also material considerations for planners in the decision-making processes. Such a strategic, holistic and synergistic approach has been successfully adopted by the municipality of Freiburg.

The development control function of planning can also be useful in delivering zero carbon development. It can be prioritised in the planning process, which helps to reduce development time-lines and building costs. This approach has been adopted by the American municipality of San Diego. Planning controls can be used to require that new development is linked to existing LZC infrastructure (where it exists) or is located close to a LZC energy supply. It can be used to manipulate urban form so that the introduction of LZC infrastructure becomes more technically and economically viable. For example in Stockholm the municipality enforced a policy which raised development densities to support the expansion of the existing district heating and public transport systems.

The planning process can also be used to raise awareness of zero carbon development options within communities and amongst producers. The planning system involves many parties in decision-making processes. In many ways it provides an excellent vehicle through which debate can take place, partnerships can be forged and energy literacy raised. Planning can be instrumental in bringing key players (i.e. house-builders, utilities, ESCOs, politicians, local businesses and residents) together to discuss potential partnerships for delivering zero carbon development. It can enable the transfer of ideas and expertise between key players, which will facilitate learning and help to deliver optimal development solutions. Discussion may also help to build an informed view and acceptance of new technical systems amongst the local community. Planners can disseminate the lessons learnt from demonstration projects to the wider local, regional, national and international communities. Malmö, Stockholm and Freiburg illustrate how the planning process (discussion, awareness raising negotiation and consensus building) can be used to facilitate and generate support for zero carbon development.

The spatial dimension of planning is important, because location influences the context (political, economic, cultural, environmental, institutional and technical) in which the regimes (house-building and energy industries) operate and this has an enormous impact on the viability and possible options for zero carbon development. Thus, it is important that any regulatory tool designed to deliver zero carbon development takes this spatial dimension into account.

The flexibility of planning as a regulatory tool is also important (although it can also be a weakness as explored in earlier discussions). This flexibility and allows other development priorities to be considered and given primacy over the zero carbon objective, particularly where future development is threatened. Finally the localised nature of planning allows innovative instruments to be tested in a spatially restricted area. Thus, planning instruments can be tested in contexts where they are more likely to be successful without threatening development in the wider region.

Strategic planning

The coordination of development with decarbonised energy systems is crucial for the delivery of zero carbon homes. The municipalities of Stockholm and Freiburg provide good examples. Historically in Stockholm spatial and infrastructural planning has been coordinated by the municipality. Thus, the optimal solutions for the provision of energy, water, waste and transport infrastructure to new development sites were considered during the planning process. There is nothing particularly remarkable in this, however, close collaboration between the municipally owned utilities (energy, water and waste) – and the urban planning department did result in the development of the extraordinary closed-loop energy system.

This energy system demonstrated the important link between urban form and the provision of LZC energy. Urban densities, mixture of land use, population size and the availability of resources (wind, biofuel, hydro-power) outside of the city limits all influenced the technical viability of the energy system. Density influenced the efficiency of the district heating and solid waste collection systems. It also influenced solar access in the city.

The mixture of land uses within the city limits increased supply of raw materials to the energy system, energy storage capacity and the overall operational efficiency of the system. The size of population affected both demand for energy and supply of resources to power the closed-loop system. The availability of agricultural land beyond the city limits also provided a source of energy – biofuel. Thus, the strategic planning of the energy system alongside new and existing development was essential for the successful implementation of the closed-loop system.

The importance of municipal control over planning and utility functions should not be under-estimated. Certainly this was crucial for the strategic coordination of both in Stockholm. Since energy provision is no longer in the control of the municipality (after Stockholm Energi was taken over by Fortum Energy in 2002), coordination has become more difficult. Also the role of planning changed and is now focused on coordinating and encouraging the collaboration between the key stakeholders (i.e. utilities, developers, community and municipality) in the development process. To an extent this more deregulated model (resulting from the privatisation of the utilities and reduction in planning powers) has undermined the more strategic approach to spatial and infrastructural planning adopted previously.

At a strategic level there is an environmental programme, an action plan to reduce greenhouse gas emissions, mitigation and adaptation plans for climate change, and an energy plan. The aims outlined in these plans are discussed with developers submitting planning applications. Planners try to encourage (rather than force) developers to take this on board when designing and planning a new development. The incentive for the developer is the publicity and marketing potential which stems from being involved in more innovative projects. This approach produces more ad hoc results.

However, the municipality can still control the spatial distribution of development and urban form. It is now focused on increasing urban densities in its bid to reduce carbon emissions from the city, whilst allowing it to grow. There is currently a large demand for new accommodation in Stockholm (200,000 units approximately) which can be catered for by increasing densities to an extent. However, the municipality is expecting an increase in migration into Stockholm putting further pressure on land. Thus planners are now starting to identify new growth areas surrounding the city (adopting a polycentric growth strategy) into which development should be focused. If these areas are built at high densities with mixed uses this should facilitate the development of district heating systems and limit non-commute trips.

Freiburg provides another example of how strategic planning can be used to deliver zero carbon development. In 1986 the City of Freiburg developed an energy supply concept which aimed to protect the climate, protect resources, and reduce pollution, without using nuclear power. This was to be achieved in several ways: reducing energy demand (thermal insulation, low energy construction and power-saving devices), increasing efficiency of energy production (cogeneration and district heating) and generation of renewable energy. In 1996, the climate concept was introduced which required a 25% reduction in CO_2 emissions by 2010. In 2007 this was updated and a new target was set to achieve a 40% reduction by 2030. Various key areas were identified in the climate action plan as having potential for delivering this reduction including municipal development planning (Figure 10.4).

Thus, the climate action plan has informed the strategic (zoning) plan and urban planning decisions in Freiburg. An analysis of the impact of the

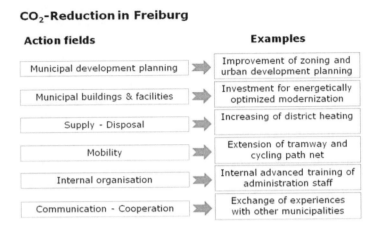

CO$_2$-Reduction in Freiburg

Action fields		Examples
Municipal development planning	⇒	Improvement of zoning and urban development planning
Municipal buildings & facilities	⇒	Investment for energetically optimized modernization
Supply - Disposal	⇒	Increasing of district heating
Mobility	⇒	Extension of tramway and cycling path net
Internal organisation	⇒	Internal advanced training of administration staff
Communication - Cooperation	⇒	Exchange of experiences with other municipalities

Figure 10.4 Areas targeted for CO$_2$ emission reduction in Freiburg.
Source: Freiberg City Council, 2009.

strategic land use policies on energy consumption, production and potential CO$_2$ emissions within the municipality was conducted as part of the process for creating the plan. Forecasting techniques were used to determine possible outcomes. Programmes to monitor the impact of these policies on energy consumption and CO$_2$ emissions are also now being put in place. Thus, the introduction of targets, forecasting and monitoring processes have helped to deliver a step-change in how land use planning is used to tackle CO$_2$ emissions in Freiburg.

The involvement of the local energy company (Badenova) with the municipal steering committee has enabled a two-way discussion about how best to achieve these CO$_2$ emission reductions within the city (Figure 10.5). Their suggestions have been fed back to the city planning working group. Badenova has been involved in the creation of both the climate action and strategic land use plans. It provides planners with the information needed to determine the best approach to delivering a low carbon energy supply to the locality or to specific developments. The company also advises developers on the optimal energy systems for new developments, which comply with local planning requirements. This approach means that planners in Freiburg do not have to be technical experts in energy planning. Their close working relationship with Badenova enables them to work with experts to identify the best technical options for existing and new development.

The Freiburg and Stockholm examples teach us a number of important lessons. Mandatory municipal CO$_2$ emission reduction targets incentivise

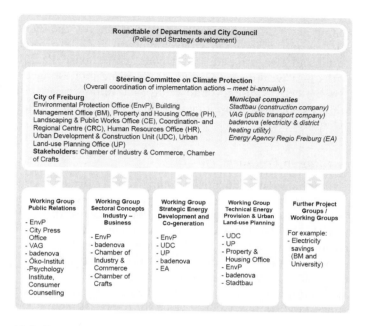

Figure 10.5 Decision-making structures in Freiburg.

Source: Freiberg City Council, 2009.

action to be taken at a local level. The role of planning in achieving these targets can be established through an action plan. This gives strength to planning authorities to take action to reduce CO_2 emissions from the built environment and transport sectors. The assessment of spatial development plans against CO_2 emission reduction targets is critical.

A baseline survey of current CO_2 emissions, energy infrastructure, built form and potential LZC energy sources can be used to construct an action plan. The results of baseline surveys can be used to forecast future emissions for different development scenarios. Thus forecasting can be used to identify potential solutions for encouraging carbon reductions. This process should inform the strategic development plan, as should the feedback from the monitoring process.

The relationship between the energy provider and the planning authority is also very important. Ideally the two should work together on the delivery of zero carbon development. This maximises the effective use of resources and ensures a more co-ordinated, strategic approach to development and energy infrastructure.

Zoning and reform codes

Land use zoning and reform codes can be used to specify the inclusion of LZC technologies and design in new developments. Euclidean zoning, performance-based and design-based (smart code) codes exist. Each has different strengths and weaknesses (Table 10.4). Some interesting examples are offered by the USA (Colorado and California) and Germany, not least the sustainability code being developed by the Rocky Mountain Land Use Institute in Denver.

Euclidean zoning in Freiburg

In Freiburg a combination of Euclidean zoning and performance codes have been used to encourage the strategic development of low carbon districts, solar homes and renewable energy capacity. Potential sites for wind energy installations and solar developments have been identified in the zoning plan – Euclidean zoning (Figure 10.6, see colour plates). This provides developers with a clear indication of the sites on which the construction will be prioritised, and thus offering greater certainty in the process.

However, this approach can be rather inflexible, particularly considering the lifetime of the zoning plan (20 years for the latest plan in Freiburg). Strategies for tackling carbon emissions (outlined in the Freiburg climate action plan) may alter over the period, perhaps due to changes in consumption patterns, national policy instruments or local energy sources.

Thus optimal development strategies may well alter over that period. Euclidean zoning does not provide the flexibility to reflect these changes. It also segregates land uses so that they become disconnected. Yet the

Table 10.4 Codes and zoning

Euclidean Zoning	❖ Emphasis on separation of use, quality, and procedures: '..fire, contagion, disorder..'
	❖ Can be inflexible and stifle creative development
Performance Code	❖ Anything, anywhere . . . if can mitigate
	❖ Emphasis on environmental protection
Design-based /Smart Code	❖ Focus on public realm and form vs. uses
	❖ Highly prescriptive; little focus on natural resources
Sustainability Code (2010)	❖ Covers broader range of topics
	❖ Integrates natural and man-madesystems
	❖ Draws on useful features of other codetypes (design, procedures, etc)
	❖ Based on a sustainable comprehensiveplan and civic engagement
	❖ Tailored regionally to climate andecology

Source: Rocky Mountain Land Use Institute, 2007.

integration of land uses and urban infrastructural systems is central to a more holistic approach to zero carbon development.

Energetic performance standards in Freiburg

Energetic performance standards for residential development were also introduced in Freiburg (Chapter 5). The plan requires that by 2011 all new development will reach a minimum energy house II standard on privately owned sites and passive house standard on municipally owned sites. These performance-based criteria establish review parameters for proposed development projects. Previous performance standards have proved a useful tool for achieving energetic (or CO_2 emission reduction) goals throughout Freiburg.

Performance standards are aspatial, unlike Euclidean zoning. They are intended to provide flexibility, rationality, transparency and accountability, better accommodating market principles with environmental objectives. They are not prescriptive, and so they enable a number of different approaches to achieving the same energetic goals which reflect and are compatible with the local context. This provides space for innovation.

However, enforcement of performance standards is a more complex and resource intensive process than for Euclidean zoning. It requires those monitoring development have a technical understanding of energetic systems, or that complex models to test the effectiveness of systems are developed. For performance-based standards it is also more difficult for house-builders to determine what is technically required. To develop the expertise in-house needed to deliver zero carbon development can be costly and time-consuming. In contrast for those with access to appropriate technical expertise the flexibility offered by performance standards is helpful. For those without access to energy expertise more prescriptive criteria (i.e. design/smart codes) are easier to understand and implement. However, performance standards enable developers greater flexibility in delivering the required outcomes within local contexts and thus optimise local resources and circumstances.

A design code for solar access

A form or design-based code offers considerably more flexibility in building uses than Euclidean codes. A design-based code is a means of regulating development to achieve a specific urban form. They create a predictable public realm by controlling physical form primarily, with a lesser focus on land use, through local regulations. The Boulder solar access ordinance provides an example of where design-based code is used to optimise use of solar energy in a city or neighbourhood.

Solar access is an important issue for some forms of zero carbon development. Rising pressure on urban areas to increase densities and building heights is impacting on the potential for generating solar energy. Solar access ordinances can address this problem.

Many American states passed solar access laws in the 1970s after the oil crisis. Currently, 34 states (including Colorado) and about a dozen municipalities have some form of solar access law. As solar energy systems become more affordable and available to mainstream property owners, solar access is re-emerging as a regulatory area in need of clarification and coordinated, thoughtful enforcement. At least 15 of the 25 major American cities participating in the Solar America Cities programme are in the process of reviewing their solar access laws.

Planning departments have developed an array of zoning ordinances for new construction that protect solar access and solar rights (for example City of Sacramento, City of Sebastopol and Marin County, all in California). These place design constraints on new developments. For example they may require:

• east–west street and building orientation (typically within 30 degrees of the east–west axis);
• landscaping that complements solar energy systems;
• dedication of solar easements for all newly constructed buildings.

The degree of prescription varies. However, house-builders are required to design developments that maintain solar access and do not impact on access to surrounding development. A variety of design options exist, as demonstrated by the plans for the GEOS development in Colorado (Figure 10.7, see colour plates). New tools are being developed to aid the designer in identifying the optimal design option for maximising solar access. The most advanced is the sub-division energy analysis tool (SEAT) developed by the US National Energy Research Laboratory.

SEAT is an energy analysis tool. It does not identify potential designs but it does estimate the impact of different street layouts, orientation of buildings, provision of green space, street widths, position of frontages, roof space and building characteristics on the ability of a development to conserve and generate energy from a solar source.

Boulder (Colorado) has implemented a solar access ordinance which guarantees access to sunlight for homeowners and renters in the city. This has been achieved by setting limits on the amount of permitted shading by new construction. A solar access permit is available to those who have installed or who plan to install a solar energy system and need more protection than is provided by the ordinance. For new developments, all units which are not planned to incorporate solar features must be sited to provide good solar access and not shade adjacent structures. They must also have roofs capable of supporting at least 75 ft² of solar collectors per dwelling unit. The city is zoned into three different areas, each with different solar access requirements dependent on existing urban form.

The solar access ordinance is interesting because it tackles solar access at an area level, rather than a building level. It considers the impact of new development on solar access in surrounding areas. It deals with maintaining access for both new and existing stock. In Boulder, there is also some acknowledgement that degree of solar access varies with existing urban form and function. The solar access ordinance helps to ensure design integrity over a longer-term period.

Access design codes could also be developed for district heating systems and possibly other renewable energy technolgies (e.g. micro-wind, micro-hydro, geothermal etc). For example, in cities with district heating systems, new development could be required to connect to the local network. In addition the code could be used to ensure that the form of the development (particularly in terms of layout, density and mix of uses) optimises the operation of the district heating system. Equally, design guidelines to optimise access to wind, hydro or geothermal energy in cities, reinforced by a permitting system which ensures long-term design, integrity could also develop. However, being too prescriptive would seriously limit potential.

The sustainability code

Currently a sustainability code is being developed by the Rock Mountain Land Use Institute (RMLUI) for Colorado. It combines a number of elements of the previous codes discussed in an effective manner. It addresses a range of environmental objectives including increasing energy efficiency of development and encouraging the production of renewable energy. The code is also tailored regionally to reflect local variation in climate and ecology (which varies significantly in the State of Colorado). This offers significant advancement on existing codes.

The sustainability code tackles delivering sustainable development in three ways:

*   Removing obstacles: Most modern codes create barriers to sustainability, often unintentionally. For example, small wind turbines and solar panels are often prohibited by residential zoning regulations, height controls, or design standards.
*   Creating incentives: Some sustainable technologies are relatively new and experimental — like green roofs. Zoning codes can foster increased density and other incentives to encourage use of such technologies.
*   Enacting standards: While removing obstacles and creating incentives will be important, no zoning code can succeed without mandatory regulations that require certain actions or prevent harm.

(RMLUI, 2008)

The sustainability code offers a menu or toolbox of options for delivering sustainable development. Within this toolbox various approaches could be adopted to reduce CO_2 emissions in urban areas. These are outlined by the sustainability code. Planning departments must assess how this might be best achieved in their jurisdiction. For example the best approach may be to remove existing obstacles to the installation of LZC technologies in residential areas created by development restrictions (for example in conservation areas). It might be that the inclusion of LZC technologies in new development needs to be incentivised perhaps by reducing house-builders' costs (by waiving planning fees or reducing development time-lines for LZC development). Regulations can also be used to encourage solar access (and wind access) within urban areas or preserve sites with potential to generate renewable energy (Table 10.5).

A key strength of the sustainability code is that it provides flexibility in choice of strategy for achieving various environmental objectives. These strategies can be modified by a planning authority to reflect local resources, issues, priorities and needs. It also identifies a range of options depending on different levels of difficulty ranging from a bronze (easiest tools to implement) to a gold standard (toughest tools to implement). The problem with the sustainability code is perhaps that it is too all encompassing. It provides a menu of options for achieving a range of environmental, social and economic objectives. Planners will need to have clearly identified objectives and an awareness of the compatibility of the instruments they choose to implement in order to be successful. This places considerable responsibility on planners and will certainly require external technical input to identify the best options. Similar problems for planners emerged with the introduction of the Code for Sustainable Homes in the UK (Williams, 2008a).

One tool developed by NREL may be able to assist in this – the renewable energy optimisation model (REO model). The model determines the best mixture of renewable energy technologies for a development. This is based on access to renewable energy resources, technology characterization (cost and performance), economic parameters (discount rates, fuel escalation rates), economic incentives (state, utility and federal incentives) and mandates (executive order, legislation). However, this tool does not consider the impact of urban form on optimal solutions. New tools are needed to determine optimal spatial strategies for reducing CO_2 emissions. Monitoring will be essential to determine how successful the package of measures chosen is.

The planning process

The planning process can be used to provide leverage for zero carbon development. Expediting the process of obtaining planning permission for zero carbon development can be used to reduce net development costs to house-builders. Planners can also co-ordinate the activities of those involved in delivering zero carbon development, ensuring a more holistic approach to the provision of infrastructure (as for example in the Stockholm Process). The process itself can also be used to encourage learning amongst key stakeholders about how to deliver zero carbon development. Furthermore it can be used to develop community engagement in zero carbon development projects (as was the case with Vauban in Freiburg).

Table 10.5 Sustainability Code: a toolbox of options for achieving reduction in CO_2 emissions

	Remove obstacles	Create incentives	Regulate
Solar energy	❖ Permit solar collectors as by-right accessory use (including historic districts)	❖ Over-the counter permitting and fee waivers ❖ Allow applicants to 'earn' additional density or height by incorporating solar concepts into a project's overall design	❖ Solar access at site level ❖ Require a minimum percentage of solar-oriented lots or buildings in new developments ❖ Require a minimum percentage of energy in new developments to come from solar
Wind energy	❖ Increase height limits ❖ Allow small turbines in a wider range of zone districts including industrial, urban, commercial, large-lot residential, and suburban zone districts ❖ Allow large-scale turbine as a by-right use subject to performance standards to speed, and reduce costs, of permitting ❖ Allow energy produced by a large turbine on one property to be used off-site by property owners who record formal agreements	❖ Identify suitable sites in comprehensive plans ❖ Lower or eliminate zoning and permitting fees for utility WECS ❖ Use district-wide building height limits to protect wind access and increase predictability for those that invest in WECS ❖ Map areas with the best wind potential and restrict new uses to those that are locally acceptable in conjunction with small turbines	❖ Preserve areas withwind potential ❖ Require that new developments of high energy consuming uses generate on-site energy using renewable resources such as geothermal, solar, or wind

Source: Modified from Rocky Mountain Land Use Institute, 2007.

Expediting the planning process in San Diego

One of the main barriers to LZC carbon development is cost. Cost is influenced by the price of LZC technologies, risk to investors and cost of borrowing. If planning can reduce some of these costs, LZC development would be more economically viable. The length of the planning process, combined with the uncertainty and risk associated with any new form of development (without a proven market) means that it is more difficult and expensive for developers to raise sufficient capital for LZC projects.

Currently the time-line for the approval of LZC projects (or in fact any non-standard form of development) tends to be significantly longer than for standard development forms. As a result the cost of processing an application for LZC development is likely to be substantially more. The length of the planning process in particular increases the net build cost of LZC projects substantially. The longer the planning process, the more interest the developer pays on their investment without a return. Thus reducing the length of the planning process can provide a significant financial incentive to a developer to build LZC projects.

The benefits of fast-tracking are clearly demonstrated in San Diego County, California. In this example the planning applications for developments where 50% of the electricity needs of a development are provided by solar energy are fast-tracked. This has meant that the application processing time has reduced on average by 75% for those projects which included solar technologies. This has saved developers finance charges on loans which covered the costs of the solar systems installed (Farhar et al, 2004). The policy has also led to an increase in applications for solar houses in San Diego County and is being piloted elsewhere in California and the USA as a method to encourage deployment of PV technology.

Expediting the planning process works as an incentive for LZC development particularly well where development time-lines are long (as in the USA). However, in the UK where pressure has been placed on planners to increasingly shorten the development time-line for all development, there is less room for manoeuvre. Here preferential treatment of applications for LZC development could be helpful at least in providing investors with greater financial certainty.

The 'Stockholm process'

The model for city planning – the 'Stockholm process' – created through the development of Hammarby Sjöstad was ground-breaking. In principle the 'Stockholm process' is an iterative, dynamic and collaborative process which brings developers, municipalities and those delivering the infrastructure to work alongside each other at the earliest possible stage in the development process. The planning authority in this model co-ordinates and encourages all the different interests in the plan, rather than enforcing the vision. It is also stimulates a learning process amongst developers and utilities.

The Hammarby project had a very clear environmental vision. In general terms this included reducing energy consumption as well as recycling water and waste. The city formed a development administration for Hammarby with its own project budget, a CEO and an environmental unit. The group had visioning, planning and facilitation functions. The development administration brought together the municipality, developers and utilities to work on a single vision for Hammarby Sjöstad and was able to apply for national and city funds for the development.

An overall vision for the project was developed by the group. The vision for the strategic LZC infrastructural system was produced by the energy, water and waste partnership. It was for the 'Hammarby Model' to be twice as effective at energy production, waste recovery and energy conservation as similar projects not using the system. The master plan for the site was developed alongside the infrastructural system by planners in the project group.

Twelve development districts were identified and handed over to a designer and builder. Competition (technical competitions) between developers was encouraged to try and achieve the best possible environmental design. This level of competition encouraged significant improvements in terms of design. Open meetings with all the developers putting in proposals for the site were held. Developers had to present their projects every couple of months to their peer group. This enabled the transfer of information between those working on the site and within the industry. Discussion between the utilities, municipality and developers was also facilitated through meetings. Thus, the housing developers were aware of the high-quality infrastructure being provided in the development and realised that the housing stock would have to reflect this design quality.

This degree of coordination was possible for Hammarby Sjöstad because the city owned the land and the utilities. Both gave the city leverage and enabled the co-ordination of the new development with LZC infrastructure. The privatisation of utilities in Stockholm has made coordination between key development stakeholders more difficult for subsequent projects. Greater dialogue and negotiation is required between the development administration and private utilities to achieve common goals. The issue here isn't about whether the city or a private company owns a utility, but more that there is a problem with single-issue organisations.

The joint creation of an energy plan for the city (similar to that in Freiburg) has helped to overcome this problem to an extent. Policies to increase energy supply to the city and change to low/zero carbon energy sources are set out in the plan. This creates some consensus between the energy company and the municipal planning authority about how to proceed, by providing guidelines for future development. Their joint involvement in the production of the plan also ensures that they both have vested interest in its successful delivery.

For the Royal Stockholm Seaport project the 'Stockholm Process' is being updated. The target for the project is to achieve zero carbon status. Thus, the initial objectives set are more testing. There are also more stakeholders involved with the project. A similar approach to the delivery of the strategic vision is being taken and the development administration is coordinating the approach. Again the processes of discussion and learning are being facilitated within the project. A common vision is being reached through this more consensual process.

In addition, a 'procurement tool' has been introduced to enable delivery. By acting as a facilitator for the whole project the municipality has coordinated a procurement approach for expensive LZC technologies, by buying at scale to reduce costs. Thus, the municipality procures LZC technologies on behalf of developers, who then buy the technologies from the municipality. This has proved particularly helpful for smaller developers who could not afford the LZC technologies alone. Information about the new LZC technologies is being made available to the developers through various discussion fora organised by the municipality.

Thus, the planning process can provide a vehicle through which key stakeholders can be bought together to discuss the vision for a development and optimal solutions for delivering that vision. Involving key stakeholders in this process ensures they have invested in the outcomes and are supportive of the project. With so many 'single-issue stakeholders' involved in a project it is important that these single issues are strategically coordinated. Planners are best positioned in the development process to achieve this. Of course this approach is likely to be more successful if the municipality can offer incentives to the other key stakeholders in the process (e.g. land, access to development funds, municipal procurement, etc) to cooperate.

The 'Freiburg Process'

The 'Freiburg Process' is all about the engagement of the community in planning new developments. The process engages the community in visioning and design consultation exercises. It also involves the community in the ongoing operation of new districts. This process has been shown to encourage community support for more innovative development models and increase long-term resident interest in the project. This process was adopted for the development of Vauban district.

Three key groups were involved in the planning of Vauban: Project Group Vauban, City Council Vauban Committee and Forum Vauban. A host of other actors also had the opportunity to feed into the planning process (Figure 5.14). Forum Vauban played a key role in the participative planning process. It brought together citizens, architects, engineers, financial experts, experienced managers of co-building projects and other partners.

It acted as the hub for the exchange of ideas, concerns and expertise amongst these groups. Private building owners, *Baugruppen* and development companies were informed through meetings, exhibitions and publications about plans for the development, and were invited to discuss them with the forum. This approach resulted in a strengthened commitment to ecological and social objectives of the plan amongst private building owners and *Baugruppen*.

The municipality and Forum Vauban jointly organised meetings to enhance citizen participation in the planning process. More than 50 workshops were held for citizens. Some workshops were to raise awareness of ecological and socially conscious design. Others were to discuss possible development options. The initial development plan for Vauban was substantially modified on the basis of the input received from these workshops. The modifications to the plan included:

- the addition of a car-free project in the neighbourhood;
- the promotion and support of *Baugruppen*;
- the designation of areas for passive-houses;
- and the inclusion of a central market place and a community centre.

Interestingly, citizens appeared prepared to adopt more a radical plan than was first outlined by the municipality. Thus, their participation in the process had actually enhanced and expanded the social and ecological agenda for Vauban. It also helped to build the social capital needed to operationalise collective energy solutions. Involvement of *Baugruppen* also enabled a degree of self-determination over the energy systems installed in new development. It should be noted that the Freiburg situation is fairly unique both in terms of the cultural context and economic incentives available to citizens for the deployment of LZC systems. The residents of Freiburg are engaged in local decision-making processes; they are empowered and support a sustainability agenda. In addition the availability of federal and local grants encourages the deployment of LZC technologies. In more conservative, dis-empowered communities, where priority is not given to the sustainability agenda or where subsidies for LZC technologies are unavailable, this approach would have produced a very different outcome.

The participative approach to planning and development used in Vauban was very resource intensive, particularly for the municipality (Donn, 2011). It engaged many different actors through a range of techniques. Involving such a large number of actors in the consultation process inevitably lengthened development time-lines, and thus the cost of development. The cost of the forum itself was not insignificant, approximately US$2,000,000 from 1995 to 2001. The Freiburg process also relied on people giving up their time to be involved (another resource cost to be factored in). However, the costs were outweighed by the gains. Citizen involvement in the decision-making and planning process for the new community ensured their long-term interest and support for the project. There are resource implications for planning authorities considering adopting this process as well as consequences for the speed of future development (Donn, 2011).

Summary of good practice

These examples illustrate that planning tools can be used to deliver zero carbon development (Table 10.6). Planning tools co-ordinate energy resources with development and encourages the transformation of urban form which supports and complements the introduction of LZC technologies. Modifications of the planning process, zoning and design codes can all be used to reduce the cost of zero carbon development. The planning process can also be used to raise zero carbon expertise amongst producers and consumers, as well as to encourage local support for new LZC systems.

Planning provides useful tools for delivering zero carbon development. It is a more flexible regulatory tool which acknowledges the need for a variety of approaches to delivering zero carbon development in different local contexts. Yet planners are still largely reliant on private investors to deliver zero carbon development. Additional leverage can be given to planning through the introduction of mandatory CO_2 reduction targets, local financial incentives, and the municipal ownership of resources.

The introduction of mandatory CO_2 reduction targets for planning departments provides greater incentive for planners to encourage zero carbon development. Targets offer planners the flexibility to determine the

Table 10.6 Planning tools for delivering zero carbon development

Good practice	Co-ordination	Urban form conducive to ZCD	Reducing cost of ZCD	Developing human capital
Local CO_2 reduction targets for planning	☑	☑		
Joint process of creating spatial plan	☑			
Euclidean zoning for ZCD or identification sites for RE	☑	☑	☑	
Energy code (performance based)		☑		
Solar access code (design-based)		☑		
Sustainability code (combination)		☑	☑	
Expediation of the planning process			☑	
The 'Stockholm process'	☑			☑
The 'Freiburg process'				☑

best strategy for achieving carbon reduction in relation to the local context (resource availability, existing infrastructure and building stock, energy consumption patterns, etc) in which the development is embedded. Such a system places more responsibility on planners to assess optimal strategies for carbon reduction. This may be achieved across a number of land uses including housing.

Local financial incentives might also be used to provide greater leverage for planning in delivering zero carbon development. Subsidies could be offered for marginal sites (i.e. those with low market value) to overcome the costs of additional technical systems. Examples include local subsidies provided for passive house development in some German cities and the climate smart grants supplied for low cost homes in Boulder.

Municipal ownership of land can help to provide leverage for zero carbon development. BedZED, Hammarby Sjöstad, B001 and Vauban were all built on municipally owned sites. Land ownership enables municipalities to impose environmental requirements on developers, whilst they benefit from the lower land costs. However, where there are limited municipal sites the scope provided by this tool is very restricted (as is the case in the UK where many municipally owned sites have been sold off).

Municipal ownership of utilities (particularly energy) could also help provide leverage for zero carbon development. If planning and utility functions are both in-house, better co-ordination between energy efficient development and LZC energy systems may be achieved (as was the case in Stockholm and Freiburg). Revenue can also be raised by the municipal utility to invest in LZC infrastructure.

A municipal utility will have more holistic objectives (i.e. environmental and social as well as economic) than a privatised utility which focuses on profit. If mandatory carbon targets are applied to municipalities this will provide further impetus for municipal energy companies to address emissions. If other utilities (i.e. water and waste) are also controlled by the municipality, then it may be possible to create closed-loop energy systems.

Municipal housing companies (or even publicly subsidised housing programmes, for example social housing in the UK) could also provide an opportunity for testing innovative forms of zero carbon development. The municipality can directly impose targets on municipal housing to reduce CO_2 emissions. Again this may be under-pinned by local mandatory carbon reduction targets or even carbon trading systems. The municipality can offer municipally owned sites to housing companies at a price which reflects the additional build cost associated with the inclusion of LZC technical systems.

Planning's future role

Planners have a significant role to play in the delivery of zero carbon development (Figure 10.8). Certainly this role is not to impose energetic standards

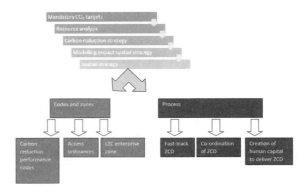

Figure 10.8 Planning for LZC development.

Source: Author's own.

on new buildings. This can be more successfully achieved using building code (as demonstrated in Sweden). Planning's role is to deal with the bigger picture, the interaction between a development, the surrounding urban fabric and the bioregion. It is important to consider bioregions rather than administrative areas since renewable energy sources can be transferred and stored across administrative boundaries. Solutions for carbon reduction in an urban environment might be more effective (technically and economically) at a regional scale.

Planners set the strategic development agenda. They are in an excellent position to create spatial strategies for reducing CO_2 emissions. A resource analysis of a region – strategic mapping of energy sources, storage capacity and infrastructure – provides a baseline indication of the potential for reducing CO_2 emissions. It can guide a planning authority in the creation of its strategic carbon reduction strategy. The carbon reduction strategy focuses on reducing consumption, improving energy production efficiency, developing renewable energy sources, or all three. The strategy reflects the environmental (natural and built) characteristics of the bioregion[7]. The impact of the carbon reduction strategy can be tested using a strategic modelling tool. Such a model a can be used to identify how changes in urban form or development patterns enable the implementation of more effective LZC energy systems.

Once a strategic carbon reduction strategy has been established it needs to be made operational through the planning process, spatial development plan and enforcement of code. Emphasis here on the strategic nature of the plan is important. Detailed requirements for energy systems to be provided for specific sites are not useful. The suitability of technologies may change over time, as may access to LZC energy sources. A more general indication in the spatial plan of where new development should be focused to support an existing LZC energy system or to support the development of a new LZC energy source would be helpful.

This could be reinforced by the introduction of carbon reduction performance codes (CRECs). The performance codes would be based on a zone's potential to reduce carbon emissions (as determined by the carbon reduction strategy). The CRECs will ensure that sites performed to their capacity, without specifying the technological system. However, some form of long-term protection of the effectiveness of the systems used is needed. Possibly access ordinances (or a similar regulatory tool) could be used to ensure long-term effectiveness of a LZC energy system once installed.

A code could also be developed to encourage the formation of LZC enterprise zones. These would be zones in which zero carbon development and supportive industries could operate side by side. All zero carbon development would be fast-tracked through the planning process (thus reducing costs to the developer). There would be no regulatory restrictions preventing the inclusion of zero carbon technologies into the built fabric (increasing certainty to the developer and other investors). Tax breaks (tax credits) or other financial incentives would be offered to low carbon developers and industry locating in the zone. This would help to encourage the construction of zero carbon development. It would also increase the local expertise in LZC technologies, eventually creating a zero carbon hub for development and industry.

In terms of process it is important that those investing in development and new energy systems have some security. The planning system can offer this, firstly by prioritising zero carbon development. Secondly, zero carbon development can be fast-tracked to reduce the development costs. The coordination of development and resources is essential. It is important that key actors for delivery are involved in the creation of the carbon reduction strategy as well as plans for implementation. This can be coordinated by the planning authority.

The involvement of key stakeholders (developers, utilities and the community) in the process of building zero carbon development increases their expertise. It is important that this knowledge is disseminated more widely within the construction and energy industries. Planners also have a role to play in the dissemination, learning and consensus building processes in communities. Engaging communities in these processes can help to build their support for more innovative forms of development and may help zero carbon development to be deployed more widely.

Planning has a role to play in the strategic co-ordination of development, infrastructure and resources as well as in the co-ordination of key stakeholders in delivering zero carbon development. It needs to provide certainty for investors through the strategic plan and design codes. Planners need to facilitate the learning process for professionals, investors and citizens so that they understand the options for achieving zero carbon development and how to deliver them. The planning process needs to be designed to encourage community consensus and support for zero carbon development.

Chapter 11

Living with zero carbon

Introduction

In this chapter we investigate what it might be like to live in a zero carbon home and how it could impact on quality of life. We also discuss how households interact with these new and complex technological systems. Technology alone is unlikely to change the lack of energy awareness and social motivations underlying current energy consumption. Far deeper changes in society will be needed to deliver low carbon (let alone zero carbon) lifestyles amongst those living in zero carbon homes. A change in role for households from energy consumers to 'energy citizens' (as defined by Devine-Wright, 2004; Morris, 2001) is explored and ideas for encouraging this shift are developed.

Living in a zero carbon home directly reduces CO_2 emitted by households through heating (or cooling) their home and using appliances. This can occur without any real changes to lifestyle as long as residents operate the technologies effectively, although the interaction between residents and LZC technical systems are important. A zero carbon house is a very complex technical system, composed of a number of different technical subsystems that relate to the building itself and the wider heating and electricity systems. There are a diversity of models that can be classified as zero carbon homes (Chapter 2) ranging from the fully autonomous system (possibly combining a passive house with solar heating and electrical systems) to one entirely dependent on an external renewable energy supply (possibly managed through a smart grid).

Different levels of household interaction with technologies are implied with this diversity of models. In some instances households are merely involved in the decision to choose a low carbon tariff, whilst in others they may be involved in the operation, management and maintenance of the energy system itself. Different models require different levels of awareness and expertise to operate effectively. The public are generally accustomed to centralised models for energy provision, which requires very limited involvement. Yet zero carbon homes lend themselves to a decentralised, decarbonised energy system. In this scenario homes can become power generators. Such a system requires considerably more user involvement in its operation, as households become producers and managers of energy. There are significant long-term social and environmental benefits with adopting this approach which will be explored in this chapter.

The case studies demonstrate a range of problems that have been encountered in the technology–consumer interface. Technological defects (common to complex systems and new technologies) have reduced public trust in new technical systems. There are also concerns about the efficiencies and reliability of new technologies. Another issue raised by the case studies is that some of those living in zero carbon homes have been removing technologies or altering building design in a way that reduces energy efficiency. Problems with residents being responsible for the long-term management and maintenance of systems have also been highlighted. Difficulties sourcing replacement technologies and lack of technical expertise amongst households are a considerable barrier to the widespread adoption of these technical systems. However, the most serious problem (and possibly the most difficult to tackle) is the rebound effect.

Living in zero carbon homes may affect the quality of life of those occupying them. Quality of life indices including comfort, convenience, affordability, personal freedom, privacy, safety and security may all be affected by the use of various LZC technologies. There are comfort, convenience and affordability issues for those living in passive houses. There are potential convenience, privacy, personal freedom and security issues for those residents connected to a smart grid. Quality of life is central to a consumer's decision to live in a zero carbon home, and to stay living there. Thus, these conflicts produced by the introduction of new technical systems need to be resolved. It could also be argued that the perception of those using the systems has been coloured by their experience of using a centralised energy system. The centralised energy system has been designed to offer the consumer comfort, convenience, affordability, personal freedom, privacy and safety. Thus, the consumer has come to expect these qualities to be delivered by all energy systems. However, the current energy system cannot offer security in a world with steadily decreasing fossil fuel resources, nor does it offer the potential social and environmental benefits of a decentralised energy system.

The invisibility of energy (Hedges, 1991; Egan, 2002) and disengagement of the public from decision-making and involvement in energy systems has eroded energy literacy. Energy consumers are unaware of their own energy consumption patterns, the cost of energy, the environmental impacts of energy consumption and low carbon alternatives. In a centralised energy system people have largely been excluded from participating in decision-making processes which have been left to the experts. The responsibility for managing energy supply, distribution and consumption rests entirely with energy companies rather than the public. Those involved in the design, installation and operation of energy systems also limit the need for public involvement. The public are seen as a potential barrier to the implementation and effective operation of energy systems, rather than a useful addition. Centralised decarbonised energy systems could offer a useful approach to delivering a reduction in household production of CO_2. Such an approach sits better with current culture, institutional and technical systems. It would not require a paradigm shift in the current landscape. Thus, it would not require people to change their behaviour. This approach was adopted by the B001 and Hammarby energy systems. However, for a long-term change in energy consuming or CO_2 producing behaviour the decentralised approach offers significant benefits.

The introduction of zero carbon homes as part of a decarbonised, decentralised energy system will not only reduce CO_2 emissions, it may encourage a long-term change in energy consuming behaviour. Furthermore it may also have social benefits, helping to rebuild social capital within communities centred on community energy production and generate greater empowerment. However, this would mean a major shift in terms of the role of the public in energy systems from 'passive consumer' to 'active participant' (or energy citizen). This would require a major cultural change (both amongst the public and within the energy industry), the creation of new institutional structures to support a decentralised energy system, as well as significant political and financial support during the early phases of deployment. Options for encouraging this paradigm shift are discussed.

Household interaction with technical systems

Household interaction with the various technical systems that constitute a zero carbon home can affect energy consumption patterns and the production of CO_2. If technologies are not used effectively, are removed or not maintained the impact on household energy savings and CO_2 emissions can be considerable. Interaction with technical systems can also help to increase household energy literacy; however, if the system is too complex it may simply be confusing. Technologies for monitoring energy consumption and CO_2 production may prove helpful in raising energy literacy, but the type of information that is provided and the way it is provided is critical to changing behaviour. The way in which households react to technologies (like smart metering, smart grids and passive houses) may influence whether they help to reduce energy consumption and CO_2 emissions or increase them.

Complex systems

Zero carbon homes are particularly complex energy systems, because they comprise several technical sub-systems. These technical sub-systems could be combined in a number of different ways to produce a zero carbon home

(Chapter 2). This can create considerable diversity in the technical system which can be called a zero carbon home. The lack of standard model for a zero carbon home means that every time a household moves they will potentially have to learn how to use a new energy system. This is time-consuming and may be beyond the ability of some households.

The involvement of several sub-systems in a zero carbon home can mean that many players may be involved in its delivery. It also increases the number of parties involved in operating and maintaining the system. Potentially this creates issues with co-ordination, particularly where systems need to maintained, upgraded or expanded. In this scenario there is likely to be some concern about who the point of contact is for the household if technical difficulties are encountered.

The greater the household's involvement in energy decision-making and the operation of systems the more complicated they will seem. It is hard enough for many households to make the decision to change their tariff or even an energy efficient light-bulb, let alone be involved in managing their energy supply, producing or storing energy. Decision-making is time-consuming and requires a degree of expertise that may well be beyond many households.

The smart grid provides an excellent example of this. Here the household is involved in a variety of processes: energy management, producing energy and storing energy. Households interact with metering systems in the home and complicated online energy management systems. Households have to make all sorts of decisions for example what energy sources to use; when to consume and store energy; which appliances to use, to switch off and when. Households connected to the smart grid may also produce renewable energy which they then feed-back into the grid. The energy produced must be monitored, managed and renewable energy technologies maintained.

Electric vehicles can be used by households to store energy as well as for transport. Households have to judge how best to utilize these vehicles to manage energy most effectively. Decisions about when to store energy, when to release it to the grid and when the vehicle is actually needed for transportation all have to be made. Operating and managing all of these smart technologies effectively is likely to be complicated and time-consuming. However, it does offer a considerable degree of individual control over energy management which will appeal to some. It also helps to increase energy literacy amongst the public which is critical for delivering LZC communities.

Certainly some of these energy management decisions can be made by utilities operating smart grids, based on a few preferences indicated by households. However, some concern has been expressed by some households about lack of individual control over energy systems in these circumstances. Yet many households find smart technologies overly complicated and time-consuming to use.

At the opposite end of the spectrum is the closed-loop system used in Hammarby, based on the 'deficit view' of the household. This system requires minimum input from households. The utilities and waste authority manage and maintain the system. It is simple to use and the number of household –technology interfaces are limited. The only real responsibility for the households is to use waste chutes effectively. The household can of course optimise their energy consumption by including metering in the home but this has not been included as a standard technology.

In this situation the household remains energy illiterate, isolated from decisions about consumption and unaware of the issues surrounding energy production. This is part of the reason that energy consumption in Hammarby Sjöstad is considerably higher than was predicted by energetic models. Certainly the planning department in Stockholm has recognized this problem and is now requiring in the new low carbon development at the Royal Seaport in Stockholm that all units have energy meters fitted. It is hoped that this will encourage lower energy consumption.

Technical defects

Technical defects reduce the public's trust in new systems and reinforce the public's fears about the reliability of new technologies. One of the greatest concerns voiced by those surveyed in the UK about LZC energy infrastructure was its lack of reliability, particularly where renewable energy technologies were included in the system. This problem is compounded by a lack of service providers who are willing and able to repair and maintain LZC energy systems and limited availability of replacement technologies. This can make rectifying problems in LZC energy systems time-consuming and expensive.

Once the public's trust in energy systems has been reduced by a technical defect it is often hard to regain. An excellent example of this is the lack of public trust in passive houses demonstrated in Sweden, which has grown from the technical difficulties encountered with low energy houses built during the 1970s in the Swedish housing programme (Chapter 3). The technology has moved on since then but the Swedish Passive House Institute faces a real problem overcoming public distrust of passive houses.

Technical defects can occur in any energy system. The problem for energy systems that adopt new technologies or even entirely new structures (as with a decentralised energy system) is that the public are pre-disposed to be sceptical about them. This scepticism is justified if there are operational difficulties. Thus, it is important to avoid these difficulties in the early stages of deployment, and to have systems in place which will quickly address them. Developing stable supply chains for new LZC technologies and building the capacity within the energy industry to manage and maintain systems long-term is vital.

Maintenance of technology

The long-term maintenance of zero carbon homes and their associated infra-structure is a key issue. Gradually utilities are beginning to offer mainte-nance packages for the micro-generation systems they own (e.g. Xcel Ener-gy's maintenance package for solar collectors or PV cells) placed on public buildings and domestic properties. New energy service providers are also beginning to emerge who offer management and maintenance packages, but capacity is still limited, certainly in the UK, USA and Sweden. New technical systems also tend to be expensive to maintain, because both the technolo-gies and expertise needed to repair systems are relatively scarce; as scarcity reduces this problem should recede.

Within centralised energy systems suppliers tend to hold a 'deficit view' of the public as energy users. They are seen to be disengaged from energy systems. This has led to the construction of an energy system and associated processes which minimise public engagement (Devine-Wright, 2006). Thus, the public are not acclimatised to involvement in the maintenance of energy systems. In the case study countries there appears to be a strong public pref-erence for low maintenance energy systems or for utilities to maintain energy systems. The reasons given by residents living in LZC developments are their lack of technical expertise, difficulties accessing suitable replacement technologies, as well as the time and effort involved in maintaining these systems. As technologies become more sophisticated and complicated this reluctance to involve to residents in maintenance could well grow. Certainly there seems to be a potential gap in the market here for property companies, ESCOs and utilities to fill.

Maintaining design integrity

Maintaining the design integrity of zero carbon homes long-term is a con-siderable problem. Without covenants or mandates which require that the design integrity of a building is maintained, its long-term energy efficiency cannot be assured. Product legislation may help by ensuring that only energy efficient products and systems are available to the market (Chapter 9). Access ordinances can be used to ensure that changes to urban design do not impact on a building's access to a renewable energy supply (Chapter 10). Building regulations can be used to ensure that new and refurbished homes are built to high energetic standards (Chapter 9), but it is difficult to regulate residents' interaction with the LZC technologies provided in the privacy of their own home.

The removal of LZC technologies from homes is also an issue, which was highlighted by a study of a low carbon development – Greenwich Mil-lennium Village – in London (Williams, 2008a). Here various appliances designed to reduce resource consumption were actually removed from units by residents, largely for aesthetic reasons' and were replaced with less efficient alternatives. Residents blamed a lack of available low energy alternatives that conformed to their aesthetic preferences and budget. Certainly there is an issue with scarcity of supply and lack of diversity of LZC products available, although it might be possible to over-ride this problem through product legislation. However, conserving LZC technologies in homes might be best encouraged by increasing energy literacy amongst the public. This can be achieved through providing monitoring and feedback.

Monitoring and feedback

Monitoring energy consumption and providing feedback to the household is key to behavioural change (Darby, 2006; Fischer 2008). The current 'invisibility' of energy to the household creates a significant barrier to changing behaviour, as they tend to be removed from both the process of producing energy and their consumption. In other words many households have no idea how much energy they consume or of its environmental impact. Monitoring and feedback systems go some way to addressing this problem by providing a valuable tool for increasing their energy literacy. However, providing households with information alone will not necessarily change behaviour and this may need to be reinforced through tariffs, personal carbon rationing and so on.

A variety of approaches towards monitoring and feed-back can be adopted (Table 11.1). Information interventions (for example energy audits and workshops to improve energy literacy) which are one-off awareness raising events offer an approach. Targeted information – personal energy audits and identification of energy-hungry devices – has been shown to have beneficial behavioural effects. However, more generalised workshops for raising energy literacy have proved less useful and energy savings have been limited.

Metering to provide feedback on current energy usage also helps to raise energy literacy amongst households. Using actual usage data appears to be more effective in changing behaviour. Energy savings of between 0% and 20% have been reported from metering schemes. In addition to usage data, metering can provide useful feedback to households on their production of energy (if fitted with energy generating technologies). Interestingly, this has been shown to be effective in encouraging a reduction in energy consumption (Farhar and Coborn, 2006). Frequent or continuous reporting of data appears to have the greatest impact. The length of time metering schemes operate also influences energy savings: the longer metering is used the greater the savings and the more likely it is to engender a long-term behavioural change amongst households.

Combining metering with information interventions, as is the case for eco-team operated by Global Action Plan, appears to be particularly successful in encouraging long-term energy savings (Staat et al, 2004). Goals for reducing consumption are set for households, identified through initial energy audits. Information interventions offer specific behavioural recommendations for reducing energy consumption tailored to a specific group. Consumption is measured over a six-week period and energy usage data is then compared with baseline data and with others in the eco-team. This allows normative and historical comparison of data which provides added incentive for those in the eco-teams to reduce energy consumption.

Smart meters can produce a range of information: for example the number of energy units consumed, the overall cost of consumption, the CO_2 emissions produced by a household, or all three. The units used will depend on the desired outcome (i.e. is the aim to reduce energy consumption, CO_2 emissions or expenditure on energy?) and the motivations (i.e. environmental or economic or both?) of those suppliers and households using them.

The variation in energy consumption patterns over a 24-hour period or throughout the year can also be monitored. This helps the household to determine where energy savings can be made or costs can be reduced. For example by shifting load from peak to off-peak hours a household can reduce energy costs. It also highlights options for reducing household CO_2 emissions, by switching load to periods when the energy mix favours LZC energy sources and when LZC energy can be stored.

Smart meters can provide energy consumption data for individual appliances. This can provide a useful indication to a household of where savings can be made. It helps to identify which appliances could be replaced to maximise energy efficiency. It can motivate households to alter usage patterns and thus to reduce the quantity of energy consumed. The data can also be used by utilities to manage energy usage remotely or to offer advice to households about specific appliances.

The smart grid can use the data produced by smart meters to manage energy supply and demand effectively. Without the right price or regulatory signals this will tend to be driven by economic effectiveness. However, given the right price and regulatory signals utilities could equally use the data generated by smart meters to reduce CO_2 emissions. Smart metering does provide households with a large amount of useful information which they can use not only to achieve energy and cost savings, but also enable them to determine how best to reduce CO_2 emissions. Thus, smart metering offers a state-of-the-art monitoring system which can be used for positive environmental benefits and greatly enhancing energy literacy. However, operating such a complex system effectively does require a considerable degree of sophistication.

In summary, monitoring and feedback mechanisms tend to be most effective when they provide actual usage data. The frequency with which consumption is monitored influences the energy savings made. More frequent monitoring achieves greater energy savings. When goals to reduce energy consumption or carbon emissions are set by the household this enhances the effectiveness of monitoring. If monitoring occurs over a longer period it is more likely to bring about a long-term change in energy consuming behaviour amongst households. Specific recommendations proffered to households on the basis of monitoring exercises which highlight how they can reduce consumption have also been found to be very effective. Monitoring and feedback greatly enhance the energy literacy of households. It can also help with the social norming process, as providing data to households which allows normative or historical comparison encourages a change in consumption behaviour.

The rebound effect

Increase in household energy efficiency produced by a technical system (a low energy house, the smart grid, a district heating system, etc) results in households being able to afford to consume more energy (and produce more CO_2 emissions) – this is the rebound effect. For example a reduction in expenditure on energy produced by energy efficient design may lead to a household increasing indoor temperatures or using more appliances. It could free household income for more travel or other energy consuming activities which might not always be compatible with using renewable energy sources. Improvements in the energy efficiency of the supply and distribution systems may also increase the quantity of energy households consume.

This is exemplified by the smart grid where there is evidence to suggest the efficiencies of the Boulder smart grid could lead to an increase in energy consumption and production of CO_2 unless carefully managed (Johnson, 2010). This could be encouraged by utilities in order to generate more revenue, unless incentives to reduce consumption are offered. Thus, given the wrong economic incentives or insufficient carbon incentives smart grids could potentially increase carbon emissions (Johnson, 2010). However, smart grid can change household behaviour using price signals and feedback. In this instance policy instruments will be needed to encourage utilities to switch their objective from maximising energy consumption towards minimising CO_2 emissions, perhaps through carbon trading schemes or carbon reduction targets (Chapter 9). Alternatively households could be persuaded to change their behaviour using personal carbon rationing. This should encourage households to use smart technologies to reduce their CO_2 emissions.

Quality of life

Living in zero carbon homes may negatively impact on at least six quality of life dimensions: comfort, convenience, affordability, privacy, personal freedom, safety and security. This is likely to make the prospect of living in zero carbon homes less appealing to all but those most dedicated to carbon

Table 11.1 The impact of monitoring on energy savings: a review of research findings

	Intervention	Savings	Reference
Information interventions	Identification of appliances consuming most energy with feed-back 3 times per week	15.1% reduction in energy usage	Becker (1978)
	Workshop based information about energy saving measures	No savings	Geller (1981)
	Energy audits	21% reduction in electricity usage	Winnet et al. (1982)
Feed-back on current energy usage	Energy consumption shown as cost per hour	Range between 12%– 0% reduction	McClelland and Cook (1979)
	Frequency of feedback influences energy savings	Continuous feedback yields a 12% savings and monthly feedback yields 8%	Hutton et al (1986)
	Time-of-use pricing with continuous feedback	20% reduction in electricity consumption	Chassin and Kiesling (2008)
	Daily feedback is better than weekly or longer intervening periods	13% reduction in electricity consumption feedback provided daily	Winnet et al (1982)
	Comparative feed-back	Electricity savings of 8% and gas savings of 17% over a period of 2 years	Staats et al (2004)
	Feed-back on production of energy (from PV solar panels)	Reduces energy consumption	Farhar and Coborn (2006)

Smart metering	Multi-information smart metering[1]	Energy consumption reduced by 9% during the test period	Ueno et al (2006)
	Smart metering	The specific energy-use reductions achieved range from 5% to 20%, with a median of approximately 6%	Fischer (2008), Faruqui et al (2009)
	Price signals and feedback	Reduces energy demand between 5–15%	Johnson (2010)

Source: Compiled based on Pratt et al, 2010.

1 The information display provided a variety of outputs, including daily load curves for each appliance, percentage of overall consumption, patterns of consumption over ten-day periods, and various recommendations for saving energy.

reduction. Overcoming these problems is central to generating demand for zero carbon homes.

Comfort

If zero carbon homes are to compete with existing housing models they will need to be just as comfortable. A constant, ambient indoor temperature, hot water, fully functioning appliances and lighting are critical to the success of a zero carbon home. Household expectations of what is 'comfortable' seems to escalate as technology improves, energy prices fall and affluence rises, as evidenced by the 6 degree increase in stock mean temperature in the UK between 1970 and 2009 (Chapter 2). Increasing 'energetic expectations' may be addressed to an extent by technological improvement in the energy efficiency of systems and substitution of fossil fuels with low carbon energy sources. However, as the global population expands and becomes more affluent, technology alone cannot offer a long-term solution. Ultimately household expectations must be addressed, perhaps through education, an increase in energy price or introduction of personal carbon allowances.

The low carbon technical systems themselves may have a negative impact on household comfort. Two examples are given here: decentralised renewable energy systems and passive houses. It may be difficult to supply energy throughout a 24-hour period from systems that are reliant on decentralised renewable energy sources. This can be tackled through the inclusion of storage capacity (i.e. pumped-hydro, compressed air, batteries or fuel cells) back-up power stations (often currently operated using fossil fuel) in the grid, and smart grid technologies but this is an expensive option (as demonstrated by the Boulder smart grid). It can also be partially addressed by spreading the peak energy load across a 24-hour period, for example by ensuring a mixture of land uses are connected to the energy system, whose peak demand fall at different times throughout the day. Alternatively, this problem might be tackled by addressing expectations and encouraging households to adopt consumption patterns that better reflect the variation in energy supply using the tariff system.

The second example is proffered by passive houses in Northern Europe, where several issues have arisen in post-occupancy surveys. The airtightness of passive houses can increase internal condensation and dampness. This can encourage the growth of mould, which in turn may have a negative impact on the health of occupants. Passive houses can be designed to overcome this problem by increasing air changes and introducing dehumidifiers. Low occupancy can also be a problem for households living in passive houses in cooler climates. The passive house uses free heat gains (delivered externally by solar radiation and internally by heat emissions from appliance use and occupants) to increase internal temperatures. Thus, for residents who live alone or households where occupants are absent throughout the majority of the day passive houses can be too cold. Of course back-up heating and cooling systems, operated using LZC energy could be used to overcome this problem.

Convenience

Convenience is central to modern lifestyles. Thus, technologies incorporated into zero carbon communities must be convenient to use, maintain, repair and replace if they are to be popular amongst households. Alternatively, property management companies or ESCOs will be needed to operate, manage and maintain the LZC technologies on behalf of the household. This point was very clearly demonstrated by low energy housing projects in the UK (Williams, 2008a; ICARO, 2009).

Residents living in Greenwich Millennium Village (GMV) encountered various problems both operating and replacing energy efficient technologies in their flats (Chapter 3). When GMV was constructed the supply chains for various low carbon technologies incorporated into the design (for example triple-glazed windows) were not well developed. This created difficulties for residents when replacing or maintaining technologies. Thus the ongoing operation and repair of the technologies was time-consuming, difficult and inconvenient. Greater access to LZC technologies will be needed if the design integrity of zero carbon homes is to be maintained. Supply chains for new LZC technologies could develop over time, driven by demand or product legislation.

A further lesson learnt from GMV was that residents did not want to be involved in time-consuming processes such as: connecting to electricity grid, finding a buyer for the surplus energy generated on site, sourcing unusual LZC technologies, training, maintaining energy systems and getting consensus amongst residents for operational decisions. Certainly the more cash-rich and time-poor residents preferred energy or property management companies to deal with the operation and maintenance of LZC technologies and energy systems (Williams, 2008a; ICARO, 2009). However amongst the cash-poor, time-rich residents there was greater interest in being involved in the management and operation of LZC energy systems, particularly if some form of remuneration was available. Pay-back from energy production, managing and maintaining the system could offer two sources of income for the less affluent households in a resident-managed model.

Even with utility-managed energy systems convenience may be threatened. The smart grid in Boulder provides a good example of this. To maximise CO_2 savings from the smart grid it is important to optimise the composition of the energy generation mix. The greatest CO_2 savings can be made if there is high penetration of renewable energy into the smart grid. It was calculated for the Boulder smart grid that if 50% of the energy consumed by customers was generated from wind, this could result in up to 23% reduction in CO_2 emissions (Johnson, 2010). However, peak generation of wind energy in Boulder occurs during the night. Thus, in order to reduce CO_2 emissions households have to be encouraged to operate appliances at night or to store the energy generated at night for use during the day time in plug-in hybrid vehicles. This is certainly less convenient for the household than the usual 'demand-response' system and will mean lifestyle changes.

Affordability

Zero carbon lifestyles must be affordable if they are to be attractive. Initially the capital cost of building to a zero carbon standard will be higher (Chapters 2, 3 and 6). However, it is expected that this additional expense can be recouped through reduced operational costs. The energy produced from a zero carbon development can be sold back to the grid, thus helping to generate a return. In addition, as energy prices rise, zero carbon homes should become more affordable (and even profitable).

Of course there has been considerable concern about the pay-back times for LZC technologies and high upfront capital costs. In addition, evidence to support higher resale values being commanded for these properties has been very limited to date. High capital costs, long pay-back periods and lack of evidence of higher resale values have been identified as presenting the greatest barriers to the wider adoption of zero carbon homes.

The GEOS team sought to develop an affordable zero-net energy home, with a short pay-back period. The technological package chosen for GEOS was based on the financial incentives[1] available, the local climate (300 days of sunshine a year) and geology. The most cost-effective technological package that could deliver zero-net energy was chosen. The break-point at which it was more cost effective to install renewable technologies rather than to increase the energy efficiency of the building envelope was calculated, based on the costs of energy, technology and the incentives available. Net energy consumption was reduced by a combination of energy efficiency measures (60% of the reduction) and the generation of renewable energy (from geothermal and solar sources – Figure 11.1).

The Colorado climate meant that cooling systems weren't needed in the GEOS development. It was sufficient to design buildings to maximise shading in the summer months (a less costly option). However, heating was very important. Initially the GEOS team did consider solar heating systems, but they were found to be too expensive (both for individual buildings and at community level). Instead a geothermal heating system was adopted. The most appropriate scale at which to install the geothermal heating system was considered (again largely based on cost). Initially a district heating system for the whole development was the preferred option. However, because of the way in which the development had to be financed, it was not cost effective to build the system in one for all 250 units. Thus smaller-scale heating systems serving around 5–6 units were developed.

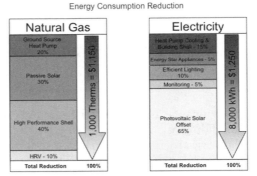

Figure 11.1 Achieving zero-net energy in GEOS.

Source: GEOS presentation to USGBC, 2010.

The energetic improvements made to a house in the GEOS development (over and above that required by the local building regulations) were estimated to cost an additional $45,000. But the monthly operational costs (mortgage and energy bills) were calculated to be less. Additional costs for green construction were included in the mortgage where the interest is tax deductible. This, combined with lower utility bills, produced a zero-net energy home, which costs no more to own than a comparable home without the LZC technologies (Stenftenagel and Klebl, 2010 – Figure 11.2).

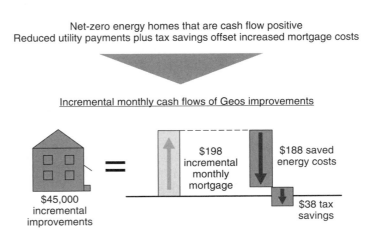

Figure 11.2 Net zero cost for the GEOS development.

Source: Stefenagel and Glavis, 2010.

Of course there is no blue-print for the most cost-effective technological package to achieve zero-net energy or zero carbon standards in housing. The GEOS package will not be appropriate in all circumstances, although the GEOS team do suggest it would be the most economic for Colorado. The most affordable technological package for achieving the same standard will vary with environmental, technological and economic factors. However, similar calculations can be made by producers and will need to be made if zero carbon homes are to find the mass market.

Privacy

Personal privacy also appears to be central to perceived quality of life, at least in Europe and the USA. The introduction of smart grid systems may create privacy issues for households. Smart grid systems operate effectively because they generate a large amount of detailed data about household usage of energy as well as decentralized production of renewable energy. Without this level of detail systems could not function efficiently. Smart grids can be 'hacked' into and they hold a significant amount of personal data. For example they produce detailed information about people's daily habits, the appliances they own and so on. This is not information most people want to become publicly available as it can reduce their personal privacy and security.

In some American states (e.g. Florida) this information has also been used to encourage social norming. Certainly it has been shown that normative data can provide a useful stimulus for reducing household energy consumption. One American university published all household energy data on-line so that people could look up their neighbours' usage. The idea was that households would use this information to assess their current level of energy consumption against their neighbours and seek to address it if necessary. However, issues have been raised concerning individuals' privacy and security with this degree of detail.

Providing normative data is helpful in influencing behaviour, although the question is the degree of detail that is necessary to produce a positive behavioural change amongst households. It is useful for households to know how their energy consumption compares with best practice and average households in their area, but providing too much information compromises privacy and personal security (Reed, 2010).

There is an issue about who should own the data produced from a smart grid (Quinn, 2009; Reed 2010). If a utility owns the data then the customer cannot control access to that information. The utility might sell information to other edge-of-service-providers (ESPs) for example, further reducing personal security and leading to unwanted approaches from ESPs. Conversely the utility may restrict access to personal information thus making it impossible for ESPs to gauge markets for their services and products that might be essential for the smooth operation of a LZC energy system. Some have suggested the possibility of households owning their personal data and thus controlling who has access to it (Reed, 2010). Certainly this issue of privacy and ownership of personal data will need to be addressed if smart grids are critical to the delivery of zero carbon homes.

Personal freedom

Personal freedom is also an important factor influencing perceived quality of life in Europe and the USA. The smart grid and district heating systems provide two good examples of where conflict between the introduction of zero carbon technical systems and personal freedom might occur. Concerns about the impact of the smart grid on personal freedom were highlighted by research in the USA and UK (ICARO, 2009; Reed, 2010; Farhar, 2010). Households could opt for utility-controlled, remote energy management services. This enables utilities to control appliance usage and times at which energy is delivered to a household remotely. The utility's decision will be based on the households' tariff, peak load and system capacity. Thus households may find that their appliances are switched off during periods of peak consumption if they are on a low energy tariff. This cannot be over-ridden by the household unless they change their agreement with the utility. This degree of utility control will affect personal freedom to use energy in the home directly, but it is of course the household's choice to opt for this service.

District heating systems in Europe are not subjected to the same competition laws as electricity supply. Thus, monopolies for heat provision have formed particularly in urban areas (e.g. E-ON in Malmö, Fortum in Stockholm, Utilicom in Southampton) and new housing developments (e.g. Barratt Homes are currently working with EDF, Utilicom and E-ON on projects). This means that households have to buy their heat from the only local heat provider, which of course restricts competition and choice. From a household's point of view this does not lead to the most cost-effective provision of heat. From a provider's viewpoint it is the only way to secure the finance needed to build, install and operate the district heating systems. One way to overcome the problem is for a third party (e.g. municipality) to provide the distribution network through which a variety of heat providers could supply the needs of the population. However, this option is expensive and risky. Yet restricting choice for heat provision could meet with consumer resistance (as demonstrated by B001, Malmö).

Safety and security

There is mounting concern about the security of fossil fuel supply and energy prices. This has led to growing interest in autonomous, individual renewable energy systems (e.g. solar housing in California). However, there is also concern about the intermittency of an energy supply based on decentralised renewable systems (Painuly, 2001; Reiche, 2002; Jardine and Ault, 2008). There are safety issues surrounding the connection of many smaller generators to the grid and the potential for power surges (Painuly, 2001; Reiche, 2002; Jardine and Ault, 2008). To an extent these problems could be addressed through the introduction of a variety of storage systems and smart grid technologies (Chapter 2).

In a decarbonised, decentralised grid a larger number of smaller energy generating facilities would also need to be safeguarded and maintained. It is important that installations are maintained and serviced regularly to obviate safety risks. Utilities, ESCOs, community energy cooperatives or private individuals would need to ensure that technical systems were regularly maintained. It is also important that sites and technologies are secure. Installing hydrogen fuel cells, hydrogen storage facilities, mini nuclear power plants or any energy producing facility in local communities could potentially be extremely risky and would need to be secured.

Concerns range from terrorist threats at one extreme and to problems with vandalism at the other. Certainly utilities installing LZC energy systems have already encountered problems with vandalism. The security of smart grid information creates another risk. The availability of personal household data online (occupancy and appliance ownership information) increases the potential for petty crime (Farhar, 2010). There has been discussion about how to best secure this information. There is still a great deal more research that needs to be done in this area to ensure the safety and security of decentralised decarbonised energy systems.

Moving on

There are many conflicts between aspects of quality of life (comfort, convenience, affordability, privacy, personal freedom, safety and security) and the new technical systems needed to deliver zero carbon lifestyles. Interestingly the value given to these aspects of quality of life appears to be derived from the technical system that many households have become accustomed to, which has arisen largely for economic reasons. However, the benefits of these more centralised and highly industrialised systems (e.g. convenience, comfort, affordability, etc) have been sold to the population and are now the basis on which households form opinions about new technical systems. Thus, the technical systems and social attitudes towards them have co-evolved together.

Centralised and industrialised production systems for energy and housing (fossil fuel energy systems and mass produced housing) developed for economic and pragmatic reasons. Both the house-building and energy industries assume a 'deficit view' of households, driven by individualistic and self-interested values. Households seek convenience and often a passive role in decision-making processes, delivery of services and products. Current industrial regimes presume that the public are driven by maximising utility (energy performance, cost reduction, etc) rather than social and environmental goals, a view that is contested by various academics (Devine-Wright, 2006; Grove-White et al, 2000). However, this view of has greatly influenced the built environment and infrastructure systems that we see around us today.

To a large extent the technical system (the built environment and energy systems) has driven the changes in the social system. Passive technological systems have produced passive consumers (although this process is self-reinforcing of course). To break this cycle new technical systems are needed, which encourage greater involvement of households in managing and producing energy. Yet for these technical systems to be successful a significant shift in the social system is needed. Households will need to be empowered, in order that they become more engaged in decision-making processes and activities within their communities. In the next section we discuss how this might happen.

Energy citizens

Zero carbon homes actually provide an opportunity to move away from the centralised model for supplying and consuming energy (in which a household is a purely an energy consumer) towards a decentralised model in which a household can become actively involved in and responsible for the management of LZC energy systems (thus becoming 'energy citizens'). This is the 'surfeit' approach. This degree of involvement could help to develop energy literacy and raise energy awareness amongst the public (Dobbyn and Thomas, 2005; Farhar and Coborn, 2006; Roy et al, 2007). It could increase public acceptance of new LZC technical systems (Faiers and Neame, 2006) and empower households so they play a role in tackling environmental problems and generating income for themselves and the community. This could help to encourage long-term change in values and behaviour, essential if energy consumption and associated CO_2 emissions are to be tackled and the rebound effect avoided.

Thus building zero carbon homes could assist in the process of creating 'energy citizens'. Significant technical, economic, social and institutional changes would be needed to support a shift from energy consumers to 'energy citizens' (Table 11.2). Technical systems would need to evolve to support the distributed production of low carbon energy, for example through the introduction of smart technologies and renewable energy storage facilities (Chapter 2). Pricing systems to benefit small producers of low carbon energy would be required (Chapter 9). Industrial restructuring to support distributed generation and supply of renewable energy would be essential (Chapter 8). New institutions (community energy co-operatives)

Table 11.2 A summary of facets of social representations of energy system evolution

Facet	Evolution of a centralised system	Evolution of a decentralised system
Technological	Centralised, large-scale, automated, 'hard' /technical	Decentralised, smaller-scale, user engagement, 'soft'/socio-technical
Environmental	Use hydrocarbon technologies and nuclear energy	Use renewables
Governance	Top-down, centralised institutions, private sector led, exclusive, representative democracy, expert knowledge	Bottom-up, greater role for local and regional institutions, community cooperatives and cross-sectoral partnerships, inclusive, participatory democracy
Human	Consumer/deficit, ignorant, lazy, passive, individualistic, self-interested, personal utility maximiser, egoistic values, disempowered	Consumer/citizen, aware, motivated and engaged, active, socially embedded, motivated by a range of values (including biospheric and altruistic), empowered
	Passive consumer	Energy citizen

Source: Devine-Wright, 2006.

that enable the community to operate energy systems collectively (and more efficiently) would also be helpful.

The community energy co-operatives would be motivated not only by profit (as with most privately owned utilities) but also by well-being, quality of life and environmental issues. A more participatory approach could develop through the creation of these co-operatives, helping to empower households and the wider community. Thus, there are social as well as environmental benefits associated with adopting this approach. 'Energy citizens' already exist in some countries, for example in Germany where there is a history of participatory democracy, community ownership, active citizenship and prioritisation of environmental issues. Examples include the *Baugruppen* and community energy cooperatives in Freiburg. In contrast, countries where systems of governance have tended to be top-down, paternalistic and exclusive (for example the UK) and industry has taken a deficit view of the public, households have become accustomed to a more passive role. Here there may be considerable difficulty in encouraging the social shift needed to create active, 'energy citizens'.

Models for involving the consumer (households in this instance) in the production and management of energy – co-provision – are many and varied. However, they can be classified in three ways:

- in terms of consumer involvement;
- in terms of energy providers involvement;
- in terms of the provision process itself.

The role of the consumer

Sauter and Watson (2007) describe a range of consumer roles – 'normal consumers', 'citizen consumers' and 'co-providers'. 'Normal consumers' are passive consumers. Currently, the majority of the population in Europe and the USA are 'normal consumers'. Thus, they take no part in the design, operation or management of energy systems. This group tend to choose energy providers based on cost and service reliability (Figure 11.3). 'Citizen consumers' are active in that they choose their energy supply based on social and environmental objectives (as we have seen this is a small percentage even in locations where 'green consumers' reside, e.g. Boulder and Freiburg). This group could also encompass consumers who allow utilities to install LZC technologies in their home or community, consume the energy, but play no part in the generation, management or maintenance of energy. The 'co-providers' ('energy citizens') can be involved in the production of LZC energy, the design of LZC energy systems, and/or their management.

The role of the energy provider

Sauter and Watson (2007) also suggest that this spectrum of consumer roles can be combined with different roles for utilities/ESCOs when considering micro-generation. Sauter and Watson (2007) suggest three models:

Consumer role	Type of consumer	Motivation	Example	Energy praxis
Passive	Normal consumer	Pragmatic – cost and reliability of energy supply	NA	Low
	Citizen consumer	Social and environmental – "ethical energy"	Green energy tariffs - Freiburg (Germany) and Boulder (Colorado, USA)	
		Economic and environmental	Consumer provides site for generation of LZC energy Excel energy PV cells (Boulder Colorado, USA)	
Active	Energy citizen or co-provider	Economic, environmental and social	Residents in Vauban district and GEO's development (once completed)	High

Figure 11.3 Consumer roles.

Source: Author's own.

the 'company control', 'plug & play' and 'community microgrid' models. These demonstrate a spectrum of involvement on the part of the utility (or ESCO) but are by no means comprehensive in terms of the options available (Figure 11.4).

The utility has greatest influence in the 'company control' model whilst the consumer is largely passive. The model is based on the notion that companies might use fleets of micro-generators as a substitute for central power generation – i.e. as a virtual power plant (Sauter and Watson, 2007). Consumers merely provide the site for energy generation and are not involved in the operation of the LZC technologies installed by the energy company. This model is unlikely to offer any real motivation for behavioural change or raise energy literacy amongst consumers.

The 'plug and play' and 'community micro-grid' models substantially increase consumer involvement in the production and management of energy. For the 'plug and play' model, consumers own and finance energy generating technologies and export energy to the grid. They tend to manage their own energy consumption to maximise the quantity of energy exported to the grid when the financial return is good. This approach helps raise energy literacy amongst consumers (Farhar and Coborn, 2006). They become more aware of their own consumption patterns, the value of energy and how to improve their own energy efficiency in order to maximise returns.

The 'community micro-grid' is a more complicated model. Many micro-generation units (owned and financed by consumers – households, businesses, industries and other organisations) are connected to a micro-grid. Each control their unit and manage the supply–demand balance within the

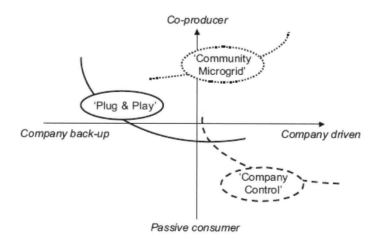

Figure 11.4 Deployment models for microgeneration.[2]
Source: Sauter and Watson, 2007.

micro-grid. Utilities/ESCOs may also play a role in the management and operation of the micro-grid, but essentially they act in partnership with the consumers. Together these actors will form a community energy company, or alternatively the community may operate alone and form a community energy co-operative.

Significant benefits accrue by involving energy providers in the process. They bring expertise, financial resources and experience to the table. Their involvement also reduces the risk to the investor. Thus it is easier to raise finance for projects which include energy providers. However, they will have different priorities to the community, focused largely on profit unless otherwise compelled by policy instruments (Chapter 9). However, partnerships between energy providers and the community have been quite effective in delivering social, environmental as well as economic goals.

The energy provision process

The role of the consumer and utility in the process of LZC energy provision (Figure 11.5) also creates a further series of models for co-provision. If consumers have a passive role then they will not be involved in any stage of this process, all stages will be delivered by the utility/ESCO. The Boulder smart grid encourages consumers to play a role in generating their own energy and managing consumption. However, the utility is still involved in the entire provision process. BedZED residents were also involved in the production and management stages of the energy provision process. In Vauban residents were involved in producing energy, as well as designing, managing and maintaining the energy system. In contrast residents in B001 and Hammarby were removed from the entire provision process. For these consumers energy will remain 'invisible'.

The case studies suggest that there are three important points in the provision process which can affect consumer behaviour: producing energy, designing and managing the energy system (Figure 11.5). Consumer involvement in managing an energy system increases consumer energy literacy encourages a reduction in energy consumption and possibly a switch to LZC energy sources. The monitoring process raises consumer awareness of consumption and production patterns. Managing consumption and production gives the consumer the responsibility to take decisions over how much energy they will consume, store or produce. Making consumers responsible for energy management is central to changing behaviour.

Consumer involvement in the production of energy also plays an important role in changing behaviour. Not only does it increase consumers' energy awareness it also provides additional motivation to reduce personal consumption, since lowering personal consumption increases the quantity of energy available to sell to other consumers. If the revenue from the energy produced returns to the local community (either as private individuals or

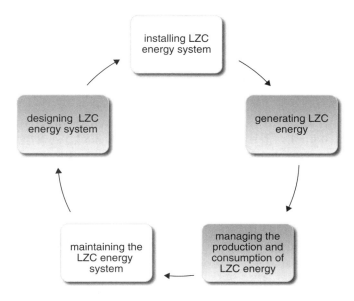

Figure 11.5 The process of energy provision.

Source: Author's own.

the community as a whole) this could provide sufficient incentive to change behaviour. It will increase energy literacy in the community and, through a social norming process, encourage others to become involved.

Involving new communities in the decision to install a LZC energy system as part of the design process can also be very effective. Communities that have opted to install LZC energy systems or adopt LZC design principles into their new development appear to have more vested interest in its success. Certainly this seems to be true in Vauban where residents have been supportive of the low carbon concept from the start (Chapter 10).

However, in the case of solar homes in California it was found that consumers preferred that house-builders made the decision to include new solar systems in units on their behalf (Chapter 3). They did not want to be involved in the decision-making process, due to their perceived technical ignorance. They were happy with the end product and most sought homes with PV for their next purchase. Energy consumption also reduced amongst these households. This suggests involvement in the decision-making process, at least initially, is not always important for future adoption or successful operation of LZC systems.

In B001 and Hammarby residents were not involved in the decision to install LZC technologies or adopt LZC design in their communities. The energetic efficiency of the development was lower than expected. This was blamed at least in part on the lifestyles of those living in the units and the fashion in which they interacted with the technologies. If the residents of B001 and Hammarby had been involved in the decision-making process to incorporate LZC energy systems in the development, they may have had a greater interest in reducing their energy consumption, although it is likely that metering would have been equally effective.

Consumer involvement in the installation and maintenance of LZC energy systems may also increase energy literacy. However, the level of technical expertise required to install and maintain a LZC energy system and lack of access to supply chains create significant barriers to the involvement of most consumers in both processes. There is no real evidence that involving consumers in either process will have a significant impact on energy consumption. Thus it is debatable, considering the time and effort it would take for most consumers to develop the necessary expertise, whether it is worth it.

A great deal more research is needed in this area to determine the relative benefits of encouraging consumer involvement throughout the energy provision process, in terms of reducing energy consumption and CO_2 emissions. The focus to date has largely been on management and metering. The examples given above highlight the diversity of approaches that are likely to be needed in order to cater for a range of groups with differing abilities, attitudes and preferences.

The role of social capital in delivering 'energy citizens'

Social context plays a critical role in the emergence of 'energy citizens', community energy cooperatives. Here it is argued that social capital is fundamental to the emergence of 'energy citizens' because it empowers them to act. Social capital is the 'glue' that binds social networks together. It influences the type, number and strength of the social bonds and interactions in a community. Where social bonds are strong, there is greater trust between individuals in a community and greater reciprocity. These bonds enable communities to work together to tackle environmental problems, share resources and exchange ideas more effectively. Communities also develop shared values, behaviours and norms. This is the social context in which 'energy citizens', community energy co-operatives or community energy companies can operate most effectively (Figure 11.6).

Social networks are useful conduits through which information can be passed and they can facilitate learning and be used to increase energy literacy amongst residents. The dissemination of information through social networks also offers a powerful tool for changing residents' values and energy-consuming behaviour through a social norming process. The stronger the bonds between those living in the local community, the more feasible it is to

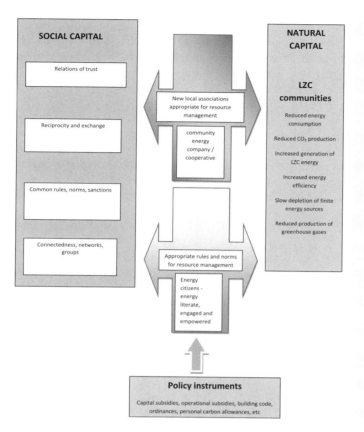

Figure 11.6 The role of social capital in creating LZC communities.
Source: Author's own.

implement community-wide infrastructural solutions to the delivery of low carbon energy and form community energy co-operatives or companies.

By strengthening social bonds within a community, trust can build. This encourages residents to act reciprocally, to share resources and work together to tackle collective action problems, such as reducing energy consumption or generating LZC energy. Thus, building social capital within communities can empower them and promote the appropriate rules and norms for resource management, enabling the creation of new local associations for the management and production of LZC energy. This can be further encouraged using regulatory controls and financial incentives including personal carbon allowances, mandatory carbon reduction targets for utilities, capital and operational subsidies for small-scale producers and so on (Chapter 9).

Trends in social capital differ dramatically between the case study countries (Table 11.3). In the UK and USA social capital is declining, whilst in Sweden and Germany it is increasing. In the UK and USA declining levels of inter-personal trust suggest that encouraging households to form community energy cooperatives/companies may be difficult. Certainly there is evidence to support this, including the limited number of community energy cooperatives in the UK and USA.

In Germany social capital is increasing from a low base. Levels of inter-personal trust are increasing (and are now higher than that found in the UK and USA). Also there appears to be an increase in informal sociability and formal participation in the community, manifested in *Baugruppen* and community energy cooperatives for example. Higher levels of trust, sociability and participation all help to provide a suitable social context in which community energy cooperatives can emerge, particularly in combination with the financial incentive offered by the capital and operational subsidies (Chapter 9).

In Sweden social capital is increasing from a high base. The Swedes have a long history of participative democracy, more collaborative housing models and lifestyles. Today high levels of inter-personal trust, informal socialising and participation in single-issue and environmental groups suggest that the Swedes would certainly be interested in forming community energy cooperatives. However, there is currently a lack of financial incentives for decentralised energy in Sweden. Thus, community energy cooperatives/companies have not emerged yet.

Regardless of the social capital at a national level, it is possible to generate social capital in communities. Building local social capital will encourage public engagement in community activities and help to create energy citizens. The development of new zero carbon communities provides a very good

Table 11.3 Trends in social capital in case study countries

Country	Social capital trend	Detailed trends
United Kingdom	Stable or declining from a high base	– Most types of associational membership have increased since the '50s. But anincreasing gap between the 'well connected' middle class and the working class. – Some shift towards self-help or single-issue organisations. Also some decline inmembership of traditional women's groups, political parties etc. – No clear evidence of decreased levels of informal socialising (but time spent visitingfriends is down especially among full-time male workers). – Declining levels of inter-personal trust

United States	Declining from a high base	(1959: 56%; 1995: 31%) and of trust inpublic institutions, especially amongst the young. – Declining associational membership. E.g. two thirds of Americans attended club meetings in the mid-'70s. In the late '90s, two thirds never attended. – Intensity of participation has fallen even more (fewer meetings, reduced willingness to assume leadership roles etc). – Declining levels of political, civil and religious engagement. Not compensated by growth in single issue movements e.g. environmental, civil rights groups. – Falling levels of informal socialising (having friends for dinner etc). – Declining levels of inter-personal trust (1981: 55%; 1998: 33%), especially amongst the young
Germany	Increasing from a low base	– Evidence of increasing inter-personal trust (1981: 32%; 1997: 42%). – Increasing levels of formal participation and informal sociability. – Falling membership of trade unions, political parties and church organisations. – Disengagement of young people. – Trend towards more transient and personalistic involvement.
Sweden	Increasing from a high base	High levels of organisational membership. 92% of Swedes belong to a voluntary organisation. Some evidence that social organisations have displayed increasing vitality with single-issue groups growing in importance. – Inter-personal trust has risen (1981: 57%; 1997: 67%) as has informal socialising. But: – Active involvement in political organisations has declined, as have religiousmovements and women's organisations. – Growth is concentrated in leisure, sports, cultural, and environmental organisations. – Some evidence of lower levels of affinity. – Declining levels of trust in political institutions in recent decades.

Source: Performance and Innovation Unit, 2002.

opportunity for developing this level of engagement. Involving residents in the a variety of processes leading to the creation (community formation, visioning, planning, designing and financing) and eventually management of new communities can help to build social capital (Williams, 2005a; Melt-zler, 2000). Using social contact design principles within new communities can further reinforce this (Williams 2005b).

Thus the design of communities and the processes operating within them can encourage greater social interaction between residents. Social interaction enables the exchange of resources, support and ideas. It encourages the formation of strong social bonds between residents, that providing a network through which social norming can occur. As relationships strengthen this builds trust between community members, and feelings of belonging and efficacy grow which in turn encourages greater engagement in community activities. This cycle is described by Metzler (2000) in his model for empowerment (Figure 11.7). Willingness to be engaged in community activities needs to be developed more widely in society if 'energy citizens' and community energy cooperatives are to become a reality. The development of new zero carbon communities could provide an opportunity to create social systems conducive to greater public engagement in the stewardship of energy.

To move away from 'deficit' towards 'surfeit' models for zero carbon communities will require that the households are more engaged in the design, production and operation of the built environment in which they live. This

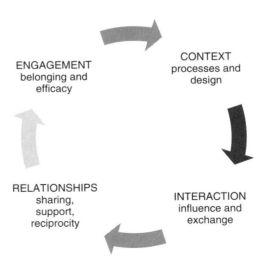

Figure 11.7 The empowerment model.

Source: Metzler, 2000.

will require that the social context (alongside the technical, cultural, institutional and political context) supports this degree of engagement. Thus it is important to rebuild social capital within communities. The existence of cohousing (Sweden, USA, and UK), *Baugruppen/Baugemeinschaften* (Germany) and community energy cooperatives (Germany, USA, UK) provides evidence that this is entirely possible.

Zero carbon lifestyles: a paradigm shift?

Achieving lower carbon lifestyles within the existing system (social and technical) is perfectly feasible, through efficiency measures and substitution of fossil fuels with low carbon energy sources. Thus low carbon lifestyles can be delivered through centralised, decarbonised energy systems (decarbonised through fuel substitution in combination with tri-generation and co-generation technologies) linked to extremely energy efficient houses. In this scenario, household involvement in decision-making processes and the operation of these technical systems will be minimised. This 'accommodator approach' is consistent with the existing paradigm.

However, taking the 'accommodator approach' will not address energy consumption nor will it address the values, expectations and motivations underlying current energy consumption patterns. Ultimately increasing the efficiency of technical systems is likely to produce the rebound effect, particularly as affluence rises. The capacity to produce all forms of energy is limited by the resources and technologies available at any one time. Combine this with an increase in population and affluence globally and it is all too apparent that consumption will need to be addressed if zero carbon targets are to be achieved. To avoid the rebound effect the values, expectations and motivations under-pinning consumption patterns need to be addressed. Thus, a new approach is required.

To move towards zero carbon lifestyles will require a paradigm shift in the existing technical and social systems. Households will need to transform from being passive consumers to engaged energy citizens, who are willing and able to be involved in decision-making processes and resource management within their communities. This should be encouraged through the social context and technical systems. The production of zero carbon homes and communities would provide the technical system in which residents could adopt zero carbon lifestyles. However, the technical system would need to be embedded in a social context conducive to resident engagement in energy stewardship, (i.e. one in which local social capital is well-developed). In fact the co-evolution of the social and technical systems is likely to produce a range of possible models for achieving zero carbon lifestyles. This diversity is important, if the socio-technical systems are to be compatible with the context in which they are embedded. Yet again this points towards the fact that there is no blue-print for zero carbon communities.

Chapter 12

A time for change

Current challenges and opportunities

The environmental imperative to move towards a decarbonised global society is clear. Stern said back in 2006: 'There is still time to avoid the worst impacts of climate change, if we take strong action now' (Stern, 2006). Several years on and very little has happened. Governments still shy away from international agreements on mandatory carbon reduction targets. They are concerned that mandatory carbon caps will slow economic growth. Yet the decoupling of GDP from CO_2 emissions is possible through dematerialisation and substitution. Nevertheless powerful vested interests in the energy industry are resistant to a regime change and there is little political support for mandatory international CO_2 reduction targets.

Regardless, fossil fuels are running out and national energy security will steadily reduce as the supply becomes scarcer. Increasing scarcity of fossil fuels will require that we re-think the way in which new development is planned. Of course this will not only be in terms of buildings and their energy supply systems (as with zero carbon homes). Development patterns, transport infrastructure, the integration of utilities and waste infrastructure, the local provision of goods and services, radical changes in consumer expectations and lifestyles will all need to be considered in an energy-constrained world.

Several trends could provide potential opportunities for growth in the deployment of zero carbon systems:

- major development programmes (in China, India, Middle East, etc);
- the scarcity of fossil fuels (energy prices and security);
- growing environmental awareness;
- economic growth and investment opportunities.

Major development programmes (in China, India and the Middle East) could provide the stimulus needed for the wider deployment of zero carbon homes. For example, the mega-cities currently being built in China are providing the Chinese with an opportunity to build their capacity to deliver zero carbon systems at scale. Building at scale has helped to build the expertise and establish supply chains for new technologies needed to deliver zero carbon systems. It has also helped to drive down prices. Thus the cost of introducing new zero carbon systems in Chinese cities is rapidly reducing. Meanwhile the Chinese are becoming the biggest producers of low carbon technologies (e.g. solar hot water collectors[1]). The Chinese will of course be able to export these zero carbon systems back to Europe and the USA should development in these regions pick up.

The increasing scarcity of fossil fuels and problems with energy security will also create a stimulus for the deployment of zero carbon homes. Scarcities will drive up prices of fossil fuels radically, which will help to generate demand for low carbon energy alternatives (renewable energy and nuclear) amongst energy generators, suppliers and the public. It will increasingly drive a market for energy management services and very energy efficient homes amongst the public. Fossil fuel extractors will also have to begin to develop a more diverse energy portfolio if they are to flourish. Thus increasing scarcity of fossil fuels provides an opportunity for zero carbon homes. The problem is that carbon emissions need to be tackled now if irreversible climate change is to be avoided.

There is growing interest, awareness and concern about environmental issues in society. As a result of education, greater access to information and recent experience (exposure to resource wars, climatic changes and extreme weather events, energy crises, black-outs, etc) society is becoming increasingly aware of the problems created by the consumption and scarcity of fossil fuels. For a variety of reasons an increasing number are seeking cleaner and more secure alternatives. There is also an increase in interest amongst consumers in 'green' products and services. Thus, there is likely to be growing demand for zero carbon homes in the future.

The current global recession has highlighted the folly of nations relying on financial services, financial markets and increase in land / property value as the basis of economic growth. It has become increasingly apparent that there is a need to widen the existing economic base of many countries by creating new manufacturing, knowledge and service-based industries. The environmental crisis provides a stimulus for developing new 'green' industries. For example green industries are being seen as a core part of the American strategy for widening its economic base and growth. Zero carbon homes could potentially generate a range of employment opportunities (designing, constructing, managing and maintaining these new technical systems) across a number of sectors.

Zero carbon homes could also provide households with the opportunity to invest in energy. The lack of security offered by investment on the stock exchange, property, from pensions and low interest rates for savers, means small private investors are searching for more secure and profitable investment options. Investing in individual or community energy systems could provide a good investment option, particularly if the wider fiscal and regulatory framework is supportive (as in Germany). In the long term the value of these investments is likely to grow as the price of energy rises.

All of these trends could help increase the popularity of zero carbon homes and lead to wider deployment.

Lessons so far...

Lessons learnt from the research presented in this book are many and varied. In technical terms there is no real reason why zero carbon homes cannot be built now. Highly energy efficient buildings, housing developments that generate their entire energy supply from renewable sources, and a range of effective renewable energy technologies already exist. Certainly technical solutions for decarbonising new build housing are available. It is retrofitting appropriate LZC technologies in the existing stock which poses greater technical problems. As is often the case the real barrier to implementation in new development is the resistance within the existing industrial regime to change and the unwillingness of government (particularly at an international scale) to enforce it.

The progress so far in delivering zero carbon homes is very limited (Chapter 6). In fact few examples of LZC development currently exist. Where examples do exist there is little evidence that the concepts, knowledge and systems developed are propagated more widely by industry or government. Often examples of best practice remain exactly that, or worse still there is a reversion to the old fossil fuel-guzzling models.

Even with significant public expenditure on LZC energy systems and housing the results are often disappointing. This is largely because the existing industrial regimes and incumbent technologies are still better supported than the newly emerging alternatives. Also the vested interests in industry, particularly in the energy industry are often so powerful that they can quash any competing technical system that undermines their market dominance (Chapters 7 and 8).

An important question now is who should fund the expansion of LZC energy systems – the energy and house-building industry or national governments? The bodies through which the bills are incurred will affect the distribution of payments. However, ultimately the bill will be paid by the population, consumers or tax payers. The manner in which funds are raised for new LZC infrastructure will be largely based on the political ideology of the governments in power.

In Europe and the USA the rate of new development has slowed in recent times. Applying new technical systems to existing communities is significantly more problematic than integrating them into new communities. A whole range of technological, institutional, political, cultural and economic barriers slow the transfer of new socio-technical systems to existing cities, towns and neighbourhoods. As house-building stagnates in Europe and the USA there has been limited opportunity to apply these LZC technological systems to new developments.

The performance of exemplar projects has also often been disappointing (Chapter 5). The scale of carbon savings, increases in energy efficiency or generation of renewable energy achieved in practice are often significantly less than predicted. There is a disconnection between theory and practice resulting from difficulties in implementation and over-optimistic modelling. Addressing both implementation and modelling is important if these exemplar projects are to be a success and become more widely adopted.

Lack of demand for LZC products (zero carbon homes, energy systems and energy) and services is hugely influential in terms of the wider deployment issues (Chapter 6). Even in locations where 'green consumers' reside demand is limited. This highlights the absurdity of relying on markets alone to drive the changes required within the energy and house-building industries to deliver zero carbon homes.

Major increases in the price of fossil fuels and carbon quotas will start to generate greater market demand for LZC technical systems (Chapter 9). Carbon quotas are already in place in Europe and there has been a significant increase in the price of fossil fuels globally. However, so far both have been insufficient to encourage the wider deployment of LZC technical systems. One answer lies in addressing the issue of vested interests, by encouraging the most powerful in the energy industry to diversify their portfolio, both in terms of fuel type and services offered.

The introduction of the zero carbon policy may eventually influence the geography of development and impact on urban form, in a manner similar to the motor car (Chapter 10). There is no blue-print for a zero carbon home (Chapter 2). A zero carbon home is a complex technical system. It can be constructed by combining a variety of sub-systems (building and energy systems). The optimal technical system will vary dramatically with location. This variation is affected by the energy resources available, existing infrastructure, urban form, regulatory controls and fiscal incentives, local culture, expertise and institutions. This local variation may affect where development occurs (i.e. the geography of zero carbon development), whilst urban form will affect the type of zero carbon system used (Chapter 10).

Policy instruments designed to encourage the delivery of zero carbon homes will need to allow for a diversity of technical solutions (Chapter 9). Thus, more prescriptive approaches should be avoided. This degree of local diversity makes a zero carbon home a difficult technical system to mass-produce. It creates considerable industrial resistance to adoption and deployment as each project has to be considered in its local context. Different technical systems will require that producers form partnerships with a wider range of suppliers and support services. A larger skills set will be required amongst producers. Replication of systems reduces costs, due to the time and resources saved through using existing suppliers, sub-contractors, previous knowledge and experience. The bespoke nature of each system makes them an expensive and time-consuming product to create (Chapters 7 and 8). The diversity of models for zero carbon homes is also likely to create difficulties with the user–technology interface (Chapter 11). Citizens may have to learn to use many different complex technical systems throughout their lifetime.

A related debate which has been highlighted in the research focuses on the role of the household in ensuring the successful operation of a zero carbon home (Chapter 11). Most of the bespoke LZC developments highlighted throughout this book have failed to achieve their carbon reduction targets. This has been attributed in part to households' inability to operate LZC technologies effectively (Chapter 11). The rebound effect has further compounded this problem. It is argued in the literature and by this research that if households could become 'active energy citizens' (rather than being 'passive energy consumers'), this would help to increase energy literacy and address consumer behaviour. It would also encourage public acceptance of LZC technological systems (Chapter 11). Thus encouraging households to become energy citizens could help to achieve long-term carbon reductions.

However, it is also argued that the cultural shift needed for the majority of citizens to become more engaged in the process of energy generation and management is so dramatic (not to mention the changes in industry and technology required) that in the short term it is simply not a practical solution. On the other hand, entirely passive systems (e.g. the Hammarby system) imposed on the population won't address the motivations, values and attitudes underlying consumer behaviour. Nor will they raise energy literacy or increase acceptance of LZC technologies amongst households. However, passive systems are more compatible with existing lifestyles and the collective societal experience of energy systems (Chapter 11).

The importance of public policy instruments in delivering zero carbon homes has been demonstrated by the case studies (Chapter 9). Certainly a more interventionist approach is needed if zero carbon homes are to become more widespread in the short to medium term. It is extremely important to consider the principle of subsidiarity in relation to the appropriateness of the various policy instruments available. When addressing global issues (carbon reduction, peak oil and energy security) and the operation of multinational companies (particularly in the energy industry), international policy instruments would be the most effective.

However, these instruments need to allow for local variation in approach to the provision of zero carbon homes. They also need to provide some significant imperative for industry to change. Without this the culture, structure and practices of both the energy and house-building industries are unlikely to alter significantly in the short to medium term. At a national and local level the types of public policy adopted by governmental bodies will of course depend on the context in which they operate, for example the political system, the availability of energy sources, institutional structures, urban development patterns, existing infrastructure and culture. Thus developing a toolbox of policies suited to a range of contexts is appropriate.

A policy instrument which reflects the spatial variation in context is also useful for delivering zero carbon homes. Planning is a more locally specific tool which can consider and also reflect local needs, resources, socio-economic circumstances, culture and so on, when determining the appropriateness of different LZC energy systems (Chapter 10). Planning also considers the relationship between the LZC system and its surrounding built environment (neighbourhood, community, region). It can be used to manipulate urban form to support existing and new LZC energy systems (Chapter 10). It also co-ordinates the integration of new LZC development with the existing built environment and energy systems (Chapter 10).

Planning balances local economic, social and environmental concerns and ensures that 'public good' is delivered. Thus it is an appropriate tool for implementing localised carbon reductions through a number of sectors including housing. It can also provide direct incentives for zero carbon development by shortening development time-lines, requiring zero carbon development through zoning codes or encouraging the creation of zero carbon enterprise zones. Planning can help to create partnerships between actors (community and industry) involved in the delivery of zero carbon development. It can also provide a vehicle for community engagement which may help to create the 'active energy citizens' who will live in zero carbon homes and communities (Chapter 10).

Lessons for practice

The research presented in this book provides some indication of how we can move towards implementing a zero carbon homes policy and indeed zero carbon development in the future. Technological options for achieving this objective are diverse, ranging from entirely autonomous, off-grid energy-plus houses to low energy houses connected to a renewables super grid. In reality a blue-print for a zero carbon home does not exist, nor is it a useful concept. However, the research highlights several lessons for practice. These can be summarised as follows.

The technical systems which constitute a zero carbon home must reflect the local context in which they are embedded if they are to be successful. The symbiotic relationship between zero carbon systems and the surrounding bioregion is particularly important. Systems need to be simple to operate and replicate. Yet there needs to be a diversity of models to reflect the range of preferences demonstrated amongst potential consumers. Markets for zero carbon homes need to be established, through demonstrating their relative advantages. The symbiosis or partnerships between stake holders in the delivery and operation of zero carbon homes is essential. The success of zero carbon homes depends on their long-term resilience to technological and cultural change, economic shocks and environmental disasters. Thus, appropriateness, simplicity, diversity, demonstrating relative advantage, symbiosis and resilience are the basic principles which should under-pin the delivery of zero carbon homes.

Appropriateness

A successful zero carbon system will reflect the technological, environmental, political, cultural and institutional context in which it is set (Figure 12.1). Incumbent and planned technical systems (e.g. district heating, smart grid, renewables super grid, etc) will greatly influence the best models for delivering zero carbon homes in any given location (Chapter 2). Thus it is important to understand the technical systems currently operating and those planned for the future in any given locality.

A zero carbon system is more likely to be dependent on local access to renewable energy sources and storage capacity than a fossil fuel system. Thus, technical options for zero carbon homes are influenced by the local environmental context. Local climate, geology, hydrology, relief and vegetation will all influence the availability of local energy sources and storage systems required for the delivery of zero carbon homes. Equally, local infrastructure (energy systems and built environment) and urban form will influence which technical systems are optimal (Chapter 10). Thus, an audit of potential local energy sources, distribution and storage systems would be helpful in providing an indication of the optimal solutions for delivering zero carbon homes.

Technological options for delivering zero carbon homes should reflect the political system in which they emerge (Chapter 9), whether it is a more laissez-faire or an interventionist model. The most appropriate technological options for any given location will depend in part on the fiscal incentives and regulatory framework imposed by governmental institutions. Both can offer investors greater certainty, resulting in the wider deployment of zero carbon systems. Thus, an assessment of the fiscal instruments and regulatory mechanisms supporting different zero carbon systems would be helpful in making a case for different technical options for delivering zero carbon homes in any given locality

The technological options chosen locally to deliver zero carbon homes should reflect local socio-cultural norms. Public attitude towards energy, degree of energy literacy, and willingness to be involved in energy provision and management will influence whether passive (deficit model) or active energy systems (surfeit model) are most suitable for delivering zero carbon homes in any given location (Chapter 11). It is important to offer a range of options to cater for a diversity of interests. It is also important to ensure

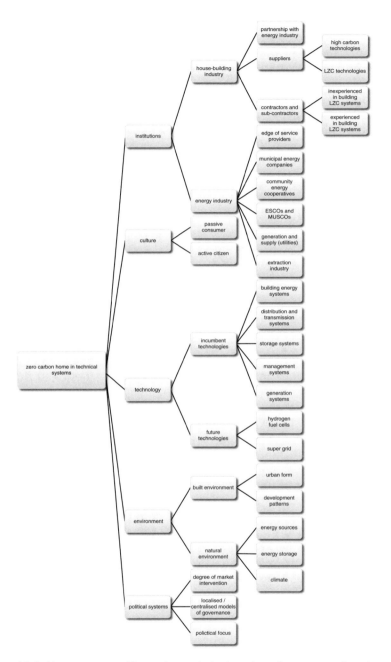

Figure 12.1 How context affects the technical options for zero carbon homes.
Source: Author's own.

systems are compatible with the socio-cultural context in which they are set if they are to be successful.

Local differences in the structure, culture and practices of institutions involved in the delivery of zero carbon homes will also affect the application of different zero carbon systems (Chapters 7 and 8). Where there is institutional inertia which resists, change, existing systems and institutions will need to form the basis for the future delivery of zero carbon systems. Where new niches have occurred, resulting from some degree of innovation amongst existing or new players, alternative systems may develop.

In summary, zero carbon homes (and their supporting systems) must be designed with the local context in mind if they are to operate successfully.

Simplicity

Technologies in zero carbon homes must be simple to operate. The interface between the 'user' (household) and the technological system (the house, smart meters, smart technologies, micro-generating devices, etc) must be uncomplicated. Technologies should be intuitive to use and the output from monitoring systems easy to understand (Chapter 11). This maximises efficiency and potential for raising energy literacy amongst households (essential for a long-term reduction in energy consumption). It also maximises market demand and opportunities for deployment.

The simplicity principle holds true for both passive and active systems. For passive systems the interactions between the household and the technology should be minimised either through design or the involvement of a third party in installation and operational processes (e.g. utilities, ESCOs, property management services). It is important that residents have a single point of contact to deal with ongoing operational issues. For active systems resident involvement should be focused on those processes for which they have adequate resources, expertise and capacity to affect, as well as bring about improvements in energy literacy (Chapter 11).

In addition, the supply system for zero carbon homes needs to be simplified, as complicated supply models will limit deployment (Chapter 7). Sustainable, simplified supply chains for LZC technologies and energy are crucial. Partnerships between industries are needed to design, assemble and operate zero carbon developments. Where possible it is useful to simplify these partnerships and ensure that all actors are using their existing skills and expertise to greatest affect.

Diversity

Consumers have a range of requirements influencing their decision to rent or purchase accommodation. Thus a diversity of models for zero carbon homes is required to cater for demand and maximise markets (Chapter 6).

However, providing consumers with a diversity of models complicates the design and production processes. Furthermore it limits the potential for industrial standardisation and cost reduction (Chapters 7 and 8).

Diversity may also complicate operational issues. If households are presented with a number of different household-operated energy systems throughout their lifetime this may create some confusion and difficulties in using the systems effectively. However, as long as the user-technology interface is similar the operational issues can be reduced (Chapter 11). In fact the GEOS experience suggests that there will be limited variation in the types of technical system used within the same bioregion (Chapter 5).

It is important to offer the market diversity in terms of the accommodation, rather than the zero carbon system interface (Chapter 11). Offering a range of accommodation options in different locations will increase the appeal of zero carbon homes to an expanding group, and lead to wider deployment (Chapter 6).

Symbiosis

Symbiosis (inter-dependency and cooperation) between actors in industry, government and the community is central to supplying and operating zero carbon homes effectively. Suppliers, utilities, developers, builders, ESCOs, community energy partnerships, municipalities, IT specialists, property management services, energy technology specialists and many more will be involved in the delivery of zero carbon homes. No single actor can provide all the expertise and resources needed to deliver this complex system. Thus it is essential that key actors work together in partnership to provide the systems and support services needed to deliver zero carbon homes. It is also critical that these actors work with the community to ensure successful operation.

Symbiosis between actors supports the innovation needed to deliver new LZC systems. It enables actors to share resources and information, creating positive feedback loops and synergies resulting in the creation of new systems. For example, actors in the energy industry may share market information regarding current energy consumption patterns, to enable long-term investment and growth in new support industries. Cooperation between utilities (actors involved in energy, water supply and managing waste streams) could enable the creation of a 'closed-loop' energy system (e.g. the Hammarby model). If actors operate purely competitively these cooperative relationships cannot form, positive feed-back loops are not established and innovation is stifled.

There is also symbiosis between a new development and the environment in which it is set. New development will consume resources from the bioregion (natural and man-made) in which it sits. It can also link into existing LZC infrastructures. For example, local natural resources, climate and storage systems may influence the technologies used in a new development as was the case for the GEOS development (Colorado). Equally, new development can be used to support existing LZC energy systems. For example, in Stockholm new development was being used to increase population densities in less populated areas to enable the expansion of the existing district heating system. It can also be used to generate LZC energy for existing stock. For example, zero carbon housing in the UK can provide LZC energy to existing stock either from on-site generation or even from remote generation. Thus, zero carbon developments should be considered as part of a wider bioregion.

Relative advantage

The relative advantages of living in a zero carbon home are environmental (reduce resource consumption and emissions), economic (reduce energy costs, energy security) and possibly social (opportunity to live within a community with similar values, ethical). Markets for zero carbon homes are currently limited (Chapter 6). The capital cost of zero carbon homes may limit market demand, but costs will reduce as volume of production increases. Targeted marketing via property agents or through social networks can both be used to increase public awareness of the relative advantages of living in zero carbon homes (Chapter 6).

It has been argued that in order for markets to expand the relative advantage of living in a zero carbon home must be demonstrated through increased production of units, as well as improved marketing strategies. More households experiencing living in zero carbon homes would provide feedback to potential markets, helping to eventually achieve critical mass.

A further key to wider deployment is in addressing competition from the incumbent energy technologies. Whilst powerful vested interests in the energy industry continue to support fossil fuel systems and fossil fuel price remains relatively low, some form of intervention will be needed to encourage market interest in zero carbon systems. Extraction quotas, carbon quotas, carbon tax, public investment programmes, capital and operational subsidies could all be used to address this problem (Chapter 9).

Resilience

Long-term resilience is essential for any sustainable system. All zero carbon housing models need to adapt to changing circumstances over the long term, particularly technological innovation, climatic changes, economic shocks or cultural trends. It is important that the systems installed are as adaptable and flexible as possible, to limit technological obsolescence and waste of resources in the future.

For example, by using electricity grids a variety of technical options for decarbonising the energy supply can be accommodated. An electricity grid allows the connection of a variety of small- and large-scale LZC energy generators, particularly if combined with smart technologies. Passive houses are also more compatible with the electric grid than heat networks. The versatility of systems is important if they are to be resilient.

The built environment is also constantly changing. This can impact on the resilience of LZC systems. For example solar access may be impeded by the height of adjacent new development. Depopulation of urban centres may render district heating systems uneconomic. Equally, households may reduce the design integrity of their zero carbon dwelling by removing LZC technologies (Chapter 11). Safeguards to ensure the resilience of energy systems are needed (e.g. using access ordinances, as suggested in Chapter 10).

Thus, the key lessons for practice are summarised in Figure 12.2. To ensure wider deployment zero carbon homes will need to be cost effective, efficient and reliable. The technology – user interface will need to be simple to use and provide informative feedback to increase energy literacy. The technical system itself will have to reflect the context in which it is found and work synergistically with its environment. Ideally although the technical systems used may be diverse, the user – technology interface should be similar. Finally, the technical systems chosen will need to be able to easily adapt to technological, environmental, economic and cultural change.

Lessons for policy

A variety of policy instruments (regulatory, fiscal, educational) will be needed to encourage the production and effective use of zero carbon homes. Policy instruments will be crucial in ensuring zero carbon homes have the relative advantage over incumbent technologies. Policy instruments are needed to ensure that zero carbon systems can compete with the incumbent fossil fuel systems (for example using carbon taxation, carbon quotas, fossil fuel quotas). They will be needed to offer a relative advantage both to producers and consumers (for example tax credits for developers building zero carbon homes or stamp duty removal for consumers buying zero carbon homes). Without this assistance zero carbon homes will remain uncompetitive.

Policy instruments to ensure the resilience of new LZC energy systems and zero carbon homes are essential (for example access ordinances, infrastructure levy, monitoring programmes, peer group learning). A long-term view of the most appropriate technical solutions at all scales is needed based on climatic forecasts, future technical and cultural trends. Policy instruments themselves will need to offer long-term support for the formation of these new technical systems (for example the 20-year feed-in tariff in Germany, product legislation, carbon taxation) and ensure that future development is compatible with them (for example access ordinances). Policy instruments to ensure that households do not interfere with the design integrity of zero carbon homes are also needed to ensure long-term

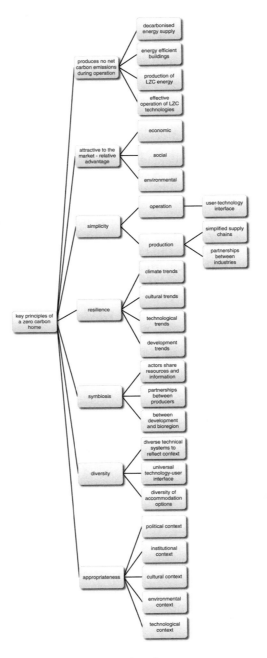

Figure 12.2 Key principles of a zero carbon home.

Source: Author's own.

resilience (for example personal carbon allowances, peer group learning, monitoring programmes).

Policy instruments to simplify supply chains (for example product legislation) and encourage industrial partnerships (for example the zero carbon standard) to facilitate the production of zero carbon homes are required. A supportive framework to encourage the creation of new institutions (for example ESCOs or MUSCOs) that can simplify household involvement in the operation of zero carbon developments is needed (e.g. capital and operational subsidies).

Policy instruments (for example planning policies) should also be used to encourage symbiosis between new zero carbon developments and their bio-regions (natural and built environment). Planning to ensure the most effective use of resources and infrastructure in the bioregion is needed. Policy instruments can be used to encourage new and existing communities to support each other in the creation of LZC energy systems (for example zero carbon homes policy and infrastructure levy). They can be used to produce industrial partnerships (particularly the sharing of resources and information between industries) and industrial symbiosis (for example by imposing carbon reduction targets on industry, carbon trading or carbon taxation, introducing educational programmes).

The scale at which these policy instruments are most effective will vary. Some barriers will be common to all. For example, internationally there is a need to address the competitiveness of non-fossil fuels. Ideally policies to encourage a shift from fossil fuels to LZC energy would be introduced internationally (international extraction and carbon quotas). However, the importance of the local context in achieving the symbioses described above and providing technical systems that are appropriate to the local environment, culture, politics and economy also suggests that in some instances local policy instruments will be more useful.

There are no one-size-fits-all policy solutions to delivering zero carbon development. Policy solutions will be dependent on the context in which they operate. They will also need to reflect the diversity of models which can be used to achieve zero carbon homes. A policy toolbox is needed which can be used to identify appropriate policy options for deploying zero carbon homes depending on the context (political, institutional, cultural, economic and environmental) in which they operate and on political objectives.

A policy toolbox for implementing zero carbon homes is presented in Figure 12.3. Policy instruments that tackle supply and demand as well as producers, regulators and consumers at a variety of scales are included. The toolbox presented here is by no means exhaustive, but it does draw out the policy instruments which have been successfully used in the case study countries to implement LZC housing and energy systems. It also highlights the policy instruments that are conspicuously lacking (e.g. extraction quotas and bioregional planning).

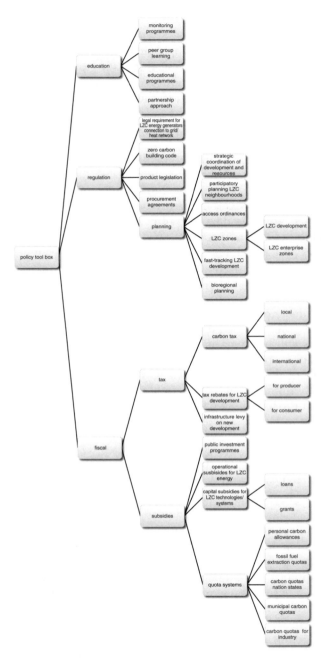

Figure 12.3 A schematic representation of the policy toolbox.

Source: Author's own.

The policy toolbox provides options for delivering zero carbon homes in different contexts. The tools are not mutually exclusive; most can be used in combination to achieve the desired outcome. The combined impact of different tools requires further investigation. Most of the policy instruments presented in the toolbox have been used to deliver LZC development in the case studies (e.g. carbon quotas, carbon tax, subsidies). However there are some which have only been trialled for a short period (e.g. personal carbon allowances) and others for which there are no working examples (e.g. extraction quotas). More research is needed to determine the impact of these policies. The transferability of policy instruments between contexts also requires further investigation.

A series of scenarios can be used to demonstrate how such a toolbox might function (Figure 12.4). A series of four opposing scenarios for the deployment of zero carbon homes have been identified: state-versus market-led; centralised versus decentralised energy systems; industry versus citizen-led; rapid versus incremental. These scenarios reflect a range of political, technological and cultural contexts as well as outcomes.

State-led versus market-led models

Different political contexts impact on the types of policy instruments that can be used to deliver zero carbon homes. This is demonstrated through the

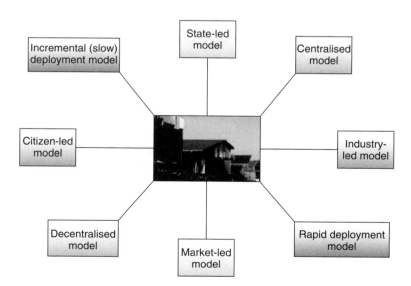

Figure 12.4 Zero carbon scenarios.

Source: Author's own.

comparison of state-led and market-led models for delivery. The state-led model uses public investment and regulation to stimulate industrial transformation and the deployment of zero carbon homes (as in China). The state invests directly in building capacity within industry to supply zero carbon systems at scale. This initial investment will help to develop efficient LZC technologies and produce them at scale. It will help also to build the skills, expertise and supply chains needed to deliver zero carbon systems. This is further reinforced by the introduction of new building programmes.

Alongside direct investment the state introduces a regulatory framework which ensures new zero carbon systems are used in the built environment. Product legislation and building codes can be used to encourage the deployment of zero carbon systems in the built environment as part of the building programme. Both can be used to eliminate energy-hungry, carbon-emitting products and systems from the supply chain. To ensure that new systems are used effectively by households, some kind of monitoring (provided through smart technologies) and training programmes will also be needed.

The market-led model relies on demand to stimulate the transformation of industry and the deployment of zero carbon homes. Thus, state intervention (regulation and public investment) is minimised in the market-led model. Fiscal rather than regulatory policy instruments are preferred. Quota systems are generally favoured since quotas offer industry greater flexibility in delivering carbon reduction targets. Tools to raise the price of fossil fuels and the value of carbon will help to create demand for zero carbon homes and decarbonised energy.

Personal carbon allowances, industrial carbon quotas and carbon trading can be used to increase the value of zero carbon products and services. Industrial carbon emission quotas provide industry with the incentive for reducing carbon emissions throughout the life-cycle of products and services. Carbon trading offers further economic motivation for industries to invest in the research and development of low carbon alternatives, as well as scaling up small demonstration projects.

Personal carbon allowances will stimulate public demand for zero carbon homes and decarbonised energy. This could be further reinforced through the introduction of energy monitoring systems (smart grids), which provide the consumer with all the information required to manage their energy consumption and CO_2 production.

Centralised versus decentralised decarbonised energy systems

Different technological contexts also influence the policy instruments used for delivering zero carbon homes. The decarbonisation of centralised energy systems largely relies on increasing efficiencies within the system (perhaps through the introduction of smart grids) and encouraging the development of renewable and nuclear power plants. It also implies a shift towards electricity, away from gas and localised heat networks.

Industrial quotas for fossil fuel extraction can be used to encourage the energy industry to develop new nuclear and renewable capacity. Industrial quotas for CO_2 emissions (from generation and supply) can be used to encourage the energy industry to develop its LZC portfolio and manage the energy supply more efficiently. This should ensure the effective use of smart grids by energy companies to curb CO_2 emissions, rather than encouraging an increase in demand for cheap energy.

Carbon trading systems also provide the energy industry with a financial incentive to decarbonise supply. This can be further reinforced through the introduction of carbon tax. Both increase the value of carbon and thus increase the relative price of fossil fuels when compared to renewable and nuclear energy. These instruments in tandem can provide a landscape in which fossil fuels and LZC energy sources can fairly compete.

The encouragement of decentralised, decarbonised systems will require a completely different set of policy instruments. A zero carbon homes policy in itself can help to encourage decentralised production of LZC energy and localised supply systems. However, this needs to be supported by many other policy instruments.

Legislation to ensure grid connection is fundamental, without this a decentralised system cannot develop. Smart-grid technologies will help to ensure a smooth transition, allowing an increase in the number of small-scale, renewable energy producers that can be safely connected to the grid, without having to significantly increase spinning capacity (or some form of energy supply back-up).

Financial support for small-scale generators, ESCOs and community energy cooperatives is also critical. Without subsidies small-scale generators will not be able to compete with large energy companies. State operational and capital subsidies aimed at small-scale generators, ESCOs and community energy cooperatives can provide the financial support needed. Subsidies reduce risk to investors, thus enabling long-term investment in decentralised LZC energy. Alternatively, larger energy companies could be encouraged to financially support small-scale generators, by introducing carbon and fossil fuel extraction quotas for industry.

The introduction of personal carbon allowances can encourage individuals and communities to become generators of LZC energy, particularly if implemented in combination with carbon tax and monitoring programmes (to raise energy awareness and literacy). This will encourage the formation of community energy cooperatives and ESCOs. Households will also become more aware of the importance of managing energy systems effectively, encouraging greater engagement with complex smart-grid systems.

Bioregional planning provides a useful tool for encouraging the creation of locally appropriate zero carbon energy systems. It can also be used to ensure a co-ordinated local approach to development and the provision of zero carbon energy. Planning controls (for example access ordinances) can also be used to ensure the resilience of local energy systems, even in urban areas undergoing considerable development. Local planning authorities can help to co-ordinate approaches to delivering zero carbon development between the community and producers (i.e. energy companies, house-builders, etc). They may also collect an energy infrastructure levy from developers (which can be used to construct local zero carbon energy systems) and plan local zero carbon energy systems. Mandatory carbon reduction targets for local authorities ensure the engagement of the planning authority in this process.

A municipal model for decentralised energy systems is the most appropriate in urbanised countries. Municipal zero carbon energy systems might be encouraged through the introduction of mandatory municipal carbon quotas. This provides incentive for the municipality to encourage and invest in zero carbon energy sources, the introduction of energy management systems and the improvement in energy efficiency of new and existing stock. It also provides incentive for municipal planners to coordinate development and zero carbon infrastructure effectively. The construction of such a zero carbon energy system might be funded through a local carbon tax paid by local energy consumers. It could also be funded through a development tax (energy infrastructure levy) paid by developers, if there was adequate new build development in the community. A further option may be the creation of a municipal energy company (or at least a company in which the municipality is a key stakeholder) that can raise finance for LZC projects through energy provision.

Industry-led versus citizen-led models

Different cultural contexts affect the policy instruments used to deliver zero carbon homes. In a culture where citizens have largely adopted a passive approach to energy, industry-focused policy instruments may be more appropriate. In contrast where citizens are more open to active engagement in the operation, management of energy systems and generation of energy policy instruments to support them in those activities could be more appropriate. Equally, the policy approach adopted will of course relate to desired outcomes.

Industry focused policy instruments are needed to deliver an industry-led model for the construction and deployment of zero carbon homes. Product legislation and building code are critical for ensuring that capacity (supply chains, construction processes, skills and expertise) is developed in the construction industry to deliver zero carbon homes. Procurement agreements may also help to build more stable supply chains for new technologies.

Developing the expertise and skills needed to deliver zero carbon homes could be assisted through state-subsidised educational programmes, peer group learning or industrial partnerships. Until production and supply systems have been scaled up, some capital subsidies (loans, grants, public investment programmes) – tied to the zero carbon requirement – may also be needed.

It is also crucial that the energy industry decarbonises supply if zero carbon homes are to be a realistic goal (particularly in densely developed urban areas). The policy instruments already discussed for encouraging centralised and decentralised LZC energy supply would be appropriate tools for delivery.

To encourage a citizen-led approach requires that there is some motivation for citizens to consume LZC products (energy and homes) or to be involved in the processes of managing or generating LZC energy. Carbon rationing (PCAs) or carbon taxation could be used to increase demand for LZC energy and zero carbon homes. It may also encourage citizens to use smart technologies, manage their energy consumption more effectively and even generate LZC energy (individually or collectively).

Educational processes (particularly real-time monitoring) to raise environmental awareness and energy literacy can produce further motivation. Citizens also need to be presented with an opportunity to become more engaged. Introducing a zero carbon building code ensures that new units at least will offer this opportunity. Product legislation to ensure the availability of LZC technologies also helps to ensure that citizens can obtain the technologies needed to manage and maintain LZC systems. Legislation requiring that small-scale producers are connected to the energy grid also provides citizens with the opportunity to become LZC energy producers.

However, citizens' capability (financial resources, skills and expertise) may limit their involvement. Thus policy instruments which subsidise the capital and operational cost (at least initially) of these new technical systems are required. Instruments to encourage new institutions that combine citizens and expert energy service providers are also needed. This will help to overcome limited expertise amongst residents and issues of raising finance particularly for community infrastructure.

The formation of these institutions will also be encouraged through fiscal incentives for example, carbon tax and subsidies. The municipality may provide a useful vehicle for enabling this kind of partnership. Municipal LZC energy systems managed, owned and controlled through a joint partnership between the municipality (and its citizen stakeholders) and energy provider, enables community involvement in decision-making and operation as well as both partners benefitting from the proceeds. In new build development the planning process is a useful mechanism through which citizens can become involved in the decision-making process.

Rapid deployment versus slow deployment models

Desired outcomes will also influence the types of policy instrument that are most suited to the delivery of zero carbon homes. Here policy instruments that will induce rapid and incremental deployment of zero carbon homes are discussed.

The rapid deployment of zero carbon homes and LZC energy systems can only be achieved by tackling the powerful vested interests in industry, particularly the energy industry. Stimulating market interest in new technical systems can be a very slow process, particularly when its delivery requires significant attitudinal and behavioural changes. In addition, the degree of institutional and technical lock-in in the energy industry is likely to prevent the widespread introduction of these technologies, even where demand is demonstrated.

Demand alone cannot drive the changes needed in industry to deliver zero carbon homes. Thus, policy instruments will need to be focused on tackling supply (and the vested interests in industry) rather than demand (and citizen preferences). Most energy companies operate at a supra-national scale. Thus, the governance of these institutions is most appropriate at an international scale. International policy instruments will ensure that vested interests are addressed and the energy industry is transformed, rather than encouraging energy companies to operate only in areas where there is no regulation.

International industrial quota systems that limit the extraction of fossil fuels and the generation of CO_2 emissions from the energy industry are needed to encourage a rapid shift towards decarbonised energy systems. This could be underpinned by an international carbon trading system which would provide further economic reward for those energy companies moving towards LZC sources, systems and services. The alternative might be to introduce an international carbon tax. However, this is unlikely to create a sufficient disincentive for the rich and powerful vested interests in the energy industry to alter the existing regime, unless the rate of taxation was extremely high. This cost is also likely to be passed on to consumers creating adverse distributional effects. Also an international carbon tax will not cap carbon production.

An international building code requirement for zero carbon building will also be needed for some parts of the international construction industry to overcome industrial lock-in. It provides incentive for the industry to innovate, establish new supply chains, construction practices, partnerships and expertise needed to deliver zero carbon buildings. It also provides security for investors. There is significant international variation within the construction industry, thus an international building code could help to unify quality in this area.

An international regulatory approach is unlikely to be acceptable to governments or powerful vested interests in industry. This has been demonstrated by the continued lack of success in agreeing global mandatory carbon reduction targets at recent climate change talks. It would take brave leadership and the creation of a robust international regulatory framework to deliver successfully. An incremental approach is more likely to be acceptable to these institutions, although the pace of deployment will be far slower. A more incremental approach will focus on generating demand for zero carbon homes, encouraging examples of good practice and scaling up those examples.

Policy instruments that can be used to generate demand include carbon tax, personal carbon allowances and monitoring programmes (discussed earlier). Local policy instruments provide an interesting option for encouraging pockets of innovation. Examples include municipal carbon quotas, municipal carbon tax, energy infrastructure levies, local building codes and local subsidies. This approach addresses existing industrial regimes but in a more piecemeal way, allowing them to test a variety technical options before scaling up. Subsidised development programmes also provide the opportunity for industry to test new technical systems. Once successful prototypes have been delivered, national policy instruments can be developed to encourage scaling up. Policy instruments that can address industrial lock-in then become critical to delivery.

A future road map for zero carbon homes

Ultimately the zero carbon home is one small part of a much more complex global system. This system is controlled by a myriad of actors, across a range of sectors. In order for zero carbon homes to scale up and become part of main stream development, a supportive zero carbon global system will need to be established. This means that changes throughout the system, not just within the energy and construction industries, are needed. Greater investigation into the inter-dependencies between actors and sectors in achieving a zero carbon system is needed, in order for a more holistic approach to the delivery of zero carbon homes to be adopted. Without this holistic approach, zero carbon demonstration projects will not scale up.

The decarbonisation of the energy supply system is needed over the coming decades. New development should play a role in delivery. Certainly, new buildings and communities offer the opportunity to generate and store LZC power locally. The aim for new housing should be that buildings produce enough LZC energy to cater for all space heating/cooling requirements, water heating, lighting, appliance use (and an increase in appliance use as predicted) and transport needs (via electric vehicles). This is considerably more than is currently required by the zero carbon homes policy in the UK, but is feasible.

As existing supply infrastructure (power stations and grid network) needs updating and replacement, LZC alternatives should be used. A LZC grid should be developed alongside the existing grid system, in the form of community micro-grids and international renewables super-grid systems. These grids will eventually need to be linked at a national level. Certainly as gas supplies dwindle, these systems will become increasingly essential. These

Table 12.1 Policy toolbox for different scenarios

Model	Fiscal policy	Regulation	Education
State-led	Public investment programmes	Zero carbon building code, product legislation, planning (zoning)	National monitoring and educational programmes
Market-led	Carbon trading, carbon tax	Personal carbon allowances; national carbon quotas	Monitoring programmes; smart grids
Centralised	Carbon trading, carbon tax	Industrial quotas (suppliers, generators and extraction industry)	None
Decentralised	Local capital and operational subsidies; municipal carbon tax and energy infrastructure levy	Zero carbon building code; grid connection legislation; industrial quotas (suppliers, generators and extraction industry); municipal quotas; personal carbon allowances; planning	Monitoring programmes; smart grids
Industry-led	Carbon trading, carbon tax; capital and operational subsidies; energy infrastructure levy building programmes	Zero carbon building code, product legislation, grid connection legislation, procurement agreements; Industrial quotas (suppliers, generators and extraction industry); municipal quotas; personal carbon allowances; planning	Educational programmes, peer group learning; partnership approach
Citizen-led	Carbon tax; capital and operational subsidies	Personal carbon allowances; zero carbon building code, product legislation, grid connection legislation, planning	Monitoring programmes
Rapid deployment	International carbon-trading systems	International industrial quotas (suppliers, generators and extraction industry); International zero carbon building code	None
Slow deployment	Municipal carbon tax; local capital and operational subsidies, and energy infrastructure levy; public investment programmes	Municipal quotas; personal carbon allowances, local LZC building codes	Monitoring programmes; educational programmes, peer group learning; partnership approach

changes to existing technical systems will not occur without supportive policy instruments.

International (mandatory) extraction quotas or carbon quotas could be
used to produce a wholesale transformation of the energy industry and
encourage the decarbonisation of the energy supply that feeds the built environment. International extraction quotas target the source of problem, the
powerful vested interests in the fossil fuel industry. They would reduce the
rate at which fossil fuels are extracted and could encourage a shift towards
greater production of renewable energy. However, this approach would
require an international organisation (like the United Nations) to administer
and enforce such a system. It would also require that an international agreement on extraction quotas could be reached.

Carbon quotas and an international carbon trading system (exemplified
by the existing European system) provide an alternative approach. This system could be supported through the introduction of a carbon tax within
nation states, the revenue from which could be used to subsidise zero carbon
systems. Already significant problems have been encountered in agreeing
mandatory carbon quotas internationally. Ultimately, this lack of agreed
quotas will undermine the carbon trading system. Both binding extraction
and carbon quotas are likely to be politically unpopular, difficult to enforce
and will take a degree of courage to enact. Thus, alternative options are
needed.

In the absence of any global agreement, progress on an ad hoc basis will
need to be made at both the national and local levels. The production of zero
carbon systems may be used as a stimulus for national economic growth
(e.g. USA, Europe). Zero carbon systems may also be integrated into new
building programmes (e.g. China). Nations investing heavily in zero carbon
systems either as a mechanism to encourage economic growth or as part of
a new building programme will no doubt export technologies produced and
expertise developed globally. This would help to deploy zero carbon systems
more widely.

This approach could be further reinforced through the introduction of
international product legislation requiring the production zero carbon technologies or the use of zero carbon systems in the built environment. The
product legislation model adopted by the European Union for electrical
goods could offer a useful model. Such a model would produce new markets
for zero carbon systems within the European Union. It would also affect the
products of those wishing to trade in Europe (e.g. exports from China and
USA).

Cities can also provide exemplars for zero carbon systems. They can act as
hubs for innovation (in terms of policy and practice) and provide an incentive for other cities to adopt similar approaches. Increasingly the world population is becoming urbanised. Thus, the application of zero carbon systems
in cities is likely to impact on the activities of and encourage greater energy

literacy amongst more people than those applied in less populated areas. Cities also have a significant impact on global carbon dioxide production. Thus targeting systems in cities will have a significant impact on global warming.

Cities are often able to act autonomously to implement innovative low carbon policies and technical systems. Thus, in countries where governments are less progressive cities can act autonomously to tackle carbon dioxide emissions. For example, some cities have introduced mandatory carbon reduction targets and carbon trading systems. Several US cities are linked with the EU emissions trading scheme, whilst in China several cities are trialling internal cap and trade systems for carbon. The construction of new mega-cities also provide the opportunity for new zero carbon systems to be implemented at scale, which reduces production costs and means the systems become available to a wider audience.

Exemplar low carbon cities tend to emerge as a result of several factors:

- a willingness to innovate and take risks;
- political leadership;
- significant public investment;
- the existence of multi-interest groups to co-ordinate development;
- public support;
- and supportive policies.

It is important to provide a policy framework in which the exemplar zero carbon cities sit, in order to encourage development of more exemplar cities. National policy instruments have often underpinned the innovative approaches to development and the adoption of zero carbon systems locally. They may also lead to other cities following suit. However, it is also important to have localised policy instruments which reflect the local context in terms of delivering zero carbon systems. This is the strength of having a toolbox approach.

This book provides detailed insight into the problems facing those trying to implement a zero carbon homes policy. Of course this could be more widely applied to zero carbon development. It provides a comprehensive analysis of the barriers and opportunities available. It investigates market potential and provides greater insight into the policy instruments that may usefully encourage the wider deployment of zero carbon development. It informs our understanding of the paradigm shift needed, both cultural and institutional, in order to deliver zero carbon development. Overall it offers a road map towards the delivery of zero carbon homes.

Notes

1 Introduction

1 In this area a rise in temperature could increase crop yields and tourism, whilst reducing the need for winter heating and winter mortality rates
2 Europe currently imports 28% of its gas from Russia and will continue to rely on its vast reserves of gas for the foreseeable future.
3 During its life-cycle a building will consume approximately 20% of its energy budget during construction and disposal phases, whilst the majority of energy will be consumed during operation (i.e. 80%).
4 In Sweden 808 kilograms of oil equivalent (Kgoe) per capita of energy are consumed in the residential sector producing 0.3 metric tonnes CO_2 per capita. In Germany 775 Kgoe per capita of energy are consumed in the residential sector producing 1.3 metric tonnes CO_2 per capita (OECD, 2007 and IEA, 2007).

2 Zero carbon homes: the technological response

1 The terms 'zero-net' and 'net-zero' energy buildings are interchangeable.
2 For standard buildings approximately 80% of emissions are produced during operation. However, for low energy/passive buildings the majority of emissions are produced during construction and demolition.
3 By 2015 the EU requires that all new buildings will conform to passive house standard. The European Energy Performance in Buildings Directive required that all European countries develop a strategy (Energy Efficiency Action Plan) for achieving low energy or passive house standard by 2009.
4 Total primary energy consumption in a passive house is lower by a factor of between 2 and 4 than levels in new buildings across Europe (Feist et al, 2001).
5 All the building parts for walls, roofs and floors are insulated with U-values within 0.10–0.15 W/m² per K.
6 All thermal bridges must be avoided in the construction of a passive house. A construction is said to be 'thermal bridge free' if the maximum bridges are under 0.01 W/m per K.
7 Windows in a passive house are especially efficient. The U-values for windows are 0.70–0.85 W/m² per K.
8 To ensure sufficient ventilation passive houses are supplied with mechanical ventilation. There are controlled air exchanges of 0.40 times per hour in a passive house.
9 The heating and cooling of passive buildings typically include a heat exchanger. Often this will be combined with a heat-pump or a highly efficient small heating system.

10 Different studies indicate that floors can have a cooling effect in the hot seasons. This indicates that floors should be less insulated in cooling-based climates. However, the roof will have a larger impact since the roof is heated by both outdoor temperature and direct sun radiation. In cooling-based climates there is hence an increased need to balance the values and to use energy performance in the regulation (IEA, 2008).

11 The carbon intensity of an energy source includes both direct emissions (from conversion processes) and indirect emissions stemming from activities such as mining, processing, transportation, production and extraction of the raw materials needed for manufacturing processes. The level of emissions can vary, depending on the fuel quality, plant efficiency and specific technologies used.

12 Calculating the carbon intensity of nuclear power is also affected by enrichment and fuel-rod production.

13 Wind, hydroelectric, biogas, solar thermal, biomass, and geothermal, estimates taken from Pehnt (2006). Diesel, heavy oil, coal with scrubbing, coal without scrubbing, natural gas, and fuel cell estimates taken and Gagnon et al (2002). Solar PV estimates taken from Fthenakis et al (2008). Nuclear is taken from Sovacool, 2008. Estimates have been rounded to the nearest whole number

14 The life-cycle estimates suggest that nuclear and renewable energy has significantly lower carbon intensities than energy generated from fossil fuels. Thus countries with a fuel mix based on renewable and nuclear energy are likely to have less carbon intensive energy systems.

15 The scale of CO_2 savings will vary between countries / regions as it is dependent on the efficiency of the incumbent energy system and fuel mix.

16 The colour scheme used on the graph denotes the following: green = large-scale district heating network; grey = medium-scale district heating network; pink = small-scale district heating network; blue = stand-alone renewable heating / cooling technologies.

3 Innovative housing programmes

1 Recent changes in government have resulted in a change in policy for house-building.

2 Unregulated emissions are now excluded from the definition of zero carbon in the UK. This has altered since the recent change in UK Government in 2010.

3 In reality the operational phase of a building generates the majority of carbon dioxide emissions (80–85%). However, as the energy efficiency of structures improves and the energy supply decarbonises, the emissions produced during other phases of the buildings lifecycle will become increasingly important.

4 Hierarchy of measures: energy efficiency parameters; carbon mitigation on-site or near-site; off-site low and zero carbon energy; and a buy-out fund to be invested in LZC carbon energy or efficiency measures.

5 Greenwich Millennium Village is a large development of low energy homes built very close to the central business district of London and next to the River Thames (i.e. a prime urban location). It was supposed to demonstrate the commercially viability of building to higher environmental standards and to test the market.

6 Delivered an energy reduction of 32% and primary energy reduction of 87%.

7 The location of the development (i.e. with excellent access to public transport); mixture of uses (providing work units and communal social space on site); the use of LZC technologies (insulation, triple glazing, PV cells, CHP system, etc); building design (passive building design, individual recycling facilities); site layout (orientation of units and high densities); the use of LZC energy system (CHP and district heating system); resident education and communal activities (e.g. car-pools).

8 The carbon emissions reduction target (CERT) requires energy suppliers to deliver measures that will result in overall lifetime carbon dioxide savings of 185 MtCO2 by 2011. Suppliers are required to deliver energy efficiency improvements (energy performance contracts) to customers, as well as increasing their capacity to generate renewable energy (delivery contracts – installation and operation). Thus it provides the energy industry with the incentive to overcome its internal inertia towards renewable energy. It is expected to lead to energy supplier investment of over £3 billion, the formation of ESCOs within existing utilities and the emergence of new players in the market.

9 The Renewables Obligation requires electricity suppliers to source a proportion of their supply from renewable generators. This offers stakeholder incentive and should stimulate production and innovation within the industry. Suppliers can alternatively pay into a buy-out fund to meet the obligation. Since 2004 renewables operators (independent of size) have been entitled to receive renewable obligation certificates (two ROCs for every 1,000 kWh) which they can also sell to electricity supply companies to help them achieve their obligation.

10 The Low Carbon Buildings Programme (LCBP) is a capital grant scheme for encouraging the use of renewable energy technologies in buildings. It follows on from the Clear Skies Programme. Both were made available to the domestic sector. During the first round of the LCBP grants were available to households to make energy improvements or install renewable technologies. However, there was less funding available from the LCBP to households than through the Clear Skies Programme. During the second phase of the LCBP funds will no longer be available to households, which will further restrict adoption of renewable technologies in the domestic sector. At the time of writing there are no capital grants schemes which house-builders can access.

11 A feed-in tariff (FIT) offering financial support to low carbon generation of electricity in projects up to 5 MW was introduced in 2010. The feed-in tariff offers high investment security coupled with low administrative and regulatory barriers. The revenue generated by the FIT, subsidises capital and operational costs and offers key stakeholders an incentive to invest. It should help to overcome the inertia within the energy industry to decentralised renewable energy and result in the entry of new participants into the market.

12 The cost of installing PV (pre-rebates) is 3 times the price considered for market breakthrough, so fiscal incentives are needed to encourage widespread deployment (Navigant Consulting, 2008).

13 Southern California Edison, Pacific Gas and Electric Company (PG&E), San Diego Gas and Electric Company, PacifiCorp, Sierra Pacific Power Company, Bear Valley Electric Service Division of Golden State Water Company, and Mountain Utilities.

14 Green mortgages have not been widely used in the residential market. Reasons cited for this include: lack of knowledgeable lenders willing to become a Fannie Mae partner and provide the required documentation and paperwork; lack of trained people who can substantiate the energy features of the home and estimate the expected cost savings; active residential real estate market with extremely low interest rates; Predicted cost savings are sufficiently low for a residential property that this may not make a large difference in eligibility for a given loan amount. In commercial properties, these savings can be much larger and such loans are more prevalent for these buildings

15 The electricity may be generated from photovoltaic (PV) systems, wind turbines, landfill-gas facilities, small hydroelectric generators, geothermal energy systems and other renewable-energy technologies.

16 This constituted a net increase in Sweden's housing stock of 650,000 new apartments and houses
17 A prerequisite for the Miljonprogrammet was the pension reform of 1959. Significant equity built up as a result of the pension reform which the Swedish government used to finance the housing programme.
18 The German government reduced the subsidy for single-family houses a few years ago.
19 For multi-family houses the payable rents are low and for new building rents must be higher (8–10 €/m²) to re-finance the construction costs. In some regions nobody can afford the rent due to high levels of unemployment and decreasing net incomes
20 The low energy standard is KfW-55/70
21 20% of the energy requirement for electricity and hot water must be sourced from renewable sources for new buildings and 10% for old buildings.
22 KfW is the development bank of the Federal Republic of Germany working on behalf of the German Government.
23 The monies for loans offered by KfW are raised partly through the capital market and partly through direct government subsidy.
24 That equates to an increase from 0.2% to 0.5% in market share between 2005 and 2006.
25 Loans are available to individual home-owners, housing companies (for rental units), small / medium-sized developers or energy installation companies.
26 Electricity from renewable sources is exempt from the tax, if the producer uses it, or if it comes from a network or an electric line that is exclusively fed by renewable sources. The law does not, however, exempt all electricity from renewable sources from the electricity tax. This is mainly due to legal and technical reasons. The government uses the tax revenue from renewable energy sources to promote the production of renewable energy.

4 Low/zero carbon energy systems

1 Fortum is a state-owned Finnish energy company.
2 MUSCO is a multi-utility service company. Such a company could plan, manage and operate a number of urban/utility systems including energy, water, waste and transport.
3 In 1991, Sweden introduced a carbon tax affecting the use of oil, coal, natural gas, liquefied petroleum gas, petrol, and aviation fuel used in domestic travel. Industrial users paid half the rate and certain high-energy industries were fully exempted from the carbon tax. In 1997 and 2007 the tax rate was raised. In 2007, the tax was EUR 101 per ton of CO_2. The full tax is now paid for transport, space heating, and non-combined heat and power generation. Owing to the many exemptions, oil accounts for 96% of the revenues from the tax.
4 The city of Freiburg owns 33% of the shares and the communities of the region own 20% of the shares
5 100,000 solar roofs programme is a capital subsidy to encourage the installation of solar technologies on new and existing buildings.
6 Feed-in tariff is an operational subsidy for the generation of renewable energy – for more details see Chapter 9.
7 According to the EU Commission, the global market for environmental technologies and services grew from €300 billion in 2000 to €740 billion in 2010.
8 The governments of Switzerland, France and Germany decided to bring heavy industry into the upper Rhine region during the 1970s to generate economic growth and

employment opportunities in the failing region. It was recognised such an expansion would require a great deal of energy. Thus the idea was to construct nuclear plants to power the new industry. If the plan had gone ahead, then the region would have had the highest density of nuclear power plants globally. However, there was a great deal of local resistance to the plan from both the Germans and French. Today municipalities on all sides of the borders (Swiss, German and French) work together against installation of nuclear power in the region.

9 Freiburger Energie-und Wasserversorgungs-AG (FEW).

10 The electricity supplied to Boulder's citizens is carbon intensive. Although electricity constitutes less than half of the endpoint energy use in Boulder, it accounts for over 80% of the total GHG emissions associated with consumption of electricity and natural gas. This is because of heavy reliance on coal-fired power stations. Thus the carbon intensity of electricity needs to be addressed.

11 Renewable portfolio standard is a state-wide incentive for increasing renewable energy production.

12 Affordable PV cells: if solar photovoltaic systems can be installed for $1 or $2 per watt by 2017 (the current price is around $8–$9 per watt), photovoltaic electric production could be more affordable than today's conventional power sources. This will also encourage the deployment of solar homes.

13 Xcel Energy is researching the production of hydrogen from wind energy. If the state can harness and store energy generated by the wind in the process of producing hydrogen, it could become a more reliable and productive source of power. In addition building transmission lines into Wyoming would help Colorado utilities use the variable wind patterns in the two states to increase wind capacity.

14 Concentrated solar power includes storage and dispatch capabilities for utilities, potentially allowing it to offset base load and intermediate energy production. The San Luis Valley is an ideal location for a CSP project.

15 Geothermal heat offers a great opportunity for some communities in Colorado (e.g. city of Arvada where the GEOS development is being built).

16 There are tremendous opportunities for Colorado to tap into small-scale hydropower potential without the need to build large dams.

17 Accenture, Current Group, Gridpoint Inc, OSIsoft, Schweitzer Engineering Laboratories, SmartSync Inc, Ventyx and Xcel Energy.

18 This is where the partners provide funding for all or part of an initiative in return for a share of the intellectual property and enhancements to, creation of, their products and services.

19 i.e. the need to ensure that future generations had access to essential resources and a healthy living environment.

20 Also known as the Kyoto Resolution.

21 Wind Source is a green tariff offered to customers by Xcel. It is the largest voluntary renewable energy programme in the USA. It costs the average household less than $25 / month to power their home from 100% renewable energy.

22 Amendment 37.

23 The solar reward programme provides subsidies for systems varying in size from 5 KW to 2 MW over a 20-year period at a rate of $2/watt. To date over $104 million has been paid in incentives to customers and more than 38 MW of solar PV has been installed in Colorado through the solar rewards programme.

24 Thirty-four contractors were in attendance. This programme cost approximately $20,000, to conduct the training, in 2007 and an additional $10,000 dedicated to evaluation and follow-up in 2008.

25 Many of the residents are staff /students at the University of Colorado or work in energy-related or environmental institutions. Thus it is perhaps not surprising that the majority of the population voted for the tax.

26 Voluntary purchases of utility-provided wind power are exempt from the tax.

27 Compared with a tax rate of $0.004/kWh for commercial customers, and an average business will pay $3.80/month. The city council had the authority to increase the tax after the first year up to a maximum permitted tax rate of $0.0049/kWh for residential customers.

28 There has been some controversy over whether this was adequate and if the commercial sector should make a substantially larger contribution. However, there was some concern as various businesses threatened to move from the city if higher taxes were imposed.

29 About 1,500 homes have benefitted from the residential programme funded by the CAP tax to date. However, the overall effect of the programme in reducing carbon emissions has not been sufficient to meet the city's target. It seems that it has fallen short because the majority of the residential programmes focused on performing building audits and not on implementation of energy efficiency measures (CAP Assessment, 2009). However, it might also result from the limited funding available.

30 Rebates total approximately $50,000 for 500 kW of photovoltaics installed.

31 In most cases, no more than 50% of the total project cost had been granted. For the first grant cycle of 2008, the city received 10 applications requesting a total of $260,000, and awarded a total of $65,000 which has been used to install 161 kW (kilowatts) of PV plus two solar thermal systems.

32 The loans were financed by a $40 million bond issue that allowed Boulder County to make loans for eligible energy efficiency and renewable energy projects. Of the $40 million, $28 million is designated for residential property owners and $12 is designated for commercial property owners.

33 Incorporating anticipated Xcel rebates and federal tax credits.

34 Colorado solar ordinance (HB 1149) in May 2009, which required builders of single-family homes to offer solar as a standard feature to all prospective homebuyers. Builders are required to give the buyer the option to either have a photovoltaic system or a solar water heating system installed on their new home, or to have all the necessary wiring and/or plumbing installed so that they can easily add a solar system at a later date. The builder must also provide the buyer with a list of every solar installer in the area, so the buyer can obtain expert help in determining if their home's location is suitable for solar and what the estimated cost savings would be. This has not yet been adopted by Boulder.

35 The UK is also encouraging decentralised energy systems (to an extent through the feed-in tariff and renewable heat incentive) but the bulk of energy supply is still expected to come from centralised sources.

36 This section is particularly focused on the time period 2000–2009. It should be noted that in 2010 a change in political power meant some changes to the policies affecting the nuclear and wind industries in the UK, although the overall approach appears to have remained largely the same.

37 In the UK the carbon intensity of the fuel supply is 2.26 tonnes CO_2/toe compared with 2.16 tonnes CO_2/toe for Europe.

38 The carbon intensity for gas is 0.19 kg CO_2/kWh compared to 0.43 kg CO_2/kWh for electricity.

39 Building regulations have led to a dramatic reduction in space heating by a factor of four since 1985 (Lowe, 2007). Housing built since the millennium in the UK is on average between 40 and 50% more energy efficient than housing stock built before 2000.

40 Data for electricity generation and fuel inputs are from http://www.dti.gov. uk/¢les/¢le18945.xls (accessed 6 November 2006). Additional data on fuel inputs

and carbon emission factors are from the UK Greenhouse Gas Inventory 1990 /2004. Submission 2006. Background Data for Fuel Consumption (http://www. naei.org.uk/reports.php) (accessed 6 November 2006).
41 1,102 MWe increase (+19 %).
42 737 MWe increase (+35 %) in onshore wind capacity and a 192 MWe increase (+49 %) in offshore wind capacity.
43 98 MWe increase (+7 %).
44 A 49 MWe increase (+15 %).
45 This assumes that the average household consumes 4700 kWh/year.
46 Assuming a CO_2 off-set of 430g/kWh.
47 Currently offshore wind is dominated by two turbine manufacturers, Siemens and Vestas.
48 In 2009, 262 schemes equating to 7419 MW were held in the UK planning system.
49 i.e. larger projects: projects over 50 MW which are determined under Section 36 of the Electricity Act.
50 Without existing nuclear power stations, the UK total annual carbon dioxide emissions from all energy use would be 5–12% higher than today (if fossil-fuelled power stations had been built instead). However, as discussed in Chapter 2, nuclear power produces significantly more CO_2 than renewable energy sources (e.g. solar, wind, biomass, hydro-power).
51 The 40% equates to 200 TWh requiring about 30 GWe of nuclear capacity.
52 The coalition government appears to be following suit.
53 Suppliers can alternatively pay into a buy-out fund to meet the obligation. Since 2004 renewables operators (independent of size) have been entitled to receive renewable obligation certificates (two ROCs for every 1,000 kWh) which they can also sell to electricity supply companies to help them achieve their obligation.
54 Carbon Trust's innovation programme and funding for new low-carbon technology enterprises, Offshore Wind Capital Grants Programme, Low Carbon Buildings Programme, Bio-energy Capital Grants and Bio-energy Infrastructure Schemes, Marine Renewables Deployment Fund, Carbon Abatement Technology Demonstration Programme and the Hydrogen and Fuel Cell Demonstration Programme.
55 Germany is a major producer of onshore wind energy and France is the largest producer of nuclear power.
56 Currently the UK renewable energy subsidy is approximately £1 billion annually – £0.012 billion spent on research and development. This compares with £1 billion for a carbon capture and storage plant and £75 billion for nuclear decommissioning.

5 Low/zero carbon neighbourhoods

1 It was previously used for manufacturing industry and shipping
2 Local Investment Program (1998–2002) a fund offered by the Swedish government to subsidise projects that were aimed at energy and resource efficient technologies.
3 Hammarby was projected to cost around 20 billion kr (Inghe-Hagström, 2002) of which the City paid 4 billion kr (Wastesson, 2002). The total investment is by others estimated at approximately 15 billion kr (Nattrass and Altomare, undated).
4 In comparison with the Swedish standard is approximately 270 kWh/m2/year (Persson and Kjellgren, 2000)

5 Compared with the UK where house-builders will have to work with utilities to plan and fund LZC infrastructure for new developments.
6 Similar results were noted in a comprehensive study of Stockholm environmental habits in 2004 (Ivarsson 2005).
7 The cost of an apartment in Hammarby rose from SEK 8,000 /m2 during the first phase to SEK 30,000 /m2 in the second phase (Wærn 2003).
8 The Royal Seaport will be fossil fuel free by 2030. The Stockholm Royal Seaport development when complete will consist of 10–15,000 new apartments and 30,000 workplaces with a district heating/cooling infrastructure.
9 The aim is to switch the CHP plant to using biofuels in the next five years. The plant is located next to the harbour so that sea transport can be used to deliver wood to the plant.
10 For example bathroom tiles which lose their pattern when too much water has been used. Another example is lamps that are on when electricity consumption is low, but go off if consumption is too high.
11 Red line = phase 1 of B001 project; black line = entire Western Harbour development project (all will eventually be developed).
12 250 million kr (£15 million) from the local investment programme.
13 The standard set for B001 was far less stringent than that set for Hammarby. However, the difference is connected with how you calculate the energy produced within the property or on the site. In Hammarby only the energy outsourced from other energy suppliers is counted, whilst B001 the energy produced and used or recovered within the site is also counted.
14 ENORM energy model.
15 It was found that the low estimated values pre-supposed a relatively large proportion of electrical energy used in buildings.
16 Split incentives between investors and energy end-users (e.g. between a landlord and tenant). The term split incentive refers to the potential difficulties that arise when two parties engaged in a contract have different goals and different levels of information. A common example is referred to as the landlord–tenant problem. This problem occurs when the landlord provides energy-using appliances, but the tenant pays the electricity bill. In this situation, there is little incentive for the landlord to choose the most energy-efficient appliance.
17 *Baugruppen* are groups of citizens planning to build their own accommodation. They are similar to cohousing groups. Residents are involved in financing the project, visioning exercises, group formation and designing their development. Various tenure, financing and management options exist. *Baugruppen* are also known as *Baugemeinschaften*. Similar models do exist in a few other major cities in Germany (Munich and Berlin), but they were pioneered in Freiburg and Tübingen.
18 Latest zoning plan deposited in 2010.
19 Primary energy demand for passive house $\leq 120\,kWh/(m^2{\cdot}a)^2$; LEH1 $\leq 40\%$ maximum EnEV 2009; LEH2 $\leq 55\%$ maximum EnEV 2009; standard from existing zoning plan = 65 kwh/sqm/annum
20 EEWärmeG 2009 – Renewable Energy and Heat Act 2009.
21 Project Group Vauban deals with the administrative coordination of the local groups involved in the Vauban project
22 Council Vauban Committee is the main platform for information exchange, discussion and decision preparation for the Vauban project.
23 Forum Vauban is the local citizens association and legal body for the extended participation process for the Vauban project.

24 High performance building shell reduces natural gas use by 40%: airtight, less than 0.1 natural air changes per hour; sips construction with r-50 roofs, r-30 walls, r-5 windows; geo-assisted heat recovery ventilator reduces natural gas use by 10%; no furnace needed for the passive house.

25 Passive solar orientation – reduces natural gas use by 30% – homes aligned east to west; minimise apertures to north; solar overhangs on south; deep porches and deciduous trees at east and west.

26 Initially the 777 m² PV (108 kWp) was to be used to power 40 electric vehicles. However, due to a lack of electric vehicles in the development the power is now being used to heat hot water and power appliances in the residential units.

27 The woodchip was to be sourced locally. The system requires 1,100 tonnes per year sourced from local tree-surgeons, from parks and gardens.

28 Two skins of double-glazing to south elevation and triple-glazing for all other elevations.

29 Super insulation – 300 mm insulation jacket around each terrace.

30 Passive solar gain – Most of the residential glazing faces south to receive maximum sunlight. Unheated double-glazed sunspaces form an integral part of each dwelling. In summer the outer windows open to create open-air balconies. Ground-floor levels of northern blocks are stepped up by 700–2000 mm, reducing overshadowing of ground floor windows.

31 The brief for the site required the development of up to 305 habitable rooms. Further conditions were placed on the site requiring the purchaser to provide a football pitch and clubhouse, and contribution towards social housing provision in the area.

32 Sutton Council engaged environmental economists Aspinwall and Co to place an independent financial value on BedZED's benefits over the conventional competitor. The highest environmental factor that could be valued turned out to be reduced CO_2 emissions during an imputed 20–25 year operational life. Based on 50 ECU/tonne (the marginal cost of meeting the EU's target for CO_2 reduction), the value of the ZED scheme over the conventional competitor was between £100000 and £200000.

33 Very few residents have an electric vehicle. This is partly because of the cost and technical capability of electric vehicles. However, it is also because of the limited infrastructure available outside the community to charge vehicles.

34 The main technical problems with the CHP were as follows: the design of new and untested equipment (e.g. the automatic ash removal); the reliability of some equipment that needed to operate continuously (e.g. the woodchip grabber and slide valves); tar condensing from the wood gas, exacerbated by cooling of the plant when shut off at night.

35 The biomass CHP plant was equipped with automatic de-ashing. It was envisaged that weekly attendances would be required for receiving woodchip deliveries, checking and filling oil and water levels, and scheduled maintenance should be carried out on a quarterly basis. However, in practice the BedZED CHP required full-time manning with frequent downtime for equipment modifications.

36 Exus Energy ceased trading and the future of the company is uncertain.

37 If the exterior sunspace windows are opened wide in the summer, and the interior windows closed, the house stays pleasantly cool.

6 Markets for zero carbon homes

1 Somewhere between research and development (to find the most effective models) and demonstration phase.

2 A warm rent includes the energy cost in the rental price of a unit. The energy cost is calculated as a function of the unit size.
3 i.e. the need to ensure that future generations had access to essential resources and healthy living environment.
4 A private wire electricity system is one that is off-grid and privately owned by a community, ESCO or private individual or company.

7   Transformation of the house-building industry

1 House-building is publicly subsidised (through low interest loans and public ownership of land) in Sweden and thus public bodies have greater control over build quality.

8   Transformation of the energy industry

1 Generators are responsible for producing the energy used in homes. Distributors and transmitters are the owners and operators of the network that transfers electricity from the point of generation to the home. Suppliers are the companies who supply and sell electricity to the consumer.
2 A survey of ESCO activity in Europe showed that there were approximately 20 ESCOs in the UK whilst in Germany there were 500–1,000 (Vine, 2003). Numbers are far greater in Germany largely due to the long-term financial incentives (capital grants and feed-in tariff) offered to ESCOs (Bertoldi et al, 2006).
3 Sydkraft was a Swedish energy company owned by communities in southern Sweden and pension funds. Sydkraft also developed the bespoke B001 energy system in Malmö.
4 Badenova is a public-private utility. It is made up of approximately 40 municipal energy companies from Freiburg and surrounding towns in the region. The public sector owns 53% of its shares.

9   Instruments for change

1 About 1,500 homes have benefitted from the residential programme funded by the CAP tax to date. However, the overall effect of the programme in reducing carbon emissions has not been sufficient to meet Boulder City's target. It seems that it has fallen short because the majority of the residential programmes focused on performing building audits and not on implementation of energy efficiency measures (Fehrer and Evans, 2009). However, it might also result from the limited funds raised through the CAP tax.
2 The problem of grid connection is now being addressed in the UK.

10   A spatial dimension

1 Hydrogen fuel cells are currently very expensive and inefficient, whilst batteries are only suited to storing smaller amounts of renewable energy.
2 Energetic systems refer to the technological systems involved in the generation, supply and storage of energy.
3 The Merton Rule requires that 10% of the energy consumed by a new development is generated by renewable sources on site. This applies to new housing developments with ten or more units or sites over 0.5 hectares in area (although thresholds vary between authorities).

4 The Code for Sustainable Homes provides sustainability standards (an accreditation system) for all new homes. It sets voluntary standards for a number of environmental objectives including on-site generation of renewable energy. Code level 6 requires zero carbon emissions from the development.

5 In the Mayor's 2004 Energy Strategy, the London Energy Partnership was tasked with setting up Energy Action Areas to act as exemplar low carbon developments in London. Four pilot EAAs were set up in 2005 to demonstrate how to deliver low-carbon urban developments that incorporate renewable energy and improved energy efficiency measures. In 2008, a new initiative was announced to create ten Low Carbon Zones.

6 Low carbon zones – neighbourhoods in which a range of approaches to reducing carbon emissions across several sectors are tested and demonstrated. These zones are expected to act as catalysts for the wider deployment of zero carbon technologies, policies, businesses and so on within the urban environment.

7 For example the potential supply of renewable energy, the density of development, mixture of land uses, orientation of sites, over-shadowing from buildings in urban areas, existing energy infrastructure and the energy efficiency of existing stock.

11 Living with zero carbon

1 Financial incentives were being offered to households by Xcel Energy for installation of PV and federal tax credits for the production of renewable energy.

2 The three models are:

'Plug and Play' model – the micro-generation unit is owned and financed by the homeowner. Within this model, consumers may change their consumption pattern in response to the reward mechanism: they might choose to maximise their revenue through exporting as much electricity as possible into the grid under a scheme of attractive export rewards, or they could choose to maximise their on-site consumption, if export rewards are low.

'Company Control' model is based on the notion that companies might use fleets of micro-generators as a substitute for central power generation – i.e. as a virtual power plant. This model involves a more passive consumer who only provides the site for the microgeneration unit, but it is owned by an energy service company (ESCO) or traditional energy utility.

'Community Microgrid' model – micro-generation units are connected to a microgrid. Consumers control their unit and manage the supply-demand balance within the microgrid. Their incentive to do this is that they own shares in the community energy company.

12 A time for change

1 China is the world's biggest solar water heater producer and user (Wang, 2010). Since 1980, solar water collectors have undergone rapid development in China with an annual average growth rate of 30%. China now produces the greatest quantity of solar water heaters in the world. By 2008, 100 million square meters had been installed and by 2010 it was expected that this would rise to 150 million square meters (Wang and Zhai, 2010).

Bibliography

1 Introduction

European Environment Agency (2005) 'Sustainable use and management of natural resources', EEA Report No 9/2005.

European Environment Agency (2009) 'Greenhouse gas emission trends and projections in Europe 2009', Report No 9/2009.

Geller, H. (2003) *Energy Revolution: Policies for a Sustainable Future*, Washington, DC: Island Press.

International Energy Agency Statistics Division (2006) 'CO_2 emissions from fuel combustion', Paris: IEA.

International Energy Agency Statistics Division (2007) 'Energy Balances of OECD Countries (2008 edition) and Energy Balances of Non-OECD Countries (2007 edition)', Paris: IEA. Available at http://data.iea.org/ieastore/default.asp (viewed April 2010).

International Panel on Climate Change (2000) 'Special report on emissions scenarios', Intergovernmental Panel on Climate change, Cambridge: Cambridge University Press. Available at: http://www.grida.no/climate/ipcc/emission/index.htm (viewed April 2010).

Lowe, R. (2009) 'Policy and strategy challenges for climate change and building stocks', *Building Research and Information*, vol 37, no 2, pp 206–212.

Milmo, C. (2010) 'Concern as China clamps down on rare earth exports', *The Independent*, 2 January 2010. Available at http://www.independent.co.uk/news/world/asia/concern-as-china-clamps-down-on-rare-earth-exports-1855387.html (viewed April 2010).

Population Division of the Department of Economic and Social Affairs of the United Nations Secretariat (2005) '*World Population Prospects: The 2004 Revision*', Dataset on CD-ROM. New York: United Nations.

Population Division of the Department of Economic and Social Affairs of the United Nations Secretariat (2008) 'World Population Prospects: The 2007 Revision', New York: United Nations. Available at http://www.un.org/esa/population/ordering.htm (viewed April 2010).

Stern, N. (2006) *Stern Review Report on the Economics of Climate Change*, London: HMSO.

US Department of Energy (October 2009) 'Buildings Energy Data Book: 2.4 Residential Environmental Data'. Available at http://btscoredatabook.eren.doe.gov/ (viewed April 2010).

US Energy Information Administration (2007) 'International Energy Outlook 2007', Washington, DC: United States Department of Energy. Available at http://www.eia.gov/oiaf/archive/ieo07/index.html (viewed April 2010).

US Energy Information Administration (2010) 'International Energy Statistics database', Washington, DC: United States Department of Energy. Available at http://www.eia.doe.gov/cfapps/ipdbproject/IEDIndex3.cfm?tid=91&pid=46&aid=31.

Williams, J. (2006) 'Innovative solutions for averting a potential resource crisis – the case of one-person households in England and Wales', *Journal of Environment, Development and Sustainability*, vol 9, pp 325–354.

2 Zero carbon homes: the technological response

Allen, S., Hammond, G. and McManus, M. (2008) 'Prospects for and barriers to domestic micro-generation: a United Kingdom perspective', *Applied Energy*, 85, pp 528–544.

DESERTEC Available at http://www.desertec.org (viewed January 2010).

Devine-Wright, P. and Devine-Wright, H. (2006) 'Social representations of intermittency and the shaping of public support for wind energy in the UK', *International Journal of Global Energy Issues: special issue on Intermittency*, vol 25, no 3/4, pp 243–256.

Dobbyn, J. and Thomas, G. (2005) 'Seeing the light: the impact of microgeneration on the way we use energy: qualitative research findings', London: Hub Research Consultants.

Ecofys VII (2007) 'U-Values for better energy performance of buildings', Report for EURIMA-European insulation manufacturers association, Carsten Petersdorff, Thomas Boermans et al, 11/2007.

Electric Power Research Institute (2008) 'The green grid: energy savings and carbon emissions reductions enabled by a smart grid', Palo Alto, CA: EPRI.

Electricity Storage Association, 2010. Available at http://www.electricitystorage.org (viewed January 2010).

Enkvist, P., Naucler, T. and Rosander, J. (2007) 'McKinsey Report – a cost curve for green house gas reduction', *McKinsey Quarterly*, vol 1, pp 35–45.

European Environment Agency (2008) 'Energy and environment report 2008', EEA: Report No 6/2008.

European Union (2002) 'Energy performance in buildings', EU Directive 2002/91/EC (updated 2010).

Europe Supergrid, La Tene maps. Available at http://www.latene.com/index.php/1/category/6/electricity-generation-and-transmission-maps/ (viewed January 2010).

European Wind Energy Association (2010) 'Powering Europe: wind energy and the electricity grid', Report, Brussels: EWEA.

Faiers, A. and Neame, C. (2006) 'Consumer attitudes towards domestic solar power systems', *Energy Policy*, vol 34, no 14, pp 1797–1806.

Farhar, B. and Coburn, T. (2006) *A New Market Paradigm for Zero-Energy Homes: The Comparative San Diego Case Study*, NREL Technical Report in Two Volumes. Volume 1: NREL/TP–550–38304–01, Volume 2 (Appendixes): NREL/TP–550–38304–02.

Feist, W., Peper, S. and Görg, M. (2001) 'CEPHEUS-project information No. 36 – Final technical report', Project Reference Number: BU/127/DE/SE/AT.

Greenpeace (2005) 'Decentralising power: an energy revolution for the 21st century' Amsterdam: Greenpeace International.

Greenpeace (2008) 'False hope: why carbon capture and storage won't save the climate', Amsterdam: Greenpeace International.

Hermelink, A. (2009) 'How deep to go: remarks on how to find the cost-optimal level for building renovation', report by ECOFYS, comissioned by European Council for an Energy Efficient Economy.

Hydrogen storage systems website. Available at www.hydrogenics.com (viewed January 2010).

Ibrahim, H., Ilinca, A. and Perron, J. (2008) 'Energy storage systems – characteristics and comparisons – a review article', *Renewable and Sustainable Energy Reviews*, vol 12, no 5, pp 1221–1250.

International Energy Agency Statistics Division (2008) 'Energy technology perspectives – scenarios and strategies until 2050', Paris: IEA.

International Panel on Climate Change (2001) 'Special report on land use change and forestry', Intergovernmental Panel on Climate change, Cambridge and New York: Cambridge University Press.

International Panel on Climate Change (2005) 'IPCC special report on carbon dioxide capture and storage', Cambridge and New York: Cambridge University Press.

Mckinsey (2008) 'Carbon capture and storage – assessing the economics', report published by Mckinsey and Company.

National Energy Technology Laboratory (2007) 'A vision for the modern grid', report by the National Energy Technology Laboratory for the U.S. Department of Energy Office of Electricity Delivery and Energy Reliability (March 2007).

Passive-on project (2010) Available at http://www.passive-on.org/CD/5.%20Long %20Description/Passive-On%20-%20Long%20Description%20-%20English. pdf (accessed January 2010).

Pratt, R. G., Balducci, P. J., Gerkensmeyer, C., Katipamula, S., Kintner-Meyer, M. C. W., Sanquist, T. F., Schneider, K. P. and Secrest, T. J. (2010) 'The smart grid: an estimation of the energy and CO_2 benefits', Pacific Northwest National Laboratory, January 2010 (PNNL–19112).

Pöyry, Faber Maunsell (AECOM) *The Potential and Costs of District Heating Networks* – a report to DECC by *Pöyry* Energy Consulting and *Faber Maunsell (AECOM)*, 5 May 2009.

Sovacool, B. (2008) 'Valuing the greenhouse gas emissions from nuclear power: a critical survey', *Energy Policy*, vol 36, no 8, pp 2950–2963.

Tinkler, M. J. (2009) 'Electricity storage: a key component of our emerging energy future', Presentation to Third Industrial Revolution: Canadian Executive Roundtable Meeting Toronto, Ontario.

United Nations (2010) *UNSD Energy Statistics Yearbook*, United Nations.

US Energy Information Administration (2010) 'International Energy Statistics database', United States Department of Energy – Washington, DC. Available at http://www.eia.doe.gov/cfapps/ipdbproject/IEDIndex3.cfm?tid=91&pid=46&aid=31

Watson, J., Sauter, R., Bahaj, B., James, P., Myers and Wing, R. (2006) 'Unlocking the power house: policy and system change for domestic micro-generation in the UK', UKERC and Sustainable Development Commission.

Williams, J. (2008a) 'Greenhouses for the growth region', *Journal of Environmental Planning & Management*, vol 51, no 1, pp 1–34.

Williams, J. (2010) 'The deployment of decentralised energy systems as part of the housing growth programme in the UK', *Energy Policy*, vol 38, no 12, pp 7604–7613.

3 Innovative housing programmes

Bukowski, Anja (2009) – Vice President of KfW Bank – interview 11/09/09.
Department of Communities and Local Government (2010) 'Housing statistics'. Available at www.communities.gov.uk/housing/housingresearch/housingstatistics/housingstatisticsby/housebuilding/livetables/ (viewed February 2010).
Department Energy and Climate Change Statistics, Available at http://www.decc.gov.uk/ en/content/cms/statistics/source/source.aspx (viewed February 2010)
Farhar, B. and Coburn, T. (2006) *A New Market Paradigm for Zero-energy Homes: The Comparative San Diego Case Study*, NREL Technical Report in Two Volumes. Volume 1: NREL/TP–550–38304–01, Volume 2 (Appendixes): NREL/TP–550–38304–02.
Farhar, B., Coburn, T. and Murphy, M. (2004) *Large-production Home Builder Experience with Zero Energy Homes*, July 2004, Report for National Renewable Energy Laboratory NREL/CP–550–35913.
Federal Ministry for the Environment, Nature Conservation and Nuclear Safety (2009) Energieeinsparungsgesetz (EnEG 2009) (Energy Conservation Ordinance/Act).
Federal Ministry for the Environment, Nature Conservation and Nuclear Safety (2009) Erneuerbare-Energien-Wärmegesetz (EEWärmeG 2009) (Renewable Energies Heat Act).
Feist, W., Peper, S., Görg, M. and von Oesen, M. (2001) 'Klimaneutrale Passivhaussiedlung Hannover-Kronsberg', CEPHEUS Projekt information 18, Passivhaus Institut, Darmstadt, Germany.
Go Solar website. Available at http://www.gosolarcalifornia.org (accessed February 2010).
Grahl, Wolfgang (2009) – NCC Deutschland GmbH – interview 15/09/09.
ICARO Consulting (2009) *Understanding Consumer Attitudes to Sustainable Community Infrastructure*, London: Green Buildings Council and Zero Carbon Hub.
Ingrid Vogler (2009) GdW – Bundesverband deutscher Wohnungs-und Immobilienunternehmen e.V. – interview 16/09/09.
Jakob, M. (2006) 'Marginal costs and co-benefits of energy efficiency investments: the case of the Swiss residential sector', *Energy Policy*, vol 34, no 2, pp 172–187.
Jones, E. and Leach, M. (2000) 'Devolving residential energy efficiency responsibility to local government: the case of HECA', *Local Environment*, vol 5, no 1, pp 69–81.
Ko, J. and Fenner, R. (2007) 'Adoption of energy efficient innovations in new UK housing', Proceedings of the Institution of Civil Engineers, *Energy Journal* 160, Issue EN4, pp 151–163.
Nässén, J. and Holmberg, J. (2005) 'Energy efficiency – a forgotten goal in the Swedish building sector?' *Energy Policy*, vol 33, no 8, pp 1037–1051.
Nässén, J., Sprei, F. and Holmberg, J. (2008) 'Stagnating energy efficiency in the Swedish building sector – Economic and organisational explanations', *Energy Policy*, vol 36, no 10, pp 3814–3822.
National Association of Home Builders Research Centre (2005) 'Zero energy home

project – ZEH Preliminary Market Analysis General Investigation of the Residential Appraisal Industry', Report by NAHB Research Centre, Marlborough, South Carolina.

Navigant Consulting (2008) 'Improved PV business models for zero energy new homes: stimulating innovation in the California marketplace' Report for California Energy Commission CEC–500–2007–090.

Passivhaus Kompendium, 2007 ISBN–13: 978–3000202308

Schnieders, J. and Hermelink, A., (2006). CEPHEUS results: measurements and occupants satisfaction provide evidence for Passive House being an option for sustainable building. *Energy Policy*, vol 34, pp 151–171.

Townshend, T. (2005) 'From inner city to inner suburb? Addressing housing aspirations in low demand areas in Newcastle and Gateshead, UK', *Housing Studies*, vol 21, no 4, pp 501–521.

Waters, M. (2007) 'Environmental sustainability: is it HIP?' Working Paper (Reading: College of Estate Management).

Williams, J. (2006) 'Innovative solutions for averting a potential resource crisis – the case of one-person households in England and Wales', *Journal of Environment, development and Sustainability,* vol 9, pp 325–354.

Williams, J. (2008a) 'Greenhouses for the growth region', *Journal of Environmental Planning & Management*, vol 51, no 1, pp 1–34.

Williams, J. (2010) 'The deployment of decentralised energy systems as part of the housing growth programme in the UK', *Energy Policy*, vol 38, no 12, pp 7604–7613.

World Wide Fund (2003) 'One million sustainable homes: moving best practice from the fringes to the mainstream of UK housing', WWF.

Woodward, Simon (2009) – Chief Executive of Utilicom – interview (24/07/2009)

Zero carbon hub database, Available at http://www.zerocarbonhub.org/examples (viewed February 2010).

4 Low/zero carbon energy systems

Allen, S., Hammond, G. and McManus, M. (2008) 'Prospects for and barriers to domestic micro-generation: A United Kingdom perspective', *Applied Energy* 85 (2008) pp 528–544.

British Wind Energy Association (2009) 'Wind Energy in the UK State of the Industry Report', BWEA, London.

British Wind Energy Association (2010) 'What does the Round 3 announcement mean? Briefing note on offshore wind energy', BWEA, London.

British Wind Energy Association (2010) 'UK Offshore Wind: Staying on Track Forecasting offshore wind build for the next five years', BWEA, London.

Department energy and climate change (2008) 'White paper on the future of nuclear power', HMSO, London.

Department energy and climate change (2009a) 'Digest of United Kingdom energy statistics: chapter 7: renewable sources of energy', HMSO, London.

Department energy and climate change (2009b) 'A prevailing wind advancing UK offshore wind deployment', HMSO, London.

Department of Trade and Industry (2006) 'Our Energy Challenge Power from the people: Microgeneration strategy', HMSO, London.

Diaz-Rainey, I. and Ashton, J. (2008) 'Stuck between a ROC and a hard place? Barriers to the take-up of green energy in the UK', *Energy Policy*, vol 36, no 8, pp 3053–3061.

Farhar, B. (2009) 'The Xcel SmartGridCity Project: Community Context and Household Perceptions', Presentation for RASEI Brown Bag (November 11 2009).

Farhar, Barbara (2010) – Institute of Behavioral Science, University of Colorado – interviewed 20/04/10.

IPSOS/Moray (2010) 'Public attitudes to the nuclear industry', report published by IPSOS/Moray 30 November 2010.

Johnson, Rebecca (2010) – RASEI, University of Colorado Smart Grid Project – interviewed 28/04/10.

Lipp, J. (2007) 'Lessons for effective renewable electricity policy from Denmark, Germany and the United Kingdom', *Energy Policy*, vol 35, no 11, pp 5481–5495.

Local Governments for Sustainability (2009) 'Long-term strategies for climate protection in Green City Freiburg – ICLEI case study 104', ICLEI, Toronto, Canada.

Lowe, R. (Ed.) (2007) 'Climate Change: National Building Stocks', *Building Research and Information* vol 35, no 4, pp 343–484.

Lutzky, N. (2004) The Environmental and Solar Sector in the Freiburg Region, BNL Consultancy report commissioned by the City of Freiburg im Breisgau (January, 2004).

Painuly, J. (2001) 'Barriers to renewable energy penetration; a framework for analysis', *Renewable Energy*, vol 24, pp 73–89.

Ragwitz, M. and Held, A. (2006) Renewable energy policy in Europe: the international feed-in cooperation, optimization and better coordination of national policy instruments', *Refocus*, vol 7, no 6, pp 44–47.

Reed, Adam (2010) – University of Colorado – Research Fellow, Center for Energy and Environmental Security (CEES), University of Colorado Law School – interviewed 24/04/10.

Reiche, D. (2002) 'Renewable energies in the EU member states in comparison', in Reiche, D. (ed.) *Handbook of Renewable Energies in the European Union*, Peter Lang Verlag, Frankfurt/Main, pp 13–24.

Runci, P (2005) 'German system and diffusion of renewable energy', Technical laboratory report PNWD3526.

Shorrock, L. and Utley, J. (2003) 'Domestic energy fact file 2003', Building Research Establishment, Watford, UK.

The Hammarby Model – Hammarby website Available at http://www.hammarbysjostad.se/ inenglish/pdf/Kretslopp%20eng%2009%202009%20300ppi. pdf (accessed September 2010)

World Nuclear Association (2010) available at http://www.world-nuclear.org/info/inf84.html (accessed 09/03/10).

WSP Environment and Energy (2009) 'City of Boulder – Office of Environmental Affairs – Climate Action Programme (CAP) Assessment', WSP Environment and Energy.

Wustenhagen, R. and Bilharz, M. (2006) 'Green energy market development in Germany: effective public policy and emerging customer demand', *Energy Policy*, vol 34, no 13, pp 1681–1696.

5 Low/zero carbon neighbourhoods

Anders, Linden (2009) – Passivhaus Centrum (Sweden) – interviewed 04/06/09.

Antonoff, J. (2007) 'Energy planning for a sustainable neighbourhood an energy-plus neighbourhood in Seattle's south downtown', report prepared by International Sustainable Solutions.

Axelsson, K., Delefors, C. and Söderström, P. (2001) 'Hammarby Sjöstad – en kvalitativ studie av människors faktiska miljöbeteende och dess orsaker', Renhållnings-förvaltningen, Stockholm, Sweden.

Bioregional (2009) *BedZED Seven Years on: the Impact of the UK's Best Known Eco-village and its Residents*, Bioregional.

Brick, K. (2008) 'Follow up of environmental impact in Hammarby Sjöstad', report published by Grontmij AB, Stockholm, Sweden.

Building Research Establishment (2002) 'BedZED – Beddington Zero Energy Development', Sutton: General Information Report 89 (Best Practice Programme), BRE, Milton Keynes, UK.

C40 cities http://www.c40cities.org/bestpractices/buildings/freiburg_housing.jsp (accessed 05/04/11).

David Khan Studio (2009) *GEOS project brief.*

Disch Architects http://www.rolfdisch.de/ (accessed 06/04/11).

Exploateringskontoret (2005) Stockholm City, The Hammarby Model. Stockholm: Exploateringskontoret.

Forum Vauban. Available at http://www.forum-vauban.de/bilder/graphic.jpg (accessed 10/03/11).

Glavis, Stu (2010) – Realtor for Boulder Green Properties – interviewed on 19/04/10.

Graham, Trevor (2009) – Head of Malmö City Council's Sustainable Development Unit – interviewed 25/05/09.

Hagström, I. (2003) 'Från Minneberg till Hammarby Sjöstad', in E. Eriksson (ed) *Stockholms stränder. Från industri till bostäder*, St Erik: Ordfront & Samfundet.

Hellman, Johnny (2009) – Environmental Manager NCC Construction (Sweden) – interview.

Ivarsson, J. (2005) 'Stadsdelsinvånarna om Miljö och miljövanor i Stockholm 2004', en undersökning genomförd av USK på uppdrag av Miljöförvaltningen, Utrednings- och statistikkontoret, Stockholms stad.

Magnuson, L. (ed, 2004) 'Boendes livsmiljö i en citynära stadsdel – exempel Hammarby Sjöstad', Gatu-och fastighetskontoret.

Nässén, J., Sprei, F. and Holmberg, J. (2008) 'Stagnating energy efficiency in the Swedish building sector: economic and organisational explanations', *Energy Policy*, vol 36, no 10, pp 3814–3822.

Nattrass, B. and Altomare M. (undated) 'The Natural Step Organizational Case Summary: Construction industry in Sweden – JM and The Hammarby Sjöstad Project', Stockholm: The Natural Step.

Nilsson, A. and Elmroth, A. (2005) 'The buildings consume more energy than expected', in *Sustainable City of Tomorrow: Experiences of a Swedish House Exposition*, Stockholm: Swedish Research Council for Environment, Agricultural Sciences and Spatial Planning, pp 108–9.

Persson, A. and Kjellgren, T. (2000) *Energy efficiency and environmental awareness integrated in every day living*, SBC, Sweden.

Preiser, K. (2009) 'Maximising public and private strengths through partnership in developing renewable energies', presentation on behalf of Badenova.

Risén, J. (2007) A case study: Hammarby Sjöstad. Available at http://www. zigersnead.com/blog/wp-content/uploads/2007/11/hammarbysjostad_casestudy_ jonasrisen.pdf (accessed 11/03/11).

Rosén, Per (2009) – E-ON energy Malmö (Specialist District Heating) – interviewed 26/05/09.

Stenftenagel, A. and Klebl, N. (2010) – Adam Stenftenagel Principal and Founder of Sustainably Built and Norbert Klebl Master Developer for GEOS – interviewed on 03/05/10.

Stoll, Thomas (2009) – City of Stockholm Strategic Planning (Hammarby and Stockholm Royal Seaport) – interviewed 02/06/09.

Svennberg, Kaisa (2009) – Swedish Environmental Research Institute – interviewed 05/06/09.

Twinn, C. (2003) 'BedZED', *Arup Journal*, 1/2003, p 12.

Vestbro, D. U. (2002) 'Modernism versus sustainable development', in D. U. Vestbro (ed) *Architecture as Politics: the Role of Design and Planning for Peace and Sustainable Development*, ARCPEACE International Architects Designers Planners for Social Responsibility in collaboration with the Div. of Urban Studies/Built Environment Analysis, The Royal Institute of Technology, Stockholm.

Wærn, Rasmus (2003) 'Ritat vid vatten', in E. Eriksson, (ed) *Stockholms stränder. Från industri till bostäder*, St Erik: Ordfront & Samfundet.

Wastesson, G. (2002) 'Exploateringsprocessen', in *Hammarby Sjöstad – BoStad02*. Stockholm: Hammarby Sjöstad, Gatu-och fastighetskontoret.

Williams, J. (2006) 'Innovative solutions for averting a potential resource crisis – the case of one-person households in England and Wales', *Journal of Environment, Development and Sustainability*, vol 9, pp 325–354.

Williams, J. (2008a) 'Greenhouses for the growth region', *Journal of Environmental Planning & Management*, vol 51, no 1, pp 1–34.

6 Markets for zero carbon homes

Bienert, S., Schützenhofer, C., Leopoldsberger, G., Bobsin, K., Leutgöb, K., Hüttler, W., Popescu, D., Mladin, E., Boazu, R., Koch, D. and Edvardsen, D. (2007) *Integration of Energy Performance and Life-Cycle Costing into Property Valuation Practice*, IMMOVALUE project final report.

Department of Communities and Local Government (2008) 'Research to assess the costs and benefits of the government's proposals to reduce the carbon footprint of new housing development', London: HMSO.

Diaz-Rainey, I. and Ashton, J. (2008) 'Stuck between a ROC and a hard place? Barriers to the take-up of green energy in the UK', *Energy Policy*, vol 36, no 8, pp 3053–3061.

Eichholtz, P., Kok, N. and Quigley, J. (2009) 'Doing well by doing good? An analysis of the financial performance of the green office buildings in the US', Royal Institute of Chartered Surveyors, London.

Farhar, Barbara (2010) – Institute of Behavioral Science, University of Colorado – interviewed 20/04/10.

Farhar, B. and Coburn, T. (2006) *A New Market Paradigm for Zero-energy Homes: The Comparative San Diego Case Study*, NREL Technical Report in Two Volumes. Volume 1: NREL/TP–550–38304–01, Volume 2 (Appendixes): NREL/TP–550–38304–02.

Farhar, B., Coburn, T. and Murphy, M. (2004) 'Large-production home builder experience with zero energy homes', July 2004, Report for National Renewable Energy Laboratory NREL/CP–550–35913.

Glavis, Stu (2010) – Realtor for Boulder Green Properties – interviewed on 19/04/10.

Grahl, Wolfgang (2009) – NCC Deutschland GmbH – interview 15/09/09.

ICARO Consulting (2009) *Understanding Consumer Attitudes to Sustainable Community Infrastructure*, London: Green Buildings Council and Zero Carbon Hub.

Laustsen, J. (2008) 'Energy efficiency requirements in building codes and energy efficiency policies for new buildings'. IEA Information Paper, Paris: IEA.

Lenormand, P. and Rialhe, A. (2006) 'Very low energy houses', *Green Building* (November).

Linden, Anders (2009) – Passivhaus Centrum (Sweden) – interviewed 04/06/09.

National Association of Home Builders Research Centre (2005) 'Zero energy home project: ZEH Preliminary Market Analysis General Investigation of the Residential Appraisal Industry', Report by *NAHB* Research Centre, Marlborough, South Carolina.

National Association of Home Builders Research Centre (2006) 'The potential impact of zero energy homes', NAHBRC Report No EG5049_020606_01.

Navigant Consulting (2008) 'Improved PV business models for zero energy new homes: stimulating innovation in the California marketplace', report for California Energy Commission CEC–500–2007–090.

Passive-on project (2010) Available at http://www.passive-on.org/CD/5.%20Long%20Description/Passive-On%20-%20Long%20Description%20-%20English.pdf.

PASS-NET (2009) International passive house database, published by PASS-NET.

Rogers, E. M. (1983) *Diffusion of Innovations*, New York: Free Press.

Stenftenagel, A. and Klebl, N. (2010) – Adam Stenftenagel Principal and Founder of Sustainably Built and Norbert Klebl Master Developer for GEOS – interviewed on 03/05/10.

Svennberg, Kaisa (2009) – Swedish Environmental Research Institute – interviewed 05/06/09.

Vogler, Ingrid (2009) GdW – Bundesverband deutscher Wohnungs-und Immobilienunternehmen e.V. – interview 16/09/09.

Waters, M. (2007) 'Environmental sustainability: is it HIP?', Working Paper, Reading: College of Estate Management.

Williams, J. (2006) 'Innovative solutions for averting a potential resource crisis – the case of one-person households in England and Wales', *Journal of Environment, Development and Sustainability*, vol 9, pp 325–354.

Williams, J. (2008b) 'Predicting an American future for cohousing and a more sustainable lifestyle?', *Futures Journal*, vol 40, no 3, pp 1–19.

Woodward, Simon (2009) – Chief Executive of Utilicom – interview 24/07/2009.

Zero Carbon Hub (2010) 'Marketing tomorrow's new homes raising consumer demand for low and zero carbon living: a marketing strategy for new homes', report by Zero Carbon Hub (February 2010).

7 Transformation of the house-building industry

Ball, M. (1996) *Housing and Construction: A Troubled Relationship*, Bristol: Policy Press.

Ball, M. (1999) 'Chasing a snail: innovation and house building firms' strategies', *Housing Studies*, vol 14, no 1, pp 9–22.

Barlow, J. and King, C. (1992) 'The state, the market and competitive strategy: the house building industry in the United Kingdom, France and Sweden', *Environment and Planning A*, vol 24, pp 381–400.

Bergman, N., Whitmarsh, L. and Köhler, J. (2008) 'Transition to sustainable development in the UK housing sector: from case study to model implementation', Tyndall Centre for Climate Change Research Working Paper 120, University of East Anglia, Norwich, UK.

Bramley, G., Bartlett, W. and Lambert, C. (1995) *Planning the market for private house-building*, London: UCL Press.

Clarke, L. (2006) 'Valuing labour', *Building Research and Information*, vol 34, no 3, pp 246–256.

Fawcett, R., Allison, K. and Corner, D. (2005) 'Using modern methods of construction to build homes more quickly and efficiently', London, National Audit Office.

Fox, Jacqueline (2010) – Barratt Homes Plc – interview 10/06/10.

Geels, F. (2002) 'Technological transitions as evolutionary reconfiguration processes: a multi-level perspective and a case study', *Research Policy*, vol 31, no 8/9, pp 1257–1274.

Geels, F. (2005) 'Transitions towards sustainability through system innovation', *Technological Forecasting and Social Change*, vol 72, no 6, pp 681–696.

Grahl, Wolfgang (2009) – NCC Deutschland GmbH – interview 15/09/09.

Halse, A. (2005) 'Passive houses in Norway', MSc Thesis, University of Oslo, Oslo, Norway.

Hellman, Johnny (2009) – Environmental Manager NCC Construction (Sweden) – interviewed 03/06/09.

Jakob, M. (2006) 'Marginal costs and co-benefits of energy efficiency investments: The case of the Swiss residential sector', *Energy Policy*, vol 34, no 2, pp 172–187.

Kemp, R., Rip, A. and Schot, J. (2001) 'Constructing transition paths through the management of niches', in R. Garud and P. Karnoe (eds.), *Path Dependence and Creation*, Mahwah, NJ: Lawrence Erlbaum Associates, pp. 269–299.

Ko, J. (2007) 'Driver and barriers for adoption of energy efficiency innovations in new UK housing'. MPhil thesis, Cambridge University, Cambridge, UK.

Ko, J. and Fenner, R. (2007) 'Adoption of energy efficient innovations in new UK housing', Proceedings of the Institution of Civil Engineers, *Energy Journal*, 160, Issue EN4, pp 151–163.

Linden, Anders (2009) – Passivhaus Centrum (Sweden) – interviewed 04/06/09.

Lowe, R. and Oreszczyn, T. (2008) 'Regulatory standards and barriers to improved performance for housing', *Energy Policy*, vol 36, no 12, pp 4475–4481.

National Association of Home Builders Research Centre (2005) 'Zero energy home project – ZEH preliminary market analysis general investigation of the residential appraisal industry', report by *NAHB* Research Centre, Marlborough, South Carolina.

Ørstavik, M., Bugge, T. and Pedersen, T. (2003) 'Bare plankekjøring? Utvikling av en overordnet innovasjonsstrategi i BAEnæringen?', STEP report 21–2003, Oslo: STEP.

Rotmans, J., Kemp, R. and van Asselt, M. (2001) 'More evolution than revolution: transition management in public policy', *Foresight*, vol 3, no 1, pp. 15–31.

SmartLIFE (2007) *International Network of SmartLIFE Centres: Design Solutions for Sustainable Construction in New Build and Refurbishments in the UK, Sweden and Germany*, Cambridge: SmartLIFE.

Smith, A., Stirling, A. and Berkhout, F. (2005) 'The governance of sustainable socio-technical transitions', *Research Policy*, 34, pp 1491–1510.

Stenftenagel, A. and Klebl, N. (2010) – Adam Stenftenagel Principal and Founder of Sustainably Built and Norbert Klebl Master Developer for GEOS – interviewed 03/05/10.

Svennberg, Kaisa (2009) – Swedish Environmental Research Institute – interviewed 05/06/09.

Vogler, Ingrid (2009) GdW – Bundesverband deutscher Wohnungs-und Immobilienunternehmen e.V. – interview, 16/09/09.

Williams, J. (2006) 'Innovative solutions for averting a potential resource crisis – the case of one-person households in England and Wales', *Journal of Environment, Development and Sustainability*, vol 9, pp 325–354.

Williams, J. (2008a) 'Greenhouses for the growth region', *Journal of Environmental Planning & Management*, vol 51, no 1, pp 1–34.

Zero Carbon Hub (2010) 'Marketing tomorrow's new homes raising consumer demand for low and zero carbon living: a marketing strategy for new homes', report by Zero Carbon Hub (February 2010).

8 Transformation of the energy industry

Bertoldi, P., Berrutto, V., de Renzio, M., Adnot, J. and Vine, E. (2003) 'How are EU ESCOs behaving and how to create a real ESCO market?' Working Paper.

Bertoldi, P., Hinnells, M. and Rezessy, S. (2006) 'Liberating the power of energy services in a liberalised energy market', Proceedings of EEDAL 2006 Conference, London, June.

Butson, D. (1998) 'Financing options for renewable energy', in *Investment in renewable energy, Institution of Mechanical Engineers*, Professional Engineering Publishing.

Convery, F. and Redmond, L. (2007) 'Market and price developments in the European Union Emissions Trading Scheme', *Review of Environmental and Economic Policy*, vol 1, issue 1, pp 88–111.

Devine-Wright, P. and Devine-Wright, H. (2006) 'Social representations of intermittency and the shaping of public support for wind energy in the UK', *International Journal of Global Energy Issues: Special Issue on Intermittency*, vol 25, no 3/4, pp 243–256.

Droege, P (2009) *100 Per Cent Renewable – Energy Autonomy in Action*, London and New York: Earthscan.

Energy Futures Australia (2004) 'The generic models for electricity industry structure', Energy Futures Australia Ltd (31 August 2004).

Geller, H. (2003) *Energy Revolution – Policies for a Sustainable Future*, Washington DC: Island Press.

General Accounting Office (2000) 'Tax incentives for petroleum and ethanol fuels', GAO/RCED–00–301R. Washinton, DC: GAO.

Goldberg, M. (2000) Federal energy subsidies: not all technologies are created equal. Washinton, DC: Renewable energy policy project.

ICARO Consulting (2009) *Understanding Consumer Attitudes to Sustainable Community Infrastructure*, London: Green Buildings Council and Zero Carbon Hub.

Jochem, E. (2000) 'Energy end-use efficiency, in *World Energy Assessment: Energy and the Challenge of Sustainability*, New York: United Nations Development Programme.

Johnson, Rebecca (2010) – RASEI, University of Colorado Smart Grid Project – interviewed 28/04/10.

Rogner, H. (2000) 'Energy resources', in *World Energy Assessment: Energy and the Challenge of Sustainability*, New York: United Nations Development Programme.

Turkenburg, W. C. (2000) 'Renewable energy technologies' in *World Energy Assessment: Energy and the Challenge of Sustainability*, New York: United Nations Development Programme.

Vine, E. (2003) 'International survey of energy service companies', unpublished, Lawrence Berkeley National Laboratory, Berkeley, CA.

Williams, J. (2008a) 'Greenhouses for the growth region', *Journal of Environment, Development and Sustainability*, vol 51, no 1, pp 1–34.

Williams, J. (2010) 'The deployment of decentralised energy systems as part of the housing growth programme in the UK', *Energy Policy*, vol 38, no 12, pp 7604–7613.

9 Instruments for change

Bukowski, Anja (2009) – Vice President of KfW Bank – interviewed 11/09/09.

Commission of the European Communities (2008) 'The support of electricity from renewable energy sources', SEC (2008) 57 Commission staff working document, Brussels, 23.1.2008.

Daly, H. E. (1974) 'The economics of the steady state', *American Economic Review*, vol 62, no 4, pp 15–21.

Federal Ministry for the Environment, Nature Conservation and Nuclear Safety (2007) 'EEG – The Renewable Energy Sources Act: The success story of sustainable policies for Germany', Berlin: BMU.

Federal Ministry for the Environment, Nature Conservation and Nuclear Safety (2009) Energieeinsparungsgesetz (EnEG 2009) (Energy Conservation Act).

Federal Ministry for the Environment, Nature Conservation and Nuclear Safety (2009) Energieeinsparungsverordnung (EnEV 2009) (Energy Conservation Ordinance).

Federal Ministry for the Environment, Nature Conservation and Nuclear Safety

(2009) Erneuerbare-Energien-Wärmegesetz (EEWärmeG 2009) (Renewable Energies Heat Act).

Fehrer, D. and Evans, E. (2009) 'Climate Action Programme (CAP) Assessment', Boulder, CO: City of Boulder Office of Environmental Affairs.

Foxon, T. J., Gross, R., Chase, A., Howes, J., Arnall, A. and Anderson, D. (2005) 'The UK innovation systems for new and renewable energy technologies', *Energy Policy*, vol 33, no 16, pp 2123–2137.

Grahl, Wolfgang (2009) – NCC Deutschland GmbH – interviewed 15/09/09.

Jacobsson, S. and Lauber, V. (2006) 'The politics and policy of energy system transformation – explaining the German diffusion of renewable energy technology', *Energy Policy*, vol 34, no 3, pp 256–276.

Johansson, B. (2006) 'Climate policy instruments and industry – effects and potential responses in the Swedish context', *Energy Policy*, vol 34, no 15, pp 2344–2360.

Lipp, J. (2007) 'Lessons for effective renewable electricity policy from Denmark, Germany and the United Kingdom', *Energy Policy*, vol 35, no 11, pp 5481–5495.

Mitchell, C. and Connor, P. (2004) 'Renewable energy policy in the UK 1990–2003', *Energy Policy*, vol 32, no. 17, pp 1935–1947.

National Association of Home Builders Research Centre (2006) 'The potential impact of zero energy homes', NAHBRC Report No EG5049_020606_01.

Navigant Consulting (2008) 'Improved PV business models for zero energy new homes: stimulating innovation in the California marketplace', Report for California Energy Commission CEC–500–2007–090.

Ragwitz, M. and Held, A. (2006) 'Renewable energy policy in Europe: the international feed-in cooperation, optimization and better coordination of national policy instruments', *Refocus*, vol 7, no 6, pp 44–47.

Reed, Adam (2010) – University of Colorado – Research Fellow, Center for Energy and Environmental Security (CEES), University of Colorado Law School – interviewed 24/04/10.

Roberts, S. and Thumim, J. (2006) 'The ideas, the issues and the next steps', Report for DEFRA, Centre for Sustainable Energy (November).

Stern, N. (2006) 'Stern Review Report on the Economics of Climate Change', London: HMSO.

Vogler, Ingrid (2009) GdW – Bundesverband deutscher Wohnungs-und Immobilienunternehmen e.V. – interview 16/09/09.

Williams, J. (2008a) 'Greenhouses for the growth region', *Journal of Environmental Planning & Management*, vol 51, no 1, pp 1–34.

Williams, J. (2010) 'The deployment of decentralised energy systems as part of the housing growth programme in the UK', *Energy Policy*, vol 38, no 12, pp 7604–7613.

Wüstenhagen, R. and Bilharz, M. (2006) 'Green energy market development in Germany: effective public policy and emerging customer demand', *Energy Policy*, vol 34, no 13, pp 1681–1696.

10 A spatial dimension

Brook Lyndhurst (2004) 'Skills and Jobs from Renewable Energy Policies and Targets', London: Greater London Authority.

City of Boulder (2005) 'Solar Access Guide', Boulder, CO: Boulder Building Services Centre.

City of Freiburg, Department of the Environment, Education and Facility Management (2007) 'Climate Action Plan', City of Freiburg, Germany.

City of Freiburg, Department of the Environment, Education and Facility Management (2006) 'Land Use Plan', City of Freiburg, Germany.

Donn, Thorsten – City of Freiburg, Planning Department – presentation 17/02/2011.

Farhar, B., Coburn, T. and Murphy, M. (2004) 'Large-production home builder experience with zero energy homes', July 2004, report for National Renewable Energy Laboratory NREL/CP–550–35913.

GEOS Team (2010) 'The Planning of *GEOS*: America's Largest Net-Zero Energy neighbourhood'. USGBC Colorado Green Building *Conference*, Denver, CO.

Local Governments for Sustainability (2009) 'Long-term strategies for climate protection in Green City Freiburg – ICLEI case study 104', Toronto, Canada: ICLEI.

Owens, S. (1990) 'Land use planning for energy efficiency', in J. B Cullingworth (ed.) Energy, Land and Public Policy, New Brunswick: Transaction Books, p 66.

Rocky Mountains Land Use Institute (2004) 'Smart codes – just how smart?', Presentation by the RMLUI, Denver, CO.

Rocky Mountains Land Use Institute (2008) *Framework – Sustainable Community Development*, RMLUI, Denver, CO.

Williams, J. (2010) 'The deployment of decentralised energy systems as part of the housing growth programme in the UK', *Energy Policy*, vol 38, no 12, pp 7604–7613.

11 Living with zero carbon

Becker, L. J. (1978) 'Joint effect of feedback and goal setting on performance: a field study of residential energy conservation.' *Journal of Applied Psychology*, vol 63, no 4, pp 428–433.

Chassin, D. P. and Kiesling, L. (2008) 'Decentralized coordination through digital technology, dynamic pricing and customer-driven control: the grid-wise test-bed demonstration project.' *The Electricity Journal*, vol. 21, no 8, pp 51–59.

Darby, S. (2006) 'The effectiveness of feedback on energy consumption: a review for DEFRA of the literature on metering, billing and direct displays', Oxford: Environmental Change Institute, University of Oxford.

Devine-Wright, H. and Devine-Wright, P. (2004) 'From demand side management to demand side participation: towards an environmental psychology of sustainable electricity system evolution', *Journal of Applied Psychology*, vol 6, no 3/4, pp 167–177.

Devine-Wright, P. and Devine-Wright, H. (2006) 'Social representations of intermittency and the shaping of public support for wind energy in the UK', *International Journal of Global Energy Issues: special issue on Intermittency*, vol 25, no 3/4, pp 243–256.

Dobbyn, J. and Thomas, G. (2005) 'Seeing the light: the impact of microgeneration on the way we use energy: qualitative research findings', London: Hub Research Consultants.

Egan, C. (2002) 'The application of social science to energy conservation: realizations, models and findings', Washington, DC: American Association for an Energy Efficient Economy, Report E002.

Faiers, A. and Neame, C. (2006) 'Consumer attitudes towards domestic solar power systems', *Energy Policy*, vol 34, no 14, pp 1797–1806.

Farhar, Barbara (2010) – Institute of Behavioral Science, University of Colorado – interviewed 20/04/10.

Farhar, B. and Coburn, T. (2006) *A New Market Paradigm for Zero-energy Homes: The Comparative San Diego Case Study*, NREL Technical Report in Two Volumes, Volume 1: NREL/TP–550–38304–01, Volume 2 (Appendixes): NREL/TP–550–38304–02.

Faruqui, A., Sergici, S. and Sharif, A. (2009) 'The impact of informational feedback on energy consumption – a survey of the experimental evidence', *Energy* (in press). Abstract (Working Paper Series) available online at http://papers.ssrn.com/sol3/papers.cfm? abstract_id=1407701.

Fischer, C. (2008) 'Feedback on household electricity consumption: a tool for saving energy?', *Energy Efficiency*, vol 1, no 1, pp 79–104.

Geller, E. (1981) 'Evaluating energy conservation programs: is verbal report enough?' *Journal of Consumer Research*, vol 8, no 3, pp 331–335.

GEOS Team (2010) 'The Planning of *GEOS*: America's Largest Net-Zero Energy neighbourhood', Denver CO: USGBC Colorado Green Building *Conference*.

Grove-White, R., Macnaghten, P. and Wynne, B. (2000) 'Wising up: the public and new technologies', report by the Centre for the Study of Environmental Change, Lancaster University, Lancaster.

Hedges, A. (1991) 'Attitudes to energy conservation in the home – report on a qualitative study', London: HMSO.

Hutton, R. B., Mauser, G. A., Filiatrault, P. and Ahtola, O. T. (1986) 'Effects of cost-related feedback on consumer knowledge and consumption behavior: a field experimental approach', *Journal of Consumer Research*, vol 13, no 3, pp 327–336.

ICARO Consulting (2009) 'Understanding consumer attitudes to sustainable community infrastructure', London: Green Buildings Council and Zero Carbon Hub.

Jardine, C. and Ault, G. (2008) 'Scenarios for examination of highly distributed power systems', *Journal of Power and Energy*, vol 222, no 7, pp 643–655.

Johnson, Rebecca (2010) – RASEI, University of Colorado Smart Grid Project – interviewed 28/04/10.

McClelland, L. and Cook, S. W. (1979) Energy conservation effects of continuous in-home feedback in all-electric homes', *Journal of Environmental Systems*, vol 9, no 2, pp 169–173.

Meltzer, G. (2000) 'Cohousing: Towards Social and Environmental Sustainability', unpublished PhD Thesis, Department of Architecture, University of Queensland, Brisbane.

Morris, D. (2001) 'Seeing the light: regaining control of our electricity system', Minneapolis, Minnesota: Institute for Local Self-Reliance.

Painuly, J. (2001) 'Barriers to renewable energy penetration; a framework for analysis', *Renewable Energy*, vol 24, pp 73–89.

Performance and Innovation Unit (2002) '*Social Capital*' a Performance and Innovation Unit Report, London: HMSO.

Pratt, R. G., Balducci, P. J., Gerkensmeyer, C., Katipamula, S., Kintner-Meyer, M. C. W., Sanquist, T. F., Schneider, K. P. and Secrest, T. J. (2010) 'The smart grid:

an estimation of the energy and CO_2 benefits', Pacific Northwest National Laboratory, January (PNNL–19112).

Quinn, E. L. (2009) 'Smart metering and privacy: existing law and competing policies, a report for the Colorado Public Utilities Commission', Colorado Public Utilities Commission (docket no. 09I–593EG).

Reed, Adam (2010) – University of Colorado – Research Fellow, Center for Energy and Environmental Security (CEES), University of Colorado Law School – interviewed 24/04/10.

Reiche, D. (2002) 'Renewable energies in the EU member states in comparison', in D. Reiche (ed.) *Handbook of Renewable Energies in the European Union*, Frankfurt/Main: Peter Lang Verlag, pp 13–24.

Roy, R., Caird, S. and Potter, S. (2007) 'People centred eco-design: consumer adoption of low and zero carbon products and systems', in J. Murphy (ed.) *Governing Technology for Sustainability*, London: Earthscan, pp. 41–62.

Sauter, R. and Watson, J. (2007) 'Strategies for the deployment of micro-generation: implications for social acceptance', *Energy Policy*, vol 35, no 5, pp 2770–2779.

Staats, H., Harland, P. and Ham, W. (2004) 'Effecting durable change – a team approach to improve environmental behaviour in the household', *Environment and Behaviour*, vol 36, no 3, pp 341–367.

Stenftenagel, A. and Klebl, N. (2010) – Adam Stenftenagel, Principal and Founder of Sustainably Built and Norbert Klebl Master Developer for GEOS – interviewed 03/05/10.

Ueno, T., Sano, F., Saeki, O. and Tsuji, K. (2006) 'Effectiveness of an energy-consumption information system on energy savings in residential houses based on monitored data', *Applied Energy*, vol 83, no 2, pp 166–183.

Williams, J. (2005a) 'Sun, surf and sustainability – comparison of the cohousing experience in California and the UK', *International Planning Studies Journal*, vol 10, no 2, pp 145–177.

Williams, J. (2005b) 'Designing neighbourhoods for social interaction – the case of cohousing', *Journal of Urban Design*, vol 10, no 3, pp 195–227.

Williams, J. (2008a) 'Greenhouses for the growth region', *Journal of Environmental Planning & Management*, vol 51, no 1, pp 1–34.

Winett, R. A., Love, S. Q. and Kidd, C. (1982) 'The effectiveness of an energy specialist and extension agents in promoting summer energy conservation by home visits', *Journal of Environmental Systems*, vol 12, no 1, pp 61–70.

12 A time for change

Stern, N. (2006) 'Stern Review Report on the Economics of Climate Change', London: HMSO.

Wang, R. Z. and Zhai X. Q. (2010) 'Development of solar thermal technologies in China', *Energy*, vol 36, no 11, pp 4407–4416.

Wang, Z. (2010) 'Prospectives for China's solar thermal power technology development', *Energy*, vol 36, no 11, pp 4417–4420.

Index

In this index tables and figures are indicated in bold; notes by n.; colour plates by cp.